Anti-Externalism

Joseph Mendola

OXFORD
UNIVERSITY PRESS

OXFORD
UNIVERSITY PRESS

Great Clarendon Street, Oxford OX2 6DP

Oxford University Press is a department of the University of Oxford.
It furthers the University's objective of excellence in research, scholarship,
and education by publishing worldwide. Oxford is a registered trade mark of
Oxford University Press in the UK and in certain other countries

© Joseph Mendola 2008

The moral rights of the author have been asserted

First published 2008
First published in paperback 2013

All rights reserved. No part of this publication may be reproduced, stored in
a retrieval system, or transmitted, in any form or by any means, without the
prior permission in writing of Oxford University Press, or as expressly permitted
by law, by licence or under terms agreed with the appropriate reprographics
rights organization. Enquiries concerning reproduction outside the scope of the
above should be sent to the Rights Department, Oxford University Press, at the
address above

You must not circulate this work in any other form
and you must impose this same condition on any acquirer

British Library Cataloguing in Publication Data
Data available

Library of Congress Cataloging in Publication Data
Data available

ISBN 978-0-19-953499-9 (Hbk)
ISBN 978-0-19-967968-3 (Pbk)

Anti-Externalism

For Allan Gibbard and Jaegwon Kim

Acknowledgments

I am grateful for help from Lily Griffin, Rowena Anketell, Patrick Arens, Bill Bauer, Catherine Berry, Tim Black, Brent Braga, Al Casullo, David Chavez, Ben Churley, Mark Cullison, Mark Decker, Cullen Gatten, John Gibbons, Danielle Hampton, Abla Hasan, Leo Iacono, Clayton Littlejohn, Tim Loughlin, Sally Markowitz, Peter Momtchiloff, Victoria Patton, Guy Rohrbaugh, J. D. Trout, Mark van Roojen, Kate Walker, and several anonymous referees. Thanks to Blackwell for permission to reuse material from my articles 'A Dilemma for Asymmetric Dependence', *Nous* 37 (2003), 232–57, and 'Papineau on Etiological Teleosemantics for Beliefs', *Ratio* 19 (2006), 305–20.

Contents

1. Introduction — 1

Part I: On Some Misleading Cases

2. Externalist Cases and Internalist Theory — 23
3. Internalist Cases and Externalist Theory — 55
4. The Real Moral — 77

Part II: Mind-Based Externalism and Sensory Content

5. Against Etiological Semantics — 103
6. Non-Etiological Mind-Based Externalism — 143
7. Qualia and Sensory Content — 173

Part III: Language-Based Externalism and Thought Content

8. Private Language and Privileged Access — 223
9. Language, Truth, and Inference — 253
10. Qualia Empiricism — 305

Bibliography — 329
Index — 347

1

Introduction

The truth is that when I daydream about green umbrellas in light rain, it does not require umbrellas, rain, anyone else, or any history. Likewise when I have such a desire, belief, or experience. But this old view is now unpopular.

Internalism is the view that all the conditions that constitute a person's thoughts and sensations are internal to their skin and contemporaneous, inside and now. Things outside my wall of skin *cause* my sensations and thoughts, and many of my thoughts are *about* the outside. But things outside are not constitutive parts of those mental states; they are not part of what makes them up. Let me be more precise. First, mental states of one type, say beliefs, often differ in content, much as declarative sentences differ in meaning. Consider beliefs that grass is green and that rain is wet. Beliefs can be about different things, and present the same things in different ways. It is because of this that they veridically or non-veridically represent. Second, some ways of typing mental states, say as knowledge and hence as true, clearly involve external conditions. And so now I can put it this way: According to internalism, my mental states of crucial and characteristic types—for instance my beliefs, desires, and sensations—would exist and retain their characteristic contents even if there were nothing outside me and no past, as long as what is currently inside my skin were unchanged.

Externalism is the denial of internalism. It is the view that features of a person's external environment or history are part of what constitutes that person's beliefs, desires, and sensations. The natural kinds around me, the machinations of my linguistic community, and my learning or evolutionary history are some of the external resources that might partly constitute my experiences and thoughts.[1]

---

[1] Mendola (1997) calls experiences 'thoughts' to stress their intensionality and capacity for falsehood. But here I will deploy more familiar terminology.

In one dark or golden age, perhaps only Hegel was an externalist. But now almost everyone is. This is a mistake. Externalism is false. Internalism is true. Or so I will argue.

Externalism is a mistake that matters. This is partly because it abets errors about the nature of our minds. The dominance of externalism has created a false theoretical complacency. We think we know roughly how our minds work, even if we haven't gotten the details right yet.

That story goes like this: Language is a social phenomenon, and much of our thought involves language. Our sensory states are causally responsive to the external world, and carry information about its states. Our neurophysiology links our sensory states and motor responses in complicated ways, but it surely links what we see with what we do, and what we hear others say with what we say. So the meanings of words and the information carried by sensory states seem obvious semantic resources to ground the contents of our mental states, even of thoughts deep in our brains.

But, as we will see, this plausible sounding story is largely false. The social features of languages and the information born by our sensory states are irrelevant to the contents of our beliefs, desires, and experiences. While mistakes about *where* our thoughts and experiences are may not seem antecedently important, they naturally lead to significant mistakes about *what* our thoughts and experiences are, and hence about what we are.

Externalism also supports a dangerous epistemic complacency. We should be cautiously suspicious of cozy, flattering arguments that we all agree in the truth, though such arguments are hard to resist. Externalism naturally suggests that the contents of our beliefs reflect the shared meanings of our words and the real nature of our world, so that our beliefs are mostly shared and mostly true. That may be one root of its popularity. But in fact even the superficially similar beliefs of different individuals differ in substantial and interesting ways. And in fact the beliefs of our ancestors clearly involved a whopping dose of falsehood, so that we have every reason to believe that our own still may.

1.1

There are commonsense motivations for externalism. When I sense things, my mind seems open to the world. The rain on the street seems to help constitute my seeing it, so that if something else were there in place of the rain, that other thing and my internal state of openness would constitute my seeing something else. When my eyes are open, it is as if I'm a hole into which the world falls.[2]

And we report our psychological states in sentences that appear to report relations to objects outside us. I see a taxi, or hear a siren. I hope the daffodils are wet. What's more, these are sentences of public languages like English, which have publicly determined meanings. I can think whatever I can say, and what I say by my English words is not a matter for my private and idiosyncratic determination.

But these commonsense motivations are not decisive. I dream of a green barn on a golden hill, or hallucinate some lurid parachute, and yet there aren't such things. I believe that Persephone is not the Easter Bunny, while yet there is no Persephone or Easter Bunny. And the public meanings of English words are reflected at least to some degree in the internal capacities of English speakers. What's more, remember how many different things can be said by different people through the same English words, for instance 'I love you.' Remember how adept we are at picking generally agreeable words that mask our real disagreements.

So we need to dig a little deeper. There are ancient theories of the mind and of language that underwrite some features of the commonsense motivations for externalism. For instance, Aristotle and his medieval friends said that a green bowl has a visual form, a certain shaped green, which can be taken up by someone's visual sense when there is an intervening medium of air that is in the state of activity that is light. And they held that it would then help constitute a sensory experience of such a green bowl. This story may sound consistent with internalism, but, according to traditional Aristotelian conceptions, the green form had to come from some perceptible object that actually had the color. Such a color form was supposed to be transmitted across the air, and it is obvious that there is nothing green in the intervening air; so it was thought that air didn't transmit the colors themselves, but rather so-called 'species' of colors, species that are essentially dependent in being on the genuine colors had only by colored objects of perception. And so sensory perception of the color of an object was thought to involve sensible species that are ontologically

---

[2] Apologies to Sartre.

dependent on the color of the object seen. This conception of perception in turn suggested a model of dreams, memories, and hallucinations in which sensible species emitted in the past from perceived objects help constitute mad, memorial, or dreaming experience now. And this model is externalist in a second way.

So externalism is ancient. But between us and this commonsense paradise falls the shadow of Galilean science. Aristotle was wrong. Common sense is wrong. Objects out there in the world don't have just exactly the properties humans experience them to have, no more and no less. Rather, objects out there have merely mass, charge, and motion, or some other appropriately measurable and Galilean properties. And sometimes those objective and Galilean properties can't be plausibly identified with the properties that we humans naively seem to experience. At the very least, some apparent features of experienced properties aren't objective and Galilean. Bluish purple and reddish purple are very similar colors in our experience. But they correspond to very different wavelengths of light and also to very different physical surfaces.

In its initial flowering, Galilean science denigrated the reality of the very colors we see. Galileo called colors 'mere names'.[3] And while philosophers have developed less radical but more complicated responses to the relevant facts, still belief in a Cartesian or empiricist veil of ideas standing between us and the external world was not simply a result of individualist social or religious doctrine, or of an unhealthy fixation on radical doubt. It was rather a natural reaction to the realization that in large part we cannot believe our eyes. It is not surprising that internalism became prominent among philosophers with the rise of Galilean science. While that new science taught us to favor observation over authority, it also suggested that our experience was much more dramatically misleading about the nature of the world than Aristotle thought.

There are contemporary externalist stories about perception that roughly resemble Aristotle's but are consistent with our contemporary Galilean conception of the objects of sensory perception. But they must be more baroque than simple Aristotelian conceptions. They involve various unexpected subtleties and hostages to fortune. Our Galilean conception of the world implies that some things that seemed obvious to Plato and Aristotle

[3] Galileo (1957: 274).

should no longer seem obvious to us, and externalism is one of those things. So appropriate motivations for externalism have now become of necessity more complex.

1.2

One thing that sometimes motivates contemporary externalism is despair about the possibility of a plausible account of our mental states that does not rest on the information of sensory signals or the meanings of sentences in public languages. Still, this motivation is inadequate, because there is a plausible internalist alternative.

I call the correct internalist view 'qualia empiricism'. According to qualia empiricism, the content of thoughts is crucially dependent on the content of sensory experiences. If we presume the truth of an internalist account of the content of my sensory experience, then my thoughts would depend on my contemporaneous and internal conditions only. That's what I mean by empiricism. And according to qualia empiricism, sensory contents are determined by, indeed identical to, qualitative features of our sensory experience that are themselves internally constituted. Sensory contents are internally determinate 'qualia'.

Let me explain. It is not like anything to be some new boots. But it is like something to be a rabbit or a human. In particular, it is like something to have sensory experiences of particular sorts. That specifies the qualia of such states. According to qualia empiricism, what it's like to hear an alto saxophone, what it's like to see colorful eggs in a basket, determines the contents of such sensations. What's more, qualia are internally determinate. By this I mean that someone's current qualia are wholly constituted by contemporaneous conditions internal to their skin.

Don't be alarmed. I'm not pushing dualism. Qualia empiricism, as developed here, is a physicalist story.[4] The internal conditions that constitute my qualia, sensations, and thoughts are *physical* conditions inside my skin. Indeed, I will presume throughout this book that only physicalist accounts

---

[4] Indeed, I will presume a type physicalism that Kim (2005) calls ontological physicalism plus reductionism. Part Two of Mendola (1997) develops a similar story suited to Aristotelian naive realism and qualia dualism, while its Part Three considers interpretation difficulties of physics that are ignored here.

are plausible contenders. I will presume that the same basic physical resources that make up the vast universe of insentient stars and galaxies make up my measly experiences and thoughts. As our Galilean science of mass, motion, and force has progressed, and delivered a plausible unified account of everything else in the vast world, including life and the complicated machinations of our neurophysiology and of what we do, it has become implausible to suggest that our minds are especially exempt from physical constitution.[5]

So the proper internalism about qualia is physicalist, I will presume. And the particular way in which our internal physical states constitute our qualia and hence sensory contents indeed reveals a second sense in which my positive view is qualia empiricism. The relations of constitution that link internal physical states and qualia are known empirically, I believe.

Perhaps it will further dampen alarm to note that the specific story about sensory content that I will tell has an architecture that is not very unorthodox. Current externalist physicalist orthodoxy embraces two competing positions regarding the contents of sensory states, to which my proposal is cleanly and plausibly related.

According to the first orthodox position, while most features of our apparent sensory contents are constituted by the nature of the paradigmatic environmental causes of our sensory states, by the information about the real world that such states carry, still there are some features of such contents that should be isolated and given a different explanation. Consider for instance the apparent similarity of reddish purple and bluish purple despite their very different environmental causes. This similarity isn't naturally explained by features of the environmental causes of our sensory states. Such qualia are characteristically given an internalist explanation by the first orthodox position, since the beauty of externalism is that it can use all the resources available to internalism, and more besides.

The second orthodox externalist position denies the plausibility of a differential and internalist treatment of some qualia. It treats all suitably apparent features of sensory contents in the standard externalist way, as constituted by paradigmatic environmental causes.

I will occupy a third position, which is yet suggested by the two standard options. Like the second orthodox position, I deny the possibility of a

---

[5] But for resistance to physicalism see Chalmers (1996).

differential treatment of some features of sensory contents. But I favor an internalist physicalist story such as the first orthodox position deploys for the qualia that it picks out for special treatment. The difference is that I deploy such a story across the board, for all features of the contents of our sensory experiences. Few fans of the first form of orthodoxy contemplate a serious semantic role for the qualia that they treat in an internalist manner. But our sensory experiences of reddish purple and of bluish purple do seem to have a semantic or representational similarity.

Internally determinate contents of sensory experience are the basic semantic resource on which mental content rests, I claim. The principal root is *not* information and *not* the socially-determined features of sentence meanings. This is a kind of empiricism, and empiricism has a hoary tradition. But empiricism of even the most general sort, which roots thought contents in sensory contents, may seem alarming. And my specific form, which rests heavily on internally constituted qualia, may seem even worse.

There are various ways this worry can arise. But focus for the moment on one famous one. Wittgenstein is widely thought to have conclusively disposed of such views as qualia empiricism, by focusing our attention on the linguistic medium of much of our thought, and the social features of language.

But he did not dispose of them. We will return at length to Wittgenstein's famous Private Language Argument against such an empiricism,[6] indeed to many Private Language Arguments. I will take these arguments quite seriously. But we will see that they fail to show that internal conditions like those that in fact constitute our qualia do not play the important semantic role in which I deploy them. In fact, our discussion of Private Language Arguments and forms of externalism rooted in social features of languages will yield various clues about the properly sophisticated internalist empiricism. Qualia empiricism can hijack much of the detailed ingenuity of externalists, by modulating externalist mechanisms into internalist variants.

This strategy will deliver a qualia empiricism that is different in a general way from traditional forms of empiricism. Traditional empiricism was not only a theory about mental content, but about evidence and confirmation. In its paradigmatic forms, it deployed qualia as characteristic

[6] Wittgenstein (1968).

evidence for perceptual beliefs, to which other beliefs were held to have characteristic evidential relations. But qualia empiricism has a different form, in which confirmation and other epistemic phenomena play a much less significant role. For one thing, qualia do not constitute evidence for allied perceptual beliefs, but rather something like truth-conditions for those perceptual beliefs. What's more, our capacity for imagination involving qualia helps provide us with an ability to entertain quasi-perceptual thoughts for the truth of which we have no actual evidence at all. That ability in turn helps root our capacity for thoughts of complex three-dimensional ways that the world might concretely be. It also helps root our capacity for thoughts that involve language and are of even greater complexity.

It is unlikely that my qualia exhaust my evidence. And, in any case, these various complex capacities give us the ability to form many thoughts for whose truth we have and even could have very little evidence. And so one moral of our discussion will be that even an empiricist philosophy of mind should become more independent of epistemology.

1.3

Despite its sketch and defense of qualia empiricism, this book has a negative goal that is at least as significant. I defend qualia empiricism in part simply to reassure externalists who think that there is no remotely plausible physicalist alternative to their views, to undercut that particular externalist motivation. If qualia empiricism is a false idol of my idiosyncratic cave, still another central claim of this book can stand.

My main negative point is that, despite current fashion, we have no good reason to believe that externalism is true. In fact, on balance we have some reason to believe that it is false. Externalism is not supported by any good arguments, and there are good arguments against at least its familiar forms. While there are arguments that appear to support externalism, their probity does not survive close examination.

This somewhat indirect strategy is necessary for internalists. We need not only alternative positive views of mental content in the face of what is now a surprisingly monolithic externalist orthodoxy. We also need new forms of argument against externalism. There are three familiar arguments against externalism, which I will call the Argument from Introspection, the Argument from Explanation, and the Argument from Science. But they are insufficient.

Crudely put, the Argument from Introspection is an argument, or cluster of arguments, that a person has privileged or introspective access to, or a priori knowledge of, the contents of their own thoughts, but not to the conditions that externalists hold necessary to the constitution of those thoughts. The Argument from Explanation is an argument, or cluster of arguments, that thoughts explain behaviors, and that what's merely contemporaneous and internal explains behaviors.

These two arguments are not decisive, because externalists have developed a variety of complex responses that leave these claims in doubt. For instance, some suggest that external conditions fix not only the contents of introspected thoughts but also of introspecting thoughts, so that externalism is consistent with introspective access to contents. And some propose alternative conceptions of explanation, in which an action directed at a particular external object requires an explanation that is similarly external. Because of the possibility of such replies, viable anti-externalist arguments of these two general forms must be that *specific* kinds of introspection or explanation are inconsistent with externalism, and so these arguments turn on plausibly deniable subtleties. We will return to these two clusters of arguments in Chapter 8, but they are not themselves decisive.

The third familiar argument against externalism—the Argument from Science—is partly methodological. Some internalists think that it is not the business of philosophy to resolve such issues as the nature and location of thought, which should be properly left to empirically-based psychology and neuroscience. And they also think that such science is or will be dominantly internalist.

Science does matter. The truth of internalism is neither a priori nor necessary. There is a way that the world might have been, the way Aristotle conceived it to be, in which externalism would have been true.[7] And the reasons for believing Aristotle wrong are dominantly empirical. What's more, I will appeal to the neuroscience of vision and other sciences to flesh out my positive sketch of qualia empiricism.

---

[7] Fisher (2007) describes hypothetical physical conditions under which externalism would be true.

But still the Argument from Science isn't a quick and royal road to internalism. A crucial problem is that this sort of strategy is even more popular on the other side, with externalists.[8] For every internalist who claims to be deferring to cognitive science, there are two externalists who do the same.

Philosophy, including philosophy of mind, should be scientifically informed and engaged, but not subservient; it is indeed in many areas continuous with scientific activity. Philosophers should be reluctant to dismiss science as irrelevant if they don't know it, and for that matter to bow to well-funded research programs just because they are institutionally successful. It can be argued that we should work harder at avoiding these extremes, but that is not the problem with the Argument from Science that I have in mind. The problem is that, even if we take our current cognitive science and psychology as gospel, the deference-to-science strategy doesn't work right now, for internalists or externalists. That is because it doesn't now clearly cut one way or the other, or at the very least there is no consensus on how it cuts.

External conditions do play a natural role in some current psychological theories, for instance in evolutionary psychology or learning theory. But on the other hand, such theories don't assure a role for external conditions in *constituting* mental content. And while some neurophysiological and psychological theories seem consistent with internalism, still many theories in areas that are intuitively relevant to content, for instance the study of perception, are hard to apply to the internalism−externalism debate. That is partly because we do not agree about which current psychological theories are successful in these areas, or indeed whether any are. But it is mostly because sober philosophers significantly but plausibly disagree in relevant interpretations of even particular target psychological theories.[9] Empirical findings and empirically-rooted theories can often be translated into various idioms variously favorable to one side or the other, perhaps with a change of emphasis, but with little change in significant content. For instance, the empirical developments that I will deploy in support of qualia empiricism can be rephrased in ways that would seem quite hospitable to externalists.[10]

---

[8] Internalist and externalist versions of the deference-to-science strategy include Burge (1986a); Segal (1989, 1991); Davies (1991); Egan (1991, 1992); R. Wilson (1995) and (2004: 144–213); Trout (2001).

[9] See n. 8.

[10] Perhaps it seems that science should strive for a unified treatment of the widest range of phenomena. A unified treatment of hallucination and veridical perception may favor internalism, while

While science is crucial, the Argument from Science against externalism is, at least for now, no more decisive than the Argument from Introspection or the Argument from Explanation. Perhaps someday things will change. But, for the time being, I will try another tack.[11]

I will try to sap the positive motivations for each form of dominant externalism, by examining each form and its motivations in turn. While it is sociologically dominant, externalism is supported by no good reasons. Through closely examining the alleged evidence for various forms of externalism, we will incidentally uncover sufficient reason to doubt it, and some helpful resources for a plausible internalism.

1.4

There are two kinds of alleged positive motivations for externalism, aside from the mere surface motivations, despair of internalism, and appeals to science that we have already discussed and dismissed. There are reasons that reflect our intuitive responses to certain specific concrete cases. And there are general, theory-enmeshed reasons. Both of these sorts of reasons are rooted in a priori or armchair considerations, but of different sorts.

Begin with the first type of reason. The growth of argument by appeal to intuitions about concrete cases is a striking feature of recent philosophy. Perhaps this is an historical artifact of the influence of Moore, Wittgenstein, or Chisholm. Or perhaps philosophy has finally found or recovered its true method. But whatever the explanation of why we favor argument by cases, it is famous concrete cases that move most contemporary philosophers to be externalists. Externalist theories are attractive only to their partisans, but almost everyone likes the cases. So I will take these cases very seriously.

Saul Kripke's *Naming and Necessity* convinced most of us that the referent of a name is not what best fits some associated description in the mind of

---

a unified treatment of the beliefs of those with different ideologies or sense capacities may favor externalism. But these facts suggest that this strategy is indecisive. And philosophers should be wary of proposing a priori constraints on science.

[11] Mendola (1997) attempts another general argument against at least some forms of externalism. Physics shows that our sensory experience is massively erroneous, so that our external situation does not help constitute that experience.

a speaker using that name.[12] Rather, it convinced us that the referent is, more or less, the object originally baptized by that name at the beginning of a history of appropriate name-transmission that leads to the speaker's use. I think of Gödel by utterance of his name and not of Schmidt, even if all I can bring to mind is that he discovered incompleteness, and even if in fact Schmidt discovered incompleteness and Gödel just got the credit. 'Feynman' refers to Feynman and 'Gell-Mann' refers to Gell-Mann in my mouth and in my thought, even if all I know about both is that they are physicists. So thoughts mediated in this way by names seem externally constituted in part; external facts about chains of name-transmission and baptism help constitute these thoughts to have the particular contents that they do.

Hilary Putnam's Twin Earth, on which you have an identical physical doppelgänger speaking some twin of English while yet the potable stuff in the lakes is not H-O-H but XYZ, convinced most of us that the extension of natural kind terms like 'water' depends crucially on the natural kinds that are in fact in our environment.[13] Your doppelgänger is internally identical but says different things. Putnam also convinced us that there is a linguistic division of labor that governs natural kind terms, so that 'elm' and 'beech' refer respectively to elms and beeches even in the speech of someone who knows only that they are trees, via the identificatory expertise of specialists. So thoughts mediated by such words as 'water' and 'elm' seem externally constituted, because specialists and natural kinds are external. And Tyler Burge convinced us that 'arthritis' and indeed many words of our language that are not natural kind terms or names have references or extensions that depend on dominant opinion in our language communities.[14] So too our associated thoughts.

The fashion for philosophy rooted in intuitive concrete cases has characteristic dangers. To focus on a few cases can mislead, since other cases may push in different directions. The absence of a systematic account can hide crucial difficulties. The world isn't flat even if it once was an intuitive paradigm of what is flat. And there are more differences in intuitions about cases than philosophers sometimes pretend. For instance, there is empirical evidence that the Gödel case does not elicit the same intuitions cross-culturally.[15] But since it is the famous externalist cases which have

---

[12] Kripke (1980).   [13] Putnam (1975).   [14] Burge (1979).
[15] Machery, Mallon, Nichols, and Stich (2004).

done most of the work in leading most to externalism, they will be the first focus of our concern. Part I discusses these famous cases at length, and develops a unified internalist response, which is incorporated into qualia empiricism.

This internalist response is a variant of so-called metalinguistic and rigidified description views. I call it RDC, for Rigidified Description Clusters. It is presented in Chapter 2. Roughly speaking, my claim is that there is a set of properties that is constituted by the internally determinate dispositions of a speaker to be positively relevant to what counts in their judgment as the referent of a given term. And there are various relative weights of those properties in determining what counts as the referent under various conditions, also constituted by the internally determinate dispositions of the speaker. Among this set of properties, there is a subset that has relatively great weight in fixing reference, and it incorporates 1) any properties that are recognized by the speaker as analytically true of or criterial for things in that extension, 2) the metalinguistic property of being referred to by that term, and 3) any other properties that are recognized as a priori true of things in that extension by the speaker. The entire set of properties and their weights is the description cluster of the term for the speaker at the time in question. The content contributed by a term 'X' with a putative reference to thoughts it mediates for a speaker at a time can be captured by deploying one sort of rigidification of the description 'the best satisfier of their description cluster for "X" '.

This proposal will definitely require some explaining. But it is a variant of familiar proposals. What is novel is my strategy for its defense. I will defend RDC against various standing objections to such accounts, but I will admit it has a cluster of intuitive problems. However, I will argue in Chapter 3 that equally famous counterexamples to crude forms of externalism require that a viable externalism deploy responses that suffer the same intuitive problems. So they cannot be decisive.

In Chapter 4, further discussion of the famous externalist cases will somewhat ironically reveal why externalism is false in at least the forms that those cases suggest. It will also reveal that a price for holding that intuitive case-based methodology is crucially revelatory of the nature of truth and reference is to qualify the significance of those things.

RDC deploys various resources, various semantic resources, that it may seem are not available to internalists. And this may seem to provide an indirect route back to externalism. Part of my job is to deliver the resources that RDC requires in a plausible way consistent with internalism. And my development of these elements of qualia empiricism will occur in the remaining two parts of the book, by contrast with externalist alternatives.

1.5

With the famous externalist cases out of the way, there still remain more general armchair arguments for externalism. In Parts II and III, we will consider theory-driven externalism. Various apparent general theoretical reasons help motivate various versions of current externalist orthodoxy. But I will argue that all high-profile externalist theories are false, and that their theoretical motivations cannot withstand close scrutiny.

There are two broad classes of externalist theories, which correspond to two positions in a traditional debate regarding whether the intentionality—the aboutness or semantic nature—of thought or of language is prior. The first class of externalisms do not depend crucially on claims that thought content is inherited from or entwined with the meaning of public language, and the second class do depend crucially on such claims. I discuss these two classes of theories, which I call 'mind-based' and 'language-based' externalisms, respectively in Parts II and III.

Each class may seem to inherit at least one very general and reasonable motivation from naive considerations I noted earlier. But internalists can hijack these motivations.

Certainly some of our thoughts are plausibly mediated by words, in the sense that they crucially involve speaking, out loud or to oneself. And so these thoughts plausibly inherit their contents from what is at least in some recognizable sense the meaning of those words. And language seems to be a public phenomenon. But the linguistic mediation of thought is in itself consistent with internalism, since what is in some recognizable sense the meaning of our words might be internally determinate.

Some of our thoughts seem rooted more directly in our brutish capacities for sensory experience, and are even arguably necessary conditions for meaningful speech. And our sensory experience faces out into the external world, and seems to be partly constituted by what we experience. But we have already seen how a crucial role for sensory content is consistent with internalism.

While our investigation of mind-based and language-based externalisms will deepen and refine our understanding of their commonsense roots, it is important to remember that proper motivations for externalist theories must be more specific than an observation that sensory content and language are crucial to our mental states. Still, it seems to many that there are such proper theoretical motivations for externalism. They underwrite the two broad classes of externalist theories.

1.6

What I am calling 'mind-based' externalist theories, the topic of Part II, do not depend crucially on claims that thought content is inherited from or entwined with the meaning of public language. Instead, they ordinarily and naturally deploy sensory experiences or perceptual beliefs in a crucial way. Since sensory experiences or perceptual beliefs are plausibly about certain of their environmental causes, it is understandable that externalist mind-based accounts focus on causal relations. Semantic relations between what a perceptual thought or experience is about and that mental state may seem to be causal relations, and that may seem to provide some grounds for externalism, even though it is a Galilean world.

But still, the stories externalist physicalists must tell are much more complicated than the naive stories that seemed acceptable to Aristotle. The now dominant cluster of externalist accounts of the content of perceptual beliefs are what I will call causal-informational accounts. They hold that the content of a perceptual thought is its *proper* cause. And it is important to understand the need for the italicized word, and the difficulties that it involves in our physical world.

False belief, even false perceptual belief, is possible. So there may be no causes of some perceptual beliefs that can be plausibly identified with their intuitive contents. But what's more, when even true perceptual beliefs have causes, they have many causes. A veridical perceptual belief about the picture of the strange pyramid on the back of some dollar bill is causally dependent not only on the picture, but on intervening nerve stimulations, the printing press, the long dead artist, some real pyramid he once saw somewhere or a picture of it, and his parents. The cause of a true perceptual belief that is its content must somehow be distinguished from all its other causes. That's its *proper* cause. And false beliefs usually have a proper cause that isn't even an actual cause.

Aristotle might consistently speak of sensible species that link sense and object by essence. But physicalist externalist accounts of sensory content must deploy some other story about proper causes. And different contemporary causal-informational accounts differ about what makes proper causes proper.

There aren't many plausible candidate accounts of proper causes. Proper causes have some sort of priority, and one obvious form of priority is historical priority. Such an historical or etiological story is also in the rough spirit of Aristotle's very natural claims about dreams and hallucinations. The earliest contemporary story of this general sort was perhaps Fred Dretske's view that proper causes are causes during a learning period. But this has become subsumed in Dretske's later work in what is now perhaps the dominant account of mental content, the etiological teleological account, which I will call 'ET'. ET is paradigmatically represented by Ruth Garrett Millikan.[16] It holds, to speak a bit crudely, that the proper cause of a mental state is what it is its function to be caused by, where that function is determined etiologically, say by evolutionary or learning history. Chapter 5 shows that ET accounts of thought content and especially of sensory content are false. It also considers and dismisses other etiological accounts of proper causes.

Another initially plausible sort of priority that proper causes might enjoy is some sort of priority in the moment. Aristotelian ontic dependence of sensible species on sensed properties is not available in our physical world. There is spatial priority in our world, in the sense that some causes of a sensory state are closer to that state than others are. But the causal chains that link sensory states to their intuitive objects include many intervening steps, including the irradiation of sense organs, that are not the contents of those states. Still, there is one kind of priority in the moment that may provide a plausible account of proper causes. It is exploited by the Asymmetric Dependence or 'AD' account, due to Jerry Fodor.[17] This holds a proper cause to be that on which other causes are *asymmetrically*

[16] Millikan (1984).   [17] Fodor (1990b).

dependent: All the other causes are dependent on a proper cause, and it is not dependent on any of the others. This seems to promise a kind of priority in the moment that is consistent with Galilean physicalism and yet that delivers intuitive contents. Still, Chapter 6 shows that externalist asymmetric dependence theories are false. It also considers and dismisses the few remaining externalist stories about proper causes.

Chapter 7 considers three remaining mind-based theoretical grounds for externalism. Some claim that knowledge is the basic mental state, that mere belief is a kind of failed knowledge.[18] Since knowledge requires truth, knowledge of most matters is not a mental state for which an internalist account is remotely plausible. And these claims together may seem to suggest other theoretical grounds for externalism about thoughts and sensations in general. But I argue that they do not provide such grounds. Second, some favor a 'disjunctive' analysis of perceptual experience, according to which veridical experience is partly constituted by its external objects while non-veridical experience is not so constituted.[19] But I argue that the disjunctive analysis is not properly motivated. Finally, I consider the most venerable argument for mind-based externalism, which is Kant's Refutation of Idealism.[20] I argue that it does not support mind-based externalism.

The externalist causal-informational tradition is perhaps the dominant externalist mind-based route, but, given the truth of physicalism, it has no successful answer to its characteristic difficulty. And by the end of Chapter 7 and Part II we will be in position to draw a more general conclusion, that all initially plausible externalist mind-based theories are false, and hence provide no reason to believe externalism.

Chapter 7 will also present my positive internalist proposal about sensory content, which is developed by variation and generalization of an account of features of our color experience due to C. L. Hardin.[21] I call it Modal Structuralism, or MS. It can be roughly characterized as the conjunction of five claims: 1) Sensory contents are qualia. 2) Qualia are constituted by internal physical states. 3) These relationships of constitution are necessary but a posteriori. 4) To each particular mode of sensation, say color vision, there corresponds a structure of alternative possible phenomenal properties, for instance colors. And at least one way to be in a state of experiencing

---

[18] Williamson (2000). [19] Hinton (1973).
[20] Kant (1998: 326–9: B274–B279). [21] Hardin (1988: 113–86).

such a property is to be in one state of a structure of alternative possible states of our neurophysiology with appropriate possible causes and effects. 5) The semantic contribution of such sensory contents is intentional. At least (4) will require considerable explaining. But one quick way to put it is that there is a kind of modal structure shared by the experienced properties characteristic of a given perceptual mode on the one hand and the neurophysiological basis of that possible range of experience on the other.

An important guiding thread through both our positive and negative arguments in Part II will be attention to the phenomenon of color blindness. Empirical facts about color blindness help reveal that standard externalist accounts of sensory content are wrong. And the neurophysiological basis of color blindness is a crucial positive clue to the nature of Modal Structuralism, which is the true internalist story about the content of our sensory states.

1.7

There remain externalist language-based theories, which are the focus of Part III. These are theories of mental content rooted crucially in the claim that the content of thoughts is inherited from the meaning of public languages, or more ecumenically that the content of someone's thoughts and the meaning of their sentences is somehow constituted all at once. Since public languages involve other people, such theories seem quite naturally externalist.

The dominant theories in this broad class are heavily influenced by a pair of observations associated with Wittgenstein, that only public languages are possible, and that this constrains the nature of our thoughts.[22] Wittgenstein's anti-private language argument is interpreted in various ways by various theorists. But, as I said earlier, it is also thought by many to be the major objection to such a qualia empiricism as I favor, and a major motivation for externalism. We will survey many possible readings of this argument, imbedded in other discussions.

Chapter 8 quite directly considers one simple and conservative form of the Private Language Argument. It compares the Arguments from

[22] Wittgenstein (1968).

Introspection and from Explanation that some deploy against externalism, and a simple version of the Private Language Argument that is naturally deployed against internalism. In other words, it considers arguments that may seem to quickly resolve the issue between internalism and externalism without recourse to my more indirect procedure. And it shows that such arguments fail, and for the same reason. That's the interesting part.

Chapter 9 considers well-developed externalist language-based theories. They share a general nature. This natural theory-driven language-based route to externalism is interpretationism. That is the view, associated for instance with Donald Davidson, that the facts about what someone thinks or means are determined by their proper interpretation, for instance by interpretations bound by principles of charity that require that ascribed beliefs be largely true. Since most of our beliefs are about things outside us, this suggests externalism. Since public language is often the medium of interpretation, and since some theories require simultaneous interpretation of language and thought, or even prior interpretation of language, this also reveals ways in which the meaning of public language may be entwined with or determine thought content, and hence other grounds for externalism. As we will further see, interpretationism also suggests many readings of the Private Language Argument.

Along with Davidson's view, a principal focus of this chapter is the well-developed externalist proposal of Robert Brandom. These two externalist theories span a range of semantic proposals encompassing suggestions of both Wittgenstein's early and late work. Davidson focuses on truth-conditions for sentences, and Brandom on proper use, and it will be helpful for us to explore this range. Chapter 9 will show that interpretationism and language-based theories in general provide no proper motivation for externalism. But it will also discuss many helpful resources that I will borrow from language-based externalists and modulate into internalist variants to help build up my positive account of the third key component of qualia empiricism.

I call that third component Non-Epistemic Internalism, or NEI. NEI, which is assembled in Chapter 10 from our previous discussions, and contrasted with some contemporary alternatives, bridges the basic semantic resources provided by MS and the detailed requirements of RDC. It does this by developing internalist echoes of various externalist mechanisms in what will turn out to be a non-epistemic mode. NEI puts much less emphasis than traditional empiricism on epistemic phenomena like evidence and justification.

1.8

Here's a summary map: Qualia empiricism, which is the conjunction of RDC, MS, and NEI, is the internalist truth.

Part I considers case-based arguments for externalism. It develops RDC as an internalist response to these cases. Its only real problems are shared by all viable forms of externalism.

Part II argues that mind-based externalist theories are false. It develops MS as an internalist alternative. And it does both these things through a consideration of color blindness.

Part III critically discusses language-based externalist theories, and develops NEI by internalist variation of their various mechanisms. NEI is considerably less epistemological than traditional forms of empiricism.

We will end up with a plausible internalist proposal, no reasons to believe that externalism is true, and everything coming up roses.

PART I
On Some Misleading Cases

2

Externalist Cases and Internalist Theory

While externalism is sometimes theory-driven, its dominant roots are the famous intuitive cases of Putnam, Burge, and Kripke.[1] This chapter rehearses these externalist cases, and propounds a single internalist response. It has a cluster of intuitive problems. But Chapter 3 argues that equally famous counterexamples to crude externalism require that a viable externalism deploy responses that suffer the same intuitive problems. In Chapter 4, further concrete cases reveal that externalism is false.

But let me better explain the structure of this argument. The famous externalist cases span a natural range of intuitive problems for internalism, and express certain pressures towards externalism. Some intuitive differences between thoughts do not seem to be internal differences: Externalism seems better placed to deliver the intuitive difference between Darwin's perceptual belief and that of his internal twin, when they each spy qualitatively identical yet distinct roses, in opposite ends of London. And some intuitive similarities between thoughts do not seem to be internal similarities: Two very different conceptions of human origins may seem to have only the phenomenon itself in common.

Still, there are also cases with which any properly developed externalism must deal. Some intuitive differences between thoughts do not seem to be external differences: Internalism seems better placed than simple externalisms to deliver the intuitive difference between beliefs about Venus in its guise as the morning star and in its guise as the evening star. And some intuitive similarities between thoughts do not seem to be external

[1] Putnam (1975); Burge (1979, 1982); Kripke (1980).

similarities: The thoughts of those who share a conception of the present king of Venus share no royal referent.

There are natural externalist resources to deploy against these internalist cases. Indeed, since externalism can field all the resources of internalism plus more besides, it can always treat its difficult cases just as any internalist would. But there are also natural internalist resources to deploy against the externalist cases. The rosaceous thoughts of Darwin and his twin share one sort of relatively general content. And if we must deliver some difference in their contents, still there is an internal difference between Darwin and his twin, since they are different people. And if the ideological differences between two people are sometimes irrelevant to the shared content of their thoughts, yet those people may have a more abstract internal similarity.

Still, there are intuitive difficulties that face internalist treatments of externalist cases. As we will see in this chapter, such treatments involve a somewhat unintuitive multiplication of forms of thought content, a somewhat unintuitive understanding of the subject matter of certain thoughts, and some tension with our ordinary practices of belief ascription. But, as we will see in the next chapter, a suitably developed externalism, which adequately treats the characteristic internalist cases, must suffer exactly the same three intuitive difficulties. So they cannot be decisive.

Since externalism can deploy all the resources of any internalism plus more besides, it may still seem poised to win. But, as we will see in Chapter 4, externalism introduces characteristic factors into thought contents that do not properly belong there. It introduces differences that are not suitably intuitive differences between thoughts.

Many details of my discussion may seem familiar. But what is crucial is the arrangement of these points, how they work together. The ground that we must cover is well trod, philosophers have mostly made up their minds on these topics, and we do not live in a patient time. But I must request your patience while I arrange all our ducks for a single snapshot.

2.1

We always remember the famous cases of Putnam, Burge, and Kripke. But we do not always remember all the levers of their mechanisms. So let me proceed slowly.

Putnam's key examples involve natural kind terms. The first is Twin Earth, which has, it is important to remember, *two* steps.[2] 'Twin Earth is *exactly* like Earth... [except] that the liquid called "water" is not H_2O but a different liquid whose chemical formula is...XYZ.... XYZ is indistinguishable from water at normal temperatures and pressures.... [I]t tastes like water and it quenches thirst like water.... [T]he oceans and lakes and seas of Twin Earth contain XYZ and not water,... [and] it rains XYZ on Twin Earth.'[3] If an Earth spaceship in our chemically savvy times crosses to Twin Earth, its crew will at first assume that, locally, 'water' has the same meaning as on Earth, but after discovering the chemical difference will withdraw that claim. The crew on a Twin Earth ship will behave symmetrically. The Twin Earth word 'water' refers to XYZ, and not to H_2O. Our word refers to H_2O, and not to XYZ.[4]

So far, all may agree. But there is a second step.

[R]oll the time back to about 1750. At that time chemistry was not developed on Earth or Twin Earth. The typical Earthian speaker of English did not know water consisted of hydrogen and oxygen, and the typical Twin Earthian speaker of English did not know 'water' consisted of XYZ. Let $Oscar_1$ be such a typical Earthian English speaker, and $Oscar_2$ be his counterpart on Twin Earth. You may suppose that there is no belief that $Oscar_1$ had about water that $Oscar_2$ did not have about 'water'. If you like, you may suppose that $Oscar_1$ and $Oscar_2$ were exact duplicates in appearance, feelings, thoughts, interior monologue, etc. Yet the extension of the term 'water' was just as much H_2O on Earth in 1750 as in 1950; and the extension of the term 'water' was just as much XYZ on Twin Earth in 1750 and 1950.[5]

The terms of the chemically unsophisticated and internally identical Oscars differ in reference. This is merely a claim about word reference and not about thought content, but most now accept the extension of this case to thoughts mediated by words.[6] As honest internalists, I think we should admit the intuitive force of this extension. We should admit that the internally identical Oscars apparently differ in their thoughts.[7]

But it is important that there are *two* intuitive pressures against internalism invoked by Twin Earth. First, the chemically unsophisticated Oscars are

---

[2] Putnam (1975: 223–5).   [3] Putnam (1975: 223).   [4] Putnam (1975: 224).
[5] Putnam (1975: 224).
[6] Putnam (1995: pp. xvii–xviii). The extensions are McGinn (1977) and Burge (1982). Burge's presentation of Twin Earth elides the preservation of reference over time.
[7] But for internalist resistance, see Segal (2000).

causally *en rapport* with different stuffs. Second, each Oscar must share reference over time with his own chemically-sophisticated descendants. This suggests that internalism is wrong in two different ways. Error One is its inability to deliver some differences between thoughts, differences due to the natural kinds in environments. Error Two is that its natural focus on individual ideology to capture content clashes with a need to preserve reference and thought content over time or within language communities despite significant differences in ideology.

Two errors are worse than one, but this complexity leaves room for quibbling. Error Two is invoked by other famous cases, and the recognition of Error One is often identified as the specific legacy of the Twin Earth case. So it is worth considering that first element in a pure, isolated way. We have some intuition that differences in the things with which we are causally *en rapport* generate intuitive differences in thought content, even when internal factors like ideology are shared. But isolated from the other elements of the original Twin Earth case, such factors are less intuitively forceful. Consider twin Oscars staring at qualitatively identical pigeons that differ merely in some bare haecceity. All can grant that their thoughts are about different pigeons, but those differences in reference or *de re* thought are intuitively and easily factored out of the rest of the thought content they share. They each believe of a grey pigeon that it is filthy, but believe that of different pigeons. Or consider thoughts mediated by the indexical word 'I', which in one intuitive sense shares a meaning though not a reference in the mouths of different speakers. 'Water', of course, is a natural kind term. But one crux is whether there is some analogous way to factor the Oscars' thoughts so that there is a kind of intuitive thought content that they share. It is not obvious that there is not, and Putnam's own suggestion that natural kind terms are 'indexical' suggests forms of factoring.[8] This is not to deny that the things with which we are causally *en rapport* are relevant to the contents of our thoughts in a deep way. But it does caution against generalizing very rapidly on the basis of the Twin Earth case alone to that conclusion. Twin Earth rests partly on preservation of reference over ideological differences and time. It is not a pure causal case.

And there is a second ground for caution. The twins share lots of ideology about the nature of the referent of 'water' that is met by both

[8] Putnam (1975: 229–35).

XYZ and H2O, quenching thirst and filling lakes as they do. Only stuffs meeting extensive introspectible conditions are revealed by that case as intuitively relevant to content, and indeed in a way that itself suggests a possible form of factoring.

These are not idle quibbles. Purer information-based cases, for instance Burge's cracks and shadows, have not generated the same level of intuitive consensus.[9] Nor, for that matter, is it *immediately* obvious that Twin Earth intuitions plausibly extend to all natural kind terms, let alone to all the terms in which one might attempt to capture shared ideology between the Oscars.[10] So while Twin Earth is forceful, and while a single intuitive counterexample may well be enough to show that internalism is false, we should be wary of over-quick generalization on the basis of one case.

Putnam's second famous case is also a language-based case requiring admittedly plausible extension to apply to thought content. While Twin Earth rests partly on pressures for shared reference over time within a planet despite differences in ideology, and the absence of such pressures across planets, the second case rests largely on intuitive pressures for shared reference within a contemporaneous language community despite ideological differences. That case is Elm-Beech:[11]

> Suppose you are like me and cannot tell an elm from a beech tree.... [T]he extension of 'elm' in my idiolect is the extension of 'elm' in anyone else's, viz., the set of all elm trees, and ... the set of all beech trees is the extension of 'beech' in *both* of our idiolects. Thus 'elm' in my idiolect has a different extension from 'beech' in your idiolect.... [But m]y *concept* of an elm tree is exactly the same as my concept of a beech tree (I blush to confess).... [Now l]et the words 'elm' and 'beech' be switched [in reference] on Twin Earth.... [S]uppose I have a *Doppelgänger* on Twin Earth who is molecule for molecule 'identical' with me, ... thinks the same verbalized thoughts I do, has the same sense data, the same dispositions, etc.... [Y]et he 'means' *beech* when he says 'elm' and *I* 'mean' *elm* when I say elm.[12]

This case suggests to Putnam a 'division of linguistic labor' for many terms: There are experts who know the criteria for belonging to the extension of

---

[9] Burge (1986a: 39–43).   [10] Mellor (1977); Schwarz (1978); Sterelny (1983).
[11] Perhaps this case also develops in a new way the intuition that the causal sources of distinct terms, say the teachers from whom we learn the terms, may introduce differences in contents. If so, it is also not pure.
[12] Putnam (1975: 226–7).

a term, and many others who do not. Yet the term in every competent speaker's mouth refers to just those things recognized by the experts.[13] Internalists should admit that there are intuitive differences in the thoughts of such twins on Earth and Twin Earth, and within the thoughts of each.

The third famous case is due to Burge. It depends like Elm-Beech on intuitive pressures for shared reference within a language community, but is explicitly addressed to thought content, involves errors of ideology and not merely incomplete understanding, and deploys a term that is apparently not a natural kind term and hence provides a template for possible generalization to thoughts mediated by many sorts of terms.

That case is Arthritis-Tharthritis:

> A given person has a large number of attitudes commonly attributed with content clauses containing 'arthritis' in oblique occurrence. For example, he thinks (correctly) that he has had arthritis for years.... In addition... he thinks falsely that he has developed arthritis in the thigh.... [T]he patient reports to his doctor his fear that his arthritis is now lodged in his thigh. The doctor replies by telling him that this cannot be so, since arthritis is specifically an inflammation of joints. Any dictionary could have told him the same. The patient is surprised, but relinquishes his view and goes on to ask what might be wrong with his thigh. [In a] second step... [w]e are to conceive of a situation in which the patient proceeds from birth through the same course of physical events that he actually does, right to and including the time at which he first reports his fear to his doctor.... But in our imagined case, physicians, lexicographers, and informed laymen apply 'arthritis' not only to arthritis but to various other rheumatoid ailments. The standard use of the term is to be conceived to encompass the patient's actual use.... In the counterfactual situation, the patient lacks some—probably *all*—of the attitudes commonly attributed with content clauses containing 'arthritis' in oblique occurrence.[14]

Internalists should grant that there are the intuitive pressures this case invokes, for shared reference despite ideological differences.[15] But there is room for quibbles about hasty generalization of this case also. Burge claims that his case is not isolated. He says that '[t]he argument has an extremely wide application. It does not depend, for example, on the kind of word "arthritis" is. We could have used an artifact term, an ordinary natural kind word, a color adjective, a social role term, a term for a historical style, an

---

[13] Putnam (1975: 227–9). [14] Burge (1979: 77–8).
[15] But see Segal (2000) for internalist resistance.

abstract noun, an action verb, a physical movement verb, or any of various other sorts of words.'[16] But some elements of Burge's case hobble an easy and radical generalization. For one thing, Burge presumes that the patient is generally competent with the language, that the error in question is isolated. So we cannot on the basis of his case alone immediately conclude, as some do, that the Burge-phenomenon can apply in a significant way to all or most of the terms of a speaker's language at once. And it is important to note that 'arthritis' is a word that sits on the edge. My dictionary says it is 'a condition causing inflammation, pain, and stiffness in the joints'.[17] There is a question about how we are to individuate conditions, and how we are to understand that definition. It can be read to suggest that any condition that causes inflammation, pain, and stiffness in the joints would be arthritis, or that arthritis is a particular natural disease that often does cause those things but is such that if it had other results or were found in the thigh would not count as arthritis, or even that arthritis is a particular natural disease that might conceivably cause other symptoms or move to the thigh. But let's grant Burge's deniable claims that arthritis is by definition restricted to the joints and isn't a natural kind term. Still, the fact that 'arthritis' is a disease term may mislead. For instance, Burge himself defends his view of the case, against the possible internalist response that we should interpret the patient's pre-correction thoughts on the basis of his own understanding of arthritis, in this relevant way:

The patient knows that he has had arthritis in the ankle and wrists for some time. Now with his new pains in the thigh, he fears and believes that he has got arthritis in the thigh, that his arthritis is spreading. Suppose we reinterpret all of these attitude attributions in accord with the method [suggested by the internalist]. We use our recently coined term 'tharthritis' to cover (somehow) arthritis and whatever it is he has in his thigh. On this new interpretation, the patient is right in thinking that he has tharthritis in the ankle and wrists. His belief that it has lodged in the thigh is true. His fear is realized. But these attributions are out of keeping with the way we do and should view his actual beliefs and fears. His belief is not true, and his fear is not realized. He will be relieved when he is told that one cannot have arthritis in the thigh.[18]

But it is important to notice that quick and radical generalization of Burge's case would properly require that it rest on nothing weightier than

[16] Burge (1979: 79). [17] Ehrlich, Flexner, Carruth, and Hawkins (1980: 34).
[18] Burge (1979: 95).

an unrecognized quirk of dictionary definitions. And recognition of an unknown quirk of dictionary definitions is implausible ground for rational 'relief' from medical 'fear'. We should grant the intuitive force of Burge's case against internalism, but again be wary of hasty generalization.

The last set of famous cases are Kripke's intuitive counterexamples to the description and cluster concept theories of name reference, theories that explain name reference by satisfaction of identifying properties had in mind.[19] Such cases also have a natural extension to thought content.

Kripke's first case is Feynman-Gell-Mann: The man on the Clapham bus can use Richard Feynman's name and Murray Gell-Mann's name to properly refer, while knowing only that they are both American physicists.[20] This case resembles Elm-Beech. It involves very thin or incomplete understanding.

Kripke's second case is Gödel-Schmidt:

Let's suppose someone says that Gödel is the man who proved the incompleteness of arithmetic.... Suppose that Gödel was not in fact the author of this theorem. A man named 'Schmidt', whose body was found in Vienna under mysterious circumstances many years ago, actually did the work in question. His friend Gödel somehow got hold of the manuscript and it was thereafter attributed to Gödel. On the [false views of name reference] in question, then, when our ordinary man uses the name 'Gödel', he really means to refer to Schmidt, because Schmidt is the unique person satisfying the description 'the man who discovered the incompleteness of arithmetic'.[21]

But that is obviously wrong. Like Arthritis-Tharthritis, this case involves erroneous understanding.

Kripke's third case introduces something new to us. It suggests that description and cluster concept theories of name reference across possible worlds are false, just in case anyone ever held such views. This is Modal Aristotle: We believe various true things about Aristotle that might be thought to uniquely pick him out in fact. But '[i]t just is not, in any intuitive sense of necessity, a necessary truth that Aristotle had the properties commonly attributed to him.... It would seem that it's a contingent fact Aristotle did *any* of the things commonly attributed to him today, *any* of these achievements that we so much admire.'[22] Modal reference, it seems,

---

[19] See Kripke (1980) for fuller explication.   [20] Kripke (1980: 81).   [21] Kripke (1980: 84).
[22] Kripke (1980: 74–5).

depends on factors that aren't in the head. Our talk of Aristotle is connected with the man himself, and he himself is carried over into the hypothetical situations that we discuss by deploying his name.

Despite my reservations about hasty generalization, honest internalists should admit that all six cases—Twin Earth, Elm-Beech, Arthritis-Tharthritis, Feynman-Gell-Mann, Gödel-Schmidt, and Modal Aristotle—suggest that internalism is false.

2.2

But there is a viable internalist response to all six externalist cases, which is at least roughly familiar. In other words, there is a viable notion of what is called 'narrow' or internally determinate content, despite the cases. It must be developed in some detail to evade certain difficulties, and even when so developed retains some intuitive problems. This chapter will develop that response by a sequential consideration of the famous externalist cases and of standing objections to such a view, and will isolate the few genuine problems for later treatment.

The famous externalist cases involve the mediation of thought by language. They are immediately relevant to thoughts whose medium is language. And the response we will end up with is a variant of three classes of familiar internalist views of reference sometimes called 'rigidified description accounts', 'metalinguistic accounts', and 'cluster theories'. Bluntly and too crudely put, it is this: There is a set of properties that can be ascertained a priori by a speaker to be positively relevant to whether something is the reference of a particular term that they use. And there are different relevant weights that those properties have in determining reference, which also can be ascertained a priori by the speaker. Among this set, there is a subset that have greatest weight in determining reference, and it includes 1) any properties that are recognized by the speaker as analytically true of or criterial for the referent, 2) the metalinguistic property of being referred to by that term, and 3) any other properties that are recognized by the speaker as a priori true of the referent (as for instance I may recognize my own existence). Call all that mechanism 'the description cluster' of the term. The content contributed by a term 'X' (that has at least a putative reference) to thoughts it mediates involves a rigidification of a description rooted in that cluster. It can be captured by something like 'the actual best satisfier of the description cluster for "X"'.

I will develop and explain this proposal in this section and the next, by working sequentially through the famous externalist cases, and by showing how its various features arise out of their details. Along the way, we will consider the objections to such a proposal that are incorporated in the classic papers in which those cases are found. Section 2.4 will consider other objections to such an account.

Begin with the Feynman-Gell-Mann and Gödel-Schmidt cases. A natural initial response to such cases is due to Russell, and is the origin of the class of possible responses that are called 'metalinguistic' responses: Perhaps Feynman is the thing called 'Feynman'.[23] Kripke considers this proposal in William Kneale's version, and notes an immediate objection and a possible fix: '[M]aybe not just one man can be called "Socrates", and some may call him "Socrates" while others may not.... Maybe only one man was called "Socrates" by me on a certain occasion.'[24]

Let's start with a first model in which 'Aristotle' means the thing named by that term, and in which terms are narrowly individuated, so that Onassis and the famous philosopher have different names that look and sound alike. For simplicity, let me assume that such a model can even be applied to last names.

The application of this metalinguistic account to our two initial cases is quite straightforward, and apparently delivers the intuitions Kripke fosters consistent with internalism. To each name 'X' there corresponds the following definite description: the thing named by 'X'. That, for all we have seen so far, can express a so-called narrow content, internally determined. Feynman is the thing named by 'Feynman'. Gell-Mann is the thing named by 'Gell-Mann'. Gödel is named by 'Gödel' even if he didn't prove incompleteness.

That initial proposal naturally suggests a variety of objections, and so it must be modified. Kripke explicitly states two.

First, as a theory of name reference, this account is circular.[25] But, I reply, we are not attempting to develop a reductive account of name reference, but an internalist account of thought content consistent with the

---

[23] Russell (1956: 251–4) and (1919: 167–80); Kneale (1962). [24] Kripke (1980: 68–9).
[25] Kripke (1980: 68–70).

intuitive force of Feynman-Gell-Mann and Gödel-Schmidt. So Kripke's first objection is not directly relevant in our argumentative context.

Still, you may feel that it is indirectly relevant. While Kripke is discussing names in particular, still it may seem that the point of his case easily generalizes to many sorts of terms. And descriptions apparently determine reference only by means of the references of the terms deployed in the descriptions. And so any defense of internalism against Kripke's case may also seem to require a developed internalist account of how descriptive primitive terms have reference that evades the suggested generalization of his case, and this may seem impossible.

In fact, in the case that concerns us, the case of thoughts, not all the relevant 'descriptions' *are* mediated by words. In our initial model, contents are merely expressed by descriptions. But in any case we will eventually see that there is a response to each of these three points. First, I do not suggest that we generalize the simple initial metalinguistic proposal for all terms, and it will soon be evident that Kripke's cases do not generalize as easily as this objection suggests. Second, we will see in Chapter 4 that is not quite exactly the reference of terms deployed in the descriptions which is relevant to thought content, though in fact this is more of a minor qualification than a significant dissent from the importance of reference. Third, the next part will begin to sketch a positive account of the internalist content of relevantly primitive notions, in which internally determinate qualia will play a crucial role.

But what I need to stress for the moment is one aspect of my first response, that we must proceed more slowly than this objection suggests. Kripke's specific cases do not imply the quick generalization that underlies this objection, nor does he himself suggest this. We have waited for almost forty years for Kripke's 'picture' to be developed into a theory that can treat in some way that is acceptable to more than a handful of partisans the puzzles that motivated the description and cluster concept theories of names that he attacked, puzzles to which we will turn in the next chapter. This is not a criticism of Kripke's cases or discussion, but it explains why it is appropriate for me to request your patience for a few pages.

Yet there may seem to be a more immediately telling way to push the circularity worry. Perhaps the worry is that it is inappropriate to deploy a notion like that of the thing named by a term in an account of thought content mediated by that term without a more concrete and reductive proposal about what such a notion comes to. But if necessary, we can borrow the needed reductive account from Kripke himself, in the manner of those now called 'causal descriptivists'.[26] Kripke provided us with a now quite popular picture of the way that, after an initial dubbing of an object by a name, the reference of the name is preserved across an historical chain of transmission of that name from one speaker to the next, when the 'receiver of the name... intend[s] when he learns it to use it with the same reference as the man from whom he heard it'.[27] And that seems to provide the necessary reductive description of what it is to be the referent of the term. All internalists need do is claim that that description reflects the speaker's internally determinate understanding of what it is to be called by a name. After all, Kripke seems to depend on our generally shared understanding of what it is to be called by a name to deliver intuitions about his cases that support his proposal.[28] Of course, we may not be self-conscious that we have such a conception, but it seems fixed by our internally constituted dispositions to respond in various ways to various situations, and indeed Kripke's own methodology suggests that we can all become aware of it in our armchairs, if only we are confronted with the relevant hypothetical cases, which of course in some sense we were all along capable of conceiving.

Externalists may object. They may be skeptical that I can deliver the relevant mechanism consistent with internalism. But we will begin that task in the next part, a task which will encompass the rest of this book. They may also have worries about the semantic sophistication in ordinary speakers that this reply presumes. But we will return to that worry in Section 2.3, after the necessary mechanism to discuss it will be in place, and where it will be a central focus. They may also object to certain applications of this view to the ascription of thoughts to those in other possible worlds. But we will consider that objection, in Scott Soames' version, in Section 2.4, again after necessary mechanism is in place.

Subject to these possible worries to which we will return, Kripke's first objection can be avoided. Still, Kripke makes a second objection to a metalinguistic proposal, and it does suggest at least *some* generalization of his cases. '[I]n the same sense...you could get a...theory of the

---

[26] Lewis (1984: 226–7) and (1999: 353 n. 22); Kroon (1987).   [27] Kripke (1980: 96).
[28] A point due to Frank Jackson among others.

meaning of any expression in English.... Of course, anyone... knows that if "quarks" means something then "quarks are called 'quarks'" will express a truth.... But his knowledge that it expresses a truth does not have much to do with the meaning of the term "quarks".'[29]

But two replies are available. First, as I've said, for our initial internalist model to properly apply to the names, it need not also apply to all terms. Second, in light of the application of Kripke-style arguments to other sorts of terms, for instance natural kind terms, by Kripke himself and by Putnam and Burge, there is some irony in Kripke's suggestion that there are rich descriptive constraints on knowing what a quark is that are met by those whose knowledge has much to do with the meaning of the term 'quarks'. If there are descriptive conditions that must be understood by someone who is competent with 'quark', then they can play a part in a description or cluster concept theory of such a term. Now put these two replies together: Either understanding descriptive conditions is a necessary condition for successfully using a term to refer or it is not. Kripke can't have it both ways.

Of course, Kripke's second objection does underline the need for a more developed positive internalist proposal, which resolves the dilemma that faces Kripke himself here in one way or the other. But we are coming slowly back to that, through the medium of famous externalist cases that plausibly require it.

There is yet a third objection to our metalinguistic model that is implicit in Kripke's discussion and has played an important role in later discussions. Presume with Kripke that a descriptive condition 'gives the meaning' of a name only if it picks out the individual to which the name refers in all possible worlds in which that individual exists, and that it merely 'fixes the reference' of a name when it merely picks out that individual in the actual world. And remember Modal Aristotle. In particular, note that it is implausible to claim that it is an *essential* property of Gell-Mann, a property he has (so to speak) in every possible world in which he exists, to be named 'Gell-Mann'. So it would seem that such a metalinguistic descriptive condition cannot capture the meaning of a name.

There are a variety of extant metalinguistic views that can be classified by their response to this objection. Jerrold Katz suggested that we deploy a 'purely nominal bearer relation' between a thing and a name, which

[29] Kripke (1980: 69–70).

requires no contingent real conditions of the bearer of the name and hence fails to determine reference.[30] Kent Bach once suggested that, since I can name things in other worlds, the property of being called by a name is a kind of essential property of the thing.[31] More recently he has suggested that the relevant property isn't essential, and hence there is a sense in which Aristotle might not have been Aristotle.[32] Brian Loar suggested that we need not be concerned with cross-world reference in providing an account of internalist thought content.[33]

But I favor one version of a fourth response. As far as the phrase 'named by "Aristotle"' captures real concrete conditions in the world at least gestured at by Kripke, it is merely contingent that Aristotle is linked to that term in that way. Since Aristotle is only contingently called 'Aristotle' on this natural understanding, then Modal Aristotle shows that such a condition can't 'give the meaning' of that name. But we can modify that description so that it captures not only an essential property but a so-called individual essence, had only by Aristotle in any possible world. In other words, we can rigidify the description.[34]

There is more than one mechanism by which to attempt this. Felicia Ackerman and Alvin Plantinga proposed variants in which the rigidification is accomplished by deploying Plantinga's notion of an alpha-transform.[35] This turns on Kripke's notion of a rigid designator of X, which designates X in every possible world in which X exists. Where 'alpha' is a rigid-designator for the actual way things are, the alpha-transform of being the F is being the F in alpha. As Ackerman came to note, this notion may be implausibly rich to capture the content of ordinary thoughts.[36] The whole way things are seems not ordinarily invoked by a single name. Another possibility, developed by Jackson, and negatively by Stalnaker and Block, for the analogous case of 'water',[37] is an 'actual' operator, whereby the extension of 'the actual F', in any possible world, is the thing that is the unique F in

---

[30] Katz (1994: 6–7).   [31] Bach (1981: 375).   [32] Bach (2002).   [33] Loar (1976).

[34] This introduces a difference between my proposal here and the account of introspectible content in Mendola (1997), which is related to the physicalism presumed here.

[35] Plantinga (1978); Ackerman (1979b). On alpha-transforms see Plantinga (1974: chs. 4 and 5). Ackerman holds that such an account might give an a priori analysis that does not preserve sense, and hence speaks of non-descriptive connotations. We will return to this worry.

[36] Ackerman (1979a, 1980, 1985).

[37] Jackson (1994, 1998); Block and Stalnaker (1999). Searle (1983: 258) deploys this sort of terminology to explain the mechanism of using a definite description rigidified 'by fiat' to give the meaning of a name.

actual fact.[38] Depending on what is meant by actual fact, this may work. But the now most popular way to understand this phrase involves appeal to the whole actual world, and this creates problems analogous to those of the alpha-transform. So I prefer a third sort of analogous mechanism which is familiar from the work of David Kaplan: dthat [beta], where 'beta' is a description.[39] Developing Reichenbach's proposal that 'I' means the same as 'the person who utters this token',[40] Kaplan suggested in light of worries analogous to Modal Aristotle that rather 'I' means the same as 'dthat [the person who utters this token]'.[41] This has the same meaning or character in everyone's mouth, but refers to a different person in each. And it refers to that person in every possible world in which they exist, even if they never speak in some of those worlds. And it does so not by invoking the whole actual world, but by drilling through to one actual person, who may also be in other worlds. It seems that we can generalize this strategy to cover the case at hand.[42] To the term 'Feynman' there corresponds the following rigidified definite description: dthat [thing named by 'Feynman'].

But there is a complication. There are two ways to interpret this phrase and 'dthat' generally, in which the description is either incorporated or not incorporated in the content conveyed by the phrase, and while the first is what we need, the second is what Kaplan originally intended.[43] Kaplan meant that phrase to directly refer, so that the object referred to is its only semantic contribution, though he admits there is an alternative interpretation, the interpretation we need, suggested by some of his initial work, in which it 'would not carry the individual itself into a possible world but rather would carry instructions to run back home [to actuality] and get the individual who there satisfies certain specifications'.[44] In this interpretation, the semantic contribution of the phrase includes the description.

Because certain details of this mechanism will matter to us later on, allow me to rather pedantically note them now. First, of course Kaplan doesn't literally mean that we are really going to run back home to the whole actual possible world, or that we are really going to start in another

---

[38] Block and Stalnaker (1999: 1–12).   [39] Kaplan (1978) and (1989b: 521–2).
[40] Reichenbach (1947: 284–7).
[41] Kaplan (1989b: 522). Note his qualifications and Reichenbach's complications.
[42] Ackerman floats and rejects this, for reasons introduced in n. 35. See Ackerman (1989: 9–10).
[43] Kaplan (1989a: 578–82).   [44] Kaplan (1989a: 580).

possible world. A second relevant point is that dthat [thing named by 'Feynman'] in the interpretation under consideration designates the actual guy, without invoking the whole actual world, although in so doing it does not obliterate the semantic contribution of the mediating description. But a third relevant point is that when we use such a rigidified description here in actuality, so to speak, to talk about that guy even 'over there' in another possible world where he isn't named 'Feynman', we are of course merely implying that he is named 'Feynman' in actual fact. Nevertheless, we don't have to invoke the whole actual world to do so, as if it really were a single place among many that had to be specifically invoked so we can talk about it. It isn't just one place among many, but rather what there is, period. A fourth point relevant to the interpretation of this mechanism is that there are other possible situations in which such a rigidified description would drill through to a different guy than the one it nets in actual fact. All those rigidified descriptions would share a character, and hence could capture the same internally determinate, narrow mental content. But they would refer to different people. This may occasion objection, to which we will return in Section 2.4. A fifth point is that the descriptions might conceivably involve genuinely indexical elements like 'I' or 'now', so that two rigidified descriptions might share the same character, capture the same narrow and hence internally determinate content, even in this actual world, and yet refer to different entities.

Naming and Necessity is powerfully convincing, and this proposal takes some of its central contributions very seriously. First, as I noted above, the metalinguistic reference-fixing description in question can incorporate Kripke's own picture of reference-determination, at least implicitly. Second, the description in question has a form that evades possible counterexamples by being contingently but a priori true of its referent. Kripke suggests that we can know a priori the contingent truth that the standard meter is one meter long. That very stick might have been longer or shorter than one meter in length, but we can know a priori that it is in fact one meter in length.[45] The way reference to the stick is fixed assures that truth a priori, even though it is contingent. And the point seems to generalize. It is intuitively plausible that if we can ascertain from an armchair the conditions required for names to refer, which is after all Kripke's practice, then there

[45] Kripke (1980: 56–7).

are a priori ascertainable conditions that fix that thing, if anything, to which a name refers. It is, Kripke has taught us, not problematic if such conditions are merely contingent.

Objections to Kripke's treatment of the contingent a priori are possible. For instance, Albert Casullo notes that knowledge of general logical principles and semantic facts like definitions is arguably a posteriori,[46] so that it is possible that even our armchair knowledge of a simple analytic truth like bachelors are unmarried is in fact a posteriori. He furthermore suggests that in Kripke's case 'one cannot know a priori that one has fixed the reference of "one meter" by stipulation'.[47] After all, memory is involved, and memory intuitively yields only a posteriori knowledge. But there are also replies to these objections available. It is not unreasonable to think that there is better initial chance for an account of logical knowledge that is not empirical than for one that is. And armchair knowledge of the meaning of one's own terms like 'bachelor' or of the truth of claims like 'bachelors are unmarried' may well seem a paradigm of a priori knowledge, which by a very natural extension would cover the sorts of unusual semantic knowledge involved in reference-fixing by stipulation or metalinguistic descriptions. But still, the key fact from our current perspective is not about apriority in any strict epistemic sense, but about whether the relevant semantic facts and logical capacities are fixed by one's internally determinate states. It might be best to explicitly dub this phenomenon, to which I will shortly return, the 'semantic a priori'. It is not really a crucially epistemic thing. Nevertheless, it is not implausible to think that one has rough armchair epistemic access to such things, to at least a large degree, of a sort I will sketch in Chapter 8, whether that counts as strictly epistemically a priori access or not. And we can for our immediate purposes reasonably take Kripke to mean armchair knowledge by 'a priori knowledge'.

2.3

Here's where we are so far: We have a general schema for an internalist account, which rigidifies contingent (and semantically a priori) reference-fixing definite descriptions that may be metalinguistic in form. And it can

---

[46] Casullo (2003: 216). [47] Casullo (2003: 208).

deliver intuitive results in Kripke's cases, consistent with internalism, in the way I have sketched. But the other externalist cases will require further development of this so far vague proposal.

The Twin Earth case suggests that the content contributed by the word 'water' to thought on both Earth and Twin Earth is more robust than something merely metalinguistic. Putnam specifies that 'XYZ is indistinguishable from water at normal temperatures and pressures. In particular, it tastes like water and it quenches thirst like water. Also... the oceans and lakes and seas of Twin Earth contain XYZ... [and] it rains XYZ...'.[48] Perhaps such shared conditions are part of the contingent a priori reference-fixing descriptions for 'water' on both planets in 1750. It is certainly contingent that water is in the lakes, but if there was nothing in the lakes and oceans and streams faced by our ancestors then it is far from obvious that their term 'water' referred. David Chalmers has already developed the proposal that something analogous to rigidified reference-fixing descriptions may provide the proper analysis of the Twin Earth case.[49]

Still, I think that we might be wrong about some features that we take water to have in the relevant a priori sense and hence which seem relevant to fixing reference. Our current notion of water is chemically sophisticated, and its chemical form matters a lot to even ordinary speakers, so that we might find out that water is nowhere but in a small puddle in Down. But even in pre-chemical 1750 we might have been wrong in thinking that water in fact was in certain lakes, or that water was what rained on all parts of the earth. So more refinement of our proposal is required.

We must deploy something like a cluster theory of reference-fixing, in which various descriptive and metalinguistic properties have various relevant weights. This might be modeled on Searle's famous cluster-description theory,[50] which was one of the targets of Kripke's attack, or on Michael McKinsey's post-Kripkean version.[51] These are ultimately rooted, like some of Kripke's examples, in Wittgenstein's discussion of Moses in the *Investigations*, just as the *Tractatus* is the ultimate source of Kripke's concern with modality as central to meaning.[52]

So replace the rigidified metalinguistic description recently proposed with something like this mechanism: There is a set of properties that is

---

[48] Putnam (1975: 223). [49] Chalmers (1996: 59). [50] Searle (1958).
[51] McKinsey (1978). [52] Wittgenstein (1968: I 79) and (1961).

constituted by the internally determinate dispositions of a speaker to be positively relevant to what counts in their judgment as the referent of a given term (and hence is semantically a priori for them). And there are various relative weights of those properties in determining what counts as the referent under various conditions, also constituted by the internally determinate dispositions of the speaker. Normal competent adults can come to at least rough armchair knowledge of these properties and their weights for their own case, in a way I will sketch in Chapter 8, but that is not a constitutive constraint on their nature.

Among this set of properties, there is a subset that have relatively great weight in fixing reference, and it includes 1) any properties that are taken by the speaker as analytically true of or criterial for things in that extension, in a sense of 'taken by' constituted by their internally determinate dispositions, 2) the metalinguistic property of being referred to by that term, and 3) any other properties that are taken as each a priori true of things in that extension by the speaker, in a sense also constituted by their internally determinate dispositions. This should not be taken to imply that anything that is to count as a referent must satisfy *all* of these properties. There might also be a second key subset of the positively relevant properties, which are at least apparently distinct properties taken by the speaker to be positively relevant to each of the preceding three types of criteria, and so on.

Call all that, all the relevant properties and their weights, 'the description cluster' of a term for a speaker at a time. Our recent proposal rigidified a metalinguistic definite description. But now the content contributed by a term 'X' with a putative reference to thoughts it mediates for a speaker at a time can be captured by something like 'dthat [best satisfier of their description cluster for "X"]'.

Some remarks about the interpretation of this proposal: First, it invokes properties that are taken as analytically true of or criterial for things in an extension, and properties that are taken by the speaker as a priori true of things in that extension. The difference is that some things that a speaker may take to be a priori true in the relevant sense, for instance that 'I exist', are not really analytic in the standard sense. Their content or meaning assures that they are true when they are thought, but they are not truths of content or meaning in the standard sense. So the relevant sort of aprioricity is broader than analyticity. Second, I have renounced an epistemic reading of what it means to be 'taken by the speaker as a priori true' or 'taken by the speaker as analytic or criterial'. Being taken by the speaker involves the *semantic* a priori, which is to say that it is fixed by the internally determinate dispositions of the speaker, about which the speaker may be misinformed. In particular, some property is taken by the speaker as analytic or criterial or a priori true of something referred to by a particular term if the speaker is very firmly disposed not to call things that the speaker takes to lack that property by that term. The difference between being taken as merely a priori true and being taken as specifically analytic or criterial is a relatively subtle difference which depends on whether the speaker takes the thought of the claim as a condition for its a priori truth. To be very firmly disposed includes a certain range of firmness with vague borders, and so too do being taken as analytic or a priori. This is an advantage in dealing with Quine's worries about the firmness of the analytic/synthetic distinction.

This proposal seems consistent with internalism about thought content, at least for all we have seen so far. But there is a natural worry. Perhaps the elements of the description cluster are themselves subject to the Twin Earth or Arthritis-Tharthritis phenomena, and hence provide indirect routes to externalism. Still, that claim is not established by those cases themselves, since two intuitive cases do not establish a general result. And there must be some conditions on speaker competence for meaningful use of a term, and for all we know so far our proposal has articulated those conditions. But we will certainly need to return to this worry as we slowly develop this proposal.

While in 'The Meaning of "Meaning"' Putnam did not explicitly object to internalist accounts of narrow or internally determinate content of this general sort,[53] he made what might seem a telling implicit objection, by proposing what seems to be an alternative conception of speaker competence: understanding the stereotype of a term.[54] He said this: 'The fact that a feature (e.g. stripes) is included in the stereotype associated with a word X does not mean that it is an analytic truth that all Xs have that feature, nor that most Xs have that feature, nor that all normal Xs have that feature, nor that some Xs have that feature. Three-legged tigers and albino tigers are not logically contradictory entities. Discovering that our stereotype has been based on non-normal or unrepresentative members of a natural kind is not a logical contradiction. If tigers lost their stripes they

---

[53] Putnam (1988: 27) presents a later objection to which we will return.   [54] Putnam (1975: 269).

would not thereby cease to be tigers, nor would butterflies necessarily cease to be butterflies if they lost their wings.'[55]

But, I reply, it might still be semantically a priori that some tigers—the semantically central tigers, those tigers through whom an individual's reference to the entire kind passes—have or once had stripes and four legs, or at the very least it might be semantically a priori that such factors are relevant among others in the way our cluster model requires.

There is another objection immediately suggested by this treatment of Twin Earth. Most share the intuition fostered by Burge's extension of Twin Earth to thought content that the twins differ in their thoughts. But the narrow content suggested by our proposal may seem to be something that they share.

But two replies are available. First, even if two corresponding thoughts of the twins in some sense differ in thought content, still they may differ merely in reference, and that may be all that the central Twin Earth intuitions demand. Second, even if we accept Burge's full extension of the Twin Earth case to *de dicto* thought, even if we insist that any intuitive narrow content must differ between the twins, our proposal can be further refined to deliver that result. Consider its key metalinguistic element: the property of being referred to by a term.

What are terms? How are they individuated? There are a variety of different accounts with the general form I have suggested, which adopt different accounts of terms. We need an account consistent with internalism. This means that adequate conceptions of the words must be available subject to the internalist constraint. When our thought is actually mediated by words, it must be that the words themselves are internally constituted. We must speak the words understandingly to ourselves, in our mind's ear, or utter them out loud or write them in such a way that they exist at tongue's or finger's end. Such speech must occur in the specious present, or alternatively someone must have the unwinding disposition to so speak all curled up in them at the moment. But this element of internalism does not suffice to fix the proper individuation of the words in question, partly because in one intuitive sense words may be types of inscriptions. And it does not suffice to fix the various internally determinate concepts of word-individuation we might deploy in description clusters.

[55] Putnam (1975: 250).

I have already suggested that Aristotle and the shipping magnate who married Jackie have relevantly different names, but there are other similar issues still in question: If I say 'Aristotle', meaning to refer to some one thing under one description, twice within an hour, does that make the same metalinguistic contribution to my thought content or a different one? Do Putnam's twins usually have thoughts with the same metalinguistic contents or different ones?

Our model can deliver the intuitions fostered by Burge's extension of Twin Earth, if we individuate words so that the twins' metalinguistic and hence narrow contents differ. And we can. Variants of this suggestion are available for analogous cases. For instance, individual perceptual beliefs mediated by the qualitatively identical experiences of the twins involve distinct tokens of experience. Hence, as Searle suggested, it might be that the perceptual beliefs of the twins focused on local water are different in content while internalism is true, even when they aren't mediated by words.[56] Alternatively, as Schiffer suggested, it might be relevant that they are beliefs of different individuals, and probably at different times.[57] These moves are not ad hoc for internalists. If two individuals think 'I am in danger', they have thoughts with intuitively distinct narrow contents that will explain their distinct behaviors. And it is natural for internalists to explain differences in reference by available internal differences.

Despite the fact that our model can deliver the orthodox reaction to Twin Earth in this way, it is not totally unreasonable to think that it shouldn't, or at least that it doesn't need to. Despite the sociological dominance of Burge's reaction to Twin Earth, some retain Putnam's initial intuition that the twins' thoughts are the same though their references differ. So I favor an ecumenical response. We can individuate terms narrowly or somewhat more broadly, so that the twins deploy the same term 'water' and so that they don't. And so there are two kinds of narrow content, one they share and one they don't.

There are other factors that demand at least two forms of narrow content: The remaining famous externalist cases suggest pressures for shared reference within language communities, like one element of Twin Earth. And this may initially seem a problem for me. Fine individuation of metalinguistic contents may be necessary to deliver Twin Earth intuitions,

---

[56] Searle (1983: 207–8).   [57] Schiffer (1978).

but threaten too many differences when we get to these other cases. Consider Elm-Beech. The only obvious elements in the first subset of the description cluster for 'elm' are the property of being a tree and the property of being referred to by 'elm', and perhaps other metalinguistic properties that reflect Putnam's account of individual competence. If we individuate these words finely, we can explain differences between two twins in different language communities. If we individuate them broadly, we can capture similarities within communities. But we can deliver all the intuitive phenomena consistent with internalism only by deploying two sorts of narrow contents at once. Broad narrow content is shared within communities (and unfortunately across communities). Fine narrow content is not shared across communities, but not within them either.

This multiplication of forms of narrow content is a genuine intuitive problem for my proposal. There are intuitive pressures for different treatments of otherwise like cases within communities or planets on the one hand and across planets or possible worlds on the other. Given that planets can start out of communication but come into communication just like different human communities on earth, and given that the cost of a differential treatment of people on other planets or possible worlds is a real difficulty for externalists in expressing the contents of those alien thoughts, one might wonder about the depth and significance of these pressures. But they are real. We have distinguished two kinds of narrow content, and thoughts obviously can share narrow content and yet differ in reference and hence a third kind of recognizable content. But we must remain attentive to the intuitive strain of proposing two kinds of narrow content and indeed three kinds of content. Thoughts intuitively have one kind of content, and not multiple forms.

There are various ways that externalists may be tempted to buttress this intuitive worry with more theoretical objections. For one thing, while it may be relatively easy to accept that there may be multiple ways to attribute mental states, say *de re* and *de dicto* attributions, still I have claimed that content is characteristic of mental states, and hence has psychological reality, and this may make multiple contents harder to swallow. What's more, it may seem quite inappropriate for an internalist to admit that reference, which can differ while internal mental states remain the same, delivers a third kind of mental content.

But some refinement of my internalist proposal can evade these theoretical worries. I think that there is a single core type of mental content, which is internally determinate, and which is what I have called fine narrow content.[58] An easy abstraction from that core constitutes broad narrow content, and the core also fixes reference in context, subject to possible qualifications that we will consider in Chapter 4. So really there is but one central type of content, and it is internally determinate.

Despite the fact that these theoretical objections can be evaded, my invocation of several sorts of content is not an intuitive feature of my proposal. To keep this problem in mind, let me call it the 'multiple-contents objection'. It will be quite important in our later discussions.

We have one famous externalist case yet to consider. Burge's Arthritis-Tharthritis case is more complex than Elm-Beech. This is partly because there may be some other descriptive elements that are plausible constraints on competence for such a case, and indeed may be elements of the first subset of our description cluster. But it is also because the doctor and the patient may initially differ in what factors they would take to be at all relevant to the reference of 'arthritis'.

Consistent with our proposal, we should expect what is a priori in the most relevant semantic sense to potentially differ in some way from one individual to the next, and indeed to be revisable. When in Chapter 9 we consider realistic thoughts intuitively shared among those who are not twins, this will deepen the multiple-contents objection. There will be various different levels of abstraction of the broad narrow contents that different individuals share. And Arthritis-Tharthritis also further underlines the need for a distinction between what I've called semantic aprioricity on one hand and armchair epistemic access on the other. There is some internally fixed dispositional fact about the individual, modulo a certain amount of indeterminacy, regarding what corrections to their usage they would accept from others, and indeed in general about how they would assess the weight of various factors in their description cluster under various hypothetical scenarios. That constitutes semantic aprioricity. But there is also someone's sense, in the armchair at any moment, of how that would go for them. And that is of course merely a fallible reflection of semantic aprioricity. Semantic aprioricity is what really matters to internally

---

[58] This is different from Mendola (1997).

determinate thought content, and this suggests a limit to our privileged or armchair access to our thought. The patient in the Arthritis-Tharthritis case may not have privileged access prior to his visit to the doctor of the sorts of corrections he is prepared to accept. He may be surprised about himself, even about what is semantically a priori for him.

From Burge's case, let's turn to Burge's objections to a metalinguistic account. 'If the metalinguistic reinterpretation account is to be believed, we cannot say that a relevant English speaker shares a view (for example) that many old people have arthritis, with *anyone* who does not use the English word "arthritis".... This result is highly implausible. Ascriptions of such that-clauses..., regardless of the subject's language, serve to provide single descriptions and explanations of similar patterns of behavior, inference, and communication.'[59] This venerable objection derives from Church and Langford.[60]

But, I reply, our proposal is not *solely* metalinguistic. It is just that a metalinguistic property is one crucial element of some description clusters, which helps especially in Burge-style cases. All the behavioral and ideological similarities between, say, Italian speakers and English speakers to which Burge adverts are available to internalists, and help constitute at least the very close similarity of the narrow contents of those individuals across language communities. And there is indeed a third kind of narrow content, which subtracts metalinguistic elements, which those Italian and English speakers who have a robust conception of arthritis can exactly share.

This may seem an inadequate response. Perhaps the best Burge-style case against our model involves those with different very incomplete or erroneous understandings of arthritis who are also members of different language communities. There are some significant psychological differences between these individuals, which are relevant in exactly the ways Burge himself stresses in his objection. Still, this fact is discordant with our practice of belief attribution. That practice involves principles of attribution that run through someone's public language. If we are going to report an Italian speaker's propositional attitudes in English that-clauses, we will take the appropriate translation from the public language Italian to the public language English as a constraint on that attribution, whether that exactly captures his or her thoughts or not. So there is some tension between our

[59] Burge (1979: 96). [60] Church (1950).

current proposal and ordinary practices of belief attribution involving such principles. Here again is an objection that requires more treatment. So I will call it the 'belief-ascription objection' for mnemonic purposes.

Notice also that such an objection seems especially telling if we deploy very fine-grained word-individuation. An individual may think of a given person twice through the mediation of two tokens of 'Charles', but hence have thoughts that have by a very fine-grained account different narrow contents. The shared causal-functional or inferential role of those words in the psychology in question may provide grounds for yet another form of narrow content that the two thoughts share. But this further proliferation of narrow contents is certainly not intuitively desirable, and again reinforces the multiple-contents objection.

Burge's next objection is that a metalinguistic account replaces contents that are intuitively about objects with contents about words.[61]

But, I reply, our internalist proposal is not that people share only attitudes with metalinguistic contents, since there is plenty that is not metalinguistic in the cluster descriptions. And the proposal is not that there are just metalinguistic contents as distinct from object-level contents. It is that the proper understanding of object-level contents sometimes involves a metalinguistic element. Burge's presumption that metalinguistic attitudes and object-level attitudes are distinct begs the question.

Still, I should admit the intuitive difference between object-level and metalinguistic notions of content. Our intuitive sense is that thoughts that are about objects are not about their names, not even partly about their names. There are ways to mitigate this objection. A simple appeal to such intuitive strain would seem inadequate as an objection to the claim that mathematical truth consists in provability. Mathematical sentences are not intuitively about proofs. If mathematical truth is in fact a kind of provability, then what such sentences are intuitively about is a kind of shadow or ideal object thrown by the proofs. What they are intuitively about is not a good direct guide to their semantics. But, there are also ways to reinforce the objection. Here is one *friend* of narrow content on a metalinguistic proposal:

Narrow content then ends up being almost exclusively about words. Consider 'arthritis'. Is its character merely 'thing called "arthritis" in my home environment'?... The cognitive content of *arthritis* is much richer than what is provided

[61] Burge (1979: 96).

by that meager description of its character. So we must enrich the description. We might try, for example, 'disease called "arthritis" in my home environment'. But the problem is that *disease* is also a deferential concept [which is subject to the arthritis-tharthritis phenomenon]. So, for that matter, is the concept of one's home environment. So we are left with 'thing called "disease" called "arthritis" in my thing called "home environment".' But now we are back to the original problem.[62]

It is necessary for me to quibble about some details of this way of pressing the objection. Burge-style referential deferentiality does not alone establish that our model can only deliver such very thin narrow contents. Indeed, it is a caricature of *externalism* to claim that there are no internal constraints on the possession of linguistic competence for even a single term that involve comprehension of relevant descriptive conditions, let alone that there are no internal constraints on competence for all terms of a language at once. Such a radical claim is certainly not established by the intuitive cases we reviewed in Section 2.1. These constraints rooted in competence can remain in place even while deference is made regarding fine details. In particular, if the facts about what it is for something to be called by a term are not understood by someone in a gross way, we are unlikely to cede them any linguistic competence in use of that term at all. And some key facts about deference are a matter of semantic aprioricity which is internally determinate.

But, despite my quibbling, I grant the intuitive force of the general objection at hand. I grant that there are intuitive differences between object-level and metalinguistic notions. And so I grant that my proposal implies that some thoughts are about things that those thoughts do not intuitively appear to be about. This is another objection we must remember for later treatment. Call it the 'subject-matter objection'.

Burge's final objection to metalinguistic accounts returns to a point we left hanging in Section 2.2. It is this: '[M]etalinguistic reasoning requires a certain self-consciousness about one's words and social institutions. This sort of sophistication emerged rather late in human history. (Cf. any history of linguistics.) Semantical notions were a product of this sophistication.'[63] In particular, the metalinguistic notion deployed here, being referred to by at term, may seem too sophisticated to be present in children's thoughts

---

[62] Segal (2000: 115).   [63] Burge (1979: 97).

about elms and beeches. And 'dthat' is an especially problematic feature of our model in this light. Perhaps only Duns Scotus thought of such things until the second half of the last century.

But remember that our proposal is not that there are just metalinguistic contents as distinct from object-level contents, but that what object-level contents *are* involves one metalinguistic element. And it is also quite plausible that children have the internally determinate ability to call things by terms. Likewise for those early in human history. Otherwise we would not ascribe to them linguistically-mediated thoughts in any full-blown sense. And remember that semantic aprioricity is not epistemic aprioricity. Armchair introspection of our notions is a complex thing we learn gradually to do, as is armchair introspection of our allied dispositional capacities, and it should not be surprising that our ability to introspect the metalinguistic features of our thought grows with time and sophistication, and is of course fallible. What's more, an adult's notion of calling and referring may be more refined than that of a child, which is intuitively relevant to the contents of their more refined thoughts. The specific worry about 'dthat' is more plausible. But of course we might similarly doubt that fine points about modal reference are important at all to the content of thought. They seem quite sophisticated also. The notion expressed by 'dthat' seems no more sophisticated than the alleged modal features of the contents that it is introduced to capture.

Nevertheless, once again I admit the strain on our everyday intuitions exacted by my internalist proposal, which is due to its apparent vulnerability to the three named objections that are still in play. We still must properly attend to the multiple-contents, belief-ascription, and subject-matter objections. And of course I must still provide a positive sketch of how there can be sufficient internally determinate notions to fill up the relevant description clusters. The last is a task that will occupy the rest of this book.

2.4

We turn now to more recent objections to internalist proposals like mine, which are not found in the famous original externalist discussions. There are three.

Felicia Ackerman's reason for abandoning her earlier and somewhat similar suggestion is this:[64] It is possible to believe that the proposition that Hesperus is visible is identical to the proposition that Hesperus is visible without believing that the proposition Hesperus is visible is identical with the proposition that dthat [entity referred to be this token of 'Hesperus'] is visible, just as it is possible to believe that any a priori correct philosophical analysis of a notion is incorrect.

But through the mediation of words one utters to oneself, even words one fully understands, it is also possible, at least in haste and without care, to believe explicit contradictions, so this objection is not decisive. Ackerman is right that the similarity of her objection to Frege's famous worry about Hesperus and Phosphorus, which is one of the key motivating cases for internalism to which we turn in the next chapter, should give us pause. But it *is* different: Frege's problem is not Moore's paradox of analysis. One way to make my point is to note that it is possible to have armchair knowledge, at least if something like Ackerman's analysis is correct, of the proposition Hesperus is visible is identical with the proposition that dthat [entity referred to be this token of 'Hesperus'] is visible. But it is not possible to have armchair knowledge that Hesperus is identical to Phosphorus, in the case Frege envisioned where we lack an understanding that the two names are co-referential. A certain sort of externalist may think that we can. They claim that to think that Hesperus is identical to Phosphorus is merely to think that Venus is identical to Venus, which is knowable a priori even in the circumstances that Frege considers. But of course that semantic claim awaits our examination of Frege's problem. And it is certainly not obvious, nor antecedently very plausible. To put my point in a simple epistemic way is to invite resistance. It may seem that Frege's worry cuts across the a priori/a posteriori distinction. As Casullo notes, you can fail to realize that the product of 16 and 13 is equal to the square root of 43,264.[65] As someone who believes in the primary significance not of the epistemic but rather the semantic a priori, I agree. But still Frege's famous and convincing case is different. Even in the night of error, not all cows are black. Learning the identity of Hesperus and Phosphorus, in ordinary cases, is learning something that is informative about the nature of the world in a different way than figuring out that one multiplied wrong or believed in haste an

[64] Ackerman (1989: 10). [65] Casullo (2003).

obvious contradiction. Internal conditions are not sufficient to determine that the belief that Hesperus is Phosphorus is false, but they are sufficient to constitute the error in the other beliefs, or so at least it is appropriate for the internalist to assume absent further argument.[66] I grant that it may be that *some* mathematical beliefs, which are knowable a priori only by some very complicated proof, are more analogous to Frege's identity than to analytic identities. But Ackerman's abandoned analysis is not.

The second recent objection is due to Scott Soames. He objects that proposals like 'Aristotle' means the same thing as the actual thing called 'Aristotle' require that people in other possible worlds have beliefs about our own world if they are to share beliefs mediated by 'Aristotle' with us, and are hence implausible.[67] But this objection is unsuccessful.

Soames discusses mechanisms deploying 'actually' and 'dthat'. He admits the existence of an interpretation of the former, one understanding of what he calls '*actually**-rigidified descriptions', which would make his central objection unsound, but registers a secondary complaint that this interpretation implies that there will be other worlds in which the relevant description will not apply to Aristotle.[68] The same rigidified metalinguistic content when thought in that world will refer to Plato, assuming that Plato is called 'Aristotle' in that world.

But, I reply, I have not proposed that narrow content that is shared is always about the same thing, especially when thought in another world. It is no real complaint about, for instance, indexical narrow contents that they are about different things when thought in different circumstances. Of course, names are not indexicals. But for an analysis to give the meaning of 'Aristotle' it is enough for it to pick out Aristotle in all worlds in which he exists, and it is not required that the analysis capture the meaning of that word as used in other worlds. No more are such implausible conditions required for an analysis to capture the content of our thoughts. Of course, if some other people in another world refer to or think about Aristotle in some way, we can report their thoughts by using our word 'Aristotle'. In other words, our practice of cross-world belief ascription may seem to conflict with my account. But I have already admitted the intuitive

---

[66] Chapter 9 returns to Kripke's Wittgensteinian discussion of arithmetical beliefs and its implications for internalism.
[67] Soames (2002: 43–50). I will interpret this case as involving a shared broad narrow content.
[68] Soames (2002: 49).

force of the belief-ascription objection in much more straightforward forms.

But my second point is directed against Soames' central objection. It is that the correct understanding of rigidified clusters requires no invocation of the *entire* actual world at all, merely those elements of actuality that they explicitly invoke. Actual Aristotle himself, as well as his property of being called by whatever particular local terms, are present in the other worlds that Soames considers. Perhaps this itself implies that in thinking of Aristotle, locally called 'Aristotle', who is also found in our world, those in other worlds are indirectly thinking minimal things about our world. But so minimal as to be fully plausible. Soames admits this minimalism of one of the mechanisms he discusses, involving 'dthat'. But in his discussion he misses the second reading of 'dthat' that Kaplan admits and that we are deploying. He thinks that it is enough to say merely that 'dthat' 'completely obliterates the descriptive content'.[69] But it need not. This problem also defeats Soames' elaborate treatment of dthat-rigidified descriptions in the recent *Reference and Description*.[70]

The third and final recent objection to proposals of my sort, proposals that incorporate a metalinguistic treatment of Burge-style deferential concepts, is put this way by Gabriel Segal: ' "[C]alled" itself appears to be a deferential concept. Neophyte philosophers sometimes accept correction from expert philosophers in respect of their views on what is called what and on what it is for something to be called something. . . . [So perhaps internalists treating Arthritis-Tharthritis will be left only with]: "thing standing in relation R to 'disease' standing in relation R to 'arthritis' in my thing standing in relation R to 'the home environment' "? And is "relation" deferential too?'[71]

My reply to this objection, which I will call the 'deep deferentiality' objection to indicate that it involves deferentiality about basic semantic notions like reference, will come in Chapter 4. This is another objection that will require extended treatment.

But it is worth pausing for a moment to reflect on the costs and plausibility of granting that the notion of being called by a term is in this way not internally determinate. Some relevant questions: Is there any plausible natural kind in the world with which reference can be identified, and would it matter if there were? Could some a posteriori scientific

---

[69] Soames (2002: 49). [70] Soames (2005: 303–13). [71] Segal (2000: 161 n. 16).

development in linguistics or psychology show that all our thoughts are about radically different parts of the world than we thought they were? And are we comfortable with the thought that there are experts on calling? Remember that the intuitions about reference on which Putnam, Kripke, and Burge depend are supposed to be available a priori to all by suitable consultation of imagination and what we each would say in our individual armchairs. Presumably they do not claim the position of those owed deference on these notions by other philosophers. And even if the success of their cases depends on deference, is that deference to experts? Can there be experts on reference, say amongst competent philosophers who differ in intuitions about it? And if some competent members of a language community can fail to grasp the dictionary definition of 'reference' or 'being called' because of some quirk of community use, does that suggest that such quirks of community use are important to apparently basic semantic phenomena like truth and falsehood?

Nevertheless, despite these qualms and questions, this objection isn't groundless. There is a degree to which the notions of referring and being called may be subject to a generalization of the famous externalist examples, as we will see in Chapter 4. But we will also see that this would undercut the importance of the quirky referential details, and hence of details of the intuitions on which Kripke, Putnam, and Burge rely. In other words, in Chapter 4 I will attempt to turn this apparent objection into an argument for internalism.

Still, the three other named objections are also still in play. My primary response to the multiple-contents, belief-ascription, and subject-matter objections, which is developed in the next chapter, is that externalism is stuck, at the relevant level of abstraction, with the very same problems. So they *cannot* be decisive.

3

Internalist Cases and Externalist Theory

While some cases suggest externalism, there are other famous cases that pull in the other direction, and require complications of any viable externalism. Even the complicated, viable forms face certain difficulties that we will trace here. But I will not argue that these difficulties show that these various forms of externalism are false. I will simply note the identity of these problems to three that afflict my internalist proposal: the multiple-contents, belief-ascription, and subject-matter objections. On their basis, I will claim only a draw, pending the resolution of the deep deferentiality objection, and of course further development of a positive internalist view.

Begin with a crude form of externalism: Some believe, on the basis of Kripke's examples, that the reference of a name is determined by the causal-historical chain of transmission of that name between an initial act of baptism of the referent and the name's use. So perhaps the content contributed by a name to a thought that it mediates is the individual so baptized. A difference in the individual at the end of a chain will imply a difference in content.

This simple externalism faces three evident problems. One is Gareth Evans' Madagascar case.[1] But our primary focus will be the two classic objections of Frege and Russell.[2] Frege noted the existence of names that share a reference but intuitively differ in cognitive significance. For instance, Venus was named twice, once as the last star in the morning or 'Phosphorus', and once as first star in the evening or 'Hesperus'. And so, it seems, one can believe that Hesperus is Hesperus and not believe that Phosphorus is Hesperus. Russell's concern was empty names and other

---

[1] Evans (1985a: 10–11). [2] Frege (1960); Russell (1911, 1956).

apparently referring terms that yet lack a reference. One can believe that the Easter Bunny does not exist, and a robust sense of reality forbids a subsisting but not existing entity dubbed by that name.

It is sociologically remarkable that *Naming and Necessity* effectively disposed of the description theory of names and its descendants without addressing in any serious way these two central motivations for such accounts. But a truly viable externalism must say more. There are analogous problems involving kind terms, including empty terms like 'phlogiston' and the intuitive difference between the thought that water is water and that water is H-O-H. And we need externalist explanations of how an individual can properly aim to reform social use so that it eschews false theory, of what someone thinks if all the experts have been shot, and of what someone thinks when they inherit one kind term with one public meaning that yet they believe to name two different phenomena. But for reasonable brevity, I will focus on the more fully developed externalist accounts of naming, and leave the generalization to you.

There are ways to develop plausible and viable externalisms that evade the intuitive cases of Frege and Russell. But they have a cost that it is crucial that we identify.

3.1

Begin with Hesperus and Phosphorus. That case has occasioned a variety of responses from externalists.

Kripke's response to Frege's problem was to attempt to transform it from an objection to simple externalist accounts of name reference into a paradox for all of us, his 'puzzle about belief'.[3] He tried to show that puzzles analogous to Hesperus-Phosphorus flow solely from two very intuitively plausible principles that govern our notion of belief and our practice of belief ascription, independent of any philosophical theory about belief content or name meaning. If so, such cases cannot be special problems for the simple externalist.

The so-called disquotation principle is this: Barring complications involving indexicals, ambiguities, and pronomial devices, if a normal

[3] Kripke (1979).

English speaker, on reflection, assents to 'p', then he believes that p.[4] The principle of translation is this: If a sentence of one language expresses a truth in that language, then any translation of it into any other language also expresses a truth (in that other language).[5] And the analogous puzzle that is supposed to flow from those principles alone is the case of Pierre:

> Pierre is a normal French speaker who lives in France and speaks not a word of English.... Of course he has heard of that famous distant city, London (which he... calls '*Londres*') though he himself has never left France. On the basis of what he has heard of London, he is inclined to think that it is pretty. So he says, in French, '*Londres est jolie*'.... Later, Pierre... moves to... London... though to an unattractive part of the city.... He... rarely ever leaves this part of the city. None of his neighbors know any French, so he must learn English by 'direct method'.... [H]e is inclined to assent to... 'London is not pretty'. He has *no* inclination to assent to: London is pretty.... [But] he does not for a moment withdraw his assent from the French sentence, '*Londres est jolie*'.[6]

By application of the two principles, we may conclude that Pierre believes that London is pretty and Pierre believes that London is not pretty. That is the puzzle.

The close analogy of this puzzle to Frege's case may lead the unsympathetic to conclude that it is no puzzle, but rather an argument for modification of simple externalist accounts, and even of Kripke's 'picture' of name meaning. There is something in the mind that semantically distinguishes 'Hesperus' and 'Phosphorus', and something in the mind of Pierre that distinguishes 'London' and 'Londres'. But Kripke does trace a convincing link between these issues and the principles of disquotation and translation that govern intuitive belief ascription, whatever theory we prefer.

My point is that the internalist should welcome the recognition that these principles alone can generate paradox in their unrestricted application. It is no objection to metalinguistic or other internalist accounts that they sometimes require violation of such principles if such principles must be violated by any coherent account. Kripke has generally convinced us that this is so. And so it seems that the belief-ascription objection to my internalist proposal is not in fact a telling objection. At the very least, if

---

[4] Kripke (1979: 248–9).   [5] Kripke (1979: 250).   [6] Kripke (1979: 254–5).

an externalist adopts Kripke's response to Hesperus-Phosphorus, then they cannot properly field the belief-ascription objection without a lot more supporting argument.

There's another related puzzle due to Kripke:

> Peter... may learn the name 'Paderewski' with an identification of the person named as a famous pianist. Naturally, having learned this, Peter will assent to 'Paderewski had musical talent'.... Later, in a different circle, Peter learns of someone called 'Paderewski' who was a Polish nationalist leader and Prime Minister. He concludes that probably two people... were both named 'Paderewski.' Using 'Paderewski' as a name for a *statesman*, Peter assents to, 'Paderewski had no musical talent.' Should we infer, by the disquotation principle [that] Peter believes that Paderewski had no musical talent or should we not?[7]

This case suggests that, if the names that mediate thoughts are indeed sometimes what distinguish two thought contents, still it is not the individuation of names in a public language but how an individual individuates names that is relevant to that person's belief contents. It hence provides some intuitive motivation for an internalism deploying metalinguistic elements over close externalist alternatives.

And there are other relevant analogous cases. One puzzling aspect of Kripke's discussion is that he does not endorse his most intuitively forceful case, which is relegated to his notes, while his reasons for not endorsing it are not characteristically convincing. That case is Mates' puzzle:[8] A speaker can assent to a sentence and fail to assent to a synonymous sentence, if they do not understand the synonymy. Someone can believe that Jones is a doctor and not a physician. So it would seem that even if all co-referential names are in fact synonymous, a puzzle of this general sort can arise. If our concern were only to defend a simple Kripkean picture of name meaning, then the close analogy of Mates' case would seem to me to provide sufficient defense. But of course our interest is thought content. And Mates' puzzle, like the Paderewski case, suggests the psychological significance of an individual's understanding of a term and not its public meaning.

I do not claim that any of these difficulties for an externalism that adopts Kripke's suggestion about Frege's problem are decisive. Rather, on the basis

---

[7] Kripke (1979: 265).
[8] Mates (1950); Kripke (1979: 274–5 n. 15, 276 n. 23, 277 n. 28, 281–3 n. 46).

of Kripke's discussion, I think we should conclude that the belief-ascription objection is not decisive against my internalist proposal, and that we so far lack a viable externalist account of thought content that can properly handle not only Frege's case but also Kripke's analogous puzzles.

A more positive externalist response to Frege's case is preferable. There are more positive externalist responses. But their problems are quite revealing.

First is a cluster of views that hold that attitude ascriptions express relations between cognizers and linguistically-enhanced propositions. Mark Richard, for instance, has developed the suggestion that these linguistically-enhanced propositions are amalgams of structured propositions and the words of sentences, which he calls 'annotations'.[9] The belief that Hesperus has risen and that Phosphorus has risen count as distinct, since they are mediated by different words.

There are immediate surface difficulties. This view implies that people who don't share languages and hence words cannot strictly speaking share beliefs. I do not claim that this is a decisive objection; I merely note that this difficulty should have a familiar sound to the internalist fan of the metalinguistic. For one thing, because belief reports are not intuitively about the words that mediate such beliefs, it suggests the subject-matter objection. And consider more details: Richard suggests in reply to worries like these that belief ascriptions in contexts may report that individuals accept linguistically-enhanced propositions that are close enough matches to the linguistically-enhanced propositions associated with the sentences used in the ascriptions. So he accepts some violations of principles of disquotation that govern common belief ascription, claiming that ordinary belief ascriptions can be misleading in detail. And because proper ascriptions are in this way relativized to contexts he in fact deploys multiple notions of content. From within different contexts, different belief ascriptions characterize the same belief. So it would seem that the belief-ascription objection and the multiple-contents objection cannot properly be held more telling against internalism. As I said, Richard's account also faces the obvious difficulty that we aren't intuitively saying things about words when we make belief reports. In other words, it also faces the subject-matter objection.

[9] Richard (1990).

These three objections are not decisive, I think. But they are the same objections that are faced by my internalist proposal, minus the deep deferentiality objection to which we will return in the next chapter, and the need for further development of my proposal.

A second cluster of viable externalist views is the Perry-Crimmins conception that notions are unarticulated constituents of beliefs.[10] Beliefs are alleged to be concrete particulars that contain ideas and notions as constituents, so that Pierre has two beliefs that incorporate different notions. Belief ascriptions are in part about their unarticulated constituents, but the same belief-ascription sentence can be about different beliefs, which involve different unarticulated constituents. In other words, the belief-ascription objection looms. But let's look at the details.

The most recent version of Perry's view is developed in *Reference and Reflexivity*, which as we will see also presents an allied view of empty names, and is perhaps the most fully developed account in any of the clusters now under consideration.[11] It rests on Perry's general reflexive-referential account of meanings and contents, which is instructive. First, there is a hierarchy of levels of content, which differ regarding the degree to which background conditions are filled in.[12] In particular, Perry distinguishes among 1) a kind of content that all utterances of 'I'll kill you' share, 2) a kind in which some utterances of 'I'll kill you' differ, depending on who says them about whom, 3) and finally a kind in which all those utterances differ. Some of these contents are transparently metalinguistic, and there are many types of content. So the subject-matter and multiple-contents objections are in play. The second feature of Perry's account is that the truth-conditions of an utterance are relative to what background conditions are presumed. This is another route to the multiple-contents objection. The third feature of Perry's account is that what is said by a sentence, its official content, is in a wide variety of cases the referential content by default, where that is what the simple externalist accounts suggest. Fourth, this account of content is applied to Frege's problem via the Perry-Crimmins unarticulated constituents model.[13] As we might expect, this involves distinguishing the official content of beliefs about Phosphorus and Hesperus, which is shared, and other sorts of

---

[10] Perry and Crimmins (1993); Crimmins (1992). [11] Perry (2001).
[12] Perry (2001: 79). [13] Perry (2001: 92–120).

content, which are not. So it invokes the multiple-contents objection. And we have already noted how the belief-ascription objection threatens the unarticulated constituents model.

To sum up, a properly developed form of the Perry-Crimmins model shares the belief-ascription, multiple-contents, and subject-matter objections with my internalist proposal.

Richard and Perry-Crimmins appeal to mediating mechanisms of different sorts to introduce differences into thoughts about Hesperus and Phosphorus. Another class of views of this general type has been developed by Gareth Evans and John Campbell out of suggestions by David Wiggins and John McDowell on how to interpret Frege on sense.[14] Intuitively distinct thoughts mediated by 'Hesperus' and by 'Phosphorus' in someone unaware of their identity are held to involve distinct cognitive mechanisms or ways of referring, though not necessarily distinct notions or ideas.

But the abstract similarity of these proposals to the Perry-Crimmins view suggests similar difficulties. Thoughts mediated by 'Hesperus' and 'Phosphorus' are not intuitively about Venus in the guise of being referred to via certain cognitive mechanisms, but merely about heavenly bodies. So the subject-matter objection is relevant, though in this case it has a metacognitive rather than a metalinguistic target. And we deploy the same standard belief ascription involving a single name to capture the various beliefs of various individuals who differ in their relevant cognitive mechanisms. So the belief-ascription objection is again appropriate. And of course if this model is to preserve very intuitive truisms that different individuals can share beliefs mediated by such terms, other sorts of content must be deployed.[15] And so the multiple-contents objection is also relevant.

Perhaps the difficulties of the last two clusters of theories depend on the robust nature of the cognitive mechanisms that they invoke. A fourth class of externalist proposals focuses not on differences in public language terms like Richard's view, but rather on differences in mental representations, and in a way that evades a commitment to robust cognitive mechanisms.

Consider a proposal by Michael Lockwood and Peter Strawson that has been recently developed by Ruth Garrett Millikan.[16] The semantic value of a name is merely its bearer. There is no difference in *content* between

---

[14] Wiggins (1976); McDowell (1977); Evans (1985*b*) and (1982: 120–204); Campbell (1987–8) and (2002*b*: 84–113).
[15] Evans (1982: 320 n. 16).   [16] Lockwood (1971); Strawson (1974: 54–6); Millikan (1997).

thoughts of Hesperus and of Phosphorus introduced by the names, but there can be a difference in such thoughts nonetheless. For those who fail to recognize the identity of Hesperus and Phosphorus, thoughts about such are mediated by different mental vehicles, while for those who recognize the identity there is but a single vehicle. Mental terms are even more idiosyncratic than public language terms, but these terms are not fused with propositions as in Richard's proposal to form new and robust sorts of content.

But this austerity is the source of corresponding disadvantages. Coming to recognize an identity is a 'different style of informativeness' than the ordinary sort of recognition, according to Strawson. While to learn that Hesperus is identical to Phosphorus may seem on the surface like learning a new fact about Hesperus, really it is not. And so the subject-matter objection looms, though in a somewhat novel way. And the difference in vehicles introduces a difference in cognition, for instance between those who recognize an identity and those who do not, which is not officially a difference in content. But whether this is called a difference in content or something else, still nothing turns on an arbitrary decision about theoretical vocabulary. The multiple-contents objection is still in play. And because this proposal through its austerity inherits Kripke's Pierre puzzle, the belief-ascription objection assumes an especially potent form.

We might hope for some happy middle ground, between externalisms that suffer from their robust semantic mechanisms and those that are too austere. And a middle route involving pragmatics has been developed by Nathan Salmon and Scott Soames.

Salmon holds that belief involves a three-node relationship among a believer, a proposition, and a mode of acquaintance with that proposition.[17] But the proposition believed is supposed to be the whole content of the belief. A believes p if and only if there is some mode of acquaintance with p such that A believes p that way, and the proposition that Hesperus is Hesperus is the same as the proposition that Phosphorus is Hesperus. So in fact everyone who believes that Hesperus is Hesperus believes that Hesperus is Phosphorus. Anyone who realizes that Hesperus is Hesperus also realizes that Hesperus is Phosphorus.

[17] Salmon (1986, 1989).

As Salmon admits, 'It is evident that [such] consequences... do not conform with the way we actually speak.'[18] We commonly say instead of someone who doesn't assent to 'Hesperus is Phosphorus' that they do not realize that Hesperus is Phosphorus, even though that claim is supposed by Salmon to be literally false. But he provides a three-part explanation of our literally false speech. First, we have a tendency to confuse the claim that someone does not realize that Hesperus is Phosphorus with the claim that they do not recognize that 'Hesperus is Phosphorus' is true. Second, we are misled by our subject's speech to the conclusion that they do not believe the proposition in question. These two parts of Salmon's explanation seem alone insufficient. Charges of confusion in common sense can be deployed against any commonsense counterexample, including the famous cases that motivate externalism, and Salmon admits that even those who do not suffer these confusions, who are semantically sophisticated, retain intuitions contrary to his proposal. Still, there is a third element of Salmon's explanation, which does not depend on such confusions. It is hence for our purposes its most characteristic element. There is supposed to be an established practice 'of using belief attributions to convey not only the proposition agreed to... but also the way the subject of the attribution takes the proposition in agreeing to it (which is not part of the semantic content of the belief attribution)'.[19]

We should be puzzled why, if belief in fact involves three relata and if belief ascriptions ordinarily, by established practice, suggest all three, still those ascriptions yet merely convey rather than assert the existence of one of the three relata. In fact, we should be at least a little puzzled by what it means to say that such facts are merely conveyed as opposed to asserted, that they are not a part of the semantic content.[20] If belief ascriptions were also to assert the existence of the third node (the mode of presentation), then the pragmatic account would collapse into other options that we have already discussed. But the difference between assertion and what is systematically conveyed is not obviously robust in these cases. And remember that Salmon's proposal conflicts with our ordinary speech. He certainly isn't making an ordinary-language distinction.

---

[18] Salmon (1989: 248).   [19] Salmon (1989: 249).
[20] See Grice (1989: 121–2) for one classic attempt at this distinction. But the inverted Gricean mechanisms endorsed by Chapter 8 will not suffice to support it.

But let me focus on other problems with this proposal, which should sound familiar. A systematic distinction properly rooted in our practice between what is conveyed and what is asserted suggests the multiple-contents objection. Fancy theoretical terminology can always be introduced to distinguish multiple kinds of content, but doesn't eliminate the intuitive force of the objection. And what is systematically conveyed by our belief attributions according to Salmon invokes a relevant variant of the subject-matter objection. It is intuitive that belief ascriptions only systematically convey what they are about, as is suggested by some of the intuitive claims with which Salmon's proposal is in tension. But, according to Salmon, belief ascriptions convey by our practice the way the subject of the attribution takes a proposition in agreeing to it, which is not, he claims, part of the semantic content of the attribution, not a part of what it is about. And Salmon's proposal also faces the belief-ascription objection. Salmon himself admits that his proposal is in conflict with certain features of our belief-ascription practice, which he claims to involve explainable errors.

There has been an alternative development of the pragmatics strategy, which does not invoke features of our established and systematic general practice of belief ascription, and so may seem to avoid some of the problems that I have noted for Salmon's version. Soames' *Beyond Rigidity* provides perhaps the best developed instance of this view.[21] Soames distinguishes the proposition that is semantically expressed by a sentence S, which is included in the information a competent speaker would assert and intend to convey by assertive utterance of S in any normal context (that is to say any non-metaphoric, unironic context lacking ignorant participants), and information that is asserted and conveyed only in certain contexts by that sentence (for instance, given mutual knowledge of special background information). This is a general distinction, applicable in many ways. It is not a special feature of our belief ascriptions. But here is its application to the phenomena at issue: Soames' view is that 'Jones believes that Hesperus has risen' and 'Jones believes that Phosphorus has risen' semantically express the same thing, which involves a single belief content that is that suggested by a simple externalist account of name reference. But, he suggests, such sentences can be used in some contexts to assert or convey

---

[21] Soames (2002: 204–40). See also Thau (2002: 98–177).

different things, for instance given common knowledge of what somebody calls something. This is supposed to be just as when a sentence is used by a speaker ironically or metaphorically, to suggest something distinct from its literal meaning to hearers in the know. The difference with Salmon's proposal is that there isn't a *general practice* of belief ascriptions standardly conveying something, but rather there is *on particular occasions* the conveyance or even assertion of things that are not semantically expressed.

This proposal shares some worries with Salmon's suggestion. If the two beliefs in question are the same, why is there a common difference in the pragmatics of the two ascription sentences, which can regularly generate differences in what they assert? And if the two beliefs in question are different, then why is all that is semantically expressed by the two ascription sentences the same? But let me focus on the differences between Salmon's and Soames' proposals, which introduce some characteristic troubles for Soames that mostly just recapitulate our familiar worries.

First, the phenomenon of belief opacity is intuitively systematic, and is in fact a standard feature of our general practice of belief ascription. But metaphor and irony are not intuitively systematic in the same way. Salmon seems right about that, and Soames wrong. By not granting that this is a systematic feature of our belief-ascription practice, Soames faces the belief-ascription objection, though in a different way than Salmon. Second, it hardly matters that Soames claims that these factors are a part of the pragmatics of belief reports, given that they are a part of what sentences in uses *assert*. He is even more closely threatened by the multiple-contents objection and the subject-matter objection than Salmon, since he explicitly invokes more than one notion of asserted content, including one sort that is not literal meaning and engages the subject-matter objection. Third, as Salmon has noted, Soames' proposal seems to be that if a speaker asserts p, and both the speaker and the hearer have mutually recognized grounds to believe that if p then q, then the speaker asserts q. 'This assumption would entail that, under normal circumstances, there is reason to hold that one who asserts anything at all ... thereby typically also asserts a host of trivial truisms: that $1 + 1 = 2$, that snow is white, that Tuesday follows Monday, etc.'[22] But that is implausible.

---

[22] Salmon (2003: 477 n. 8).

I do not take the difficulties I have noted for Soames and Salmon to be decisive. My point is rather the familiarity of some of these worries: The pragmatics strategy relies on a violation of the disquotation principle and standard forms of belief ascription within certain contexts, in either the form proposed by Salmon or by Soames. Lois Lane will deny that she believes that Clark Kent is Superman, and ordinary speakers will not make that attribution to her. But the pragmatics approach implies that that ascription is literally correct. So the belief-ascription objection certainly seems no more properly decisive against my internalist proposal than against the pragmatics views. And we have seen in various ways that the multiple-contents and subject-matter objections are held at little distance, at no relevant distance, by the very thin, somewhat tenuous, and very theoretical distinctions between semantic assertion and pragmatic assertion in use, or between what is systematically asserted and merely systematically conveyed by our practice of belief ascription.

Let me be clear. I do not claim that any of my worries here have established that any of these strategies are not viable for friends of direct reference. But our survey of possible externalist responses to Frege's problem has revealed that viable externalisms must deploy resources similar and often identical to those deployed by metalinguistic internalism. More to the immediate point, my internalist proposal strains our intuition in ways reflected in the belief-ascription, multiple-contents, and subject-matter objections. But so do all viable externalisms that have faced up to Frege's problem, and proposed a positive solution. So these objections cannot be decisive against my internalist view.

3.2

Consideration of another class of famous internalist cases will yield the same result. Plausible externalist treatments of empty names, of Russell's problem, possess further symmetries with my internalism, and more shared difficulties. Focus especially on negative existentials involving empty names, for instance the true claims that Pegasus does not exist, that Santa Claus does not exist, and that Vulcan, the planet hypothesized to explain the Newtonian irregularities in Mercury's motion, does not exist.

Viable externalist responses to Russell's problem fall into two main categories, within each of which I will discriminate two forms. Of the four forms in question, three share the belief-ascription, subject-matter, and multiple-contents objections with my internalism. The fourth has another sort of argumentative symmetry with internalism.

Let me begin with Keith Donnellan's classic account of negative existentials. It has a metalinguistic form, which is the first form of our first main category of responses. It is this:[23]

a) When the historical explanation of the use of a name (with the intention to refer) ends...with events that preclude any referent being identified, I will call it a 'block' in the history. In [the case of Santa Claus] the block is the introduction of the name into [a] child's speech via a fiction told to him as reality by his parents. Blocks occur in other ways. For example, children often invent imaginary companions whom they themselves come to speak of as actual. The block in such a case would occur at the point at which a name for the unreal companion gets introduced by the child himself via his mistaken belief that there is a companion to name. A somewhat different example would be this: suppose the Homeric poems were not written by one person, but were a patchwork of the writings of many people, combined, perhaps, with fragments from an oral tradition. Suppose, further, that at some point in time an ancient scholar... attributed the poems to a single person he called 'Homer'.... [T]hen the block occurs at the point at which this scholar enters the picture.[24]

b) If N is a proper name that has been used in predicative statements with the intention to refer to some individual, then 'N does not exist' is true if and only if the history of those uses ends in a block.[25]

There are problems in detail with this account. Donnellan articulates pretty much what we actually believe about Homer, but we don't say that Homer did not exist. But my main point is something else:

Donnellan's account of negative existentials is straightforwardly metalinguistic. It hence faces the subject-matter objection. And notice that a different child across the street, whose uses end in a different block, fails strictly speaking to share with the first child a false belief in the existence of Santa Claus. And so the belief-ascription objection is in play. Donnellan responds by suggesting that their blocks are historically related.[26] But this is

[23] Donnellan (1974). [24] Donnellan (1974: 23–4).
[25] Donnellan (1974: 25). [26] Donnellan (1974: 26, 29–30).

in fact to grant the force of the objection, and indeed to invoke two types or levels of content.

Donnellan claims to be articulating not the meaning but merely the truth-conditions for negative existentials.[27] But that difference seems insufficiently robust to make a real difference in our context, which is the application of Donnellan's conception to the issue of thought content, since both the meaning and truth-conditions of words seem relevant to the content of thoughts that they mediate. And marking that difference itself invokes one form of the multiple-contents objection.

Still, that distinction and Donnellan's difficulties make it unsurprising that his proposal has been developed in two contrary directions. John Perry bites the bullet, in a way that makes one problem shared with my internalism quite explicit.[28] To object that thoughts that allegedly involve metalinguistic elements are not intuitively about words is to commit what Perry calls 'the subject matter fallacy', he claims. But of course if this is a fallacy when externalists have problems, then so too when internalists are needy. And we have already seen that Perry's theory of content suffers from multiple contents and some tension with ordinary practices of belief ascription.

Joseph Almog has developed the other possible route.[29] While Almog holds that the truth-maker for all true negative existentials is the same positive world, whether the negative claims invoke Vulcan or Santa Claus, still he believes that Donnellan has in fact articulated plausible '*tracking* conditions, ways of tracing how a name came to name whatever it did (if it did)'.[30] Negative existentials that invoke Vulcan and Santa Claus differ in metalinguistic tracking conditions, but have the same truth-maker. But contrary to this development of the metalinguistic proposal, beliefs in those two negative existentials do not intuitively share their dominant content. And so Almog's route constitutes another plausible target for the subject-matter objection and belief-ascription objections, though in a somewhat different way. And of course marking the distinction in question as one between truth-makers and tracking conditions does not really make the distinction between two sorts of content disappear, and so the multiple-contents objection is still relevant.

---

[27] Donnellan (1974: 25).   [28] Perry (2001: 123–72).
[29] Almog (1991).   [30] Almog (1991: 614).

The second form of our first general category of externalist responses focuses not on sentences but on the propositions that they express. It includes Kripke's famous but unpublished and generally unavailable proposal.[31] These views are not metalinguistic, but rather metapropositional.

Here is Gareth Evans' report of Kripke's proposal: 'Kripke suggests that, although the sentence "*Fa*" fails to express any proposition if the singular term is empty, one may nevertheless form an intelligible description, "a proposition which says of *a* that it is *F*", *using* the singular term "*a*" in what Kripke calls "a special sort of quasi-intentional use". Using this description, we can form the intelligible proposition "There is a proposition which says of *a* that it is *F*, and that proposition is true." '[32] The true negative existential claim that 'Santa Claus does not exist' may then be the denial that there is a true proposition that says of Santa Claus that he exists.

Notice that two sorts of propositions, and hence two sorts of contents, and hence the multiple-contents objection, are in play. And notice that this proposal suffers from the same sorts of tensions with ordinary practices of belief ascription that we might expect on the basis of Kripke's Pierre case. By such practices, if a child assents to 'Santa Claus exists', they hence believe the proposition that Santa Claus exists. And the metapropositional is no real improvement over the metalinguistic if our purpose is to evade the subject-matter objection.

This proposal has yet other difficulties that indirectly reinforce this third similarity. Evans plausibly complained that 'we are told that there is a special use of a singular term (a "quasi-intentional" use) available to those who believe the term is empty. But we are not told what this amounts to.... And since we are given no account of this use, it remains intensely problematic how it can be that, although there is no proposition expressed by "*Fa*", there can nevertheless be a proposition expressed by "There is a proposition which says of *a* that it is *F*".'[33] Evans then developed a positive account of such a special use, which is a natural and apparently necessary refinement of Kripke's 'picture'. Evans' development is parasitic on his conception that empty names may be used in specific ways in linguistic games of make-believe, as in the pretense of a story-teller.[34] 'The general idea is that someone who utters [a singular negative existential statement]

---

[31] In his Locke lectures. Published discussion includes Evans (1982: 343–72); Almog (1991); Katz (1994); Salmon (1998).
[32] Evans (1982: 349).   [33] Evans (1982: 349–50).   [34] Evans (1982: 353–68).

should be likened to someone who makes a move within a pretence in order to express the fact that it is a pretence.... [H]e is like someone who jumps on the stage and says: "Look, Suzanne and the thief over there are only characters in a play." '[35] Evans provided a three-part account of how this works. 1) When there is a true negative existential statement deploying a name 'N', there is a use of that name in a pretense such that in the world of the pretense the name refers. 2) 'Really' is a word that, when prefixed to a sentence X deployed in a pretense, produces a sentence that is true when X is not only true in the pretense but true in fact. 3) And the true negative existential 'N does not exist' is the negation of the claim that 'really N exists'.[36] Evans claimed that his account, unlike Donnellan's, is an account in which the name is used. And so it may seem to avoid the subject-matter objection. But it is used in what is obviously only an unusual sense, within the pretense.[37] And in any case, as both Evans' explication of 'really' and his analogy with a play suggests, the negative existential in question is in fact about the linguistic pretense that involves that name. This development of Kripke's metapropositional account is metalinguistic in a refined and indirect but still real sense, and so the way in which it faces the subject-matter objection is less novel than it may appear.

Turn now to our second general category of externalist accounts of negative existentials, which insist on a greater symmetry between claims involving empty names and those involving names that refer to existent entities, and so may seem to evade at least the subject-matter objection. One form of this type involves reference to implausible Meinongian entities, like a merely subsisting Santa Claus. But there is also a form that shares a suitably robust sense of reality with metalinguistic and metapropositional accounts, so let me begin with that.

David Braun has developed the suggestion that there are gappy propositions.[38] It is supposed that there are genuinely singular propositions that incorporate existing objects as constituents, and that the primary semantic role of a name is to introduce a particular object into the propositions it is used to express. But a nonreferring name cannot introduce any object into propositions. Still, it can be used to express merely gappy or unfilled propositions, with a hole where the object should be. As Braun says, such a

---

[35] Evans (1982: 369). [36] Evans (1982: 369–72).
[37] Evans (1982: 371). [38] Braun (1993).

view, unlike for instance Kripke's view, will straightforwardly explain why '"Vulcan is a planet" and "Ossian is a poet" express different propositions. A less happy consequence is that "Vulcan is a planet" and "Ossian is a planet" express the same unfilled proposition.... So the beliefs that a person expresses by sincerely uttering "Vulcan does not exist" and "Ossian does not exist" have the same... propositional content.'[39] The beliefs can be yet distinct, Braun claims, though not in any 'semantic respect'.

As we already noted in our discussion of Almog, such a structure ensures that an account will face the subject-matter and belief-ascription objections. Such beliefs do not intuitively share propositional content. And of course a distinction between beliefs that isn't called semantic but yet introduces differences in intuitive content does not make the multiple-contents objection disappear.

Because of these familiar difficulties, we should consider finally accounts that introduce special non-existent objects. They seem able to deliver roughly the right sort of intuitive subject matter. 'Santa Claus does not exist' seems intuitively to be about Santa Claus, existent or non-existent. And such accounts also seem to fit our intuitive practices of belief ascription, and by deploying merely one sort of content.

But such accounts of empty names have real problems of plausibility. Russell's view of names was partly occasioned by revulsion from Meinong. So it is not surprising that the simple view of name meaning suggested by Kripke's famous cases can evade Russell's problem by appeal to the mere subsistence of non-existing entities that are yet part of the real world. But our sense of reality should be too robust for that, certainly under the strictures of physicalism that we presume here.

Still, there is a subtler strategy than Meinong's in this general area, which has been developed by Nathan Salmon from suggestions of David Kaplan.[40]

The first element of the strategy is to develop an analogy between reference across possible situations and across time. Consider the fact that Socrates no longer exists. Then note that one can now use his name to assert a genuinely singular proposition that includes him; one can assert that Socrates was snub-nosed, and he himself seems to be part of what one asserts. There is *now* no Socrates, and hence there is *now* no genuinely

---

[39] Braun (1993: 464).
[40] Salmon (1987, 1998). This account is largely endorsed by Soames (2002: 89–95).

singular proposition that includes him, it is alleged. And yet we can obviously assert things that involve the man himself, and we can now have beliefs about him. 'Socrates' is not a genuinely empty name. Likewise, the story goes, there are actually no mere possibilia, subsistent or otherwise. But when conditions are right, we may be capable of naming particular merely possible individuals, so to speak over there in other possible worlds. And so we can actually use their names to assert genuinely singular propositions that include those merely possible individuals, and deploy their names to mediate our actual beliefs, for instance that such individuals do not exist. These names aren't genuinely empty. They are no more empty than 'Socrates'. But in neither case is any unacceptably Meinongian metaphysics required, it is alleged.

Still, there is need for a second element of this strategy. How can our talk pick out particular merely possible individuals? One way that has been suggested deploys Kripkean claims about essences, for instance the claim that we are each necessarily rooted in the very egg and sperm from which we came. Perhaps one can hence talk about the specific but merely possible individual who would have resulted from the fertilization of some actual egg by some actual sperm.

There are natural objections. Kripke's claims about essentiality of material origin are far from well established or generally accepted. And even if we grant such claims, identical twins come from the same sperm and egg. So even if it is essential to each to come from that sperm and egg, that is not an individual essence of each, not a property had *only* by that particular individual and always by that individual in all possible worlds in which it exists. So such a property cannot be used to pick out a particular individual in other worlds. And there are no other obvious resources available to deliver such individual essences. It is not intuitively impossible for twins to be born in other than their actual order, and no empirical discovery could support such a claim of impossibility. It is not intuitively impossible that there be either one without the other, and no empirical discovery could support that claim of impossibility either.

What's more, the strict analogy proposed between temporal and modal cases is untenable. Other times have a more robust metaphysical status than other possible worlds. One way to see this is to note that a strict analogy between the modal and the temporal would break the yet stricter analogy between the spatial and the temporal. It is radically implausible for me to claim that objects now in London do not strictly exist because I am elsewhere. But Special Relativity implies that at least some intuitive temporal and spatial differences cannot be treated differently. There is in fact no absolute simultaneity, which would be required if certain objects elsewhere but now strictly exist, while all recently destroyed objects do not.

But my main complaint is something else. There is a new sort of argumentative symmetry between internalism and any externalism that fields such a proposal. If mere possibilia are available to externalists as the objects of more or less direct reference consistent with the plausible metaphysical strictures of physicalism, which I doubt, then so too are they available to internalists. And so every time that an externalist is tempted to deploy two actually existing objects to introduce a difference in thoughts, then the internalist can introduce the two objects in their merely modal home, out there in other worlds so to speak. Mere possibilia are not in the appropriate sense spatially or temporally external to the cognizer, since they are not spatially and temporally located in the actual world. And even if you think that such possibilia, including other possible worlds, exist as mere abstracta in this world, which is not plausibly consistent with the physicalism we presume here, still they lack spatial and temporal locations. They are not specifically externalist resources.

Of course, we must still be able to get at them, to pick them out. And so an externalist might claim that our ability to individuate and name relevant possibilia depends on the existence of external conditions, say certain sperm out there in the world. But we can have internally determinate thoughts about external conditions, including particular sperm. And gestures at Kripke's claims about material origin do not constitute a well-developed story of how the individuation and naming of mere possibilia is generally performed anyway, which might firmly motivate a reliance on external conditions. And the very fact that the externalist proposal under consideration requires for its plausibility a close analogy between modal reference and our more or less direct reference to past objects that no longer exist, suggests a treatment of the paradigmatic externalist cases (which characteristically invoke a difference between thoughts introduced by their histories) that is yet consistent with internalism. In fact, it seems to be the very sort of treatment that I have already proposed. Remember that the sperms and eggs that produced us no longer exist. If you can work backwards in time from your current thoughts to pick out particular historical sperm that might have united with your egg to form a different person, which is what Salmon suggests, then it would seem you could also work outwards in space from your internally determinate thoughts.

But it is another symmetry with internalism that is most telling. However the story mediated by sperms and eggs turns out, it is clear that there are other ways that more or less particular and yet intuitively non-existent objects can be introduced into our thought and speech. The externalist must tell another tale about such cases. Salmon himself suggests a treatment of fictional people like Sherlock Holmes modeled on Peter van Inwagen's, in which they are abstract entities that are created when authors write.[41] Salmon says this: 'Conan Doyle one fine day set about to tell a story. In the process he created a fictional character as the protagonist, and other fictional characters as well, playing a certain role in the story. These characters, like the story itself, are man-made abstract artifacts.'[42] He suggests a similar treatment of mythical names like 'Pegasus'.

This in itself invokes the subject-matter objection, since Pegasus is intuitively a horse and not an abstract entity. Abstract entities don't have wings, but Pegasus does. And this proposal is not plausibly consistent with physicalism, especially because these abstract entities come into the world at particular times and are not constituted by any of the physical conditions that introduce them into the world. But my main point is that if myths and story-writing can introduce special abstract objects to be the objects of intuitively singular thoughts consistent with the plausible strictures of physicalism, still that is more grist for the internalist mill. If story-writing can introduce a particular referent, so too it seems can the short little tales about anything at all that we all tell to ourselves, in the mind's ear and throat, and believe. Of course Salmon will insist that not any blather with words creates a relevant man-made abstract object. But our blather about just about anything ordinarily creates as determinate a sense of its putative referent as many real novels create of many of their characters.

I think that such abstracta, like mere possibilia, are not really plausibly consistent with the physicalism we presume here. But the most important moral is that if they could be deployed consistent with a strict sense

---

[41] van Inwagen (1977, 1983).   [42] Salmon (1998: 300).

of reality, which I doubt, then they would be so cheap as to provide plentiful opportunities for the defense of internalism. Externalism can use abstracta in a variety of ways. It would be as easy to deploy abstractly intensionalized objects, Venus qua Hesperus and Venus qua Phosphorus, to defend simple externalism against Frege's problem. But internalists can with equal plausibility deploy handy abstracta with just the right properties to deliver whatever intuitions about content are desired consistent with internalism. While it may seem that abstracta can't be in the head because they lack spatial location, still by the same argument they can't be located outside of it, and hence an abstract Pegasus or Santa Claus is not a specifically externalist resource. And if the character Sherlock Holmes is an abstract object in time, still the relevant time is the time of the thought, just as the internalist requires. Of course, we have no good reason to believe that the platonic abstracta such a cheap internalism requires exist. But we have no better reason to believe in the platonic abstracta deployed by externalists.

We have surveyed the four externalist mechanisms for dealing with Russell's problem. Three share our three familiar difficulties both with internalism and with externalist treatments of Frege's problem. The fourth has different and debilitating metaphysical difficulties in our physical world. It isn't really viable, so I will set it aside. But if it were to succeed, then it would provide very helpful resources for the internalist.

3.3

And so we can conclude our discussion of externalist responses to internalist cases. The classic counterexamples to simple externalisms—Frege's problem and Russell's problem—require complications in any viable externalism. These necessary complications leave viable externalist accounts open, at the relevant level of abstraction, to the very same intuitive objections that threaten my internalist proposal, at least if we suspend for the moment the deep deferentiality objection and worries that it deploys resources unavailable to internalists.

This shouldn't be a surprise. Externalists naturally field internalist resources when they actually consider at length the cases that motivated Frege and Russell in the first place. There are differences in detail in how the various internalist and externalist cases work against the various proposals in play, of course, since Hesperus-Phosphorus is not identical to Twin Earth. But all the phenomena that all the cases invoke are very common. What's more, the contents that externalists must deploy when names are empty and when belief opacity is evident are also plausibly present when names refer and belief opacity doesn't matter, and provide plentiful resources for internalists. And while the detailed responses of viable externalisms and internalisms to particular cases may differ, some of these details seem to favor internalism. For instance, externalism naturally deploys externalist accounts of word-individuation, while internalism does not, and hence the Paderewski case is difficult for some externalist accounts. But so far I claim only a draw.

Of course, we have still to face the deep deferentiality objection to internalism. But the unlovely and unnatural contortions required of internalism to handle the famous externalist intuitive cases are the same unlovely and unnatural contortions required of externalism to handle the famous internalist intuitive cases. Multiple forms of content, some tension with familiar principles of belief ascription, and unobvious subject matter for certain beliefs are three requirements of any reasonably adult conception of thought content, internalist or externalist.

4

The Real Moral

We possess a viable internalist response to the famous externalist cases, conditional upon successful resolution of the deep deferentiality objection, and also of a general worry that internalism cannot deliver all the resources that this response requires. Sections 4.1 and 4.2 discuss the deep deferentiality objection, by a somewhat indirect route that also provides a case-based argument for internalism. Section 4.3 concerns some details of my positive proposal, and points towards the resolution of the worry about resources.

4.1

The famous externalist cases do not show that internalism is false, and the famous internalist cases do not show that externalism is false. But there remains an issue between internalism and externalism that cases can resolve.

A crucial difference is that externalism explains, while internalism ignores, certain facts about reference and hence truth. You might think that this means that externalism wins. But thought content is important to psychology in all its details. And those facts about reference and truth are psychologically unimportant. So externalism about thought content is false.

Let me put it another way: Three clusters of facts about reference and truth, three psychologically unimportant clusters, are not facts about thought content. First, reference is vague or indeterminate when thought content is not. Second, to return to the deep deferentiality objection, reference can depend on the deferentiality of our notion of reference when thought content does not. Third, reference depends on quirky and arbitrary facts when thought content does not. A suitably motivated externalism crucially differs from internalism by holding these three clusters of facts relevant to thought content. And they are not so relevant.

One apparent theoretical motivation for externalism is the thought that the primary semantic phenomenon is reference, and not those features of individual ideology that internalism invokes. But I will argue that reference in its superfine detail is not the central and most significant semantic phenomenon in which thoughts participate.

Such an argument may seem impossible. The contents of thoughts seem quite clearly to be, or at the very least to be closely allied with, their truth-conditions, with how they represent the world to be. And truth apparently depends on reference. If the references of the components of the content of a thought are unimportant, so to the same degree is its truth. So my claim may seem absurd or unbelievable. What's more, if in the end I am going to rely on such an apparently radical claim, you may wonder why I bothered to develop an internalist story about the famous externalist cases.

But it is important to note that my claim is significantly qualified. My argument is not as radical as Stich's arguments that truth and reference are of no deep importance.[1] My focus is not as radical as Chomsky's focus on internalist mechanisms that are 'pure syntax'.[2] I think that there is a degree, indeed a large degree, to which a viable internalism should care about truth-conditions and hence reference. That is why my insistence in Chapter 1 on the importance for internalism of truth rather than evidence is not mistaken, though it needs to be refined and qualified. And it is also why I needed to develop an internalist response to the famous externalist cases, cases which invoke our semantic intuitions. I mean to respect at least most of those semantic intuitions. I think that to understand someone's thoughts is to understand in some sense how they take the world to be. Whether those thoughts are in fact true or false, it is more or less to understand how the world would be if they were indeed true.

This involves something like Dan Dennett's conception of a notional world, David Lewis' analogous proposal, or Brian Loar's context-indeterminate realization conditions.[3] Clearly part of the systematic development

---

[1] Stich (1990: 113–19). One difference is that I think that semantic interpretation is always possible even when reference and truth are problematic. But my arguments reinforce Stich's contention that variants of the reference relation might be as good.

[2] Chomsky (1995). But see page 14.   [3] Lewis (1981); Dennett (1982); Loar (1988: 108–9).

of a successful internalism must be the detailed elaboration and defense of such rough conceptions. But the rest of this book is devoted to the beginnings of that task, and Chapter 2 already provided some crucial details. This is a kind of 'narrow' content, constituted by internal conditions only.

This narrow content will to one degree or another *match* the world, to adopt an unclaimed term. It will get the world right or wrong, and in various ways. When a narrow content involves indexical elements, what it should match may depend on when and where and by whom facing in what direction it is thought.

Now I can put my point this way: Sometimes we can know all the facts about the narrow content of someone's thoughts, and all the non-semantical facts about the world, including even who that someone is and where in the world they are and how they are oriented in it, and yet the facts about the match of content and world will not be sufficient to determine whether certain of their thoughts refer or are true.[4] There may yet be facts about those things that externalism and not internalism can deliver. But such facts about reference and truth are of no genuine psychological significance.

To identify people's references and to sort their beliefs into the true and the false may sometimes be psychologically revealing about them, but it can also miss important theoretical and ideological differences between them that explain notable differences in their behavior and outlook. That is uncontroversial between internalism and a sophisticated externalism that has a viable response to the famous internalist cases. But the crucial point is that sometimes the identification of references and the sorting of beliefs into true and false is not in fact relevant to what people think. Such sorting, such bookkeeping, might always make a kind of unfortunate social sense in, for instance, the culture of religious wars that preceded the full flower of the Enlightenment, when it seemed socially important to sort people into the categories of believers in one confession or another. Catholics were sometimes banned from London. But it is sometimes gross and distorting if our point is to understand one another. And sometimes it does not matter to what we think.

---

[4] All the non-semantical facts may also determine other semantical facts directly, for instance externalist features of reference. But my claim ignores such direct routes.

It may seem that only by sorting people's beliefs into the true and false, that only by identifying their references, can we learn from each other, can we communicate, can we engage together within communities, across communities, and over time in great social practices of knowledge. But I do not claim that facts about truth and reference are *never* relevant, only that sometimes they are not relevant. Sometimes if we cannot sort people's beliefs into true and false, we can still learn from and communicate with them. It is not that truth and reference in all their details are never relevant, but that when they are relevant to thoughts their relevance depends on something else. It depends on the match of narrow content and world. And narrow content still matters when we cannot sort people's beliefs into true and false.

4.2

That's my claim. Now for argument. There are, as I said, three clusters of psychologically unimportant facts about reference and hence truth.

First, sometimes people's thoughts are vague or confused in such a way that it is perfectly clear what someone thinks, vague or confused as it is, but indeterminate whether it is true or false. Perhaps there are various ways to refine the contents of those thoughts into new contents that are determinately true or false, but the original contents remain vague or confused. In such cases and in that sense, truth and reference doesn't matter to psychological semantics.

Kripke's Pierre is such a case. Kripke says:

I am fully aware that complete and straightforward descriptions of the situation are possible and that in this sense there is no paradox. Pierre is disposed to sincere assent to '*Londres est jolie*' but not to 'London is pretty'. He uses French normally, English normally. Both with '*Londres*' and 'London' he associates properties sufficient to determine that famous city, but he does not realize that they determine a single city. (And his uses of '*Londres*' and 'London' are historically (causally) connected with the same single city, though he is unaware of that.) We may even give a rough statement of his beliefs. He believes that the city he calls '*Londres*' is pretty, that the city he calls 'London' is not. No doubt other straightforward descriptions are possible. No doubt some of these are, in a certain sense, *complete* descriptions of the situation. But none of this answers the original question. Does Pierre, or does he not, believe that London is pretty? I know of no answer to *this* question that seems satisfactory. It is no answer to protest that, in some *other* terminology, one can state 'all the relevant facts'.[5]

I agree that no answer to Kripke's question seems satisfactory. But I claim that we should conclude that this reveals limits to the importance of the vocabulary in which it is posed. Once we know all the facts that Kripke allows can be expressed in other vocabulary, there is no point in knowing the answer to Kripke's additional and paradoxical question. Such facts about reference are semantically and psychologically unimportant. Indeed, in this instance, as Kripke suggests, there is no coherent determinate answer to the question, even though Pierre has beliefs.

And remember Putnam on jade: 'Although the Chinese do not recognize a difference, the term "jade" applies to two minerals; jadeite and nephrite. Chemically, there is a marked difference. Jadeite is a combination of sodium and aluminum. Nephrite is made of calcium, magnesium, and iron. These two quite different microstructures produce the same unique textural qualities!'[6] The facts about 'jade' are indeed even more complex than Putnam noted.[7] The ancient Chinese term for jades was applied, at least often, to many more materials that could be worked in roughly the same way. But most ancient jades were nephrite. Jadeite was only introduced from abroad late in Chinese history, perhaps in the eighteenth century. And jadeite was considered false jade even relatively recently in the English-speaking world.[8] But assume that Putnam is right that our own word refers equally and only to jadeite and nephrite. Now ask, like Kripke of Pierre, did an ancient Chinese artisan who made two figures, one of nephrite and one of another shiny stone, believe that they were both jade, or did he not? And did his beliefs about jade extend to jadeite? Given a suitably referential reading of those questions, they have no answers, and it doesn't matter that they don't.

So sometimes externalist conceptions force us to ask questions that there is no point in asking. Other cases of indeterminacy in reference turn on the interaction of not implausible externalist claims about community determination of reference with the obvious fact that sometimes there is more than one relevant community.

---

[5] Kripke (1979: 259). The quote elides a paragraph break.   [6] Putnam (1975: 241).
[7] Hansford (1968: 26–48).   [8] LaPorte (1996: 127).

Burge introduced the difficulty of regional idiolects. '[A] person's aberrations relative to the larger community may be normalities relative to the [smaller] one. In such cases, of course, the regional conventions are dominant in determining what contents should be attributed. At this point, it is natural to appeal to etiological considerations. The speaker of the dialect developed his linguistic habits from interaction with others who were a party to distinctly regional conventions. The person is committed to using words according to the conventions maintained by those from whom he learned the words.'[9] But this treatment has a cost. The individuation of idiolects is sometimes indeterminate or vague, and hence so are reference and truth.

Brian Loar introduced another sort of case, where communities overlap perhaps only in the speaker: 'Suppose Bert is a full member of two English-speaking communities that differ linguistically in small ways of which he is unaware. The first is ours, where "arthritis" means arthritis; but in the second "arthritis" means tharthritis.... [Still] in explaining Bert psychologically the natural thing to say is that he has just one belief, one way of conceiving what is wrong with his ankles.'[10] Segal has deployed similar cases in which a transatlantic speaker of English plausibly has references torn between dominant uses in England and the United States.[11] There are also cases with competing and differing sets of experts, and in which unbeknownst to a speaker a word has two relevant meanings.[12] In all of these sorts of cases, reference and truth may be indeterminate while psychologically-relevant content is not.

Another case, due to Perry, involves names:

Suppose you are standing in front of the philosophy department talking with your friends about Aristotle Onassis. I join the conversation and quite naturally take you to be talking about the philosopher. The issue under discussion is how much Aristotle knew about Plato, and I say, 'Aristotle knew Plato and his philosophy very well.' We might have a disagreement about what I have said. On one view, ... I have inadvertently referred to and said something false about Onassis.... One can think of the use of names in conversations as akin to anaphoric co-designation. The speaker's intention to exploit the convention already in play trumps his intention to refer to the person his guiding notion is of.... Alternatively, we could suppose

---

[9] Burge (1979: 114). Note his qualifications that follow this claim, when someone has contrary intentions.
[10] Loar (1988: 106).   [11] Segal (2000: 136–41).   [12] Segal (2000: 75).

that I have said something true about the philosopher that is irrelevant to the conversation. While *what I said* may be unclear, there is no mystery about what happened.[13]

It is reasonably clear in this case what Perry is thinking when he enters the conversation. But if we accept the externalist theoretical suggestion that it is unclear what he said, we should then conclude that what was said in that sense is irrelevant to the semantics of his psychology.

My second cluster of cases reflects an objection to my internalist proposal that we left hanging earlier. We worried that the notion of being called by a term might be subject to the Twin Earth phenomenon, or that it might be a deferential notion. Since the second possibility seems more plausible to me, I called this the deep deferentiality objection.

In the end, I don't think that it is plausible that reference is in fact a deferential notion.[14] I think that the deferentiality of reference isn't so much a fact about reference and truth as a possibility that we need to explore, and so that the second relevant cluster of facts about truth and reference involves mere possibilities. But you may disagree, which is why I am exploring these possibilities.

There are individual narrow conceptions of being called by a term, certainly in adults capable of the relevantly sophisticated introspection, which reflect internally determinate capacities necessary for full linguistic competence. But such individual conceptions may be incomplete or erroneous. The content properly contributed to a thought by one's self-conscious notion of being called by a term or even by the internally determinate capacities that it fallibly reflects may hence depend on the natural kind *reference* or the vagaries of community or expert use of 'reference'. Or at least that is the possibility that we are exploring.

I find it hard to credit the idea that the contingencies of natural kinds matter all that much in this case. I think we could not find out through empirical research that a universally-shared conception of word reference is radically mistaken.[15] But I admit there are not unreasonable grounds to worry that there is social determination of the extension of 'being called'. My goal is to convert this apparent objection into an advantage.

---

[13] Perry (2001: 136).
[14] This is not to say that other psychological or semantic notions are not deferential. On belief, see Gibbons (2001a: 14–15), but note the last paragraph of page 15.
[15] Though we might find that it is inapplicable in our world.

Kripke, Putnam, and Burge proceed largely from the armchair, and they depend on our armchair agreement. But their concrete cases made us sit up with surprise. At first, not everyone agreed with the intuitions their cases fostered. But there has been a slow and steady growth within the English-speaking philosophical community and our students of the intuitions fostered by the cases. Perhaps this suggests that we accept that there are experts about reference even among philosophers, to whom we should defer, albeit slowly and reluctantly. If those of us who were tardy in accepting these cases had been in different communities with different and internalist experts, perhaps all the references of all our words would have been subtly different all along.

If this is so, and I'm not sure it isn't so, then it is an unfortunate feature of our conceptions of reference and truth, which should not infect any accurate account of what we think. But it will take me a moment to explain why. Let me begin with a general point, which will matter to us later in more than one way.

Talk of 'experts' and the linguistic division of 'labor' may elide the dark side of the social determination of meaning. The social complexity of the city of knowledge may encompass corruption. The alleged experts to whom we defer may sometimes not have any relevant extra knowledge, but simply greater influence. They may be treated as experts because of social accidents, and not because of any greater cognitive expertise. Indeed, it is even possible that they know less than we do, but simply have more power. The propriety of social determination turns on the nature of the 'expertise' in question.

It will take a while for us to understand the relevance of this dark scenario to the case at hand, to the case of reference and truth. I think that what really happened about reference is very different: Kripke, Putnam, and Burge noted features of our internally determinate and generally shared conceptions of reference that we would otherwise have missed. Normal adults all along had the dispositions to respond to their cases as we have mostly come to respond to them. But most of us didn't realize that about ourselves. The semantic a priori was divorced from the epistemic a priori. On this conception, Kripke, Putnam, and Burge are legitimate semantic experts. They were more skilled in eliciting key intuitions and tracing out their consequences. But notice that on this conception there is no relevant social determination of our ordinary conceptions of reference and truth.

Such conceptions are fixed by what I have called semantic aprioricity for all normal adults.

So consider other sorts of legitimate expertise. Perhaps the relevant semantic experts are most of us, because most of us have always had the dispositions to respond to the famous externalist cases in the appropriate way. And so only young children and a few adults who lack sufficient semantic sophistication have semantic notions whose content is socially determined. Alternatively, if those children and adults lack a notion of reference, still perhaps their references themselves are in a very general way socially determined by the general commonsense adult conception of reference. If the rest of us responded differently to the famous cases, then they would still defer to us all, and so the references of all their terms might be perturbed by social factors.

But young children and a few semantic incompetents cannot provide a strong case for a general semantic conception like externalism. Such individuals need more training to have an ordinary adult cognitive life. It is one thing to lack an understanding of something specific like arthritis or elms, but quite another to fail to understand what it is for words to apply to things. Perhaps the less than fully competent make do with more rudimentary semantic notions than our own. But then of course they may also make do with more rudimentary relations between their thoughts or even words and the world. Their cognitive life is too different from ordinary adult life to provide much grounds for social externalism of any interesting sort.

So perhaps the best case for externalism about the notion of reference is in between. Perhaps most of us have always had the right dispositions to respond to the famous cases, but some philosophers who are generally competent yet have deviant conceptions, rooted in deviant dispositions, for instance regarding what to say about the famous externalist cases. So those who lack the intuitions generally fostered by the famous cases are by that very reason mildly semantic incompetent, and should defer.

Perhaps that is what some externalists think, though I know of none who has the crust to say it out loud. But in any case it is hard to see why such merely numerical deviance should count in itself as incompetence. There are some words that most people misunderstand.

So far we haven't found a form of expertise that would properly support social externalism about the notion of reference. That would seem to require adult experts to whom other competent adults should defer, whose expertise is rooted not merely in their numerical superiority, and not merely in their special knowledge of our ordinary and generally shared semantic conceptions, conceptions constituted by the internally determinate dispositions of most competent individual adults.

Perhaps Kripke, Putnam, and Burge knew some crucial semantic facts that most of us didn't know, beyond mere facts about our ordinary and internally determinate conceptions of reference and truth. Perhaps they had relevant expertise that required revision of our ordinary commonsense notions of reference and truth. But that scenario is quite unlikely, because then they could not properly have rested their arguments on our general intuitive response to particular concrete cases. They rather would have properly needed to convince us of the crucial general semantic facts that we had missed, and shown us how that required us to change or refine our old and faulty semantic conceptions.[16]

We have exhausted possible forms of genuine semantic expertise that could support social externalism about central semantic notions. If we want to find a scenario in which there is genuine social determination of such notions by so-called experts, then we are forced to consider a dark and unlikely possibility. Perhaps there is social determination of our notions of truth and reference, but the experts on reference and truth have no special cognitive expertise that legitimates their status as experts. We defer to them, but there is nothing that makes that especially appropriate. They have unusual influence, but no unusual expertise.

About this possibility, you should share my worries. Should the facts about the truth and reference of all of someone's thoughts at once be dependent on certain quirks of such an expert's opinions, even in the relatively small details in which I grant they may be so dependent? Do we think that truth and reference should be dependent even on those elements of expert opinion that may potentially reflect the interests of the experts, and even indeed help assure the institutional success of their theoretical views? Isn't this a reason to revise our notions of truth and reference so that they aren't so dependent?

I have to admit that I am not certain, that I don't *know*, that there aren't elements of our notions of truth and reference that are deferential

---

[16] There are elements in Burge that might be used in such an externalist argument. We will return to this point.

in this way. And I admit that my partly metalinguistic treatment of other terms cannot plausibly apply to its own terms, or at least cannot by such an iteration suitably capture the internally determinate content of metalinguistic notions. I think that Segal's deep deferentiality objection tells forcefully against a metalinguistic treatment of the deferentiality of metalinguistic notions. But remember that my aim here is merely to convince you that possible externalist elements of our notions of reference and truth are not psychologically important. And now that we have suitably isolated what they would involve, that is easy to do.

There is some internally determinate conception that each normal adult person has of what it is to be called by a term, fixed by their internally determinate dispositions to consider certain things the references of certain terms in various hypothetical scenarios, and perhaps other dispositions as well. This plays an important role in allowing a kind of internally determinate content to the metalinguistic conceptions of each such individual. But I grant that it is possible that our intuitive notions of truth and reference are deferential. And this suggests at least possible grounds for social externalism.

Still, such externalist features of the notions of truth and reference, if they exist, would be psychologically unimportant, for several reasons. First, they would be unfortunate and troubling in the ways suggested by my series of questions about the dark scenario, by the conditions required if there is to be genuine social determination of basic semantic notions. Nothing important should turn on such details, and in the ideal psychology nothing will. It is as if we inhabited a society in which the only notion or term in the vicinity of 'truth' could not by definition be applied to things a dictator didn't believe. In such a case, we'd need to clean things up a bit to do psychology and indeed to have a flourishing cognitive life. Second, since expert opinion might change, so too might the truth and reference of all our thoughts, to the degree that these things are dependent on expert opinion in the dark way we have isolated. This kind of instability would also be relevantly unfortunate. Third, there might be differing groups of experts within a community, and indeed the experts of different communities might differ, so that reference and truth were indeterminate or relativized. But that would also be too unfortunate to constrain the proper psychology.

But my next point about the notions of reference and truth is I think the most important, and indeed is relevant to our concerns even if the notion of reference isn't deferential to expert opinion. Even if there are no experts on truth and reference, indeed even if we all immediately share all the intuitions on which Putnam, Burge, and Kripke rely, even perhaps all of us in all language communities, still it is reasonable to worry that their cases reveal relatively arbitrary and quirky features of our notions of truth and reference, due to complicated and relevantly arbitrary social contingencies and historical developments or even to chance factors, and not due to deep and inevitable pressures from the nature of rationality or of social life or the world. Even if these facts about reference don't rest on unfortunate forms of deference, they may be accidents of generally shared convention. Our notions of truth and reference may be in these details highly conventional, accidental, and arbitrary, and for that reason and to that degree unimportant to any proper account of what we think.

To understand this point properly, it is perhaps easiest to turn to the third cluster of facts about reference and truth that are psychologically unimportant and hence show externalism false. They share a general character with the point of the last paragraph, but are not facts about the reference of 'reference' but rather about the references of other terms. Here we pass beyond direct discussion of the deep deferentiality objection.

This third cluster of facts all invoke a distinction between what is inevitable or natural or rational, and what is merely quirky, arbitrary, or highly conventional, about the extension of a term. To the degree that the reference or extension of any particular term is merely arbitrary in these ways, and in a way not reflected in the match of someone's narrow content and the world, it is psychologically unimportant, I claim. While the meaning of all language is conventional, and hence there is an element of conventionality in any thought mediated by words, still there are different kinds of contingency and conventionality that words can suffer. Some, but only some, involve intuitively arbitrary and unimportant constraints on the extensions of terms. And these introduce an *arbitrary* conventionality into some details of the reference and truth of our thoughts, which for that very reason are psychologically unimportant except when already reflected in narrow content.

One caveat: There is a sense in which these details are sometimes reflected indirectly in narrow content via its possible metalinguistic elements. But note that so far we have deployed these metalinguistic elements to deliver some intuitive differences and similarities between some thoughts, not to provide a crucial element of the truth-conditions of all thoughts. The metalinguistic elements of a content need not be very weighty or dominant elements in the relevant cluster, and so not very weighty in determining its match to the world, at least when there are sufficient other elements in the cluster that do match the world. The dispositions of the speaker might constitute them as especially weightless in circumstances like those we will be discussing, or at least weightless in their details that turn on quirks. Also, the relevant metalinguistic elements of some contents may invoke the speaker's understanding of terms—what the speaker means by them—and not their conventional extension, including the speaker's understanding of the metalinguistic terms in play. Or it may involve the speaker's internally determinate conception of the social facts of usage.[17] But such qualifications aside, my point is this:

In cases where the extensions of terms involve arbitrary quirks that are not reflected in narrow content, externalism may provide an account of the truth-conditions of thoughts that is more intuitive in detail than the kind of match to the world that narrow content alone can provide. But it is for that very reason incorrect, for these intuitive details are unimportant in a way that thought content is not. Two individuals may share narrow contents, and be in circumstances in which their thoughts have the same semantics and the same proper semantic values, and in which both indeed suitably match the world, but in which the thoughts don't have the same references or truth-values, simply because of arbitrary quirks of convention.

This is because sometimes those who determine the extensions of public terms aren't true experts, but are rather confused or mistaken, or even quacks or frauds. And it is because sometimes even genuine experts inherit terminology whose details are determined by the arbitrary caprice of history or the epistemically non-rational politics of past experts. As I said, there is a dark side of the division of linguistic labor, and to the social determination of meaning more generally. And arbitrariness can infect words of public languages even when the only relevant 'experts' are those who know standard dictionary meanings, because dictionary meanings also can involve arbitrary quirks.

---

[17] This might be important in Cartesian demon scenarios.

There are a variety of cases that can reveal the sorts of quirks in question. Some involve biological kinds. Here is Mark Wilson's case:

> The term 'Grant's zebra' was originally (*circa* 1820) applied to a strain of zebras native to Kenya. A set of morphologically distinct animals from Rhodesia was likewise called 'Chapman's zebra.' Later exploration showed that the two animals interbred near the Zambezi River and constituted one species *Equus burchelli*. Thus the term 'Grant's zebra' in present day English [refers to the original subspecies]. On the other hand, if zoological exploration of Africa had begun instead near the Zambezi [and Chapman's zebras had not been specially named but rather first observed near that river], 'Grant's zebra' would have naturally evolved to become the vernacular title for the entire species.[18]

This dependence on the order of discovery makes the extension of 'Grant's zebra' now too quirky and arbitrary in certain details to matter in those details to the psychological content of a thought mediated by that word in someone unaware of the details who is undisposed to grant such arbitrary features of public usage relevant weight. And it makes those details irrelevant to the thoughts of those confronted with such a zebra who lack the term, or who fail to apply it to the case at hand.[19]

Consider other cases. Some reflect the notorious theoretical controversies about the nature of species. For instance, Winston in a standard recent survey distinguishes the *phenetic* concept of species, whereby species are the 'smallest groups which are consistently and persistently distinct and distinguishable by ordinary means', *reproductive* concepts, whereby species are 'groups of interbreeding populations that are reproductively isolated from other groups', *phylogenetic* concepts, whereby species are single lineages or sets of closely related lineages occupying minimally different adaptive zones, and *cohesion* concepts, whereby species are the most inclusive population of individuals having the potential for mechanisms that limit population boundaries by microevolutionary forces like gene flow, natural selection, and genetic drift.[20] Some of these controversies imply controversies about species boundaries. And some of these controversies are conflicts among experts that the nature of the world itself evidently cannot resolve. This

---

[18] M. Wilson (1982: 572).
[19] Grant's zebra has also occasioned discussion about the semantic relevance of future external conditions, including Jackman (1999, 2005); Ebbs (2000); Brown (2000). Lance and O'Leary-Hawthorne (1997: 44–54) develop other examples. Chapter 9 discusses future determination.
[20] Winston (1998: 45). See also Ereshefsky (2001: 80–93).

provides for the possibility of further cases of our first general sort, in which reference is confused or vague when thought content is not. But when there are communities, say of biologists, in which such controversies are resolved, that will introduce arbitrariness into the boundaries of species. If a general conception of species from among many current feasible competitors comes to be adopted or denied by local experts on relevantly arbitrary grounds, for instance academic politics, that will generate a resolution of the extensions of many species at once that is equally arbitrary, and does not firmly constrain the thought contents of local non-experts.

And consider S. M. Walters' investigation of the families and genera of angiosperm taxonomy:[21]

The selection of the world's flora and the botanical literature available to Linnaeus and his immediate successors determined the main shape of the classification which we use today. Willis's generalization about the relationship between the age of a [taxonomic category] and its size... is valid enough, both for families (if size is judged by number of genera) and for genera (if size is judged by number of species). Willis, however, thought of the age of the [taxonomic category] in evolutionary terms; all that is necessary to validate the generalization is to interpret 'age' quite literally as the number of years since the particular [taxonomic category] was created *in the mind of the taxonomist*.... [W]e have no reason to think that Angiosperm classification would be substantially the same if botany had developed in, say, New Zealand in the nineteenth century instead of medieval and post-medieval Europe.[22]

[One] example of the importance of early recognition of 'kinds' of plants can be found in the fruit trees related to the apple.... Impressed by the similarity in structure of apples, pears and quinces, Linnaeus accommodated them in his single genus *Pyrus*; but it is amusing to find that tradition has triumphed after all, and modern Floras provide us again, as in seventeenth-century European works, with the four genera for apple, pear, quince and medlar. Can we doubt that, if these Rosaceous fruit trees had been unknown in Europe until the time of Linnaeus, we would happily have accommodated them in a single genus?[23]

This element of arbitrariness in the extensions of biological terms can make such features of their use of which a speaker is unaware irrelevant to the content of their thoughts mediated by such words.

Biological kinds are not the only examples. Here is Segal's summary of LaPorte's interesting discussion of gem terms: '"Sapphire", in its broader

---

[21] Walters (1961: 83). See also Ayers (1991: 82–3).
[22] Walters (1961: 74).   [23] Walters (1961: 82).

use, applies to all gem varieties of corundum... except ruby, according to most authorities. The original Greek term probably referred not to sapphires, but to lapis lazuli. "Ruby" applies only to red corundum. "Topaz" applies to aluminum silicate... no matter what the color. However, the original term, used by the Greeks and Romans, applied not to aluminum silicate, but to yellow corundum, i.e. yellow sapphire. Emeralds and aquamarines are both beryl, ... the former green, the latter blue.'[24] When someone has thoughts mediated by such terms without being aware of such quirks, and also when they think about such entities but without using the relevant vocabulary, these quirks are generally psychologically irrelevant.

Consider a recent case from astronomy. An icy object in solar orbit beyond Neptune, UB313, was recently discovered to be larger than Pluto.[25] There are little grounds to include Pluto as a planet and exclude UB313, but some question about whether to include both or neither. That there are merely 8 solar planets, and not at least 10 and probably more, and hence a refinement of the notion of a planet, was recently decided by a vote at an astronomy conference in Prague, and on no genuinely natural or world-reflecting grounds. If someone who was unaware of this situation believed in May 2006 that there were 8 planets, then I claim that the eventual outcome of this arbitrary vote isn't relevant to the psychologically relevant content of their thought, even though it decided the truth of that thought.

Sometimes it isn't the borders of a kind that are arbitrary, but whether or not there are things of a kind. There are atoms. Dalton was right, even though he thought atoms crucially, perhaps even by definition, were ultimate particles whose destruction required the destruction of matter.[26] But Priestley was wrong.[27] There is no phlogiston. In many cases Priestley's claims about dephlogisticated air are intuitively true, because they are causally rooted in real oxygen.[28] And Priestley's false conception of phlogiston, that it was a positive substance released in burning, rather than say a negative phenomenon (like a hole) that invades the air when burning occurs, seems no more obviously crucial or false than Dalton's view of atoms. And indeed some of Cavendish's utterances about phlogiston were

[24] Segal (2000: 130).   [25] Bertoldi, Altenhoff, Weiss, Menten, and Thum (2006).
[26] Dalton (1964: 162–3).   [27] Berry (1954: 19–46).
[28] Kitcher (1978) and (1993b: 97–112 and 272–90).

arguably controlled by hydrogen, as the conception of phlogiston evolved. But still, there is no phlogiston.

That is for two reasons. First, that terminology was associated with the expression of a particular view about combustion and related phenomena to which there was a contemporary competitor, Lavoisier's new chemistry, that deployed a different terminology, and with which our own chemistry is more closely allied.[29] So, to return to our other case, if Dalton had had a contemporary opponent with an influential theory that was otherwise very similar but deployed *divisible* particles called 'shmatoms', then there would be no atoms, in our best judgment. And the existence or non-existence of such a competitor related to our own views in the relevant way is psychologically irrelevant, irrelevant to what Dalton thought then.

Second, there is no phlogiston partly because Lavoisier was an extremely skilled and powerful academic operator who favored alternative terminology. Among other things, he developed a new and very successful textbook for chemistry embodying not only his own theories but his own and distinctive vocabulary.[30] This is (say in regard to what Priestley thought) a psychologically irrelevant accident of academic politics.

Try another case. Lavoisier was wrong about one thing. There is no caloric. But clearly his remarks about caloric were largely controlled by heat. And clearly Carnot's development of fundamental principles of thermodynamics in the language of caloric isn't false. Why is there no caloric? First, 'caloric' was a term associated with the conception of heat as a material which had contemporary competition deploying different terminology, and that motion conception of heat better fits our own thermodynamic conceptions and conception of energy conservation. (If you think this is not an accident, remember Dalton.) Second, because there was no brilliant and powerful propagandist like Lavoisier still attached to the old terminology in the middle of the nineteenth century. Two more psychologically arbitrary accidents, irrelevant to the content of Lavoisier's thought.

In fact, things are probably even worse for reference and truth than my simple theory suggests. There is really no reason to believe that there is a general explanation of all differences of this sort. Rather, some terminology survives and changes its associated ideology and some does not, sometimes

---

[29] Conant (1966).   [30] Guerlac (1975: 107–19); Poirer (1993: 176–97).

for arbitrary or accidental reasons, and that is partly why we say there are some things and not others. There are no witches, but there is genius. There is no evil eye, but there are curses. The world isn't flat, but the sky is blue. But, in any case, when the match of the narrow content of someone's thoughts and the world does not suffice to determine such differences,[31] then they are, in various ways explored in this section, of no psychological significance.

Fans of externalism rooted only in external natural kinds will note that two of my clusters of objections to externalism have invoked the dark side of the linguistic division of labor, and do not count against the determination of content by natural kinds. They may suggest that the twisty convolutions of the social city of knowledge should scare us out into nature and not back into ourselves. But my third cluster of objections does suggest that some features of what we often consider to be natural kinds are not very natural at all. And remember our dialectical situation. My central worry in this chapter is the deep deferentiality objection to my internalist proposal, the objection that the notions of reference and being called by a term are deferential notions. This objection is most plausibly rooted in social externalism. Indeed, it is especially implausible to claim that reference is a natural kind if it involves the arbitrary convolutions and crannies discovered from externalist armchairs.

But we have not merely answered a standing objection to my version of internalism. We have seen some new case-based reasons to believe that internalism is correct. There is the narrow content of thoughts, and there is the world. The match of narrow content and the world determines reference and truth to a degree. But to the degree that it does not, reference and truth are unimportant. And so internalism is true. Indeed, that is the *real* moral of the quirky and otherwise misleading cases of Kripke, Putnam, and Burge.

4.3

We now possess the sketch of an internalist reply to the famous externalist cases, and indeed the rudiments of a general internalist story about the

---

[31] With the qualifications noted in the ninth paragraph of Section 4.1.

contribution to thought content of words that putatively refer. It is the first of the three main components of qualia empiricism. I call it RDC, for Rigidified Description Clusters.

The story goes like this: There is a set of properties that is constituted by the internally determinate dispositions of a speaker to be positively relevant to what counts in their judgment as the referent of a given term. And there are various relative weights of those properties in determining what counts as the referent under various conditions, also determined by the internally determinate dispositions of the speaker. Normal competent adults can come to at least rough armchair knowledge of these properties and their weights for their own case, in a way I will sketch in Chapter 8, but that is not a constitutive constraint on their nature.

Among this set of properties, there is a subset that have relatively great weight in fixing reference, and includes 1) any properties that are taken by the speaker as analytically true of or criterial for things in that extension, in a sense of 'taken by' constituted by their internally determinate dispositions, 2) the metalinguistic property of being referred to by that term, and 3) any other properties that are taken as each a priori true of things in that extension by the speaker, in a sense also constituted by their internally determinate dispositions. There might also be a second key subset of the positively relevant properties, which are at least apparently distinct properties taken by the speaker to be positively relevant to each of the preceding three types of criteria, and so on.

Call all that, all the relevant properties and their weights, 'the description cluster' of a term for a speaker at a time. The content contributed by a term 'X' with a putative reference to thoughts it mediates for a speaker at a time can be captured by 'dthat [best satisfier of the description cluster for "X"]', as long as 'dthat' is understood in the proper way noted in Chapter 2.

We have already considered many objections to such a proposal. But plausible worries remain. Begin with this one:

In the last section, I claimed that there are limits to the significance of possible quirky and arbitrary features of the notions of reference and truth, especially when they are not reflected in an individual's dispositions. I also claimed more generally that there are limits to the significance of quirky and arbitrary features of the boundaries of the extensions of all sorts of terms, and hence to the reference of those terms and the truth of sentences containing them. But this presents real difficulties for me.

First, qualia empiricism is non-epistemic. It is more in the tradition of truth-condition semantics rather than that of assertion-condition semantics. I think that the basic semantic notion is not something epistemic like justifiable assertion, but rather something more like truth. So I have theoretical commitments that make worries about the notions of truth and reference a special problem for me.

Second, the notion of truth is so central to our general vocabulary of intellectual assessment that I would be very hard pressed to avoid the word 'true' in the rest of this book. And truth is basic in other ways. It is for instance one condition required for knowledge, and evidence is evidence of truth. So many other common words of intellectual assessment are as problematic as 'true'.

In the last section, I argued that 'true' is a somewhat flawed word. But I can hardly avoid it and the terms that rest on it. And of course I will use words that refer. That is my problem.

One way around this problem would be to perform some repairs on the notion of truth. Philosophers have interpreted our concepts in various ways, but sometimes the point is to change them. However, that is obviously too grandiose a job for the moment. So I adopt this optimistic stop-gap measure:

I will use the unusual word 'match' rather than 'truth' in key theoretical proposals. But when in the course of discussion I claim that something is true, or even just say something, you can assume that I assume that I have an internally determinate sense of what I am saying, to which I am ceding full authority over the suggestions of any external experts, and which I claim to involve no quirky and arbitrary extension boundaries. And so when I say that some thought or claim is true, what I'm really claiming is that it has narrow content that matches the world.

That is absurdly optimistic, and may seem grandiose in another way. But all I'm doing is assuming slightly more responsibility for my claims than is assumed by anyone who makes a philosophical proposal, in order to avoid another sort of work that is too hard and that would distract us from the issue at hand. And in the end, nothing crucial here will turn on this.

But that leads to another worry. I did not argue in the last section that *all* features of social and other sorts of external content determination were dark and unfortunate. So it is open to externalists to propose alternative repairs to our cognitive notions than those I would propose.

But this will be work for all of us, work that will almost certainly involve some revision of our intuitions about cases and some revision of our notions of truth and reference. I think that the real moral of this part is that while an appeal to cases cannot show directly that externalism ought to be accepted, it can show that some cases that may seem to support externalism do have dark and unfortunate implications, which are related to features of our notions of truth and reference that should be revised. We know that internalism is safe at least in these ways, and much work will need to be done before we know that a refined externalism can be made safe. So at least for now, internalism ought to be accepted.

You may reasonably request a somewhat clearer sense of what I mean by the arbitrary and quirky aspects of the boundaries of the extension of a term, or the dark side of the division of linguistic labor. It is natural to propose a conditional test: If some feature of the boundary of the extension of a term in a public language is due to features of social life that are not responsive to reality, then it is quirky and arbitrary. But of course we can have even very full-blooded individually-determinate beliefs about reality that are not really responsive to that reality; we can be lost in misleading evidential backwaters. And I do not think that the relevant kind of reality-responsivity is an epistemic matter, and hence that we should modify the notion of truth in some verificationist or other evidence-based direction. And some of our terms do refer to social factors of the same sorts that make other terms not responsive to reality. So I won't attempt a serious general characterization, and hope that you can gather what I mean from my cases. The lack of any obvious way to mark a general distinction between the dark and the happy features of social determination is perhaps one reason to be skeptical that a properly reformed externalism is possible.

But I don't claim that this is the final word. Clearly, Putnam doesn't conceive the linguistic division of labor to privilege quirks of expert opinion about natural kinds over the facts of nature. The kinds themselves are supposed to matter most. But notice that this reply is only available for the externalist when there are genuine natural kinds in question, and that some of our quirky kinds from the last section seem superficially to be pretty natural. And notice that there is reason to worry about granting expert quirks even defeasible status in determining reference. Burge has argued that the fact that the influence of the socially persuasive is subject to dispute and cognitive checks legitimates their influence, and indeed helps make the result of social persuasion a proper norm for the mind.[32] But it is far from clear that the notion of a cognitive check rooted in reality makes sense for many important cases, and it is not obvious that the mere possibility of dispute and cognitive checks really is sufficient to defeat the dark side of social determination.

This is one point, I think, at which the issue between externalists and internalists should now be fought, and on other grounds than intuitions about cases. But as an internalist I hasten to point out that intellectual norms for the mind would not be worsened if we all became closely aware of the nature of our agreements and disagreements, and in particular if we ceased to mistake what are in fact merely metalinguistic agreements and disagreements for more substantial forms.

Still, there are other worries about RDC. Even if we expansively consider properties to be bits of the world to which terms refer, it is clear that many words do not have the kind of referential meaning to which RDC is relevant. And yet they can mediate our thought.

But, I reply, in our discussions of externalist language-based theories in Part III, I will develop an internalist treatment of other sorts of cases. RDC is not intended even as a sketch of the contribution of all words to thought.

Another standing worry about RDC is that it is unclear how we are capable of the conception of the various properties that enter into the clusters in a way consistent with internalism. It is plausible that the conception of some properties in some clusters involves the mediation of other words. But it is also clear that on pain of an implausible linguistic idealism this cannot generally be true.

My reply to this important objection, as well as to other natural externalist worries about the resources RDC requires, will be one aspect of the rest of this book. In the next two parts, I will develop the other two positive components of qualia empiricism, and try to show how they provide, among other things, the resources that RDC requires. I will work forward from properties whose conception does not crucially involve linguistic mediation, back towards those that do. Some of the description clusters themselves have a kind of layered structure, with certain properties dependent on others, and this response will in fact work up some chains of dependence in paradigmatic clusters.

---

[32] Burge (1986b) and (2007: 151–81 and 275–315).

The next two parts also have other argumentative roles, but they are entwined with this reply. Even if the famous externalist cases are not decisive, you may think that there are theoretical reasons to favor mind-based or language-based externalism, and you may also think that some of those reasons show that RDC harbors features that are covertly externalist. Still, we will see that there is no reason to favor these theory-based forms of externalism over qualia empiricism.

PART II
Mind-Based Externalism and Sensory Content

5

Against Etiological Semantics

The positive role of this part is to develop the second element of qualia empiricism: Modal Structuralism or MS. This is an account of sensory contents as internally determinate qualia, and will help provide the resources that RDC requires. But this part also has a negative role. That is to dispose of alleged theoretical motivations for mind-based externalist theories. These roles are entwined, because mind-based externalist theories encompass the dominant alternatives to MS.

Chapter 7 sketches MS. Chapter 6 considers externalist mind-based theories in which current conditions play the crucial external role. This chapter discusses forms of mind-based externalism in which history is crucial. But first some general background:

5.1

Because sensation is the obvious place where thoughts that are not mediated by language touch the world, mind-based externalist theories naturally deploy sensory experiences or perceptual beliefs in a central role. Since sensory experiences and perceptual beliefs are plausibly about certain of their environmental causes, it is also natural that such accounts focus on causal relations between environmental stimuli and mental states as the central semantic root. The apparent plausibility of that general conception is one central theoretical motivation for externalism.

But there is an important complication faced by such accounts in our physical world. When perceptual states have causes that plausibly are their objects, they yet have many other causes, in a cascading chain. But none of those causes is naturally and inevitably the content of such a state in quite the way that naive Aristotelian theories of perception suggest. The content of my sensory state is not some irreducible green right there in my headlights with which sensible species informing my eye share an essence.

The now dominant externalist accounts of the content of perceptual states are causal-informational accounts, which hold that the content of a perceptual thought is its *proper* cause. False perceptual beliefs usually have a proper cause that isn't an actual cause, and even true perceptual beliefs have many actual causes that are not proper. While Aristotle might consistently speak of sensible species that link sense and object by essence, physicalist externalist accounts of perceptual content must deploy some suitably physicalist story about proper causes. Different contemporary causal-informational accounts differ principally about what makes causes proper.

There will be two unifying themes in our negative discussion of externalist physicalist accounts of proper causes, in this and the following chapter. The first is this:

We seek the true physicalist account of what constitutes our mental states to have the contents that they do. We seek what is in that sense a reductive explanation of mental content. And as we will see, accounts of proper causes that can be deployed to answer the characteristic difficulty of otherwise intuitive externalist causal-informational accounts face a dilemma.

They either provide a relatively robust and specific account of propriety, which hence might be deployed in a reductive and properly motivated externalist account of content, but which unfortunately turns out to involve the wrong kind of propriety to play a semantic role. Or they deploy a vague conception of propriety, which might be stretched to encompass the semantic propriety at issue for us, but which can't properly explain or reduce it in a specifically externalist way.

The various externalist accounts of the proper causes relevant to thought content, of *semantically* proper causes, are either false, or so vague as to provide no motivation to think that externalism is true. The second horn of this dilemma will be central later on, and sometimes both horns will be in play. But the first account that we will consider falls firmly against the first horn.

The second unifying theme of our negative discussion will also be an important positive clue to the nature of MS. It is color blindness. A quick sketch of facts about color blindness is the last piece of background required before we can begin the main negative arguments of this chapter.

Human color blindness is the inability to discriminate color differences that can be distinguished by normal humans. It has various forms. To understand these forms, it is useful to consider certain features of the neurophysiology of human vision.[1]

The retina of a normal human contains, in addition to 'rod' cells that discriminate light from dark, three kinds of 'cone' cells that are crucial to color vision. The visible spectrum of light spans relatively long red wavelengths and relatively short blue wavelengths. And the three sorts of cones contain three different pigments, which are maximally sensitive to different wavelengths of light. L (or long wavelength) cones are called 'red' cones, M (medium wavelength) cones are called 'green' cones, and S (short wavelength) cones are called 'blue', though in fact the red cones are maximally sensitive to the yellow region of the spectrum.

Different colors are perceived when different types of cones are stimulated to different degrees, but the details are complex. For one thing, there is a kind of opponent-processing of color stimuli, even in the retina itself. There are neural mechanisms that are sensitive to red and green as opposing colors, and others that are sensitive to yellow and blue as opposing colors. This helps explain the two more or less perpendicular diameters of the familiar color wheel, spanning red to green and yellow to blue. Red and green are in some sense opposing colors. So are yellow and blue. Orange is reddish and yellowish, and it is seen when the red-green system is tipped towards red and the blue-yellow system is tipped towards yellow. Red is seen when the red-green system is tipped towards red and the blue-yellow system is neutral.

Some forms of human color blindness are due to brain damage, and can be quite dramatic. Central achromatopsia is a disorder in which, in extreme cases, everything looks grey. But the most common forms of color blindness are due to genetic disorders that affect the synthesis of the pigments in the cones, and are less dramatic. Normal humans are trichromats: Any colored light can be matched in their experience by some combination of no more than three other lights of fixed colors, called primaries. This we might

---

[1] The standard text on color vision is Kaiser and Boynton (1996). See also Gordon and Abramov (2001); Palmer (1999: 94–142); Byrne and Hilbert (1997: vol. ii); McIlwain (1996: 183–96); Hardin (1988). On color blindness see Kaiser and Boynton (1996: 414–84); Gazzaniga, Ivry, and Mangun (2002: 172–5); Byrne and Hilbert (1997: vol. ii, pp. xx–xxiv); Hsia and Graham (1997); Nathans (1997); Rizzo, Smith, Pokorny, and Damasio (1997); McIlwain (1996: 189–91); Hardin (1988: 78 and 145–54); Pokorny, Smith, Verriest, and Pinckers (1979).

expect on the basis of the three types of cones. Some color blind people are anomalous trichromats, because the peak spectral sensitivity of one or more of their cone types is shifted. But most color blind people are dichromats. Only two primaries are required to match any color in their experience. This results from the disabling of one of the three types of cones.

The very most common sort of color blindness results from abnormalities of the L or M cones, which create difficulties in discriminating red, yellow, and green. This is called red-green color blindness. There are also forms of color blindness that involve the S cones, but they are relatively rare. And some individuals are even monochromats. But let me focus on the most common type.

Cones may be disabled to various degrees. There are those who are classified as red-green color blind who yet discriminate some greens from some reds, and both from some greys.[2] They have merely decreased sensitivity to the differences. But there are also more straightforward cases of red-green color blindness, in which reds and greens cannot be discriminated. Protanopia is lack of the pigment crucially constitutive of L cones, and deuteranopia is lack of the M cone pigment. Red-green color blindness is most commonly due to recessively inherited defects in genes on the X chromosome. Red-green color blindness afflicts more men than women because the genes for the pigments in question are located on that chromosome, and because men have only one X chromosome, while women have two. Men will be red-green color blind if they have one anomalous X chromosome, but red-green color blind women must have two anomalous X chromosomes.

The somewhat misleading name of color blindness may suggest to the unwary that all humans share color experience, and that color blindness involves a failure to discriminate some features that are present even in the experience of the color blind. But in fact there are differences between the color experiences of the normal and the color blind. Rare individuals whose eyes differ in color sensitivity, or who become color blind through injury or disease, observe and report these differences.[3] Such differences in experience will be crucial to us, so let me repeat the point. The experience of a color blind person sometimes differs from that of a normal percipient even

---

[2] Broackes (1997: 216).

[3] There are controversies about the detailed nature of these differences, but the phenomenon is clear. See Kaiser and Boynton (1996: 452–5); Alpern, Kitahara, and Krantz (1997).

when they are in identical environmental conditions, because of internal differences. And different sorts of color blindness, which involve different internal abnormalities, also characteristically involve different experiences.

Still, it is also possible to exaggerate these differences, misled in the other direction by the same misleading name. Most color blind people are not totally blind to color. The fully red-green color blind can still discriminate some colors, and they do not see all reds and greens as greys. So the differences in the color experience of most color blind people are more subtle than the name suggests. But they are real. And there are also rare sorts of color blindness, for instance in those who lack cones altogether or who have the extreme forms of central achromatopsia that I noted earlier, that involve very dramatic differences in experience.

When Chapter 7 returns to my positive internalist proposal about sensory content—to Modal Structuralism—that proposal will be rooted in these and other facts about our color experience. All the differences that plausibly constitute the differences in color experience between normal humans and those with various sorts of color blindness, when environmental stimuli are shared, are internal differences. And friends of internalism will note that if internal differences can explain these differential features of human color experience, as they must, then there is at least initial reason to hope that they can explain any other differential features of our sensory experiences.

But we will come back to that positive point only after first charting the debilitating difficulties of the dominant externalist alternatives, which deploy various externalist accounts of proper causes. Different externalist proposals suffer from various difficulties. But these theories not only span a dilemma from the reductive but false to the vague and unexplanatory, they are also incompatible in various ways with the color experience of the color blind.

5.2

There aren't many plausible physicalist accounts of proper causes. Proper causes have some sort of priority, and one obvious form of priority is historical priority. Such an historical or etiological story is even in the rough spirit of Aristotle's view about dreams and hallucinations, which is that they inherit their content from antecedent veridical experiences. Now we turn to a detailed examination of externalist accounts of proper causes in which historical conditions play the primary externalist role.

The first we will consider is now the most popular mind-based externalist theory. Teleological accounts of the contents of thoughts and sensations deploy the functions of such states.[4] Pioneers of this 'teleosemantics' include Stampe, Enç, Dretske, Papineau, Millikan, and McGinn.[5] And it is indeed not unreasonable to think that the sensory content of some pattern of neural firing is the environmental condition by which it is supposed to be caused. 'Etiological' accounts of function, for instance those of Wright, Millikan, and Neander, hold that the functions of things depend on their histories, especially their evolutionary histories.[6] And it is indeed not unreasonable to think that the function of a certain color pattern in butterflies is to evade some predator that exterminated those of the same species who lacked that pattern. 'Etiological teleosemantics' or 'ET' combines these two elements. It claims, for instance, that the content of some pattern of neural firing in a sensory system is the environmental condition that led to the natural selection of a capacity for such a pattern. This is the account of proper causes that will be our first concern. Current practitioners include Dretske, Millikan, and Papineau.[7]

Because sensation is our principle positive concern in this part, and because sensory states are the psychological states that most plausibly have distinctive evolutionary histories, I will focus primarily on ET accounts of sensation. But we will return to other applications of ET in Section 5.8.

The outline of my argument against ET accounts of sensory content can be briefly sketched.

1) According to ET, the etiologically-proper causes of sensory states are the contents of those states. And so, for instance, there can be a sensory state that falsely represents, when none of its actual causes are its etiologically-proper cause.

---

[4] Or the functions of mechanisms that produce them or respond to them.
[5] Stampe (1977); Enç (1982); Millikan (1984); Papineau (1984); Dretske (1986); McGinn (1989: 143–54).
[6] L. Wright (1973); Millikan (1984); Neander (1991a, 1991b); Allen, Bekoff, and Lauder (1998); Hull and Ruse (1998).
[7] Millikan (1984, 1993c), though Millikan (2004: 66–7) stresses that teleology only helps fix proper causes in cases of error; Papineau (1987, 1993); Dretske (1988, 1995); Matthen (1988); Jacob (1997). Criticism includes Perlman (2002) and Walsh (2002).

2) But etiologically-proper functions, including those that specify etiologically-proper causes, are characteristically retained in the face of present deformities that make it impossible to perform the functions in question. For instance, the evolutionary history of a severely deformed cow heart may give it the function to circulate blood even though it cannot circulate blood.
3) And deformed sensory states do not characteristically retain their normal, evolutionarily-specified contents. Deformation of sensory systems affects sensory contents in a way that ET implies that it would not.

Consider the color blind. Their sensory contents are different from those of the normal. And yet they share any relevant evolutionary history with the normal. The propriety defined by ET does not seem to be semantic propriety, at least in their case. And so we come to our other unifying theme, our dilemma for externalist accounts of proper causes. ET accounts of content are not vague and non-reductive, but they deliver the wrong contents.

This is just the sketch of an argument. We will need to reconsider each of its points in detail, by attention to corresponding detailed complexities of the motivations for ET accounts, and also of the different ways in which ET can be applied to deliver sensory contents. The next four sections flesh out this argument sketch. They argue in more detail that ET accounts of sensation are irreparably false, and that they are supported by no motivations that can withstand close scrutiny.

The problem for ET reflects a confusion in ET's principal rationale, and the next section will characterize that rationale, its confusion, and the problem. Sections 5.4 through 5.6 elaborate the difficulty for the range of possible ET accounts of sensory content, for the range of ways in which ET can be applied to deliver sensory contents.

5.3

It is important to distinguish rationales for ET and rationales for somewhat similar claims. History may be relevant to content even if etiologically-constituted functions are not. And there may be evolution of sensory systems and yet no teleological specification of content. Still, there is an apparent two-part rationale for ET.

First, teleosemantics has a natural plausibility. Crudely speaking, the content of a thought or sensation is held by teleosemantics to be the thing that is *supposed* to cause the allied internal representational state. The content of that representation is claimed to be the thing (or fact, or property) by which it is that representation's *function* to be caused. And such claims sound plausible.

The second half of the principal rationale for ET is the motivation for an etiological account of function. There are alternative accounts, which focus on current or future conditions rather than histories,[8] but the dominant view of functions is now the etiological view of Wright, Millikan, and Neander. According to such a view, the history of something is crucial to the constitution of its particular function. For instance, a particular history of natural Darwinian selection of a certain trait is thought to help constitute a particular function for that trait. That trait, crudely speaking, is *supposed* to do whatever it did in its history that led to its selection.

What motivates etiological accounts of function? The most forceful motivations, we will see, rest on intuitive examples. But there are also more theoretical motivations, which were dominant in the original discussion of such accounts by Wright.[9] And one theoretical motivation that is both apparently relevant to content and not obviously exhausted by the examples is this:

Non-etiological conceptions of function, for instance that of Cummins, seem to leave functions too indeterminate to play any significant role, say in fixing content. You can do lots of different things with a rake, but it seems you only know what it is really for if you know why it was made. Etiological conceptions of function promise more determinacy of function.

But it is unlikely that ET accounts of at least sensory content will find much support and comfort in this alleged theoretical motivation. In what is in various ways an irony, the majority of the discussion that sensory content has received in the ET literature involves consideration of the *objection* that the sensory perceptual states of frogs and quasi-perceptual states of marine bacteria are indeterminate in content if ET is true.[10] So

---

[8] Perhaps a function is a capacity that plays a role in the analysis of some capacity of some containing system. See R. Cummins (1975); Bourse (1976, 1977). Or perhaps a function is a disposition apt for selection. See Bigelow and Pargetter (1987).

[9] L. Wright (1973).

[10] Dretske (1986); Fodor (1990a); Pietroski (1992); Agar (1993); Neander (1995); C. Price (1998).

ET accounts of sensory content don't seem very plausibly to benefit from this general motivation for etiological conceptions of function. While it may antecedently *seem* that a particular history of natural selection would be helpful in constituting which of many possible functions a particular evolved trait has, just as the intentions of a designer may help determine the exact function of a tool that yet can be used in a variety of ways, still this hope hasn't been vindicated by experience in the case of sensory content.

Two different classes of possible indeterminacies of function were introduced into the ET literature by Dretske and by Fodor as plausible difficulties.[11] We can summarize those problems in this way: Let us presume that evolutionary history fixes that a certain neural capacity, triggered by certain kinds of environmental conditions, is had by almost all current humans, because of natural selection bearing on our ancestors[12] in circumstances that were very simple. In those past days, a single causal chain always ran from a particular sort of predator through the sensory organs and nervous systems of our ancestors in a particular way to the neural state that is the activation of that capacity, and then on to a particular sort of avoidance of the predators, and finally on to the relative increase of the affiliated genes and hence the prevalence of the trait among later humans. There were two long causal chains, one leading toward and the other away from the mental representation in question, which are plausibly relevant to its function according to ET. But exactly where on the inbound chain is the *proper* cause of the state that is its content? And where on the outbound chain (since traits are selected for their effects) is the effect centrally relevant to the natural selection in question?

Focus on the first question. Is the sensory content of that representational state supposed to be the predator or the allied irritations of our sense organs? Here is one source of possible indeterminacies of function. Furthermore, each point in the chain seems subject to a variety of possible descriptions. Which are the relevant ones? Even if evolutionary proper causes and selection-relevant effects in history can be suitably isolated, what are the proper descriptions of the cause and effect pairs? If all the predators were tigers and bears, but also the only big, fast, ferocious things in our ancestral environments, which description properly characterizes the predators in the way relevant to sensory content? Here is a second source

---

[11] Dretske (1986); Fodor (1984, 1990a).   [12] Or their traits, or their genes.

of possible indeterminacies. So there are various objections in principle to the determinacy of sensory content if ET is true.

These abstract objections are abstractly debatable, but they are vindicated by the actual course of the ET literature. A principal irony that bedevils ET accounts of sensory content is that various ET theories have focused on various parts of the relevant inbound chains as the proper causes and hence the contents of the states in question, or at the very best on the same parts under very different descriptions. Frogs snap their tongues out to ingest any small, dark, moving things that range by their eyes, because there were nutritious flies in their ancestral environments. So what's the content of the frog's sensory state when it is led to snap? Neander says it is small, dark, moving thing.[13] Millikan says it is frog food.[14] Agar says it is fast-moving, non-dangerous, dark food.[15] McGinn and Sterelny say it is fly.[16] Price says it is (catchable) fly.[17] ET accounts of sensory content, even while agreeing on the historical facts, differ regarding the functions of the relevant sensory states and hence their contents. So there is no reason to believe that a concern to avoid indeterminacy of function is going to be very helpful in motivating an ET account of sensory content in particular. It might seem that each alternative ET account has removed indeterminacy of content in a different principled way. But my point is that there are no grounds to choose amongst these various principles by appeal to evolutionary history or ET.

Perhaps it seems that we should just adopt the account that yields the right results. But there are other ironies here. It is interesting that in the case of the frog, which has received most attention, there are no strongly held and introspectively-based intuitions to help resolve the issue, even if we grant, as for instance Millikan would not, that introspection is relevant. The various accounts at issue seem curiously insulated from relative disconfirmation. We should, it seems to me, focus on cases like the human case where we at least have some strong intuitions about the content of sensory states against which our theoretical claims can rub. And in any case, my focus in this book is on human thoughts, and among sensory contents merely on the kinds that we can introspect from our armchairs. What we need here is a match between introspectible human

---

[13] Neander (1995). [14] Millikan (1991*b*: 163). [15] Agar (1993).
[16] McGinn (1989); Sterelny (1990). [17] C. Price (1998).

sensory content and the kind that some version of ET can deliver in a properly principled way.

Perhaps ET can provide that. But it certainly does not suffice to motivate ET to blandly say that it will remove some indeterminacies. We need to know which and how. And until we see that ET can deliver the right details, the alleged theoretical motivation for etiological accounts of function under consideration, that it removes at least some indeterminacies, does not provide suitable reason to believe ET.

Despite my complaint, I do not believe that we should take the disagreements among the various ET accounts of sensory content as decisive against ET. We know that there are different kinds of propriety, for instance ethical propriety and good manners. Probably there are different kinds of *telos* or function. So we should expect that there are a variety of different sorts of proper causes, given different detailed kinds of even specifically etiological functions. We shouldn't expect a univocal notion of etiological function to pick out the sole candidate content for sensory states, for it is unlikely that there is a single and univocal notion of even etiological functions.

The real problem for ET accounts comes, rather, from the opposite direction. If we are careful, we can see that the more or less specific ways in which etiological accounts as a body refine the rough and intuitive notion of a function for a representational state pull rather too determinately in the wrong direction. Etiological propriety is not semantic propriety.

But before we can properly understand the grounds for this complaint, we need to consider the other crucial motivation for etiological accounts of function, which is supplied by concrete, intuitive cases. For all we have seen so far, this is a motivation that might provide some genuine grounds for ET. And maybe it will even help flesh out the first alleged motivation in some specific way that will provide genuine support for ET. Perhaps I should note for bookkeeping purposes that these are cases that support a theoretical claim about functions that is a theory-enmeshed motivation for externalism, that unlike Twin Earth they are not direct case-based arguments for externalism. But the most important point is that these cases have an unequivocal force, unlike the more theoretical motivation we just discussed.

Here is Millikan:

[I]t is of the essence of purposes and functions that they are not always fulfilled. The fact that we appeal to purposes and intentions when applying the term 'function' results directly in ascriptions of functions to things that are not in fact capable of performing those functions; they neither function as nor have dispositions to function as anything in particular. For example, the functions of a certain defective item may be to open cans; that is why it is called a can opener. Yet it may not function as a can opener; it may be that it won't open a can no matter how you force it. Similarly, a diseased heart may not be capable of pumping, of functioning *as* a pump, although it is clearly its function, its biological purpose, *to* pump...[18]

What a thing does or can do now cannot constitute its function, rather its history must be relevant, because things that cannot perform their function may still retain it. That is the key motivating intuition behind etiological conceptions of function, and it also suggests the specific kind of determinacy that etiological accounts of function can help provide.

To push the point home, here is Neander:

Suppose there are no lions. Then suppose that half a dozen lions pop into existence, we know not how. Having stared at them in superficial amazement for some time, we eventually begin to wonder about their wing-like protuberances on each flank. We ask ourselves whether these limbs have the proper function of flight. Do they? When we discover that the lions cannot actually fly because their 'wings' are not strong enough, we are tempted to suppose that this settles the matter, until we remember that organismic structures are often incapable of performing their proper function because they are deformed, diseased, atrophied from lack of use, or because the creature is displaced from its natural habitat (the lions could perhaps fly in a lower gravitational field). On the other hand, often enough there are complex structures that have no function, for instance, the vestigial wings of emus and the human appendix. The puzzle is where among these various categories are we to place the lions' 'wings'. I contend that we could not reliably place them in any category until we knew or could infer the lions' history.[19]

Wright's original etiological account isn't rooted primarily in such cases, and indeed requires that something that has a function in the full sense can perform it. But even Wright criticizes non-etiological accounts on similar grounds: '[T]he function of the federal automotive safety regulations is to make driving and riding in a car safer. And this is so even if they actually have just the opposite effect, through some psychodynamic or automotive quirk.'[20] And he ends up proposing that there are special cases of this sort that his analysis should be extended to cover

---

[18] Millikan (1993c: 21).   [19] Neander (1991a: 179–80).   [20] L. Wright (1973: 153).

by dropping his contrary clause requiring the capacity to perform the function.[21]

Even internalists should admit, I think, that these cases have some intuitive force. And so there is at least one motivation for etiological accounts of function that might in turn provide some genuine motivation for ET.

We have traced the principal motivations for both teleological accounts of content and etiological accounts of function. And so we come back to ET, which puts them together. The content of an inner representational state is, more or less, whatever it is its function or purpose to be caused by, where that function or purpose is crucially constituted by the evolutionary history of the creature with that state, or by something that in some way mimics such a history of natural selection, for instance, it is alleged, the learning history of the individual. ET implies that two creatures that are physically identical in the moment and yet that have different histories hence may have thoughts and percepts with different contents.

This route to ET, it may seem so far, involves various presumptions and a little vagueness, but no serious confusion. Still there is a confusion, an equivocation on 'function'. Functions of things characterize what we might call their *proper* states; they specify how those things in some sense *ought* to be. But there are different sorts of propriety. The principal motivation for ET that we have just reviewed overlooks the fact that the proper causes of psychological states in the semantically relevant sense are not etiologically proper causes. This can be seen with particular clarity in the case of sensory contents. As we will shortly see, the particular kind of propriety that etiological accounts of function can deliver is not the kind that sensory misperception requires.

While I do not deny that the cases cited by Millikan and Neander and indeed by Wright have a certain intuitive force supporting the claim that at least one notion of function is etiological, my contention is that these key motivating cases put ET in a bad light when applied to sensory content. Indeed, they suggest problems even for alternative non-etiological accounts of function that attempt to preserve our intuitions about such cases, for instance those accounts that specify functions by reference to properties of average members of species.[22]

[21] L. Wright (1973: 167–8).   [22] Bourse (1976, 1977).

The task of the rest of this section is to explain why this is so in an initial and general way, before we turn to an examination of the detailed manifestations of this problem in each of the three detailed forms of ET accounts of sensory content. I don't expect you to be convinced until you see the details. But in the following three sections I will trace them out for all three forms.

The propriety plausibly rooted in history is before us. Now we need to dig deeper, and ask whether this etiological propriety is in fact the kind of propriety centrally relevant to sensory content. We cannot presume simply because a deformity of one kind is etiologically constituted that another kind will be as well. Some sorts of defects or deformities may be constituted as such by present conditions, even if other sorts are historically constituted.

So we must determine which exact sort of deformity or defect is relevant to the constitution of sensory content. Sensory error, presumably. But there are various things that might be called sensory error. Consider seeing a horse on a dark and dreary night, and taking it to be a cow. It is not unusual to claim that there is no sensory error in the strict sense in such a case, that the sensory looks and feels are as they are, and are known as they are, and are not in themselves erroneous, but that rather there is an erroneous perceptual judgment or belief. Such a case would then provide us with no genuine sensory error, no error directly relevant to the nature of sensory content itself. So we must presume a different sort of account of sensory content to develop any direct role for ET of the sort we are now considering, in which genuine sensory error is possible. It must be that the content of a sensory state itself is given by its proper environmental cause, say a certain sort of edge in the environment, so that when it is caused by other things, say on dark and stormy nights, the sensory state itself is false or otherwise in error.

Our central question is whether the kinds of deformities present in the crucial motivating examples for etiological conceptions of functions are relevantly similar to the kinds of deformities present in sensory contents that are erroneous in this way. On the surface, there are differences. The deformities present in Millikan's defective can opener and deformed heart reflect functions that cannot, because of the internal condition of the entities in question, be performed by those entities, except perhaps in wildly counterfactual environments involving low gravity and atmospheric pressure or absurdly brittle cans. Likewise for Neander's lion wings incapable of flight.[23] But the most common and intuitive cases of sensory error are quite different. They involve internal representations in intact organisms that are quite capable of fulfilling their proper tasks in many real circumstances, but that have other than their ordinary environmental causes because, say, it is dark out at the moment. The mental representations or systems in question are not deformed in the manner of a defective can opener or deformed heart. They retain their intuitive capacity to perform their allotted task.

Of course, this may only be a surface distinction. It needs more detailed consideration. But if we begin with the kind of deformity present in Neander's and Millikan's motivating cases, and try to develop close sensory analogs, then we are forced to choose between possibilities in which there is no deformity of the sorts that motivate etiological functions, and possibilities in which there is such a deformity, but a deformity that would suggest on the grounds favored by ET a very implausible kind of content.

The key motivating intuition behind etiological accounts of function is that an anatomically radically-malformed heart that cannot now pump yet can intuitively retain pumping as its function because of its evolutionary history.[24] But the representational elements of sensory capacities that seem most analogous to these intuitive cases are representational elements of anatomically deformed sensory systems that cannot now indicate the world in the normal way. And these do not at all intuitively retain their sensory content, despite the fact that they do intuitively retain their evolutionary functions[25] in the same way as malformed hearts.

This initial case is abstract and deniable. It may seem that by possessing evolutionary functions fixed by environments in which they were accurate, sensory representations have a capacity to misrepresent. But we will conclude from a detailed examination of alternative theories that span the range of possible architectures for ET accounts of sensory content that all involve the confusion of two kinds of propriety, one sort of propriety to which etiology is relevant and another sort to which it is not. An attempt to develop relevant sensory analogs of the cases that firmly motivate etiological conceptions of function will show that sensory content is crucially dependent on merely current and indeed individual conditions and not on history, because current and individual deformities of sensory

---

[23] We will later consider another reading of Neander's case.
[24] Or perhaps the intentions of some unsuccessful designer.   [25] Or creationist analogs.

systems affect sensory content in a way that ET accounts imply they would not.

There are a variety of ET accounts of what might be considered perceptual or sensory content, even if we assume, with current orthodoxy, that sensation involves inner representations, analogous to sentences or words in a language of thought. Such accounts may focus on the contents of sensory states, or perceptual beliefs, or concepts deployed in perceptual beliefs. But for the moment we are centrally concerned with sensory content in particular, leaving even perceptual belief aside. However, a second axis of differences is more important for us in this context.

ET accounts of sensory content may deploy various sorts of general architecture. For instance, they may directly ascribe to syntactically-characterized mental representations—representations characterized by their more or less intrinsic properties—etiologically proper causes that are their contents. Or they may ascribe sensory content by appeal to consuming and producing mechanisms for such representations in the cognizer, and to the etiologically determined functions of those mechanisms. Or they may focus on etiologically normal environmental conditions as those in which causes of representations are proper causes and hence contents. We will discuss these three possibilities in three sections.

5.4

ET accounts that ascribe sensory contents *directly*, as etiologically proper causes of syntactically-characterized mental representations, face straightforward counterexamples. It is ironic that examples like these bubble close to the surface in one *advocate* of such an account. There are two kinds of direct accounts, those that deploy evolutionary history and those that deploy more recent history. We will begin with the first alternative.

Fred Dretske's *Naturalizing the Mind* includes his most extensive treatment of sensory content.[26] According to Dretske, sensory experiences have proper causes and hence contents constituted as such by Darwinian histories of natural selection of sensory systems. We as a species have genetically-determined sensory systems with representational states of certain intrinsic

[26] See also Dretske (2000).

sorts that have evolutionary functions to be caused by certain things. And syntactically-characterized mental representations have sensory contents identical to their evolutionarily-determined proper causes.

But the problem with this is that the evolutionarily proper cause that some mental representation evolved to have seems irrelevant to intuitive sensory content when its causes and effects are wildly askew because of organic deformity.

We can see this by a development of Dretske's own examples. To interpret the central text, note that in Dretske's terminology sensory content is the informational content of 'representational-s' states. By way of contrast, 'representational-a' states are thoughts, for instance perceptual beliefs, which reflect our way of taking our sensory experiences and not just the contents of the sensory experiences. He apparently holds that some thoughts are 'recalibrated' experiences.

Here is the key passage:

Just as we can recalibrate a speedometer when we change the size of our tires... so also can sensory systems recalibrate when there is a change in the information an experience delivers. After wearing spectacles that make everything 'look' 30 degrees to the left, touch 'educates' vision and objects begin to 'look' to be where they are grasped. This, at least, is one way of describing the experiential change that accompanies adaptation. As we age, there is a gradual yellowing of the macula (spot on the retina) that changes the signals sent from the retina to the brain about the wavelength of light.... Despite this constant change in the information representational-s states carry, there is no corresponding representational-a change: we still see blue and yellow, red and green, *as* blue and yellow, red and green.[27]

Note closely the pressures on Dretske in this paragraph. There should be no adjustment in the sensory content of a given mental representation by training or aging on Dretske's account, since those things don't affect evolutionary history. So the case of the yellowing macula is an unacknowledged counterexample to his account, and to any similar account.[28] There is an internal representation with a sensory content that is supposed to be fixed throughout our lives because the representation has a fixed evolutionary history throughout our lives, and yet it becomes detached from the intuitive

---

[27] Dretske (1995: 20–1).
[28] Though this is Dretske's case, it may be mythical. See Pokorny, Smith, Verriest, and Pinckers (1979: 60). But see also Kaiser and Boynton (1996: 419).

causes and effects of such a sensory content through life. There is constant change as we age in the sensory contents of our states when we look at fixed objects, according to Dretske's theory, because of the yellowing macula. The particular mental syntax that is caused by a fixed environmental stimuli shifts, and yet each piece of syntax retains its evolutionary *telos*. And nevertheless we are oblivious to any change, because our behavior and introspectible experience regarding the environmental object is relevantly unchanging.

The alleged sensory content delivered by Dretske's ET in such a case has little to do with ordinary intuitive sensory content. Intuitive sensory content is stable over aging in Dretske's case and more or less by his own admission. But the kind his ET account can deliver is not.

There are other cases that may seem initially more favorable for Dretske. Put on a pair of sunglasses.[29] There is an introspectible shift in qualia. But you quickly adapt so as to match stimuli and response in the normal way, and lose your sense of any experiential oddity. Now take them off. You notice the reversion in qualia. Dretske may claim that the yellowing macula induces slow changes in sensory content like those that occur as we adapt to sunglasses, and that such gradual changes in sensory content are not introspectible and make no difference to the way in which we match stimulus and response.

But the motivation for this very evanescent sort of sensory content, irrelevant to introspection or behavior, is correspondingly evanescent. And there are other eyeglasses to consider. Notice the quote marks around 'look' in Dretske's discussion of distorting spectacles. In fact, over time individuals come to adapt at least somewhat to spectacles that initially change their intuitive phenomenal experience of things. I have such an adaptation when I buy new glasses, out at the edges of my visual field, as things that at first seem curved come to seem straight again. The natural thing to say about this is that since evolutionary history is stable over these adapting changes in sensory content, then that history does not determine content, at least not solely or significantly.[30] Indeed, the natural thing to say is that internal

---

[29] Gibbons (2005).
[30] Seager (1997: 95–6) discusses the analogous perceptual training of winetasters. And Seager (1997: 97–101) treats a case that is analogous to anatomic deformities. Phenylthiourea is tasteless to some of us, but bitter to others of us. He argues that this is unlikely to involve a difference in our evolutionary histories.

adjustments occur, which constitute a difference in experience. And yet Dretske wants to treat such cases in accord with his ET account, so he insists that there is a kind of content, properly sensory content, that is always stable throughout this adaptation, and only another kind, the content we see the state as possessing, that changes during such an adaptation.

And this alleged stable kind of sensory content would need to be much more wildly out of accord with intuitive sensory content in cases of yet more radical adaptations introduced by strange glasses that Dretske doesn't mention, although they are the most famous such spectacles. There are inverting glasses, which make everything at first seem upside down.[31] Yet over time the wearer adapts, and everything comes to seem right side up again. Dretske's view implies that the proper sensory contents of the wearer remain relevantly stable throughout the period they wear the glasses, so that the world always in fact is upside down in their sensory experience though they cease to realize it after a while, and behave and introspect just as they would if it were right-side up. But that is quite implausible. If they took the glasses off, everything would look different, indeed upside down, and only further adaptation would return things to normal.[32]

The kind of case that might plausibly motivate a role for evolutionary history in fixing sensory content for particular syntax and yet not generate the kinds of conflict with ordinary conceptions of sensory content on which I have traded here, is a case where current abilities, on one hand, don't fully underwrite its determinacy but, on the other, don't conflict with it.

---

[31] The literature on inversions is large and controversial. See e.g. Howard (1982: 512–16).

[32] There are contrary currents in Dretske. Dretske (1995: 68) requires that differences in sensory content be reflected in current discriminatory abilities. And Dretske (1988) treats the case of inversion in a surprising way. While he says *in the text* on page 67 that if through 'some reproductive accident, an individual... (call him Inverto) inherits his F-detector in defective (let us say inverted) condition [then p]oor Inverto has an RS [or representational system] that always misrepresents his surroundings: it represents things as being F when they are not...', *in accompanying footnote 9* he says: 'It should be noted that one doesn't disable an indicator *merely* by reversing the code—letting *b* (formerly indicating *B*) indicate *A* and *a* (formerly indicating *A*) indicate *B*. As long as this reversal is systematic, the change is merely a change in the way information is being coded, not a change in the information being coded. But though *A* and *B* are still being indicated (by *b* and *a* respectively), they are, after the inversion, no longer being accurately *represented* unless there is a corresponding change (inversion) in the way the representational elements (*a* and *b*) function in the rest of the system.' The first two sentences suggest that coding can be determined by current conditions. The stress in the third sentence on the way in which the representational elements function in the rest of the system suggests merely the additional relevance of the current effects of those elements. And so in the footnote Inverto misrepresents things when the effects of his representations don't fit their causes, and etiology is irrelevant. Perhaps the third sentence instead suggests that the functions of consuming and producing systems and not of particular types of mental syntax matter, despite Dretske's main claims. We will return to that architecture.

So perhaps we should look to something like color qualia inversions that are not behaviorally detectable for a genuine role for history. Perhaps with different selection histories momentary physical twins would have different visual contents, but related as qualia inversions, with the color experience of one inverted along some axis of the color wheel.

But there are other sorts of examples to consider first. In particular, consider the color blind.

Color blindness is most commonly sex-linked and inherited, due to a recessive gene located on the X chromosome. It is a defect. It isn't plausible that there was selection pressure for color blindness. The color blind and the normally sighted share any relevant evolutionary history.

This means that color blindness is in one etiological sense an abnormality. But the color blind *differ* in sensory content from the normally sighted. And while those differences perhaps imply that they differ in what would be the proper causes of their sensory states, and if we wish we can call that a difference in function, that difference is due to their current internal differences from the normal. Their history shared with the normal is irrelevant.

The unusual features of the content of the visual-experience of someone who is color blind are not plausibly fixed by their evolutionary history. And even if they sometimes undergo a particular brain activation pattern that evolved to indicate a particular color, which yet because of their unusual wiring never occurs when they look at something with that color, and never presents the intuitively relevant aspects of that color to them in a way reflected in their color-matching behavior, it is quite implausible to say that their sensory content is as in the ordinary human case just because of their shared evolutionary history. But that is exactly what the kind of ET account that we are now discussing implies.

There are two kinds of possible visual qualia in play here. Dretske's version of ET suggests that the sensory contents of the color blind may involve all normal sensory differences but have unusual cognitive effects, so that a color blind person misses some differences in their sensory contents. Their qualia are normal, but they can't introspect or act on some of the differences. But there seems little motivation to postulate a form of sensory content that is so divorced from action and introspection. And there is a second possibility. Much more plausibly, the color blind have abnormal qualia, of which Dretske's ET can give no account.

The case of the color blind undercuts even the use of evolutionary histories to fix the differences between qualia that are not intuitively reflected in current behavior. Such an evolutionary history could not help in a qualia inversion case for twins who were color blind in some limited way, because that history doesn't fit their current capacities in the right way. And of course we saw earlier that the most firmly motivated etiological functions don't merely refine but can cut against current capacities.

That concludes the main argument of this section. But we should consider complications.

First, Dretske's account of function seems at least sometimes a mixed and not purely etiological account, which requires that an entity still possess a capacity for which its ancestors were selected for that to be its function, so that a suitably deformed heart does not possess the function to pump blood. But this wouldn't help ET. It blocks the attribution, to those whose selection history and current capacities are askew, of any sensory content at all. Such are the color blind. It also undercuts the principal rationale for etiological determinants of function.

Second, while Dretske holds that recent individual histories of learning are by definition constitutive not of sensory but rather of belief content, there are alternative forms of ET that focus on such recent history.[33] And there are possible mixed views, which maintain that evolutionary history fixes a range of possible contents that is fine-tuned by more recent history. So we should consider analogs of Millikan's cases in which individual learning history assigns a representational function to a syntactically-characterized mental representation that it cannot now perform, say because of intervening injury or aging. In the training period of youth a certain mental representation was caused by straight lines, but not now.

But remember our sensory adaptation to eyeglasses. That straight lines caused a certain piece of mental syntax in our clear-sighted youth is irrelevant to its sensory content after we have first put on distorting glasses and then adapted to them. And our relatively fast adaptation to inverting or correcting eyeglasses suggests that any relevant training period is identical

[33] Kitcher (1993a); Godfrey-Smith (1993, 1994).

to the period of behavioral adjustment. This in turn implies that there is no motivation to think that any recent etiology, and not just the new behavioral tendencies, helps constitute sensory content. While some of the color blind have unusual learning histories, they also differ in their current capacities. And remember that central achromatopsia can result from a hit on the head after a normal learning history.

Perhaps, someone might insist, learning history delivers a refinement of intuitive sensory content that is consistent with current behavioral capacities, as in the Twin Earth case. But we have already disposed of Twin Earth. And remember that a role for individual history in constituting content is not automatically a role for etiological teleology in particular. But most important, recall that the firmest motivation for etiological conceptions of function involves functions that cannot now be performed, in the deep and stable way that deformed hearts and wings incapable of flight on Earth cannot perform their function in any current normal environments, and not merely in the adventitious way that you cannot see water because you happen to have weak tea in your pond today. Characteristic ET functions do not play minor roles in refining current capacities. Rather, they can cut against them, in the sense that they can be functions that there is no current capacity to perform. And to the degree that differences in learning history do not merely refine but can cut against current capacities, they seem irrelevant to sensory content, just like the evolutionary history of the color blind.

Still, perhaps it seems there is a middle ground. Etiological teleology rooted in your recent history might cut against your capacities here and now, but might not cut against your capacities tomorrow or over there. Not all etiologically improper causes are as similar as water and weak tea. Causes in the learning period might cut against your behavior and current capacities here in the dark night, and yet not cut against them tomorrow in broad daylight.

But there is no middle ground. Very firmly motivated etiological teleology involves functions that in a deeper sense cannot be performed. And there is a second point. The lack of fit of cause and behavior proposed here is evident even now in the dark and dreary night, as I stumble about and try to saddle a cow. This second point requires elaboration, but it also reflects the characteristic problem of the second possible ET architecture.

5.5

The second form of ET account fixes sensory contents by the functions of mechanisms in the cognizer that produce or consume mental representations. It assigns particular functions to mechanisms with which mental representations are in relation. And those functions help constitute the contents of the representations *indirectly*.

The problem for this type of account is that the invocation of production and consumption is a double-edged sword for ET. Inverting glasses and the color blind suggest that the actual state of contemporary mechanisms of production and consumption of a mental representation can do all the necessary work of fixing its sensory content, in the moment and irrespective of history.

But perhaps that is only a surface case. So let's try to develop possible analogs, involving production and consumption mechanisms, of the concrete motivating cases for etiological functions. Those cases involved organic deformities. There are two sorts of organic deformities that seem to be relevant possible analogs, but neither seems to put things in the right light for ET.

Remember my myopia. When I look, from at least a few feet away and with my glasses off, at the taillight on a tractor, it appears as a considerably larger, round, lacy ball. Now consider a representation, a neural firing pattern in my visual system, that occurs when that lacy pattern appears in my experience. Assume that my deformity is all anterior to that pattern, that my production mechanisms are deformed so that the neural pattern in question is indirectly evolutionary determined to properly register things of the shape of lacy balls. Notice that, in me and when my glasses are off, it is not caused by such things, but when my glasses are on it is. So its actual current causes depend on whether my glasses are on or off, regardless of my evolutionary history or even my learning history. Still, the fan of ET may say, perhaps the *function* of the production mechanisms is relevant to fixing the laciness of the content. But notice that the introspectible and sometimes false aspects of its causes that such a sensory state presents to me, the apparent laciness and shape of those causes, seem fixed in the moment by the consuming mechanisms.[34] Whether my glasses are on or

---

[34] Except for behaviorally irrelevant features like the aspects of color qualia that may be plausibly inverted in twin cases. It is not an accident that my example here is spatial. In Chapter 7, I claim

off, whether the production mechanism in question is natural but deformed or unnaturally corrected, I introspect and tend to behave on the basis of the content of that pattern in the same way. The introspectible experience is the same.

Still, that may seem an opportunity for a second sort of possible deformity, of consumption mechanisms, to yield a role for etiology. But it is the actual and not the etiologically proper state of the consumption mechanisms that determines intuitive sensory content in this case. The misrepresenting laciness when I have my glasses off affects what can be revealed even in my so-called narrow behavior, when I'm asked to draw what I see in the air with my finger. It is not specially revealed by anything that we need to take a long view into my evolutionary history or even into my relatively recent history of education to descry.

We need no recourse to evolutionary or learning history to explain that my sensory representation of things is mistaken when I have my glasses off. All that defect intuitively happens right here, as I stumble into things and draw them improperly. When I have my glasses off, the actual causes and the actual effects of my visual representations don't fit together properly. The causes and effects of my sensory representations, the actual form of the production and consumption mechanisms and perhaps their actual environmental causal antecedents, *may* be relevant to their content, but the etiological functions of those mechanisms are apparently not. This is the point that concluded the last section. Whether my myopia makes me stumble or the dark night leads me to saddle a cow, still the relevant lack of fit is evident here and now.

Once again, it is important to bear firmly in mind that forceful examples motivating etiological conceptions of function involve the inability of an entity to perform its function. But production and consumption capacities that an organism doesn't now have, but in some sense is supposed to have, are intuitively irrelevant to current sensory content.

To put it briskly, sensory deformities either affect the content of sensation in a way that can be revealed in current behavior, or they don't. If they don't, then they are intuitively irrelevant to sensory content. If they do, then no etiologically proper state of functioning is relevant to the content

that production mechanisms are relevant in the color case, but it is their actual state and not their evolutionarily ideal state that matters. We will shortly turn to another relevant example involving color qualia.

in question. This is perhaps most evident when etiologically proper and current capacities are in conflict, and so the fan of ET may once again retreat to the suggestion that etiology properly has a mere refining role. But we must remember that this isn't the sort of case that forcefully motivates etiological conceptions of function.

What *would* properly motivate the second type of ET account of sensory content would be a sensory representation that intuitively retained its *indirectly* evolution-determined content despite current deformities that skewed its actual causes and effects. But if there is some sort of anatomical malformation not only of my eyes but of what is posterior to a representation so that it has abnormal effects on other regions of my brain or motor systems, if for instance I have neural systems that evolved to produce and consume a certain specific mental representation in the presence of blue elephants that yet because of my deformity is produced and consumed in me when I look at a green silo with my glasses on and react just right, still it is the current causes and effects of that state that seem relevant to its content. The content that would be fixed indirectly by the evolutionary function of the production and consumption mechanisms is irrelevant to any intuitive sort of sensation.

Consider again the crucial case of the color blind. If a red-green color blind person can be said to retain systems of production or consumption that yet are deformed from their normal state, systems that evolved to allow certain discriminations by the differential production or consumption of distinct sorts of representations, representations that yet in fact, we will presume, introduce no differences that the person in question can notice, it is very implausible to claim that nevertheless these differences are present unnoticed in that person's experience. And if the color blind cannot be said to share such systems with the normal, then their systems of production and consumption do not plausibly possess evolutionary functions, even though they do help constitute quite specific sorts of sensory experience. If you are inclined to think, on the other hand, that recent history matters in such cases, remember what I said earlier about sensory adaptation to inverting glasses.

I have focused on relatively specific etiological functions of consumption or production mechanisms, fixing indirectly a particular code for produced or consumed representations. But more general functions may seem relevant. One way evolutionary or learning histories might help fix sensory contents would be to fix some general purpose for a sensory system, say to rule out the possibility that sensory representations as a body represent internal sensory receptor states rather than environmental conditions with which they co-vary.

But here again what is in the moment, the mental representation and consumption and production mechanisms as they are, seem able to do all the necessary work, if indeed it can be done at all in relevant moments of selection or learning history or by that history plus contemporary conditions. There is an intuitive fit between the actual effects and causal role of a sensory representation on one hand and what it is intuitively about on the other. Also, it is again important that only functions retained when they cannot now be performed securely motivate a role for etiology. And if the production and consumption mechanisms retain a general function that they cannot now perform, it is irrelevant to intuitive sensory content.

5.6

The third type of ET account of sensory content deploys external normal perceptual conditions. Sensory contents are supposed to be the causes of mental representations under etiologically proper conditions, say the conditions in evolutionary history that were in place when the appropriate representational capacity was selected for.[35] For example, it might be that visual representations have proper causes when the light is proper, and that the light is proper when it is as it was when selection pressure for such representations occurred.

But remember again that forceful motivating cases for etiological conceptions of function involve organic deformities. And when one is not in normal perceptual conditions, still one's consumption mechanisms are not defective, and indeed one has properly-formed internal production mechanisms. It is just that one happens to be in the wrong external conditions for viewing things, so that one has an image as of a horse on the basis of a cow. So the class of views under consideration doesn't deploy capacities that we cannot in some organic sense perform. And so they are distant from the forceful motivating examples for etiological conceptions of function.

---

[35] Even if perhaps those conditions were statistically abnormal in the past.

These claims may seem resistible. Neander's lions have earthbound wings, but they would work in an (in some sense) 'normal' environment that they will never occupy, in which the gravitational field was weaker.

But it is important to see that those are different sorts of normal conditions than the third ET account needs. As there are various kinds of propriety, so too there are various kinds of normalcy. In Neander's case, all the lions are always now outside of normal conditions. In Millikan's case, the heart in question is always now deformed. This is what gives these examples their intuitive motivating bite, and forces us to history as a source for intuitive functions. But the normal conditions relevant to perception are, indeed often, locally available. Sometimes in fact the light is good.

There *is* a kind of fixed deformity or mismatch with the environment in the case of the myopic and the color blind. But we have seen that such cases aren't supportive of ET, and anyway they don't provide a useful interpretation of the architecture now under consideration.

Still, resistance may continue. Perhaps normal perceptual conditions are defined as such by being the conditions in evolutionary history under which selection pressure for sensory capacities was felt. Our eyes didn't evolve because of what happened when the light was so bad that they were useless, and that negative fact may seem intuitively relevant to their content now. We might tell an analogous story involving learning.

But we already know why this is wrong. We don't need evolutionary or learning history to reveal that bad light leads vision astray, or what counts as bad light. Bad light is what makes our behavioral responses askew from their environmental causes. There is no firmly motivated role for ET available from this sort of case. As our discussion of myopia revealed, any sensory error seems fixed by the misfit between the actual causes and actual effects of the mental representations in question.

A well-motivated ET account with the architecture under discussion will assign contents by reference to normal perceptual conditions that are no longer available anywhere. But if this yields any specific contents at all, they will not be intuitive. And the color blind and eyeglass-adapted suggest that historically normal conditions are not always available to fix the sensory contents of some individuals.

There is also another problem with this sort of ET account. Such accounts have debilitating problems with Mohan Matthen's normal misperceptions, misperceptions that occur in standard conditions because of plausible design limitations.[36] As he says, 'it is possible to create a surface on which the color changes gradually, in just the way that illumination normally changes. In uniform illumination, such a surface would be perceived as uniformly colored and variably illuminated.'[37] Uniform illumination certainly counts as a normal condition of illumination. But it can support misperceptions.

Of course, such a case is abnormal in one sense suggested by etiological teleology, since it is unlikely that such cases of normal misperception had a significant role in our evolutionary history. So it might seem more sympathetic to the architecture under consideration to claim that etiological teleology will deliver normal conditions of perception that are richer than any mere restriction to normal conditions of illumination or attention such as I have supposed, to claim that normal conditions of perception will also restrict us to perceptual objects that were present in our evolutionary history. But of course any account of the content of sensory states that doesn't allow us to see things like barns, tractors, and new industrial colors has other unacceptable implications.

Furthermore, notice that normal misperceptions, along with all intuitive misperceptions, are identified as that by current failure of fit between environmental causes and behavioral responses, mediated by the current state of production and consumption mechanisms and current environmental conditions. Etiology is again irrelevant.

5.7

Our initial general worry about ET accounts of sensory content has been vindicated for all three forms. When etiological functions do real work, they ascribe the wrong contents. And ET accounts are motivated only by a confusion of two different sorts of propriety, by a bad pun on 'proper'.

We haven't yet considered ET accounts of thought content. But we have focused on what is widely thought to be the *best* case for ET. It is implausible to think most beliefs or other thoughts innate, and hence to suppose that they result from Darwinian selection in any very direct way. And traits are plausibly selected for their effects, while beliefs and other thoughts don't seem characteristically to have stable and particular effects.

---

[36] Matthen (1988: 12–13).   [37] Matthen (1988: 12).

Nevertheless, we need to consider these other ways of deploying ET. And we also need to consider theoretical roles for history that fall outside of ET. I will begin with the second task, which will bring us back in a properly motivated way to the first. And I will focus on the central case of belief.

Part I already dismissed the most standard and intuitive reason to think that history matters to belief content. Putnam's twins differ in their history in a way that does intuitively appear to introduce a difference in their thoughts. We also gave passing consideration there to analogous cases involving perceptual beliefs. But there is another *theoretical* role for history, which yet falls outside of ET.

Some suggest that the content of a mental representation that is the internal basis of a belief is its cause during a learning period, so that when such a belief is otherwise caused outside of that period, it is false. Dretske's early proposal that etiologically proper causes are causes during a learning period has been subsumed during his own development into his variant of ET, whose application to beliefs we will consider shortly. And we have already discussed learning in other ways. But we should consider alternative forms of this general conception that fall outside of ET.

Jesse Prinz has proposed that proper causes are that subset of the causes that nomologically co-vary with a mental representation that were its *incipient* causes—'the causes on the basis of which a concept was formed'.[38] He says that if 'I form a concept as a result of a perceptual encounter with monarch butterflies, that concept refers to monarchs alone, even though it is tokened when I see viceroys.'[39]

Prinz notes one natural objection to a simple learning period account, that 'children overextend their concepts during learning. For example, tokens of young children's DUCK concepts are caused by real ducks, toy ducks, swans, and geese.'[40] But he suggests in reply that toy ducks, swans, and geese will not nomologically co-vary—will not co-vary as a matter of natural law—with the mental representations in question outside of the learning period, and so the toy ducks, swans, and geese aren't proper causes. He deploys a relatively elite sort of nomologically-relevant properties to skirt natural objections to accounts with the etiological architecture he prefers.

---

[38] Prinz (2002: 249–51).   [39] Prinz (2002: 250).   [40] Prinz (2002: 249); Mervis (1987).

But there are other natural objections to learning period accounts, which interact with that otherwise helpful resource in a debilitating way. Consider cases in which we extend our concepts over time, or in which the causes during the learning period seem too limited to cover the intuitive range of a concept. Perhaps you developed a concept on the basis of interaction only with monarchs that intuitively extends also to viceroys. For instance the concept BUTTERFLY.

In fact, almost all cases of concept learning involve some generalization beyond the cases in fact encountered during learning. The proper generalization cannot be determined only by the nomological covariation in question, or the relevance of the learning period drops out. But the learning period alone may involve less than a full range of relevant cases.

Prinz suggests as a general matter that 'the intentional content of a concept is the class of things to which the object(s) that caused the original creation of the concept belong.'[41] The class determines the proper sort of generalization from learning history. But there are lots of classes. Still, perhaps Prinz means to rely on natural classes and kinds, so that the restriction to incipient causes can deliver a determinate reductive constraint on proper causes. This might also fit nicely with his emphasis on nomological covariation.

But there is a sense in which both viceroys and butterflies are natural kinds. Still, perhaps there is a particularly robust and elite sort of natural kind that fixes the relevant proper generalizations from learning history.

But then the problem is that there are cases like the concept of jade. Jade is not a robust and elite physical natural kind, but rather is standardly thought to encompass both jadeite and nephrite. The deployment of very robust natural kinds to fix the proper generalization of learning period instances cannot deliver intuitive contents in our physical world. Even Prinz' own discussion of the jade case seems to assume that the pre-scientific conception of jade did not pick out a specific natural kind.[42]

To couple learning history and natural kinds in the way that Prinz suggests will not deliver intuitive contents. Since Prinz lacks a properly

---

[41] Prinz (2002: 250).

[42] Prinz (2002: 254–5). This is not explicit, but otherwise Prinz has nothing to say about the pre-scientific notion, except that it is unusual. Perhaps he thinks that the pre-scientific notion involved deference to experts who falsely thought jade was a single natural kind. But that is implausible, and leaves the question of how those experts on Prinz' own account could coherently think that.

motivated general story of exactly how the contingencies of learning history are relevant to content that can encompass the cases he wants to include but exclude my case of the butterfly concept, his learning period account of proper causes fails.

Perhaps it is Prinz' focus on incipient causes that is the problem. Perhaps we should lengthen the content-fixing learning period into a period beyond that in which the concept was formed, in something like the way Dretske originally proposed.

But Fodor asked a relevant question about this proposal: When is the period over? Does a bell ring? If there is to be some genuine theoretical role for educational history in fixing someone's belief content, then there must be some appropriately motivated way to pick out the particular historical phenomena, the particular features of their continuous history of education, that are relevant.

In effect, that is what Millikan, Dretske, and Papineau have tried to supply in various ways by their applications of ET to thought, by developing various analogs of positive selection pressure that might conceivably play a role in fixing an etiological function for particular beliefs. And so we return to other possible applications of ET, in particular to the case of belief.

5.8

In their distinctive applications of ET to belief, Millikan develops a cognitive analog of selection pressure, while Papineau and Dretske develop two different conative analogs. Their proposals are ingenious. But there is no reason to believe in their historical aspects.

Begin with Millikan.[43] One of her two models for the application of ET to belief is the case in which one picks up a sentence from a natural language, from which she claims it derives its function. But that model is implicitly covered by our discussion of the famous externalist language-mediated cases. RDC plausibly evades any external language functions. So consider her second model. She thinks that there are cases in which people

---

[43] The central text is Millikan (1984), supplemented by Millikan (1993c, 2000). Millikan (2004) is a recent restatement in alternative terminology, and on page 85 states a key clarification. Millikan (2005) is a recent treatment of Millikan's language-mediated model.

form brand new inner terms for brand new concepts, as when Leonardo conceived the parachute, and that etiological considerations play a role in fixing content in such cases.

To understand her discussion of such cases, it is necessary to understand some of the mechanism that she deploys. While syntactic typing of inner mental terms—whereby two mental terms 'cat' and 'cat' are of the same type—is not determinate in the moment according to Millikan, there is supposed to be some sort of capacity to introduce new tokens of inner terms, tokens that are apparently of at least sufficiently determinate type even in the moment for us to speak of a particular mechanism that is momentarily determinate that generates them. Developing a new concept involves developing a procedure for introducing a new term, perhaps on grounds that certain sensory conditions obtain. And all the mechanism that requires is also supposed to be determinate in the moment.

Humans are supposed capable of forming the negations of their beliefs, and of making inferences on the basis of beliefs. But the key semantical and etiological point is supposed to be this: Millikan suggests that we have what she sometimes calls a consistency tester.[44] This ensures that if a newly introduced concept[45] yields over time a variety of inconsistent representations, say beliefs that some one thing is and is not a parachute, it will be scrapped. This individual history of testing of a new concept is supposed by Millikan to provide it with what she calls a proper function, and hence provide the inner terms that it introduces with derived functions, which according to her story are crucial to belief contents.

The consistency tester is the crucial locus of ET for new concepts according to Millikan. Her use of the consistency tester has been criticized on the grounds that either it tests for formal syntactic consistency, which is a weak constraint that doesn't yield much of a significant test for concepts, or it involves testing for truth, in which case it introduces debilitating circularities into the account.[46] These complaints aren't strictly correct, but point to another and more telling charge. The reason they aren't strictly correct is that Millikan has a few helpful resources to deploy in response. Clearly the capacities directly tested by the consistency tester are supposed to include what she calls the 'programs' or concepts for introducing the

---

[44] Millikan (1984: 142–6 and 152).
[45] Perhaps I should say 'newly introduced momentarily determinate partial basis for a concept'.
[46] Rupert (1999).

tokens into mental representations and not merely the bare syntax itself. And Millikan deploys a robust metaphysics of real property similarities and real substances,[47] and optimistically holds that a concept that passes the consistency test must track reasonably well these particular robustly realistic similarities or objects to maintain its consistency. I don't believe this, but will grant it for purposes of argument. A very robust metaphysics of intuitive *perceptible* property similarities and ordinary commonsense substances is not really consistent with physicalism, but I will also ignore that worry.

Millikan thinks that, in our robust metaphysical environment, consistency assures that over time 'natural relations' of non-contradictoriness are tracked reasonably well.[48] My complaint is that we can accept most of this story and still find no motivated role for history in determining contents by determining functions. One has at a moment various sorts of dispositions and actual causal tendencies that are relevant to how one would or does treat a mental term. One has the momentary basis of a consistency tester that would in fact test various dispositions to iterate mental terms for their consistency in various ways. And one is in an environment in which there are various natural kinds and objects that those various concepts and inner terms would variously indicate. That seems to be enough to deliver contents if the historical version of the story that Millikan tells is itself enough.

The relevant behavioral fit or misfit of real identities and mental terms is available in the here and now, just like the behavioral misfit that reveals my myopia when I bump into the furniture. The crucial work of the consistency tester is also here and now. It is important to Millikan that identity be assessed by a system that can make mistakes,[49] and this may invite thoughts of teleology and hence etiology. But this unfortunate capacity is assured for even a momentarily determinate creature in the metaphysically robust environment that Millikan assumes, by the fact that internal monitoring of identities and real identities in the world could come apart even in that moment.

Clearly Millikan holds that the *actual history* of the testing of an inner term in the life of the individual who introduces it matters to its content. She also may think that the actual history of an inner term in inferences

---

[47] In Millikan (1998) these become largely the same.   [48] Millikan (1984: 143 and Part IV).
[49] Millikan (1997: 505–6).

helps to type it. But the problem is that with all the robust resources she deploys in the moment, there is no motivation for these claims. What exactly is it that is supposed to happen in the individual's life that cannot happen in the moment?

It may be that it takes some time to display a capacity to track a continuing object, but that doesn't mean the capacity to do so isn't coiled into one's dispositions of a moment. Dispositions are clearly difficult things to treat properly, but Millikan is already up to her neck in claims about what would happen if various sensory conditions were or were not present, for instance under normal conditions for beliefs that have never occurred[50] in the history of the world.

Millikan's etiological proposal about belief contents is ingenious. But if her mechanism works, which I doubt, still it is not adequately motivated over a non-historical variant.[51]

Another possible mechanism for mimicking selection pressure by histories of education has been developed by Papineau. His key claim deserves extended quotation:

Suppose our individual psychological developments throw up new possible belief types, new ways of responding mentally to circumstances, at random, analogously to the way that our genetic history throws up mutations at random. Then we would expect such new dispositions to become 'fixed' just in case belief tokens they give rise to lead to advantageous (that is, psychologically rewarding) actions, analogously to the way that genetic mutations become fixed just in case they have advantageous (offspring-producing) results. . . . More specifically, only those few doxastic mutations which produce beliefs that are *usually* caused by circumstances in which the resulting actions are rewarding will get fixed.

Of course, even a new belief type which *is* 'learnt' in this way still won't *always* lead to advantageous action, for sometimes it will be triggered by 'abnormal' circumstances, circumstances other than the one that in the learning process ensured the belief had advantageous effects and which therefore led to the selection of the disposition behind it. My suggestion is that the belief should be counted as false in these 'abnormal' circumstances—or, to put it the other way round, that the truth condition of the belief is the 'normal' circumstance in which, given the learning process, it is biologically supposed to be present.[52]

---

[50] Though their terms may have occurred.
[51] The variant is externalist, though non-etiological. Chapter 6 considers such accounts.
[52] Papineau (1987: 66–7).

The first paragraph presumes a lot. Its implausible claims about randomness seem intended to buttress the distant analogy between evolution and learning histories. But I will focus on another point.

A key element in this story—its crucial analogue of evolutionary pressure—is what made actions in one's educational history 'advantageous' or 'psychologically rewarding'. It is desire. The behaviorally-relevant effects of a belief depend upon the desires that accompany it, and the content of those desires have a constitutive role in fixing the content of the beliefs according to Papineau, since they fix the past conditions when things were psychologically rewarding. He says that 'we ought to count the truth conditions of beliefs not simply as circumstances in which they have biologically advantageous effects, but more specifically as the circumstances in which they will have effects that will satisfy the desires they are working in concert with.'[53]

So to understand Papineau's account of belief content, we need also to understand his account of desire content.

Papineau deploys two cross-cutting typographies of desires.[54] First axis: Some are innate, while some are learned, originally as means to innate ends. Second axis: Some fluctuate in response to environmental conditions in the manner of hunger, while some do not.

A learned desire for something is not a belief about that thing's being an instrumental means to the satisfaction of the pre-existing desire that was the root of its acquisition. And a desire that fluctuates in response to environmental conditions is not a belief about the presence of these conditions. This is allegedly because the desires will not extinguish immediately upon our receiving belief-forming evidence, evidence that they fail to satisfy the pre-existing desires in the first case, or evidence that the relevant environmental conditions are not in fact helpful to the satisfaction of desire in the second case.

That is one role for belief in fixing desire. There must be prior facts about what we believe to determine whether or not our learned or fluctuating desires count as desires, because there must be prior facts about what counts as specifically belief-forming evidence.

But there is another, more important role for belief in fixing desire. Despite the range of his typographies, it is innate and stable desires

[53] Papineau (1993: 70). [54] Papineau (1984: 562–5).

that receive most of Papineau's attention. To a first approximation, the satisfaction condition of the mental representation that constitutes such a desire is the effect 'it is biologically supposed to produce', the effect for which it was selected.[55] But there is also a crucial refining detail of Papineau's account: The mental representation that constitutes a particular desire, though typed at least in part by its contemporaneous role, has a range of effects in any particular situation in both evolutionary history and in the present. But which among those relevant in its history is the satisfaction condition?

Any particular action stemming from a desire will have a sequence of potential effects which are relevant to gene bequests. As we proceed outwards, so to speak, we will go past effects (eating this piece of food, say) which are taken to be relevant only in virtue of current beliefs, on to effects (eating sweet things, increased metabolic activity) the relevance of which is assumed by natural selection but not by the agent, and ending up, if all goes well, with gene bequests. The satisfaction condition of the desire is the *first* effect (eating sweet things) which is taken to be relevant by natural selection and not by the agent.[56]

But what is not taken as relevant by the agent is a matter of what beliefs the agent has and lacks. The desire in question will not extinguish should the agent come to believe that the desire not have that crucial effect. So here there is another way in which beliefs help fix desires. This time, the content of prior beliefs, what they are about, is relevant to fixing the content of desires. The satisfaction condition of such desires depends on what the agent believes.

So there are two similar ways in which, according to Papineau, the beliefs that someone has or would have under particular conditions help determine the content or existence of their desires, one relevant to the content of innate and stable desires, and another relevant to the existence of other sorts of desires.

Let me turn now from exposition to criticism. My complaint against Papineau's ET treatment of learned beliefs, which depends in turn on his account of desire and desire content, is that it seems circular in a debilitating way. First we hear that the contents of an individual's learned beliefs depend on the individual's learning history and what counts as satisfying a desire in that history. But then we hear that this depends on what beliefs or

---

[55] Papineau (1987: 67). [56] Papineau (1987: 69).

dispositions for belief were had then. The nature of belief content depends on the nature of desire content and the existence of desire, but the nature of desire content and the existence of desire depend on belief content.

We are used to functionalism, and functionalism is not debilitatingly circular. But notice that here beliefs are only constituted as such by desires that must be prior in a quite strong sense, since desires must be present in the history that antedates beliefs. And beliefs themselves must be present in those histories. It is perhaps overly sympathetic to call this circular. It seems inconsistent. And notice that vicious circularity should not be a surprise in such a theory. It is a natural risk of using desire-satisfaction as the analog of selection in an ET account of beliefs.

Still, I have cheated a little. The structure of Papineau's account suggests not a circle so much as a vicious spiral into the past. Current beliefs depend on past desires that depend on still older beliefs, and so on. But it is hard to see what motivation there might be for such a proposal. An etiological account implies that there are cases in which the content of a mental representation will differ if merely its history differs, even though that mental representation retains all of its present factual and counterfactual causal relations. In fact, in a non-circular and genuinely ET variant of Papineau's account this would be so even within the lifetime of a single individual. It is intuitive to think that one's psychology of content gradually develops all together with one's developing dispositions, and that its nature is different at different moments because one's dispositions differ at those moments. We think older children's thoughts differ in content because their momentarily-determinate dispositions are more complex. But in the sort of case Papineau needs to motivate his account, one would be physically stable in the relevant sense, or alternatively repeat exactly the same sequence of momentary physical states and behaviors each day, and yet believe different things each day as one's history grows, and by that very fact. This is far beyond anything suggested by the famous externalist cases of Part I, even if we ignore the relevant facts that a role for etiology isn't necessarily a role for etiological teleology and that we have already disposed of those cases. Davidson's more controversial swampman case—in which his physical twin emerges randomly out of a swamp allegedly without psychological states—has approximately the right structure. But notice that Papineau's proposal should be motivated by a very specific sort of historical dependency, in which beliefs depend on temporally prior desires that depend on temporally prior beliefs. It isn't that there is someone growing into determinate beliefs and desires all at once as their history lengthens, as in the swampman case. Rather, we must specify some temporal period for the relevant semantic spiral given constant training pressure on a fixed physical structure, with desires and beliefs having stable contents for say a fixed period of days and then looping into new contents constituted by that past moment of history, and so on.

There is no reason to believe this. There are ways that desires and beliefs together plausibly constrain each others' contents. But it is more plausible to think that they do so in the moment, in the manner suggested by traditional functionalism.[57]

Dretske has attempted a kind of middle route, between the purely cognitive analog of selection pressure developed by Millikan and the robust conative story of Papineau. In this model, effects in learning histories mediated by conation are important, but these are histories of reinforcement in which the exact content and existence of desires is not crucial. Accounts with this architecture need not suffer from the Papineau spiral, but can apparently exploit the relatively close analogy between positive conation and selection pressure.

Dretske's central treatment of thought content, in *Explaining Behavior*, crucially involves a way in which learning histories are supposed to fix the identity of functions and hence of contents for the basic thoughts that Dretske calls proto-beliefs. Dretske holds them all learned, indeed that there cannot be innate beliefs more or less by definition.

His story about proto-belief content is best told in his own terminology. An 'indicator' of fact S carries the information that S, paradigmatically because the indicator is caused always and only by S, presuming certain fixed background conditions. We might say that it normally is caused always and only by S. A 'representation' R is something more, something whose *function* it is to indicate a particular S. And Dretske favors an historical account of this function. R represents S when it is recruited as a cause of certain characteristic behaviors because of what it indicates about S, and hence comes to have the function of indicating S. Later on, after it is already recruited as a cause, it can retain this function even if caused, even if normally caused, otherwise than by S.

---

[57] For more on Papineau's account see Mendola (2006*b*).

We begin with a mental representation B, that is a 'natural representation' of something F. B indicates F in the requisite way if it is lawlike that Fs cause Bs. In a later moment, after learning occurs, B is a proto-belief (with content F). A motor response M is learned, and B causes M because it indicates F. After learning, B has the *function* of indicating F and hence has F as a content. The B to M causal connection was reinforced or rewarded in conditions where F was indicated by B (and alternate effects were punished or extinguished). And this in turn was because, in that learning history, M was a happy response, and hence led to the reinforcement or reward in those circumstances F. Because in that history F was the cause of B that led the B to M connection to be reinforced, we call F the content of proto-belief B.

In this story, the goals of particular desires and the nature of particular reinforcers are not relevant to proto-belief contents. What is crucial is that it is because of B's indication of F that certain resulting behavior is reinforced in that history, not what behavior is reinforced or how it is reinforced. Of course, such reinforcement will lead over time, presuming the truth of the behaviorist learning theory on which Dretske relies, to change in the momentary causal-functional-dispositional state of the creature that learns. But learning histories are relevant to content in the way Dretske requires only if different creatures in the same momentary state yet may differ in proto-belief content because their learning histories differ in some way.

The problem is that Dretske does not provide any real motivation to think that history matters to the content of proto-beliefs in the particular way that this version of ET requires. The famous externalist cases, for instance Twin Earth, do provide some intuitive grounds to think that history matters to content. But we have already dealt with those cases. And Twin Earth intuitions are not enough to support Dretske's particular proposal. And for that matter Dretske does not firmly endorse them.[58]

What seems required to motivate a genuinely ET account with the form Dretske suggests, what might show that his talk about reinforcement and function can do real work, are cases in which dominant historical etiology suggests one content and particular reinforcing etiology suggests another, in which Twin Earth intuitions pull against the suggestions of Dretske's account.

---

[58] Sullivan (1993); Neander (1996). Neander argues that a narrow construal of content is appropriate for Dretske and teleosemantics, and cites evidence from public discussion that Dretske agrees.

But such cases are unfavorable for Dretske: Assume that most days past when you thought about what you call 'water' your thought was rooted in H-O-H, but on the few days when 'water' thoughts led you to the behavior characteristic of such thoughts, say digging a well, they were rooted in XYZ. In that case, the dominant historical etiology seems more intuitively relevant to content than the accident of when you acted. Try another case: Most days past when you looked out the window at night and saw a big cowy-looking animal that you called 'cow', it was a cow, but on the two days out of hundreds when that behavior was rewarded by candy, in fact it happened to be a bull. In this case, the dominant historical etiology of your thought seems more intuitively relevant to content than the accident of when you got rewards.

Of course, I don't suggest that you be an externalist on the basis of Twin Earth. But the famous externalist cases are more intuitive than Dretske's theoretical proposal, and in the kinds of conflict situations we are exploring they cut in another direction. Another way to put my point is that my internalist proposal for dealing with Twin Earth plausibly deploys description clusters that make the constitution of the dominant local watery stuff of greater semantic significance than the constitution of the watery stuff one happened to be looking at when one acted and was given candy. In cases where Dretske's account says anything interesting and new about the relevance of history to error, something genuinely ETish, that is not to his intuitive advantage.[59] And of course if necessary we could always hijack it for internalism in the way I just suggested.

We have seen in this chapter that etiological theories of proper causes are false. They deliver the wrong contents when they say something distinctive, and are supported by no reasons that survive close examination.

---

[59] One alternative is to deploy a tight natural connection between the represented and the reinforcer. But this faces the difficulty of snorfs and kimus from Pietroski (1992).

6

Non-Etiological Mind-Based Externalism

Perhaps there is a plausible non-etiological externalist account of semantically proper causes. But there certainly aren't many.

As I watch a purple hat blow away across a field, an account of proper causes focused on spatially immediate causes of my sensory states would yield unintuitive content: the intervening light. An account focused on the most distant causes would also yield unintuitive content: an atmospheric disturbance. An account focused on ambient natural kinds[1] would miss hats and even purple, which spans reddish purples and bluish purples associated with very different spectral profiles. While sometimes there are two sensory routes that triangulate on intuitive content,[2] still sometimes I have one eye shut, and there is often only one channel of reception for the primitive sensory properties characteristic of each sense modality.

Nevertheless, there is one non-etiological externalist theory that may seem to deliver exactly what we need. And after ET it is probably the most popular alternative.

Accounts of mental content rooted in *asymmetric dependence* hold, crudely speaking, that the content of a mental representation is the cause of that representation on which all its other causes depend.[3] That, it is alleged, is the representation's proper cause.

To speak somewhat less crudely, such accounts, hereafter 'AD accounts', hold 1) that (a) any nomic relations that obtain between, on the one hand, a mental representation and, on the other hand, various causes and possible causes of that representation that are not its content, are dependent on (b) a nomic relation between that representation and its

---

[1] Perhaps a non-etiological variant of Millikan's account. [2] Lloyd (1989).
[3] Fodor (1987: 97–127) and (1990b).

content, but 2) that the latter nomic relation is not dependent on any of the former relations. Nomic relations are relations of natural law, which involve counterfactual dependencies in a way that I will shortly explain.

There is more than one AD account; there are a range of possible accounts that share that general form. Yet we will see that all of those alternatives are false. The problem is a dilemma defined by reference to three axes of difference among possible AD accounts. Any position along the first axis requires a problematic position along one of the other two.

The first axis is that AD accounts may deploy nomic relations that differ in *scope*, which apply for instance to all individuals or merely to particular individuals and hence have in that sense relatively wide or narrow scope. The second axis is that AD accounts may deploy different conceptions of the nature of the syntax of mental representations. The third axis is that AD accounts may deploy different accounts of the grounds of the nomic relations that bind that syntax to target contents.

I will argue that AD accounts that deploy wide scope laws cannot fit with a reasonably plausible account of the nature of the syntax of mental representations, and that AD accounts that deploy narrow scope laws cannot fit with a reasonably plausible account of the grounds of the nomic relations that bind that syntax to target contents.[4] Those are the horns of our dilemma.

Section 6.1 sketches AD and its motivations, but its principal role is to introduce the three crucial axes just noted. Sections 6.2 and 6.3 reveal problems along the other two critical axes faced by AD accounts that deploy, respectively, wide and narrow scope laws. Section 6.4 considers alternative externalist accounts of proper causes.

6.1

The central feature of AD accounts is a specific conception of semantically proper causes, whose primary champion is Jerry Fodor.[5] There are forms

---

[4] Much published criticism of AD focuses on forms that deploy mere counterfactual conditionals rather than the more robust nomic relations Fodor now prefers.
[5] Perhaps Fodor (1990b: 93) is canonical.

of AD accounts that incorporate a concern with actual causal histories, but the paradigmatic forms rely predominately on nomic relations, which may be merely *hypothetical* in the sense that they link merely possible causes to merely possible effects.[6] As I said, the basic idea of such AD accounts is that the target contents of mental representations of type R are those things of type Y, among all the things that are nomically related to Rs, such that all the other things are nomically related to Rs because Ys are, and such that it is not the case that Ys are nomically related to Rs because any of those other things are. In other words, Ys are the causes or possible causes on which the others are dependent, and that are themselves not dependent on the others. The other causes are hence said to be asymmetrically dependent on Ys, in the sense that if Ys had not been causes of Rs, then the other things would not have been, but the opposite dependency doesn't hold. Such a nomic relation guarantees that Ys *would* cause Rs in various hypothetical situations. So it is true that, counterfactually, if a Y occurred in certain circumstances, then an R would occur. But this nomic relation also supports counterfactual conditionals of another sort, such that if Ys had not been nomically related to Rs, then the other causes would not have been.

Bluntly put, the idea is that if mental representations of cows are caused by horses wearing green hats then that is because cows also cause or would cause them, but not vice versa.

The primary motivation of AD accounts is to get the cases right, to provide an intuitive account of semantically proper causes. While Fodor, in his guise as the primary partisan of AD, has given other positive arguments for AD, they are not convincing. First, they involve public language cases, while AD accounts are primarily accounts of mental content: He says that if one mistakenly says 'horse' of cows it is only because it means horse, because one says it primarily of horses.[7] And he claims that the practice of paging people depends asymmetrically on the practice of naming them.[8] Second, an unsympathetic reading of these passages would suggest that Fodor's intuition that the adventitious causes of something are dependent on the content-relevant causes is merely his intuition that the first are from the semantic standpoint accidental, in other words that they are causes that

---

[6] Fodor thinks that nomic relations differ from actual causation in a second respect to which we will return.
[7] Fodor (1987: 107–8).   [8] Fodor (1990b: 96–9).

aren't contents.[9] This may make us suspicious that such an account cannot really be developed into a reductive account of content. But working out this suspicion will require that we look at the details, and see that AD accounts cannot get the cases right either, at least without deploying some very implausible metaphysics.

AD oscillates between the horns of the general dilemma that structures our discussion of externalist accounts of proper causes. It sounds good when too generally stated to securely motivate an externalist account of content. But it delivers the wrong contents when made suitably robust and reductive. However, it will be another and more specific dilemma for AD that will be our primary focus here.

There are a number of ambiguities or generalities in the sketch of AD accounts that I have given. In his guise as the principal partisan of AD, Fodor has clarified two of them in what seem to be necessary ways. After we consider these necessary refinements, we will return to other ambiguities or generalities that are relevant to our central dilemma for AD.

The first necessary clarification is this: In his development of AD, Fodor uses 'nomic' in a stronger sense than any I've yet explicitly introduced, such that nomic relations are not merely causal relations that imply counterfactuals, but also must link elite properties that in some sense 'cut nature at its joints' and are properly projectible, in other words that are the proper basis for inductive generalization. This may require some delicacy when we get to the representation of purple hats, but the resource in question is crucial for AD. There are a variety of apparent counterexamples to AD as so far specified, which suggest that the target nomic relation, relating a mental representation and its intuitive content, is asymmetrically dependent on other relations involving parts of that content or things more general than that content or things intervening between that content and its representation. Indeed, we will discuss a central instance of this objection in Section 6.3. So AD as so far explicitly characterized fails to yield intuitive contents for thoughts. Fodor's crucial response to many of these cases has been that such alternate properties aren't proper candidates for nomic relations even if they seem to suggest the relevant counterfactuals, that they aren't properly projectible and elite.[10] On the basis of passages like these, it

---

[9] R. Cummins (1989); Adams and Aizawa (1994: 239–40).
[10] Fodor (1990b: 101–2 and 109) and (1991b: 257).

might be more accurate to say that AD uses two resources together to block the characteristic problem of causal-informational accounts of content, a restriction to nomically elite properties and also asymmetric dependence itself, and not just the eponymous one. A plausible AD must adopt this fix, though we should worry whether it causes the same sorts of difficulties as Prinz' analogous mechanism.

A second necessary refinement is Fodor's reasonable insistence that the counterfactual-supporting asymmetric dependencies between nomic relations that are constitutive of content are synchronic rather than diachronic. They are dependencies that obtain at the time when the content is possessed by the mental representation and not dependencies that obtain over time. Such a clause is also important in disposing of counterexamples. This is because, for instance, a mental representation's having a content may be diachronically dependent on some history of education that is intuitively not its content. And of course this clause is what makes AD plausibly non-etiological.[11]

But there are three other generalities or ambiguities in AD that will be more important to us here. They correspond to three axes of possible AD theories that will structure our discussion. These axes are relevant to determining the exact conditions in the world required by various claims about asymmetric dependence that AD accounts must make. And they are the axes on which our dilemma for AD will be defined.

First, it is sometimes ambiguous in Fodor's formulations exactly to whom particular context-fixing nomic relations are supposed to apply. Do individuals instantiate different content-determining laws, even perhaps different laws in different moments of their individual lives? Or rather do the relevant laws apply across a linguistic community, or a species, or even to all cognizers? Whatever Fodor's commitments,[12] a consistent form of AD must adopt one such account. I'll call this 'the scope issue'. Laws that apply to all cognizers or across a species have relatively wide scope, while those that apply to individuals or to individuals at moments have relatively narrow scope.

---

[11] Another possible axis of difference among AD accounts: Fodor (1990b: 96) says that he would be satisfied to deliver sufficient but not necessary or even plausible conditions for content. But we are interested in actuality.

[12] There is dominant Fodorian view on this, underwritten by Fodor's general endorsement of apparently wide scope psychological laws, though *ceteris paribus*. But we need to consider the full range of possibilities, and will see in Section 6.2 that wide scope laws are problematic for AD.

The second structuring axis is spanned by various accounts of the nature of the syntax of mental representations, the identity of the mental representations to which an AD account is to ascribe content and hence that enter into the relevant nomic relations with target contents. It is not sufficiently clear given Fodor's various statements of AD what fixes the identity of the mental representations to which content accrues. And again, whatever Fodor's commitments, a consistent form of AD must adopt one such account. Call this 'the syntax issue'.

The final structuring axis involves a quite general issue, regarding exactly what in the world properly grounds the relevant nomic claims, and the claims of dependency among those nomic relations, which an AD account deploys. I'll call this 'the grounds issue'. Not only are there a spectrum of possible views on this issue, there are many different specific issues about such grounds we might discriminate, and which suggest a variety of different sub-axes by which to organize discussion of AD accounts. For now, I will merely note two issues that will be significant later on.

The first notable grounds issue is that physicalism is one constraint of plausibility that should govern the nature of relevant nomic dependency claims. Plausible AD accounts are physicalist, and we presume the truth of physicalism here anyway.

Physicalism generates serious constraints on AD. As I noted, what are in some sense characteristic counterexamples faced by AD seem to require in response the claim that only genuine, full-blown nomic relations among certain elite properties, perhaps including uninstantiated properties like that of being a unicorn, are relevant to content.[13] One might worry that if we take this talk of at least uninstantiated elite properties seriously, it is in some immediate tension with physicalism as an ontological doctrine. And even if, at least for instanced properties, we might reasonably hope that a distinction between properly projectible properties on the one hand and not properly projectible but yet counterfactual-supporting properties on the other might be made consistent with physicalism without deploying transcendental universals, still we might also reasonably worry that the peculiar eliteness of fully nomic properties in at least Fodor's formulations surreptitiously involves even more than mere projectibility, perhaps indeed something so rich that it cannot be delivered consistent

---

[13] Fodor (1990b: 93–5 and 100–2).

with physicalism. For now this is merely an ungrounded suspicion, but we will return to it.

A second notable grounds issue involves the differences between internalism and externalism and among different forms of externalism. Fodor works within the externalist tradition in recent writings, the general dialectical position of AD as a development of externalist information-based accounts of content suggests that this is a plausible home, and of course this is our reason for interest. But there are large elements of AD that might be made consistent with an internalist conception of what grounds content-fixing nomic dependencies. It is possible to field what Fodor calls a 'pure informational account', which requires no actual causation at all but merely nomic relations that ensure that causation would hypothetically occur under various conditions. This indeed is in one sense the most characteristic form of AD account, and something like it is suggested by some of Fodor's remarks about unicorns.[14] But, on the other hand, Fodor sometimes deploys formulations that require, if some mental representation is to represent X, that some of its type be actually caused by Xs.[15] And he also characteristically requires that some of its type *not* be caused by X's, that they have other causes, for it to mean X.[16] This second restriction is motivated by the thought that content must accrue to mental representations *robustly*, that even if caused by an inference or perceptual error a mental representation must retain its content, and this restriction has also been deployed by Fodor in response to counterexamples. It is such requirements about instanced or uninstanced causal relations that most obviously make a version of AD externalist, so that conditions external to the skin of someone are part of what constitutes that they think as they do. Perhaps this suggests that AD really belongs among the etiological accounts. But there is more than one detailed way that externalist resources may be deployed by an AD account, not only to fix the nature of actual causal histories in the manner already noted, but perhaps also to fix the content of hypothetical causal relations. For instance, if there is only H-O-H currently around in the environment and no XYZ, then it may seem that even if one hasn't actually interacted with H-O-H, still in some relevant sense one *could* only so interact. AD as it has been developed by Fodor is neither internalist nor dominantly etiological.

---

[14] Fodor (1990b: 100–1).   [15] Fodor (1990b: 121).   [16] Fodor (1990b: 118).

There is a sense in which all these axes of possibility for AD accounts, involving scope, syntax, and grounds, represent a potential richness in its basic conception. But we will see as we proceed that all the specific alternatives with which we are left after we resolve our three principal structural axes are problematic. We will see that resolving the scope issue towards the general end of the spectrum, say in favor of species-wide laws, makes it impossible to resolve the syntax issue in a plausible way that doesn't generate debilitating problems for AD accounts. And we will see that resolving the scope issue towards the specific and individual end of the spectrum generates corresponding difficulties in plausibly resolving the grounds issue. That is the dilemma for AD accounts that I will pose here.[17] The first horn is the primary concern of the next section; the second horn is the primary concern of Section 6.3.

A more detailed outline of my argument may be useful. I presume that if an AD account is true, then it assigns intuitively plausible contents to mental representations. And AD accounts must deploy either wide scope or narrow scope laws. But we will see in the next section that if the laws are wide scope, then mental representations are typed by causal-functional roles, and that if mental representations are so typed, then AD accounts assign them implausible contents. And we will see in Section 6.3 that if the laws are narrow scope, then AD accounts also assign implausible contents, as long as nomic dependencies have plausible grounds.

6.2

Fodor holds that psychological states with content involve inner mental representations in a language of thought often called 'Mentalese', a language with determinate and combinatorial syntactic structure. There are certain token words of certain specific types, as for instance 'cow' and 'cow' are two instances of the same type of word, which combine together to form sentences with specific sorts of syntactic grammar. And *any* AD account is committed to some sort of typing of the mental representations, of the

---

[17] Perhaps there are two sorts of psychological laws relevant to content, some narrow scope and some wide scope, which generate two corresponding sorts of content, narrow and wide. But each alternative would suffer from one of the two problems we will trace.

vehicles of representation. I've been calling that the syntax of the language of thought.

The nature of that syntax is crucial for AD accounts, because it is to words or sentences of the so-called language of thought that content accrues, and which are hence one set of the crucial relata bound by the nomic relations that fix content. What is supposed to determine the syntax of someone's mental representations? Fodor has long and consistently held that syntax is fixed by internalist resources, and that it is a 'formal' resource, which is to say that it is fixed independently of semantic considerations. Whatever Fodor's commitments, these seem to be reasonable constraints on the nature of mental syntax, which we should accept.

But there are three more specific accounts of syntax that we should consider. It is notable that all three are suggested at some point in Fodor's writings, and that this gliding by the principle partisan of AD hides some of the difficulties that we will shortly trace.

Written words within natural languages are typed more or less by shape, spoken words by sound profile. Such a very simple and concrete account of the syntax of the language of thought is also possible, and indeed it is suggested, though usually at arm's length, by some things Fodor says. For instance, he claims that, at least intuitively and metaphorically, 'formal operations apply in terms of the, as it were, "shapes" of the objects in their domains.'[18] And he says that for 'the purposes of a naturalist semantics the only non-question-begging reading of "cow" is #c^o^w#...' where 'cow' is a mental representation and #c^o^w# captures an 'orthographical/phonological sequence'.[19] That is the first account of syntax we should consider, that it is typed by shape or something equally concrete.

But it is somewhat more plausible, and indeed sometimes Fodor seems to propose, that syntax is typed by an *abstraction* from concrete shape. 'The syntax of a symbol is one of its higher-order physical properties. To a metaphorical first approximation, we can think of the syntactic structure of a symbol as an abstract feature of its shape.'[20]

And yet even in a footnote to that passage there is a still more plausible third suggestion, that '[a]ny nomic property of symbol tokens, however—any property in virtue of the possession of which they satisfy causal

---

[18] Fodor (1980: 64).   [19] Fodor (1990b: 112).   [20] Fodor (1987: 18).

laws—would, in principle, do just as well. (So, for example, syntactic structures could be realized by relations among electromagnetic states rather than relations among shapes. As, indeed, it is in real computers.) This is the point of the functionalist doctrine that, in principle, you can make a mind out of almost anything.'[21] This at least points towards syntax typed by causal-functional role.[22]

Whatever the niceties of Fodor exegesis, such a range of accounts of mental syntax is possible, and we need to consider the form of asymmetric dependency in light of each. As I've said, the nature of syntactic typing and the proper form of an AD account are linked, since a syntactic item is one of the two relata bound by a relevant nomic relation. I will argue in this section that more abstract and relational accounts of syntax are much more plausible if the language of thought and hence relevant content-fixing laws are supposed to be invariant among, say, all humans, that is to say if such laws have *wide* scope. But I will also argue here that this generates a serious problem when conjoined with AD as an account of content. Problems for more narrow scope accounts will be most evident in the next section, when we discuss the other relata bound by AD.

But let's begin our discussion with the simplest case, syntax-typing by literal shape, or by something equally concrete like a specific sort of quite concretely-specified neural firing pattern. My main point about this is that it is extremely implausible that the same shapes or firing patterns are present across all cognizers for the representation of, say, water, or even of a particular taste. This is assured by the reasonability of the intuitions that underlie the traditional multiple-realization problem, the recognition that those who have somewhat different neurophysiological details can yet share thoughts. And such a very concrete type-theory certainly would not be supported in such a strong and implausible form by Fodor's familiar and widely accepted arguments for the language of thought thesis: arguments from productivity, systematicity, and from the nature of mental processes.[23] Nor is the language of thought thesis very plausible if committed to such a fixed concrete typing even merely across a single species. Fodor

---

[21] Fodor (1987: 156).
[22] This is Fodor's most recent drift. See Fodor (1994: 108–9), though we might worry about the use of numerical identity there. In light of Fodor (2000: 20–2 and 28–33), these causal-functional roles would need to be relatively narrow—relevant to logical form but not to any robust conceptual role.
[23] Fodor (1987: 135–54).

himself suggests that there are primitive representations not just for sensory properties but for properties like doorknob and fire hydrant.[24] But it simply isn't plausible that all humans are fitted out with a mechanism that will assure that exactly the same firing pattern or shape is involved in the mental representation of such things. Even if, as Fodor thinks, we are innately fixed to generalize from stereotypical doorknobs to possession of the doorknob concept, we aren't fixed to represent them in exactly the same way, by exactly the same shaped tokens. How could we be? Even if the form of the syntax is fixed by the stereotypes, we interact with somewhat different stereotypes. Perhaps it might be claimed that we somehow generalize from different stereotypes to a single concept, and then that determines the shape of the relevant representation. But that would violate the formality condition.

Of course, AD accounts can abandon Fodor's other commitments. Perhaps there are only primitive representations for sensory properties. Still, brains, even brains of identical twins, plausibly exhibit different patterns of excitation and different shapes at the suitably fine-grained level. And we shouldn't forget the traditional functionalist worry that, absent the patterns of connectivity that surround it, a particular concrete firing-pattern would plausibly retain no content at all, whatever its asymmetric dependencies on target contents.[25]

We can reasonably conclude that if the laws that fix the content of a piece of syntax lock content to concrete shapes or particular firing patterns, then the laws are laws for individuals, or even perhaps merely for individuals in brief periods of their lives. This, we will see in the next section, creates certain problems for AD accounts, but not those that immediately concern us.

So let's consider the next possibility, which is syntactic typing by something a bit more abstract than literal shape. The question is which abstractions are relevant. While abstract shapes can be realized in a variety of ways, still it may seem that the disjunction of realizers should not be 'wild' or 'open'. In other words, the fan of AD might say that those abstract shapes that enter into laws are the relevant ones, are properly nomic. But there are two ways to understand this.

---

[24] Fodor (1998: 89–145).
[25] Fodor, a fan of punctate minds, might implausibly disagree.

On one hand, perhaps it is supposed to be the case that whatever types of syntax there are involving abstract shapes is set by the facts about whatever it is that is nomically tied in the appropriate way to represented properties, that we find the syntax by starting with what is represented and working back along the content-determining nomic relations it enters into. But this violates the very plausible formality condition, that syntax is fixed by other than semantic resources. If 'cow' is just whatever represents cows, then Fodor's project and most current reductive attempts at mental semantics fail outright.

On the other hand, perhaps the laws that fix syntax are independent of those that fix content. There are various ways this might be so. As Fodor himself suggests in response to arguments made by Kripke's version of Wittgenstein, arguments we will discuss in Chapter 9, it might be that certain types of syntax are fixed by the nature of the projectible and elite properties there are in the world, properties that are *candidates* to enter into content-determining laws. But of course to the inevitable degree that the relevant syntactic typings are not invariant across all cognizers, these elite properties would need to be fairly locally-based and locally-applicable. Relevant syntax might be fixed by specific and properly individualized Platonic forms hovering over particular cognizers or specific irreducible Aristotelian telē pushing out from within them. But that seems like dualism by another name. Physically acceptable narrow scope projectibility, relevant for instance to a particular individual psychology, seems an inappropriate resource to constitute eliteness if it requires violation of the formality condition. And some sort of projectibility in an individual psychology supporting laws that define syntactic identity independently of content would push this alternative towards a narrow scope version of the causal-functional form of syntactic-typing that we are soon to discuss. And as we will see in Section 6.3, narrow scope accounts face other debilitating problems. So perhaps we should consider relatively wide scope syntax of this general sort. But the problem with this route is that it is implausible that a particular piece of syntax in all sorts of cognizers has an at all reasonably concrete material specification anyway, for reasons we have already considered. If that is required by AD, then it seems plausibly false. The only form of plausible wide scope laws of this sort are abstract enough to count as full-blown causal-functional typing.

We have seen that the most plausible forms of our second sort of syntactic-typing collapse either into narrow scope accounts of the sort we will consider in the next section, or into our third sort of typing. We seem forced to the third and relational form of typing syntax if we are to avoid narrow scope laws. So let's focus there.

Let's presume that a piece of syntax is what it is because it plays a certain causal-functional role.[26] Perhaps paradigmatically, this role mirrors its narrowly logical role, its role in proper formal deductive inferences.

This causal-functional conception may seem to threaten a vicious circularity, but no more does it do so than any causal-functional scheme that characterizes some level of entities all at once, by their role in the overall system. There are a variety of different forms this causal-functional typing might take. The typing might be unique for individuals or for moments of individual lives, or correspondingly more social or universal; it might be narrow or wide in scope.[27] If the laws relevant to content are individual, we will face the problem promised in the next section. Perhaps, however, it might be that one could abstractly characterize a constituting causal-functional role for a piece of syntax that is constant across all individuals, at least say of a species.

So, at least for all we know so far, reasonably wide scope laws are plausible and consistent with AD. They just require causal-functional syntactic typing.

The primary argument of this section, however, will be that plausible wide scope and hence causal-functional syntactic typing creates a debilitating problem when conjoined with an AD account of content. Causal-functional typing and asymmetric dependence together yield unintuitive content. Here's the argument:

By an AD account of content, 'cow' means cow just when 1) it is nomically related to cow, and 2) if it is nomically related to anything else then that other relation is asymmetrically dependent on the first. But 'cow' can't mean cow unless 'cow' exists, at least in whatever potential way any currently uninstanced word in the language of thought exists. And if 'cow' is to so exist, on the conception of syntactic-typing that we are currently

---

[26] This is somehow shared in all of its occurrences, be they beliefs or desires. There are allied views on which only the belief tokens are typed in one way.

[27] Fodor's discussion of causal-functional typing in Fodor (1994) adverts to what seems to be an *individual* machine table, or at least a table for a number of machines more similar than any two humans are.

exploring, then it must be such as to be nomically related to whatever is specified in the role that fixes its syntactic type. And in addition it would be a 'cow' (given the plausible formality condition) even independent of semantic considerations, even if there were no cows and it were not nomically related to cow in the way that it is. 'Cow' cannot be nomically related to cow unless 'cow' exists in the relevant sense, and it cannot so exist unless it is nomically related to its typical syntactic cause. And by the formality condition it can and would be nomically related to that syntactic cause even if it bore no nomic relation to cow. So, according to AD, 'cow' in fact means typical syntactic cause of 'cow' and not cow. But that is the wrong content.

This objection is pressing whether the laws fixing content apply to individuals, species, or across all cognizers, as long as syntax is typed in a causal-functional way. But such a form of typing seems *required* if wide scope nomic relations fix mental content. Or at least that is so absent enormously implausible claims about constancy of the shape of particular mental representations across cognizers.

How might the partisan of AD reply? One source of possible objection to my argument is suggested by an analogy between my case and other alleged counterexamples to AD that have been discussed in the literature. Those other cases do not seem debilitating, so neither may my argument. But, I reply, there is a difference. The analogous cases are not couched in such a way as to evade defensive deployment of elite properties. For instance, while the robustness clause of the standard Fodorian formulation of AD assures that mental representations will have non-content causes, still arguably there is no law linking such causes to the representation. Seager has claimed that at least when AD is applied to natural languages malapropisms provide counterexamples somewhat analogous to my own, and Adams and Aizawa have stressed adventitious causes as problematic for AD accounts. But against these analogous cases, a partisan of AD can properly deploy the reply that the alternative property that AD threatens to nominate as content is not nomic. Still, in the case we are considering it *must* be nomic, since the syntactic types must be nomic according to AD to be bearers of content. So Fodor's characteristic response to the analogous cases can't work against my case.

Another possible source of objection is a concern that if my argument were successful, it would also be successful against functionalism generally, and it may seem that we have lots of reasons to believe in functionalism. Functionalism allows that various causal-functional roles accrue all at once to particular bits that instance them, so why can't the nomic laws that create syntax and those that fix content accrue all at once to some brain state? But, I reply, notice that the formality condition assures that the various laws in question in our case are not all on one level in this sense, and cannot accrue all at once. Those relevant to syntactic identity come first and independently. That additional dependency structure is a difference between the situations faced by AD and traditional functionalist conceptions, and it is also what generates the false assignment of content according to AD.

Despite the fact that to abandon the formality condition is to give up on one of the central working assumptions of current discussions of content, still one might wonder in this context why we shouldn't at least interpret it less rigidly than I have. Or one might attempt to modify AD to rule the particular dependency that generates my problem semantically irrelevant. So let's consider such responses, which require some modification of the basic AD account.

It may aid AD if we think of what it must presume in a stratified way, involving a staged process: There is a weak causal-functional role that fixes syntactic identity, say across all humans. That's the first part of the first level. Then, in the second part of the first level, we somehow causal-functionally characterize the particular role in which such a piece of syntax will be primarily caused in the cases relevant to content-fixing dependencies, say as a belief. So now we have a strong causal-functional characterization of one of the relata of a relevant nomic dependency, and can move on to the second stage. In that second stage, the instancing of a particular concrete piece of syntax of some sort, fitting the necessary weak role, is caused in the stronger and more particular causal-functionally characterized position, say in the belief-constituting role sometimes called 'the belief box', by the target content, and that is a matter of law, and indeed of a law on which other related nomic relations asymmetrically depend.

Note that it must be that that basic law links the target property qua that property on the one hand with the Mentalese word qua something meeting a strong causal-functional characterization on the other. Now suppose we modify AD accounts so that the content is the second-stage cause on which all other second-stage causes depend, the cause on which all the other causes depend asymmetrically once the identity of the second-stage causal relata are fixed, partly of course by the causal-functional role that fixes relevant syntactic identity.

Fodor might ask, 'What's wrong with that?' But this is an ad hoc modification of AD accounts. There is no particular theoretical motivation for this proposal other than the need to patch up an account of proper causes that isn't very securely motivated to begin with. And a second problem is that it makes claims about the forms of nomic relations and their dependency that are implausible even if coherent, and in any case a very bad fit with physicalism. If AD can escape one horn of our dilemma in this way, it runs more quickly than expected onto the second, which involves the grounds issue. Though the central grounds issue for AD is our focus in the next section, let me explain this second worry about our ad hoc revision.

On this proposal, one of the relata bound by a relevant law must be characterized partly in terms of hypothetical causal relations and partly in terms of actual causal relations to other things that are themselves characterized partly by actual and hypothetical causal relations. It is under that description that the syntax is nomically related to the target content. We don't know of any other laws like that.[28] This isn't the standard functionalist case in which all the causal-functional constraints are met all at once by a concrete realizer, where all laws target a relatively concrete entity under a concrete characterization. In the case at hand, it is rather that a first set of relations and roles create something as something to which the other causal relations can bind, but only when it is also bound by the first set. While Burge and other externalists have defended laws or at least explanations that link entities characterized relationally, they are not laws that link entities essentially characterized by *hypothetical* relations.[29] And it is striking that Fodor himself has argued that even the non-hypothetical relational properties involved in broad content can't properly figure into psychological explanations.[30]

Still, it may seem that even functionalism is at least implicitly committed to laws of this type. For instance, when something is functionally individuated as a headache, it is a headache because of its causal-functional

---

[28] Perhaps some hold that all basic laws relate *pure* dispositional properties. But physicalism precludes the laws in question here from being basic.
[29] Burge (1986a).   [30] Fodor (1987: 27–53) and (1991a).

role. And a headache may cause someone to go buy a pain reliever. So it looks like buying pain relievers enters into laws with headaches in virtue of the functional roles brain states play in order to become headaches. But, I reply, it is important to remember that a plausible revision of AD must, like AD, deploy nomic relations that link elite, projectible properties. And there is no proper law of this sort that links headaches and shopping for pain relievers. Some forms of functionalism maintain that a higher-order, say psychological, functional structure may be realized by a variety of lower-order, say biological, functional structures. But that is not the sort of dependency within a level of structure that our modification of AD requires.

Perhaps it will seem helpful that there is a more concrete way to conceive of the laws required here. The laws might link target contents not to hypothetically and relationally characterized syntax, but rather to vast disjunctions across all the possible global internal physical states realizing such syntactic states, such that a content-fixing nomic relation obtains between the target content on one hand and a disjunction across all the concrete conditions including the relational ones sufficient for the syntax to be the syntax that it is on the other. But this suggests that the content doesn't accrue just to the intuitive syntax, but to the syntax plus the whole syntactic-typing physical environment of that syntax in the cognizer. We will trace AD's necessary antipathy to disjunctive properties as properly elite and projectible in the next section. But in any case this is a very unusual and unfamiliar sort of nomic relation.

Whichever of these alternatives we adopt, disjunctive or staged causal-functional, no plausible law has this particular kind of complicated form. And there are also worries about what might plausibly ground such a law. I have noted that it is important to plausible accounts rooted in AD that the kind of laws that fix content involve genuinely elite and properly nomic properties, properties that among other things are projectible and support counterfactuals, and also important that many other kinds of intuitively causal relations not be elite in this way. The elite properties must privilege some intuitive causal relations over others in any plausible AD-based conception. But more is required by the proposal under consideration. There must be elite nomic relations among certain sorts of elite properties that together fix syntactic identity, and then a second set of elite nomic relations that link to nomic structures of the first sort in a way to fix content, and indeed there must be dependencies among such second-level relations that help single out intuitive contents by the mechanism of AD. But if eliteness is projectibility, it is hard to see how there can be the several distinct sorts of elite relations this requires. At the very least, the friends of AD should explain how laws of the very peculiar kind it would require on this option can be consistent with the fact of physicalism, how they can be in any sense constituted by, even if not reduced, to the physical. For on the surface, they cannot be delivered by all the microphysical facts. They seem rather to require physically-unconstituted Platonic properties and Platonic relations among those properties and then Platonic relations of dependency among those relations that are not constituted by anything like relatively concrete and physically respectable projectibility. We will return in the next section to worries like this about Fodor's own proposals.

Our situation so far is this: If tokens are typed relatively concretely, that plausibly requires relatively narrow scope content-fixing laws, whose cost we will assess in the next section. And if they are typed relatively abstractly, by reference to causal-functional relations, then AD fails, barring ad hoc modification, implausible laws, and what seem to be unusual forms of Platonism in serious tension with physicalism.

6.3

In this section, we will be concerned primarily with problems for asymmetric dependence created by narrow scope typing. We will consider the interaction of narrow scope typing with the grounds issue, in particular by a focus on the other relata of the relevant content-fixing nomic relations, the target contents.

The general problem we will discover here arises out of the response required by one characteristic objection to AD accounts. This crucial response is problematic if content-fixing nomic dependencies are narrow in scope. And hence narrow scope AD assigns unintuitive contents, barring some very implausible metaphysics.

Let's begin with the characteristic objection. It is at least a surface problem for AD accounts that they suggest counterintuitive contents in cases in which the nomic relation to the target property is mediated by a causal mechanism in such a way that that nomic relation seems asymmetrically dependent on the nomic relations linking the mental representation with intervening states of the mechanism. For instance, the mental representation of cows in my belief box seems plausibly nomically related to cows only because it is nomically-linked with a range of retinal stimulations that mediate my experience of cows. AD accounts implausibly imply that the contents of thoughts involving that mental representation involve disjunctions over retinal stimulations and not cows.

We need to carefully consider Fodor's response to this objection. No other response seems possible if AD is to be successfully defended. Surely it wouldn't be adequate merely to *insist* on the contrary and AD-friendly dependency.

It might still be said... that the dependence of cow thoughts on distal cows is asymmetrically dependent on their dependence on *disjunctions* of proximal cow projections; distal cows wouldn't evoke COW tokens but that they project proximal whiffs or glimpses or snaps or crackles or... well, or what? Since, after all, cow spotting can be mediated by theory to any extent you like, the barest whiff or glimpse of cow can do the job for an observer who is suitably attuned. Less, indeed, than a whiff or glimpse; a mere ripple in cow-infested waters may suffice to turn the trick.... [J]ust about *any* proximal display might mediate the relation between cows and cow-thoughts for some cow-thinker or other on some or other cow-spotting occasion.

So barring appeals to *open* disjunctions, it seems likely that there is just no way to specify an array of proximal stimulations upon which the dependence of cow-thoughts upon cows is asymmetrically dependent. And... it does seem to me that the price of intentional univocality is holding that primitive intentional states can't express open disjunctions. The idea might be that, on the one hand, content depends on *nomic* relations among properties and, on the other, nothing falls under a law by satisfying an *open* disjunction (open disjunctions aren't projectible).[31]

Such is Fodor's response, that the relevant disjunctions across proximal stimulations are open and anomic and unprojectible.

But it is important to note that here the scope issue has become crucially relevant. Fodor's response requires that the content-determining laws be wide in scope. See for instance the last sentence of the first paragraph I've quoted. For each individual at each moment there *is* a particular mechanism

[31] Fodor (1990b: 109–10). See also Fodor (1991b: 257).

present, specifying certain specific proximal stimulations that will generate mental representations of cows. Perhaps that is a disjunction across proximal stimuli, but hardly an open one. If relevant laws were very narrow scope, then it would only be because 1) it is nomic for an individual at a time that 'cow' is caused by the members of such a disjunction that 2) it is nomic for that individual at that time that cows cause 'cow'. So 'cow' would mean the disjunction over proximal stimulations after all. And that is the wrong content.

So if the laws invoked by AD are very narrow in scope, then Fodor's crucial response won't work. According to AD, 'cow' would mean the disjunction across the proximal stimuli that would cause tokenings of 'cow' in the individual in question at the time. AD would ascribe the wrong content. But if, on the other hand, those laws are at all wide in scope, then we face the problem about syntax we discovered in the last section. According to AD, 'cow' would mean typical syntactic cause of cow. AD would once again ascribe the wrong content. That is the crux of our dilemma for AD. It ascribes the wrong contents to our thoughts whether the laws it invokes are wide or narrow in scope.

That is the main conclusion of this section, and indeed of my dilemma for AD. But we should consider possible objections to my treatment of this horn. It is here that our focus on the metaphysics of the grounds issue will be most relevant.

One might object that the difficulty at hand only attends a particular class of cases, so that while it is real it is of limited significance. AD might help in other cases. Perceptual beliefs about cows *are* quite central to our concerns here, but still perhaps we should consider other relevant cases that Fodor has discussed.

It seems that the key and central cases of represented properties according to Fodor are what he calls 'appearance' properties, which receive his latest extended attention in *Concepts*. Perhaps being a cow is an appearance property. But there are also other sorts. Three examples Fodor gives are the properties of being red, being a doorknob, and being water (or at least being water for Homer, in the days before chemistry). Fodor's idea is that in the case of appearance properties, say the property of being a doorknob, things go like this: From experience of stereotypical doorknobs, we develop by a kind of generalization a mental representation of being a doorknob (and not just a stereotypical one). Indeed, he holds that it is essential to the property of being a doorknob that it is the property we 'lock on to' from initial experience of stereotypical doorknobs, presumably by an innate mechanism and such that experience of stereotypical doorknobs can be non-circularly specified by reference to their concrete sensory properties. The three appearance properties I've noted are supposed to be somewhat diverse. The property of being a doorknob is not a natural kind, and in that specific sense doesn't cut nature at its joints. The property of being water is supposed to cut nature at its joints in that sense, though Fodor maintains that pre-chemical Homer didn't *conceive* of it as a natural kind, since (we can presume) he had no idea about inner essences and would have found the notion of experts about the identity of water bizarre. Red is not a natural kind, but is unlike doorknob in that we can represent such a property in sensation even if we lack the concept, even if we can't represent it in thought. It is, Fodor says, a 'sensory property'. He explicitly holds that the property of being red and the property of being a doorknob are realized in the world itself by vast, and presumably largely unprojectible, disjunctions over basic physical properties. He says indeed that the only law in which doorknobs qua doorknobs enter is the psychological law that we lock onto them in consequence of certain sorts of experience, namely of stereotypical doorknobs.[32]

So far Fodor's account of central cases seems largely consistent with internalist conceptions of the grounds for content-fixing laws and dependencies. They are, as he says, laws about us.[33] But there are other relevant cases that suggest externalism. Fodor holds that we can come, by forming a conception of the inner essence of something like water and then deferring to experts about its nature, to have concepts of natural kinds as such. He says that, in such a case, by 'water' we will, if in a largely H-O-H containing environment even with a bit of Putnam's XYZ thrown in and even if we haven't interacted with any H-O-H, refer to H-O-H and not XYZ.[34] It seems to me that the most natural treatment of these cases for Fodor, modeled on his treatment of unicorns, is different from that he provides,[35] and makes much of the fact that we or at least our pre-chemical ancestors would have responded to XYZ as if to water if it had been around. But Fodor says that our deference to experts yields via AD the water-like

---

[32] Fodor (1998: 146).   [33] Ibid.   [34] Fodor (1990b: 115–16).
[35] And indeed Fodor (1994) claims that such twins are nomologically impossible and hence irrelevant.

substance our environment largely contains as the content of our mental representation of water, since in the largely H-O-H containing environment XYZ wouldn't cause tokenings of 'water' unless H-O-H did. So this is externalism about the grounds for the relevant nomic and dependency claims. Another relevant externalist case is Elm-Beech. And Fodor says that many of us lock on to the properties of being an elm and being a beech only through the mediation of our experts.[36] There is a kind of mechanism, containing experts, which underwrites the particular nomic relations fixing such a content for many of us.

These are the applications of AD by Fodor that are central to our concerns. But notice that all of these cases generate a particular problem of the general sort under consideration now for AD, because they involve an intervening mechanism of a particular fixed sort, at least if for argument's sake we accept the analysis of the cases that Fodor provides. 'Elm' and 'beech' might represent one's particular experts saying 'elm' and 'beech'. Similar things might be said of 'water'. And the causing of the tokening of a mental representation by the property of being a doorknob, being water, or being red is plausibly mediated for a particular individual at a time by a specific set of proximal stimuli, and indeed can only be caused by a specific range of possible proximal stimuli. Indeed, there is a deeper layer of dependency in some of these cases, for instance on the stereotypical stimuli from which we would innately generalize to possession of the concept of doorknobs. If Fodor is right to say that being a property such that we lock on to it on the basis of experience of stereotypical doorknobs is *constitutive* of what it is to be a doorknob, then he can hardly claim that it is obvious there is a mere diachronic dependency here. And he must admit that these various properties enter into psychological laws. So 'doorknob' means the disjunction across the experiences of stereotypical doorknobs. If doorknobs are supposed to be lawlike because mind-dependent, surely it is worth noting that stereotypical doorknob looks also enter into psychological laws, and in fact into those very laws that are constitutive of what it is to be a doorknob, according to Fodor.

So we can properly conclude that my argument, though initially focused on a single case, is of more than limited relevance. In all the cases that Fodor has treated and are central to our concerns, we find a variant of the

---

[36] Fodor (1994: 33–9).

problem. But let's consider other objections to my argument. Fans of AD might try to wiggle up the middle on the scope issue. For instance, they might propose that content-fixing laws are specifically invariant within language communities. But if the language of thought of an individual is constituted by their public language, then Fodor has lost perhaps his most characteristic thesis, and his arguments for it. More important, it is plausible that for a public language there are fixed distal stimuli that are the most characteristic causes for appearance concepts and also the causes on which the other and more theoretical-mediated stimuli asymmetrically depend. So the content of 'cow' in a public language, if that is fixed by AD, would probably be some disjunction across typical cows. And individuals speak quite differently, so it isn't really clear that any token-typing of mental representations rooted in public language could avoid relational typing anyway. And if it couldn't, then typical syntactic bases of inference would probably be assigned as contents by AD. So this middle thesis has some of the characteristic problems of both ends that surround it.

There is another salient middle ground thesis, that the relevant laws are laws for individuals over time. But remember that we cannot plausibly focus AD on diachronic dependencies among laws, and hence we might also properly wonder about the relevance of diachronic grounds for laws. In fact, to speak about both diachronic and synchronic dependencies among laws seems to require that laws obtain at particular times, and that seems to imply that their grounds so exist. And in any case, it seems plausible that there is enough stability of belief in individuals to make it the case that there are laws of even this cross-temporal sort linking proximal stimuli disjunctions and 'cow' for an individual. Another worry is that very concrete syntactic typing may not be available over time even for individuals.

One guiding thread in this part is the phenomenon of color blindness. And the case of the color blind suggests another salient middle ground thesis. Some of the differences between the normally sighted and the color blind may seem to be fortunate for AD. The perceptual beliefs of the color blind and the normally sighted engage the same world. And the intuitive differences in the intervening mechanisms by which the color blind and the normal lock onto the same properties out in the world apparently help assure that AD in such cases delivers the right contents, as long as the content-fixing laws are laws for all. In other words, the color blind and the normal may seem to be two mid-sized natural groups that allow us to go up the middle between the two horns of our dilemma. They stably utilize different intervening mechanisms involving different classes of proximal stimuli to get at the same world, but they may be governed by the same content-fixing laws.

But consider whether, according to such a model, the color blind are supposed to share relevant mental syntax with the normal.

Presume that they do not. Then there is a problem. Then they don't in fact share content-fixing laws with the normal. The mechanisms that mediate the locking on of the normal and the relevantly abnormal to things like surface spectral reflectances are somewhat different. If those who are color blind in a particular way have differently typed mental representations than the normal, then the peculiarities of their intervening mechanism are delivered as contents by AD. Indeed, those peculiarities are features of the mechanism in question that are unusually stable across a range of cases, across all of those who are color blind in the same way. So this in fact represents an especially virulent form of the second horn of our dilemma for AD.

But if, on the other hand, the color blind are supposed to have the same types of mental representations as the normal, then there is another problem. On the middle ground model under consideration, content-fixing laws are shared by the color blind and the normal, and so even some of the actual fixed causes of the sensory representations of the color blind violate the content-fixing roles for those states. AD provides the color blind with the sensory contents of the normal.

Indeed, on this model, if mental syntax is relationally typed, as is most plausible for wide scope situations like this, then there is likely to be an additional problem. Then it is likely that the mental representations of the color blind aren't even typed by syntactic roles they actually can fill, but rather by their in some sense ideal roles. In such a situation AD delivers typical syntactic causes in the normal as the sensory contents of the color blind. This is an especially virulent variant of the first horn of our dilemma. Perhaps it seems that sensory representations have no typical syntactic causes. But then the formality condition would plausibly be broken by such representations.

In either case, whether the color blind share normal mental syntax or not, AD is unable to deliver their sensory contents.

We have seen that my argument against AD cannot reasonably be claimed to apply to only a few unimportant target contents. And it cannot be evaded by tampering with the scope of laws in question. There is one last response that AD might deploy to save at once narrow scope laws and intuitive contents,[37] but it requires a very questionable position on the axis tracing possible grounds for claims of asymmetric dependence.

There might be an individual with a particular sort of physically-constituted causal structure that underwrites various counterfactuals and narrow scope projectibility claims rather than others, an individual incorporating a mechanism that insures that in the face of a wildly disjunctive range of environmental stimuli such as those constituting the surface spectral reflectances that normal humans see as green, mediated by a correspondingly disjunctive range of proximal stimuli, the individual's belief box will instance a particular mental word, say a token with a certain shape.

What in the world makes it the case that it represents green and not the correspondingly disjunctive proximal stimuli? The physical facts about the individual don't seem sufficient to underwrite the story that AD needs to tell here if the laws have narrow scope. There are no individual and local physical resources to sort out the target properties as elite; the disjunction over proximal stimuli supports relevant counterfactuals and is locally projectible in the relevant way. And if the relevant laws have wide scope, then we run into the difficulty with relational typing that we faced in the last section.

Still, perhaps some robust metaphysics can help. It isn't enough to postulate objective Platonic dependencies out in the world that constitute green as a nomic property from the point of view of the universe, however implausible they might be. We must deal with the color blind and not just the normally sighted. Rather, for there to be any help from metaphysically elite properties with such cases, there would have to be a kind of special Platonic idealization floating somewhere in the vicinity of each individual, involving special irreducible properties linked by irreducible nomic relations (*ceteris paribus?*) that fix that the proper idealization for semantic purposes of that particular individual focuses on cows or green rather than proximal stimuli. This is close enough to dualism

---

[37] Fodor flirts with other responses to the cow stimuli problem that are too idiosyncratic and implausible to detain us here. For discussion see Mendola (2003).

(an epiphenomenal variety with supervenience and the causal-closedness of the physical) to give the game away.

What AD would need to properly underwrite narrow scope laws that would deliver intuitive contents by asymmetric dependence only sounds at all plausibly consistent with physicalism if we ignore the issue of how physical facts are supposed to ground all the very particular nomic and nomic dependency claims AD needs for it to deliver intuitive contents. In other words, content-fixing laws that deploy hovering Platonic forms to deliver intuitive content face the same sorts of tensions with physicalism that we noted in Section 6.2 were faced by Platonic mechanisms for delivering determinate forms of syntax that can help AD evade the first horn of my dilemma.

The proper conclusion from the dilemma we have traced is that AD cannot play the central role in helping externalist physicalist causal-informational accounts deal with their characteristic difficulty. AD accounts of proper semantic causes are false.

6.4

A plausible causal-informational account of mental content must deploy some physicalist theory of proper causes. We have surveyed the principal externalist contenders of both etiological and non-etiological sorts, and seen that they are not promising. But there are other mind-based externalist theories that fit uneasily into my organizational scheme.

We have focused on the past and the present. What about the future? As it turns out, reasonably well-motivated views of this sort involve the mediation of thought by language. So we will consider these possibilities in the next part.

We face a shortage of viable externalist candidates. But sensory states are perhaps characteristically caused by what they are about. So it may seem that there *must* be *some* correct story about proper causes that an externalist causal-informational account can deploy, even if we don't yet have any idea of what it might be. But any theory of the content of sensory states, including any internalist theory, can deliver an account of proper causes. The characteristic and proper causes of a sensory state are those that match its content, but that does not imply that the characteristic causes of a sensory state constitute its content. Perhaps the order of explanation runs in the other direction. It may be hard to see where the content of a sensory state could possibly come from, if not from its causes. But it is important to notice that without an adequately reductive externalist theory of proper causes, external causal-informational stories about sensory content are bankrupt. They are no help at all. And there are internalist alternatives, for instance the qualia-based account I will develop in the next chapter.

But still, there is one last apparently externalist account of proper causes that we should consider, which fits uneasily within my temporal framework for reasons I will shortly explain. This account has been developed by Gilbert Harman, Dennis Stampe, Robert Stalnaker, and Michael Tye.[38] According to this conception, proper causes are optimal or normal causes, causes under optimal or normal conditions.

Two examples: Stalnaker proposed that causes under optimal conditions play a crucial role in constituting beliefs, though not the only role. 'Beliefs are *beliefs* rather than some other representational state, because of their connection, through desire, with action. Desires have determinate content because of their dual connection with belief and action.'[39] But beliefs have determinate content by their causal connections with the world. In particular, '[w]e believe that P just because we are in a state that, under optimal conditions, we are in only if P, and under optimal conditions, we are in that state because P, or because of something that entails P.'[40]

Tye's formulation, which he supposes to be specifically applicable to sensory contents, is this: '[F]or each sensory state, S, of a creature c, within the relevant set of alternative sensory states of c, we can define what S represents as follows: S represents that $P = $ df If optimal conditions were to obtain, S would be tokened in c if and only if P were the case; moreover, in these circumstances, S would be tokened in c because P is the case.'[41] Tye augments this proposal with an AD condition, to dispose of some circumstances that co-vary with sensory states in the relevant way but that are not intuitively perceptible.[42] And as we saw, in a narrow scope case such as Tye's formulation suggests, this mechanism does not in fact successfully eliminate inbound co-varying conditions, conditions of the causal mechanisms that intervene between the characteristic environmental

---

[38] Harman (1973, 1999); Stampe (1977); Stalnaker (1984); Tye (1995, 2000).
[39] Stalnaker (1984: 19).   [40] Stalnaker (1984: 18).
[41] Tye (2000: 136). I have suppressed a paragraph break.   [42] Tye (2000: 140).

causes of sensory states and those states. Still, that detail won't matter for our present purposes.

According to optimality accounts, proper causes are causes under optimal conditions. The crucial question, then, is what optimality is.

Like the notion of a proper cause, the notion of an optimal cause is capable of a tautological sense, which will leave the optimality conception true, but empty and unhelpful in motivating an externalist account of mental content. It is surely not enough to say that optimal conditions are whatever conditions assure that Tye's S would be tokened if and only if P, because then any account of sensory content, including my internalist proposal, will assure that such a constraint is met. Rather, a suitably reductive optimality account must deploy some independently specifiable notion of optimal conditions, which can help to non-circularly constitute content. And such a characterization must crucially involve external conditions if it is to provide theoretical grounds for externalism.

ET provides one instance of such a characterization. Perhaps optimal conditions are those conditions in evolutionary history that led to the natural selection of the mental capacity in question, at least in cases like Tye's that involve sensory contents. But we have already seen that ET accounts of optimal conditions fail. And if optimal conditions just are conditions of optimal perception as specified by ET, then optimality accounts are not a new and distinct alternative.

Tye and other proponents of the optimality account seem to want to preserve a certain generality regarding optimality. They seem to want optimal conditions to be evolutionarily determined when that is possible, and otherwise determined when it is not. But we have also considered and rejected other relatively robust externalist conceptions of proper causes that fall outside of the ET tent, along with forms of ET that encompass learning histories. What's more, an account of optimality conditions that can stretch to cover all possible externalist conceptions of proper causes would still be quite empty. It would leave all the real work of motivating externalism to the various specialists down in the trenches, developing specific accounts. And as I've said, an account of optimality that can stretch to cover all possible conceptions of proper causes, including that implied by my internalist story, has no relevant content whatsoever. This great capaciousness is one reason why the optimality account falls uneasily into my etiological/non-etiological schema.

Some writers call optimal conditions 'normal',[43] and it is conceivable that we are to take optimal conditions, at least sometimes, to be statistically normal conditions. That would be sufficiently specific and externalist to provide the optimality account with some distinctive and appropriate content. And, depending on whether or not the conditions that help constitute normalcy are historical or not, this proposal might be etiological or non-etiological. That's a second reason why the optimality account fits uneasily into my organizing framework.

But there is a serious problem with this proposal. Statistical normalcy does not constitute semantic propriety. Anxious as I am, a tree limb swinging in the wind may be the statistically normal cause of my perceptual belief 'lo, a wolf'. But that is not its content.

David Lewis, in another context, proposed that normal causes and effects within a species are relevant to the mental states of each individual member of the species.[44] And maybe that would help with the case of the wolf, if most people aren't as anxious as I am. But remember that some members of species have abnormal sensory capacities. Consider the color blind. Their abnormal experiences lack normal causes within the species, but still have content.

Perhaps, it may seem, the statistically normal cause of an individual's own psychological state is supposed to be its content. But remember again my tree limb. And remember the normal misperceptions we noted when discussing ET.

The statistical conception of optimality delivers the wrong contents, or none at all. And there aren't other plausible externalist accounts of optimal conditions or normal causes that we have yet to consider. The optimality account of proper causes only seems like a plausible alternative to ET and AD when it is left vague and very general. But when vague and general it provides no grounds for externalism in particular, since even an internalist account is consistent with a suitably tautological reading of its central claim.

We have completed our survey of mind-based externalist accounts of proper causes. None succeed. They are either empty, or suitably substantial but wrong. The dominant form of mind-based externalism is false, or at the very least we now have no good reason to believe it. It fails to

[43] e.g. Harman.   [44] Lewis (1980).

deliver any real motivation for externalism, despite its initially plausible sound.

But we still have some distance to go before we are done with mind-based externalism. There is a cluster of mind-based externalist theories that are in various ways less reductive than the causal-informational accounts we have been discussing, and that require consideration even under our presumption of physicalism. I will discuss these in the next chapter, in the guise of objections to my positive internalist proposal.

7
Qualia and Sensory Content

The second component of qualia empiricism—Modal Structuralism—is our primary focus in this chapter. MS involves five key claims: 1) Sensory contents are qualia. 2) Experiences of qualia are constituted by internal physical states. 3) It is necessary that such internal physical states be the experience of such qualia, but that is only knowable a posteriori. 4) These physical states and experiences have the modal structure architecture, which is a generalization of C. L. Hardin's proposal about color experience. 5) The semantic contribution of sensory contents is intentional.

Section 7.1 concerns the first two claims. Section 7.2 discusses a posteriori necessities. Section 7.3 develops the modal structure architecture. Section 7.4 sketches the semantic contribution of qualia. Section 7.5 presents remaining mind-based externalist theories, in the guise of objections to Section 7.4. And Section 7.6 responds.

7.1

The qualia of a sensation reflect what it is like to experience that sensation,[1] and there is an old tradition that roots the contents of sensory experience in what it is like to have that experience. But let me begin with a survey of recently dominant reductive accounts of sensory content. As we saw, the most popular physicalist accounts of mental content root the contents of internal mental states in their causal relations to proper external causes, causal relations refined by asymmetric dependence or etiological teleology or something analogous. Call such accounts of sensory content 'direct' accounts.

---

[1] There is an alternative use of 'qualia', whereby qualia include only non-representational features of experience. But the text's usage seems dominant.

In their paradigmatic form, direct accounts do not distinguish qualia from other sorts of sensory content. They simply identify whatever qualia there might be with features of sensory contents constituted by their proper external causes. Call such proposals 'simple direct accounts'.

There are natural problems for simple direct accounts, even if we ignore the conclusion of the last two chapters. Certain aspects of our experience of color, reflected in what it is like to have that experience, come apart from any plausible objective basis of color out in the world. Reddish purple seems very similar to bluish purple, but no two colors have more dissimilar objective bases. The normal and the color blind have different sorts of experience while in the same external conditions. And we do not understand how the world seems to a bat merely because we can see complicated details that the bat can hear.

At least since Galileo, it has not been uncommon to distinguish the objective basis of color out in the world from color as we experience it. Some of the subjective aspects of our experience of color seem to require other than a simple direct account. And so, as we might expect, physicalist orthodoxy has developed another branch. If we presume standard causal-informational stories about content, and note that qualia seem subjective in some details, it is natural to focus on higher-order representations of sensory states as relevant to the subjective aspects of sensory qualia.

There are a variety of these 'higher-order' representational accounts: So-called higher-order experience or inner sense accounts, such as William Lycan's, hold that qualitative experience involves a perception-like awareness of our own mental states.[2] Higher-order thought accounts, such as David Rosenthal's, hold that it involves thoughts about sensations.[3] In either of these ways, causal-informational stories about content can be deployed in another way than in simple direct accounts, and at least in that detail in a manner consistent with internalism.

But another distinction between forms of higher-order representational accounts will be more important to us. The first and rare form identifies all sensory contents with the subjective qualia constituted by representational relations of internal states to internal states. According to such a view, subjective qualia exhaust sensory contents. We will return to accounts

[2] Lycan (1996).   [3] Rosenthal (2005).

like that in a moment. But a more common and characteristic form of higher-order account denies this identity. Instead, such a view distinguishes subjective aspects of our experience of the world on the one hand from the features of sensory content that plausibly reflect the world on the other, and provides distinct accounts of each. It provides a direct externalist account of the worldly or objective or 'representational' content of our experience, and an internalist account of the merely subjective or 'qualitative' content.

This factoring involves obvious difficulties. It is important to see that there are two pressures if we presume a causal-informational account of content. One presses away from the simple direct accounts in the way I have just noted. But another presses towards them.

It is hard and unintuitive to distinguish the representational content from the qualitative aspects of our sensory experience. The way my sensory experiences of a green tree or a purple flower represent the world to be and what it is like to have such experiences seem at a minimum closely allied. That it is why Aristotle held that color just as it appears in our experience is right there on the objects of the world. Simple direct views have the intuitive advantage of always proclaiming the commonsense identity of qualia and sensory content. On the other hand, they have a difficult time explaining the obviously non-veridical aspects of our experience. Color just as we experience it to be, in which purplish blues are very similar to purplish reds, is not in fact there on the objects. Aristotle and untutored common are wrong about that. Still, factoring higher-order accounts postulate an unintuitive diremption of subjective qualia from the representational content of sensory states. They require two sorts of green as the contents of our sensation, green as we experience it and green as it is in the objects. They require very tortured factoring of experience into plausibly veridical and merely qualitative elements. The post-Galilean distinctions between color in the objects and color as we experience it, between representational and merely qualitative features of our experience of color, are not commonsense distinctions, no matter how common they now are among philosophers.

Common sense does recognize limits to the veridicality of our experience. Experienced highlights are not reflected in the commonsense colors of objects, and experienced shape is related only by projection to real shape. But the fact that there are perceptual illusions involving even shape and highlights suggests that qualia aren't radically dirempt from the representational contents of sensations, and at the very least that the division isn't immediately evident internal to sensory experience itself.

There are other sorts of cases. The sensation of pain involves qualia that may not seem intuitively representational. But we will come back to that case.

There is another natural worry about factoring higher-order accounts, even if we continue to ignore the difficulties of the last two chapters. The visual similarity of two purple roses that have very different surface spectral reflectances doesn't seem like an attendant similarity of our neurological states or sensory systems. The differences in qualia don't seem to be about our own states, but about the world. This is not a decisive objection, since we know our experience is misleading in certain ways. Still, perhaps it helps explain why there is yet another orthodox story about factoring.

It might be that there is a way we know our sensory states or their objects by having the states that isn't a matter of ordinary representation of the states or their objects but yet that somehow delivers qualia. Perhaps subjective experience is more like a kind of know how rather than a kind of knowledge that. Differences in qualitative experience that are not differences in representational content may involve different ways of *doing* that representing, and hence involve in that sense different sorts of *know how*. Perhaps this treatment also fits the case of pain.

Where are we? Simple direct externalist accounts of sensory content are implausible, not least because they cannot capture all of our experience in the world we actually inhabit. But there are higher-order and know-how accounts of the qualitative aspects of our sensory experience, which are apparently consistent with physicalism and even in some forms with internalism, and also with the obvious facts about our experience and the world. The dominant instances rely on unintuitive factoring and deploy false externalist causal-informational accounts of the representational contents of sensation. Since there is no intuitive factoring of the content of our sensory experience into the representational and merely qualitative, and because, as we saw in the last two chapters, externalist causal-informational theories are false, it would seem that both higher-order and know-how accounts should be developed into alternative internalist accounts of all the content of our sensory experience, at least if they can be. This is a third general architecture for a physicalist account of sensory content, different from simple direct accounts which do not factor and also from the sorts of higher-order or know-how accounts that do factor.

Most of the problems with externalist stories about proper causes that we surveyed in the preceding chapters seem to extend to internalist variants. So more development of know-how accounts in particular seems the most promising alternative. On the other hand, while such accounts are vaguely characterized, their very name suggests that they are not intended as accounts of all the representational content of sensory states. But however these matters of classification go, in the rest of this chapter I will develop one relatively specific possibility with the third general architecture that I have isolated.

There are simple direct accounts of sensory content. They are one orthodox alternative, and don't factor. Then there are orthodox accounts that factor, and deploy some internalist physicalist account of subjective features of our sensory experience. But these two alternatives suggest the possibility of a third, which is not widely represented in current literature, but still uses roughly orthodox resources combined in an unusual way. Like simple direct accounts, the third form of account does not factor between subjective qualia and representational features of sensory content. But like higher-order or know-how accounts, it deploys an internalist physicalist account of subjective qualia. And by deploying this architecture, the third form evades the characteristic difficulties of both of the first two forms. That is the position that I seek to occupy.

An internalist physicalist account that identifies internally determinate qualia and sensory content seems antecedently the best option available to us. And those are the first two key features of Modal Structuralism.

But these features of MS themselves suggest an immediate objection. Since the subjective qualia deployed by orthodox factoring accounts seem to many to be not merely non-veridical but even non-representational features of our experience, of no semantic significance, it may also seem that they cannot provide a plausible model for all our sensory contents. Still, it is clear that among the subjective features of our color experience is the close similarity of purplish blues and reddish blues, which is an intuitively semantic feature of that experience. Nevertheless, we will need to return at length to this crucial worry, in Sections 7.4 through 7.6.

You may reasonably wonder why I am confident that the true account of qualia, and hence of sensory content, will deploy only internal resources.

But I am not confident. I just think that we have no real reason to doubt it, not least because of the problems we discussed in the last two chapters, and some reason to believe it. Here is the reason to believe it:

Factoring is implausible. Sensory contents are qualia and all qualia should receive the same treatment. But the color blind have different qualia than those with normal color vision, even when in the same environmental conditions. And the difference between normal and color blind qualia must plausibly be constituted by internal differences between the normal and the color blind.

Put a color blind person in exactly the same external environment as a normal percipient, give them even the same external history, and they will still have a somewhat different experience of the world. So what constitutes the difference must be inside them. Even if the color blind differ in some of their relations to their environment, they so differ because of what is inside of them. And the relevant differences seem to be not only internal but current. Remember that people can become color blind.

If current internal differences can deliver the difference in qualia between the normal and the color blind, as they apparently must, then we have some antecedent reason to think that current internal differences could at least in principle deliver all differences in qualia. And factoring is less antecedently plausible than the absence of factoring. In other words, there is one set of cases, the differences in color experience of the color blind, about which we are reasonably certain that internalism is true, and we also have some reason to believe that the other relevant cases are no different.

Because color blind individuals are incapable of discriminations that the normal can make, it may seem that while their differences from the normal are internal, still what dominantly constitutes our experience is not. It may seem that internal differences merely screen off the color blind from the world, like a cataract. But that is not a plausible understanding of the differences in question. Some individuals are anomalous trichromats, and have color experience that is different from the normal in a manner other than straightforward subtraction. They can make discriminations among environmental stimuli that no normal human can make.[4] There are differences among people's color experience that are not merely intuitive omissions from the normal case.

---

[4] Kaiser and Boynton (1996: 444).

So we have at least some initial reason to believe that all sensory contents are qualia, and that qualia are constituted by internal physical states. Those are the first two elements of MS. But we have yet to properly engage with some serious worries about this suggestion.

7.2

The third feature of MS is its reliance on a posteriori necessities. This is required as a response to a standard objection to my proposal, as to any physicalist story about the experience of qualia.

Many worry that physical states, internal or external, cannot properly explain qualia.[5] In a merely physical world, constituted by the machinations of microphysical particles, it may seem that there would be no way to explain the intuitive differences between those who have our experience and hypothetical others who rather have an experience of color that is inverted along the axis of the color wheel that runs from red to green. Or it may seem that there would be no way to explain the difference between us and so-called zombies, who lack experience like ours and who it is like nothing to be, but who yet act and talk just like us. And this may seem grounds for dualism. The differences between us and the inverts and the zombies may seem to be other than physical differences. It may seem that even our physical duplicates yet might be inverts or zombies.

A now standard response to this objection involves a posteriori necessities. Physical states are supposed to constitute experience of qualia in a way that while necessary is only knowable a posteriori, so that we cannot understand in any a priori way how it is that our physical states do constitute our experience of qualia. Zombies and inverts who are our physical twins are supposed to be impossible, even though we cannot rule out their possibility in an a priori way, and so they are in some sense conceivable.

In the next section, I will express qualms about inversion arguments. And in this book I presume the truth of physicalism anyway. But still I think it is true that we cannot reason in an a priori way from someone's physical constitution to the exact nature of their experience. That is mostly for reasons explained in the next section. But another is that there is no way

---

[5] e.g. Chalmers (1996).

for us to know what it is like to be a bat—which hears by its sonar such things as we can only imagine seeing—on the basis of a priori inference from knowledge of its complete physical state. Those who deny that there is this barrier to our knowledge seem wrong. And so if, as also seems plausible, internal physical states can only constitute our experience of qualia if they necessitate such experience, that must involve a posteriori necessities.

This claim is now orthodox, but I should admit that other aspects of qualia empiricism involve me in relevant unorthodoxy. I should admit that I think we can have an understanding of other sorts of scientific relations of constitution, say of how H-O-H constitutes water, in a way that does not involve the same need for a posteriori necessities. And this asymmetry is itself sometimes used to motivate dualism. It may seem that physicalism about the experience of qualia plausibly requires a symmetry with more ordinary cases of constitution by the physical, say of water by H-O-H. A plausible physicalism may seem to require that constitution relations generally are a posteriori.

This is not correct. But to properly understand either of the physicalist options in play here, that asserting the symmetry and that denying it, will require some background. Kripke's *Naming and Necessity* is the source of famous externalist cases. And it ends with a famous argument for dualism. Nevertheless, the roots of both these options can be found there.

Perhaps the most crucial innovation of *Naming and Necessity* is an insistence on a pair of distinctions, between the epistemically a priori and the necessary, and between the a posteriori and the contingent. Against tradition, there are alleged to be contingent a priori statements and necessary a posteriori statements. For instance, identity statements involving names, such as 'Hesperus is Phosphorus', and theoretical identity statements such as 'water is identical to H-O-H' are claimed to be necessary a posteriori. And since Kripke plausibly insists that identity is in fact a relation that holds between a thing and itself, not between its names,[6] this has led most readers to conclude, and to believe that Kripke concludes, that there are not only necessary a posteriori statements but genuine necessary a posteriori propositions, propositions that are necessary but only knowable a priori. On the other hand, the fact and hence proposition that the standard meter in Paris is one meter long, which rests on the way reference to the standard

[6] Kripke (1980: 106–9).

meter is fixed, as the standard of that length, is supposed to be contingent but knowable a priori.[7]

Focus on a central application of this pair of distinctions. Kripke, along with Putnam, convinced most of us that the theoretical identity of H-O-H and water is necessary and not contingent. Most crucial for our purposes, he convinced most of us that if physical states are to constitute our qualitative experience in something like the way that H-O-H constitutes water, it must be necessary that they do so. The constitution of qualia by internal physical states and of water by H-O-H no longer seem to us, as they seemed to the physicalists of the 1950s, contingent.

Since knowledge of such constitution relations seems to be a posteriori, this suggests to many that theoretical identities generally involve a posteriori necessities. That is the first option now under consideration. But it is not that deployed by qualia empiricism, which requires a little more background.

There are those who resist Kripke's innovations. Begin with the contingent a priori. In Chapter 2, we considered an objection that Kripke's alleged cases of contingent a priori knowledge, rooted in reference-fixing, are really just examples of contingent knowledge that is not a priori. And there are even some who implausibly claim that these examples are rather necessities known a priori.[8] Another worry is that Kripke's reference-fixing mechanism is capable of delivering by a novel route a priori knowledge of necessary truths,[9] and indeed even a priori knowledge of the very necessary truths that Kripke claims are knowable only a posteriori. For instance, Casullo worries that 'on the face of it, if S stipulates that "Hesperus" is to be the planet identical to Phosphorus, then S knows a priori that Hesperus is Phosphorus', contrary to Kripke's claims.[10] My internalist semantic conception has plentiful resources to distinguish what is known by individual reference-fixing in this way and what came to be known through astronomical observation, which is one reason that it faces the belief-attribution and multiple-contents objections. But such a treatment is in tension with Kripke's own suggestion that what a mathematician knows through the a priori proof of a theorem and what a layman knows a posteriori through the mere report of the mathematician is the same, and with the semantic conceptions that support that contention.[11]

---

[7] Kripke (1980: 54–6).   [8] Soames (2003: 397–422).
[9] Jeshion (2000).   [10] Casullo (2003: 206).   [11] Kripke (1980: 159).

But other forms of resistance to Kripke's innovations are more immediately relevant to our concerns. Some have proposed that Kripke's alleged cases of the necessary a posteriori do not really involve a posteriori knowledge of necessary propositions. A recent and somewhat popular alternative account is a variant of what is called two-dimensionalism, associated for instance with Frank Jackson.[12] This suggests that statements like 'water is identical to H-O-H' express something that can be factored into two parts, an a posteriori and contingent claim like 'H-O-H is the locally dominant watery stuff' and an epistemically a priori or at least armchair claim like 'water is the locally dominant watery stuff'. In a strict sense, there are no necessary a posteriori propositions involving kind terms. And if 'water' is a rigid designator, that is only because it means something like dthat [locally dominant watery stuff].

Despite these worries, I accept, along with the current general consensus, both of Kripke's revolutionary proposals, both the contingent a priori and the necessary a posteriori. I also accept the now popular claim that while theoretical identities are necessary, they yet can be a posteriori. So the standard reply to the standard objection to internalist physicalism about qualia is available to me. But only with a little unorthodox spin required by other features of qualia empiricism, some of which implies the characteristic features of the second physicalist option I have promised.

One bit of spin, familiar from Part I, is that, partly to avoid controversies about what counts as a priori knowledge, I would rather talk about armchair access to the semantic a priori in these cases. The semantic a priori, because it depends on the conditions that make thoughts contentful, is more analogous to analyticity than it is to familiar epistemic aprioricity, though it can characteristically be accessed from armchairs. But since I basically accept Kripke's revolutionary pair of distinctions, I will suppress the terminological distractions this bit of spin would require, until we return to these issues in Chapter 10.

A second bit of spin is more important in this context. I need to quibble about some of Kripke's examples. Several key components of qualia empiricism are built on familiar foundations provided by Kripke. They are even suggested by more specific claims of *Naming and Necessity*.

---

[12] Jackson (1998). Mendola (2006a) is probably incorrect in suggesting that such variants of two-dimensionalism are paradigmatic.

But they are in some tension with some of Kripke's treatments of particular cases.

Focus on kind terms. While *Naming and Necessity* suggests that there are necessary a posteriori propositions involving such terms—for instance the identity of water and H-O-H—it also suggests that qualitative experience requires a different and asymmetrical treatment. In particular, it argues that there cannot be necessary a posteriori identities linking the experience of qualia, for instance pain qualia, and the physical bases of such experiences.

It is now orthodox to believe that Kripke was right about the general issue but wrong about qualia, that there can be necessary a posteriori identities in general, as he showed us, but also of qualitative experience and physical states in particular, which he denied. It is orthodox to believe that Kripke's model for the theoretical identity of water and H-O-H has broader application than he allowed. It is also orthodox to believe that this involves not merely necessary a posteriori statements, of the sort suggested by Jackson, but what I will call full-blown necessary a posteriori propositions, so that there is a single fact expressed by a true necessary a posteriori statement that is both necessary and a posteriori. This is the first physicalist option again.

Still, there is Jackson's alternative two-dimensional treatment of the theoretical identity of water and H-O-H, which I previously noted. We might call this the 'robust' two-dimensional account. And I think that about many cases this view is more or less correct. This is implicit in some of my claims in Part I, and will matter again in Part III. To be specific, I think that if Kripke is right that the identity of water and H-O-H is necessary, then that is only because it involves rigidification of a description cluster. On this analysis, analogous to Jackson's proposal, the claim that water could only be constituted by H-O-H rests on a reasonably deniable semantic claim that the word 'water' involves rigid designation of a hidden essential nature, a claim that was implicitly denied by physicalist philosophers in the fifties. So perhaps I should also say that what will be most crucial for our purposes is the necessity running in only one direction, not from something's being water to its being H-O-H but from its being H-O-H to its being water, or at least suitably watery. What is crucial is that H-O-H be watery in every possible world in which H-O-H exists. This fact doesn't rest, according to the analysis

I favor, on the reasonably deniable claim about rigid designation of a hidden nature. I think that this fact is, as Jackson suggests, a semantic necessity, analogous to an analyticity. I don't see how H-O-H could be watery in some possible worlds but not others. And it seems to me that in principle we can see this a priori. In Part I, we saw in effect that Kripke's notion of contingent a priori reference-fixing can go some distance towards underwriting some of the controversial aspects of this overall view. And it does allow through the use of rigidification Kripke's crucial claim that kind identities are necessary.

But I also think, contrary to the simplest form of robust two-dimensionalism, that Kripke was right that there is an asymmetry between the general case of theoretical identities and the identity of qualia and physical states. More important, he was right, or at least the orthodox interpretation of his view was right, about the general possibility of full-blown necessary a posteriori propositions, that don't rest on tricks like rigidification of description clusters. But, at least for kind terms, he had his cases backwards. While robust two-dimensionalism or something analogous provides the correct treatment of ordinary theoretical identities, I believe, and such identities in fact involve no full-blown necessary a posteriori propositions, still there are full-blown necessary a posteriori propositions that link internal physical states and our experience of qualia. The constitution of qualitative experiences by their evident physical bases is full-blown necessary but a posteriori, in a way in which the identity of water and H-O-H is not.[13] This is the second physicalist option I've suggested, which is embraced by qualia empiricism.

MS deploys full-blown necessary a posteriori identities of various qualitative experiences and their relevant internal physical bases. Or rather, to be more precise, it involves something closely analogous to that, full-blown necessary a posteriori relations of constitution by physical states of qualitative experience. Such full-blown necessary a posteriori relations underwrite the correct account of sensory content, I believe.[14] And this suffices to undercut the dualist objection that is our concern in this section.

---

[13] For a similar view of the asymmetry, but not developed by contrast with a two-dimensionalist treatment of standard identities, see Levine (1983, 1998). Another analog is Loar (1996). The one-way necessitation provided by these constitution relations defuses worries about the explanatory role of identities noted by Kim (2005: 121–48).

[14] This is a difference from Mendola (1997).

Kripke to the contrary says that the theoretical identities of water and H-O-H and of heat and the motion of molecules are a posteriori necessities, but that the identity of pain and neural c-fiber firing cannot be. But careful examination of his grounds for the asymmetry can in fact help reveal the way in which he gets his cases backwards.

Kripke says

> heat is something which we have identified (and fixed the reference of its name) by its giving a certain sensation, which we call 'the sensation of heat'.... Nevertheless, the term 'heat' doesn't *mean* 'whatever gives people those sensations'. For first, people might not have been sensitive to heat, and yet the heat still have existed in the external world. Secondly, let us suppose that somehow light rays, because of some difference in their nerve endings, *did* give them these sensations. It would not then be heat but light which gave people the sensation which we call the sensation of heat.[15]

But this treatment suggests just the factoring strategy that robust two-dimensionalism requires. There is a contingent a priori reference-fixing description linking heat to the sensation of heat. 'Heat' refers to whatever here in the actual world it is that gives us that sensation. The fact that heat gives us that sensation is a priori but contingent. Because this claim is contingent, there are telling modal objections to such a description giving the meaning of 'heat'. Still, these objections can be evaded by deploying 'dthat', in our favored reading. Heat might be 'dthat [kind that gives people the sensation of heat]'. Note also that the description Kripke proposes for heat centrally deploys a sensory property. This is favorable to qualia empiricism. On the other hand, he does suggest that at least some sensory properties like yellow are external physical properties. But, nevertheless, he says that 'yellowness is picked out and rigidly designated as that external physical property of the object which we sense by means of the visual impression of yellowness. It does in this sense resemble the natural kind terms. The phenomenological quality of the sensation itself, on the other hand, can be regarded as a quale' in the relevant sense.[16] So he does also invoke the kind of phenomenological yellow that I deploy, and which I am claiming is available to internalists.

---

[15] Kripke (1980: 131). The quote elides two paragraph breaks.
[16] Kripke (1980: 128 n. 66). The phenomenological quality is a quale in Russell's sense, and hence relevant to qualia empiricism.

Now look at the details of Kripke's treatment of pain, which is asymmetrical with his treatment of heat. He says this:

Let '*A*' name a particular pain sensation, and let '*B*' name the corresponding brain state, or the brain state some identity theorist wishes to identify with *A*. *Prima facie*, it would seem that it is at least logically possible that *B* should have existed... without Jones feeling any pain at all, and thus without the presence of *A*.... [But i]f *A* and *B* were identical, the identity would have to be necessary. The difficulty can hardly be evaded by arguing that... *being a pain* is merely a contingent property of *A*.... Can any case of essence be more obvious than the fact that *being a pain* is a necessary property of being a pain?[17]

In other words, there isn't the space between the sensation or feeling of pain on one hand and pain on the other that there is between the sensation of heat and heat, so that the factoring that Kripke suggests for heat, between on the one hand what I have interpreted as a contingent a priori reference-fixer for 'heat' and on the other hand the necessary essence of heat, is unavailable.

I agree. But I think we should conclude differently. We should not dismiss the overwhelming empirical pressure to conclude that our mental states are constituted by the physical, and that pain in particular is constituted by something relevantly like brain states, by something internal though physical. Of course, we presume physicalism here anyway, and so I'm now in the business of providing sketchy motivation rather than real argument, and there are dualists who have reasons to disagree. But the fact is that we have staggering a posteriori reason to conclude that physicalism can account at a minimum for everything in the world besides our measly little qualia, or at the very least everything concrete. So we have antecedent reason to suspect that the physical can also account for those measly qualia. And pain doesn't naturally lend itself to externalism, since pain is inside us. There is uniform empirical correlation of our internal physical states with our qualitative experience of pain, or so most of us believe. So it is antecedently plausible to claim that our pains are constituted by our internal physical states. What's more, it is in exactly a case like this, where we have radically different modes of internal and external access to one state, feeling it from the inside and seeing it from the outside through neural imaging, that we might reasonably expect a gap in our capacities to judge property identities,

[17] Kripke (1980: 146).

or the possibility of property constitution, a priori (or from our armchairs). So while these matters will require closer examination, it at least appears that any asymmetries between the constitution of qualia by the physical and the constitution of water by the microphysical are less likely to be ontic in nature than to be epistemic or semantic.

The factoring strategy that Kripke's own discussion suggests supports something resembling a robust two-dimensionalist treatment of ordinary theoretical identities, which is closely related to my proposal in Part I. And Kripke's claim that such a strategy won't fit the case of pain and brain state identity is quite plausible. But while Kripke is right that there are full-blown a posteriori necessary propositions, and Kripke is also right that there is an asymmetry between the case of qualia and the case of ordinary theoretical identities, he got his cases backwards. He was right about what matters most, in his revolutionary proposal that there are full-blown a posteriori necessities, and only wrong about the relatively trivial matter of how to distribute a few examples.

A better explanation of the asymmetry I am claiming is required, and will come in Chapter 10, where I give a sketch of the difference between our concepts of qualia and our concepts of things that can be physically constituted in a way that we can more fully understand. This analysis is based on details of qualia empiricism yet to come, but will not beg any questions, because the details of qualia empiricism on which I rely in Chapter 10 do not include the particular claim about a posteriori necessities in question here.

Beyond these details of qualia empiricism, and the arguments I have stolen from Kripke, and the need to reply to a standard objection in a way consistent with other claims of qualia empiricism, I have alluded to other reasons to believe that there are full-blown a posteriori necessities in the case at hand. The most important involve the story about the fourth element of Modal Structuralism told in the next section, whereby the reasoning that properly supports belief in certain specific relations of constitution rather than others involves crucial a posteriori elements. But another relevant point is that those who would defend accounts of the constitution of qualia by our physical states in which the relation in question is a priori, for instance hard core analytical functionalists,[18] cannot properly

---

[18] One analytical functionalist attempt is Braddon-Mitchell and Jackson (2007: 124–5). A more concessive alternative attempt is developed in Braddon-Mitchell (2003). Hawthorne (2002: 21–31) is

explain the hard time that we have in understanding a bat's experience. Perhaps they will reply that something is a priori knowable if and only if it is knowable given only the minimal experience required to have all the concepts involved, so that the barrier for us in the bat case is merely one of forming the concepts an intelligent bat would have. But there is an unusual barrier to our understanding of even the constitution of our *own* qualitative experience by the physical, when we *do* possess all the concepts in question. This is one reason that the a posteriori reasoning of the sort that I deploy in the next section seems crucial.

And so, I claim, sensory contents are qualia, and qualia are internally and physically constituted in a way that requires full-blown necessary a posteriori relations of constitution linking certain types of physical, neurological, or functional states and the existence of specific types of qualitative experiences. Those are the first three features of Modal Structuralism. These three features simply deploy orthodox resources in a somewhat unusual way. But without a more detailed story about how our internal physical states constitute experience of qualia, this trio of claims may still not seem properly believable.

7.3

The correct a posteriori internalist physicalist account of our qualia, and hence of our sensory experience, is not a higher-order representational account. And if it counts as a know-how account that is only because that class is vaguely characterized. It has what I will call the modal structure architecture, which is shared by a class of views pioneered by C. L. Hardin and Austen Clark on the basis of a general idea proposed by Bernard Harrison.[19]

Consider again color inversion arguments. It is sometimes thought that I can have no way of ruling out the possibility that my physical twin yet has an inverted color experience, for instance flipped over along the red-green axis of the familiar color wheel, with blue exchanged for yellow and with

---

similar. These proposals seem mistaken about the semantics of ordinary terms for qualitative properties, which are semantically basic in a way that forbids such complications as they deploy.

[19] Harrison (1973, 1986); Hardin (1988: 113–86); Austen Clark (1993, 2000).

other corresponding changes all along the wheel.[20] Harrison's general idea was to exploit asymmetries in color experience to show that such inversions can be ruled out.

I think that this is a good idea, but there are problems with Harrison's execution of the strategy. His proposal is focused on allegedly necessary and, it would seem, a priori features of our color terminology and experience, and he presumes too close a connection between the detailed nature of our color terminology and the structure of our sensory experience.[21] And in any case, our concern here is rather with necessary a posteriori relations of constitution linking neurophysiological or other internal physical states and qualitative experience, and Harrison does not focus on those particular sorts of relations.

But Hardin's and Clark's variants of Harrison's strategy *are* concerned to link our experience and our neurophysiology. Hardin's was developed first. He focuses on the possibility of color inverts who yet share our neurophysiology of vision. He attempts to project the structure of the normal range of possible color experiences onto the normal range of possible neural states that plausibly underlie them, on the basis of structural analogies. And he argues that we have more antecedent reason to expect, on the basis of the structure of human color experience and of our neurophysiology, that someone who has normal visual neural systems would have normal rather than inverted color experience.

Consider the methodology of this strategy. We begin with empirical data from our own experience about the nature of human color experience and from color science about what might plausibly realize human color experience. So we begin with two empirically informed and contingent constraints. And in a second a priori or armchair step, we reason that some assignments of that color experience to that neurophysiology, some such relations of constitution, are more antecedently plausible than others, without that yielding any a priori certainty that such relations of constitution hold, or any full understanding of how they do hold. Our belief that a particular constitution relation obtains is a posteriori, since it crucially rests on the fact that we have chosen, on admittedly a priori grounds, from a very limited set of possible candidate relations of constitution given to us

---

[20] Chalmers (1996: 99–101).
[21] Though he makes points about brown to which we will return.

a posteriori. Without those a posteriori limitations, we could never have reasoned in our armchairs to the conclusion that the true constitution relations obtain.

Hardin's specific proposal is this:[22] Some hues are 'unique'. Unique green, for instance, is the green that looks neither bluish nor yellowish. Since the neurophysiology of color vision exhibits an opponent-process organization, with a single system responsive to blue and yellow as contraries and another responsive to red and green as contraries, we might expect the phenomenal opposition of those colors as revealed by the familiar color wheel. And we might also plausibly identify the experience of unique green with the neurophysiological state that occurs when the blue-yellow system is neutral and the red-green system is tipped towards green. To put this in another and slightly less tendentious way, not any assignment of our pattern of phenomenal color experience to our neurophysiology is as antecedently plausible as another. Rather, the most plausible assignments would respect the structure of unique hues. They would assign unique hues to neurophysiological states in which one opponent-process is neutral, and the other is tipped in one direction or the other. And they would assign unique red and unique green to different states in which the same opponent-process is neutral. Likewise for unique blue and yellow. That greatly restricts plausible inversions of color experience.

Hardin tries to squeeze more out of this strategy. For instance, he suggests that since yellow seems phenomenally hotter than blue and red hotter than green, perhaps this reflects states of positive versus negative activity in appropriate opponent-process structures.[23] That seems more antecedently plausible. He also points out that there are more discriminable greens than reds, and more discriminable blues than yellows.[24] So perhaps we are down to just one possible inversion, in which unique red is inverted with unique yellow and unique blue with unique green.

[22] In fact, Hardin's view has assumed two forms. Hardin (1988: 113–86) is the original formulation, and shies away from robust claims about the constitution of the asymmetries among color primaries by physical differences. But Hardin (1997) is more confident. See *Philosophical Psychology* 4 (1991), for a symposium on Hardin (1988), esp. Hardin's exchange with Joseph Levine, 27–51.

[23] This idea is presented as speculative in Hardin (1988), and there is evidence for opponent-process cells that are active in both directions. But Hardin (1997) cites an unpublished paper by B. Katra and B. H. Wooten in support of the claim that summed averaged opponent-process cancellation data reflects the intuitive asymmetry between hot and cool colors.

[24] This was noted in Hardin (1988), but Clark was first to emphasize its significance.

But there are other exploitable asymmetries in color space and in our neurophysiology. Yellows are characteristically less saturated than reds. And indeed color-sensitive cells in the cortex apparently are more sensitive to relatively lighter yellows and darker reds.[25] For that matter, oranges and yellows shade into what seems the distinct color of brown, which isn't phenomenologically merely a blackened yellow or orange in quite the way that dark blues and greens are merely blackened blues and greens. And this may reflect the same neurophysiological asymmetry.

So perhaps we should expect, though without any a priori certainty or entailment, that someone with normal neurophysiology would have normal and not in any way inverted color experience. This suggests certain ways in which color qualia are constituted. And it rests crucially on a posteriori knowledge of the neurophysiology of color vision, as well as a kind of a priori or at least armchair reasoning that does not yield entailments.

We cannot tell what phenomenal experience some bat with an alien neurophysiology would have when in some particular foreign neural state, even if we know everything there is to know about bat neurophysiology. Whether we want to call it (as I recently implied) a posteriori knowledge that we must lack or a priori knowledge of which we are incapable, we don't know what it is like to be a bat. Still if we have a given understanding of the range and phenomenal structure of the possible sensory experience of someone, and an understanding of the range and structure of possible neurophysiological states that realize those experiences in that individual, we may be able to predict which phenomenal states are plausibly constituted by which neurophysiological states. Our overall inference is a posteriori because it involves crucial a posteriori elements, and it is quite fallible, but it is one we can make. It may reveal full-blown necessary but a posteriori relations of constitution linking internal physical states to qualitative experiences.

The best strategy for coming to an understanding of what physical states constitute what sensory experiences in normal humans is, I believe, to push something like Hardin's general strategy very hard for all features of normal human qualia that are not plausibly veridical, like the structure of unique hues. Once this initial generalization of Hardin's strategy is successful, we should take two more steps. We should treat the remaining

---

[25] Yoshioka, Dow, and Vautin (1996).

qualitative features of our normal human sensory experience in the same way. Then once we understand our qualia in that way, we should claim that they exhaust our normal sensory contents. I think that because of the asymmetries that Kripke recognized between the constitution of water by H-O-H on one hand and the constitution of qualia by their physical bases on the other, we should not expect to be able to understand how our neurophysiology constitutes our experience in quite the way we can understand how H-O-H constitutes water. But with luck we can come to another sort of understanding of the full-blown a posteriori necessities that link internal physical states with qualia, and hence with sensory contents.

I have some differences in detail with Hardin. For instance, there is some evidence that the experience even of yellow things by the red-green color blind is phenomenally different than normal experience in a relevant way. Some rare individuals possess one color normal and one color blind eye, and can introspect differences, and at least one such subject perceives the yellows seen by the color blind eye as orange.[26] So perhaps the tipping of at least a normal red-green system isn't necessary for experience of reddish hues. And while Hardin defends an orthodox conception of full-blown a posteriori necessities linking physical states and visual qualia, it is on the model of the orthodox post-Kripkean understanding of water and H-O-H, and I hold that the case of qualia is quite unique in this respect. Unlike Hardin, I do not think we can come to as good an understanding of how our neurophysiology constitutes our color experience as of how H-O-H constitutes water. But my main difference with Hardin is that I suggest that we deploy this type of account across the board, to underwrite all the differential features of the contents of our experience. I think we should generalize Hardin's attractive idea.

In this, I agree with Austen Clark.[27] But I have other detailed qualms about Clark's generalization of Hardin. Clark maintains that the sensory qualities involved in a particular sense are characterized solely by structural relations within the corresponding space of discriminable qualities, which the possession of neurophysiological states exhibiting isomorphic structure would fully explain, leaving no difficult gap in our understanding.[28] I think that this is too optimistic. One way to put my point is that Clark's view

---

[26] Kaiser and Boynton (1996: 452–5).
[27] On other modalities see Austen Clark (1993: 153–60); Mendola (1997: 129–35).
[28] Austen Clark (1993).

implies that we can develop what he calls an 'objective understanding' of the qualitative experience of a bat. We can do this by coming to understand the very abstract structure of its qualitative space, the structural relations among the qualities it 'hears' that are fixed by the discriminability and similarity of the properties it senses aurally and the location in that sensory 'space' of sensory primaries (analogous to unique hues). And he thinks that this objective understanding is adequate to defeat Thomas Nagel's worry that humans will never understand the experience of a bat.[29] But I think that such an abstract structural understanding is not enough for an understanding of what it is like to be a bat sufficient to defeat Nagel's worry. Another way to put my point is this: In Clark's proposal, *very* internal mechanisms of discrimination are what is crucial to the constitution of experience. Even possession of specific internal sensory receptor cells is apparently unnecessary. This allows Clark to claim that qualia inversion of intuitive sorts can occur consistent with his proposal, for instance when his very internal mechanisms are attached to sensory receptor cells in inverted ways.[30] But it seems to me more plausible to claim on the basis of our current limited information that the relevant sensory receptors, say the relevant cones, play a crucial role in constituting the nature of at least our human qualitative sensory experience. Some of Hardin's claims about the asymmetries that constitute experience of yellow, for instance the relevance of saturation, seem also to imply this.[31]

Very abstract structural similarity of the sort that Clark deploys seems insufficient to constitute phenomenal similarity. One way to try to show this is to present radical inversion cases, in which two creatures share qualitative spaces with the same abstract structure but involving very different sensory receptors. But different real human senses don't share enough structure, and wildly hypothetical cases are hard to comprehend. One relatively comprehensible and realistic inversion case that might make my point is this: Two creatures might have qualitative experience with exactly the same Clarkian abstract structure, but such that the experience of one was a left-right mirror inversion of the experience of the other. But

---

[29] Nagel (1974); Austen Clark (1993: 206–9). But note Clark's qualifications.
[30] Austen Clark (1993: 201). He doesn't talk explicitly about variations in connections to sensory receptor cells, but rather to 'stimuli'.
[31] Hardin (1988: 296–7).

this case wouldn't be accepted by Clark, for a reason that marks another difference with my proposal. He holds that sensory qualities are referred to real points in local space, so that the basic objects in which they are experienced as instanced must be genuine external positions.[32] He is not an internalist about sensory experience. But I think that the rudimentary spatial structure of our experience is rooted in our internal structure. For instance, I think that a mirror spatial inversion of our internal state would generate a mirror spatial inversion of our experience.

Despite my differences from Hardin and Clark, my proposal is closely modeled on their views. It simply adds together Hardin's less abstract conception of relevant structure and Clark's generality. I call the kind of view I share with Hardin and Clark a commitment to 'the modal structure architecture', and my particular variant 'Modal Structuralism', on the basis of a bad pun.

To each particular *mode* of sensation, say color vision, there corresponds a structure of alternative possible experienced properties, and at least one way to be in a state of experiencing such a property is to be in one element of a structure of alternative possible states of our human neurophysiology. There is a kind of *modal* structure shared by experienced properties and the neurophysiological basis of those possible ranges of experience. For instance, it is probably essential to the normal human experience of unique red that it be realized in a structure capable of alternatively providing the normal human experience of unique green. Green and red seem like quite distinct components of our experience, but they aren't as distinct as they seem. I also stress the importance of specific sensory receptor cells more than Clark does, and this may involve another doubly modal element: Assume that cones in particular are crucial to color experience, to that *mode* of experience. Then while actual external stimuli aren't crucial to our experience of color, the nature of those sensory receptors constitutes a range of dispositional truths about what *would* excite them that may be relevant to the constitution of our color experience.[33] In the case of sensory experience, not the external spatial or temporal environment but the internally constituted, doubly modal environment of a mental representation is crucial to its content.

---

[32] Austen Clark (2000).

[33] Perhaps not just specific sensory receptor cells but contrast relations to distinct sensory modalities are crucial to experience of the phenomenal properties characteristic of a sense.

MS does not reject the paradigmatic functionalist claim that at least some variety of physical structures may be capable of realizing a particular psychologically-relevant structure. But the opponent-organization that the modal structure architecture exploits is different than the usual causal-functional connections modeled on inference that most functionalists exploit. Another difference with paradigmatic forms of functionalism is that MS suggests that only a few privileged possible causal links between internal physical states are essential to the content of relevant mental representations. This is a kind of internalist analog of AD, since the relations constituting a particular experience are those on which other psychological relations involving such experience asymmetrically depend.

There is a standing objection to accounts like MS that claim that qualitative features of our experience are complexly constituted, and in particular that relations among qualitative features of our experience are constituted by relations among elements of the neurophysiological basis of our capacity for such forms of experience.[34] The objection is that qualia seem to be intrinsic and not relational properties of our experience.

I agree that it is natural to quickly conclude on the basis of the appearance of phenomenal green, green as we experience it, that it is an intrinsic property. But it is also just as natural to quickly conclude on the basis of the appearance of bluish purples and reddish purples that they involve objective similarities of objects out in the world. Natural quick conclusions on the basis of the appearances of colors are not alone sufficient evidence on these matters.

There is another relevant standard objection. The architecture of MS makes it an instance of 'the adverbial theory of perception', proposed by Ducasse and Chisholm.[35] According to the adverbial theory, when someone has a sensory image of something round and green, there needn't be anything round and green, but rather a certain way of experiencing. And that's what I think. This theory may seem to require an adverbial analysis of the deep logical form of sentences reporting sensory experiences that involves no quantification over particular objects experienced. And the objection is that such an analysis cannot explain proper inferences between such sentences, for instance from the claim that I sense a red triangle and a

---

[34] Levine (2001: 96–104). [35] Ducasse (1942); Chisholm (1957).

green circle to the claim that I sense something red, but not to the claim that I sense a green triangle and a red circle.[36]

There have been attempts to provide an adverbial analysis of the logical form of such sentences that supports the right inferences, but they are very controversial.[37] However, focus on the physical structures that realize our visual experience according to MS. Certainly your experience can have a complex spatial form, with green triangles and red circles experienced at various visual locations. And according to MS, any physical structure capable of realizing the experience of green triangles and red circles would also be potentially capable of realizing the experience of red triangles and green circles, and certainly of red things. But the key point is that, according to MS, the physical structures that realize experience of green triangles and red circles are not characteristically structures that also realize experience of red triangles and green circles, but they are all structures that realize the experience of red things. The proper inferences among the sentences in question are underwritten by inclusion and exclusion relations among the physical conditions that would constitute their truth.

7.4

We have focused on the metaphysics of MS, and hence on its characteristic differences from simple direct accounts. But there are also crucial semantic similarities.

Simple direct accounts hold that qualia are constituted by the representational contents of sensory experiences. I hold to the contrary that qualia constitute sensory contents. I believe in a contrary order of explanation. But there is a semantical view that simple direct accounts and MS share, which has received much recent discussion under the rubrics of 'representationalism' or 'intentionalism'.

The fifth key commitment of MS is to intentionalism, although not to a simple direct form. Both forms of intentionalism hold that all qualia are representational. Neither form factors sensory experiences into features with representational content and other features without. And so recent discussions of simple direct forms of intentionalism have developed resources relevant to my otherwise inverted proposal.

[36] Jackson (1975, 1977). [37] Tye (1984); Casullo (1987).

Begin with color. I claim that there is no difference between the qualia of an experience of a green object and the green that such an experience presents the object to have. The color we experience objects to have in the most basic sense is the kind of Aristotelian color that Galileo plausibly ridiculed as a basis for science. If, like many philosophers, you claim that your own dominant conception of green is of a property that standardly causes certain sorts of experiences in normal perceivers, then I grant that you have the ability to conceive such a sophisticated property. I even grant for the sake of argument that it plays a crucial role in your everyday thought, though frankly I don't believe that. Still, I deny that such a property is found in the what-it's-like of your visual experience, and hence deny that it is part of the characteristic content of your visual sensation. If you like, you can call the color that I am deploying merely 'phenomenal color' and your favorite objective causal property 'real color'. But it is phenomenal color that plays a basic semantic role in qualia empiricism.

This is an ancient and very natural view. Just read Aristotle. Just look out your window. And it still has at least a few contemporary adherents.[38]

I also think that such a treatment extends to all the basic elements of the contents of our sensory experience, to rudimentary spatial and temporal relations that are immediately experienced, to sounds, and smells, and the like.[39] In general, the qualitative content or what it's like of your experience provides it with a kind of success or truth-condition, though there are some complexities about how this works in detail. To put it officially and in the jargon of Part I, the qualitative content of a sensory state can match the world or fail to match the world.

What it's like to see a green circle puts real constraints on what conditions in the world can cause such an experience if it is to be suitably veridical. Indeed, some of those constraints suggest that some features of color experiences are generally false, for instance the subjective similarity of reddish purples and bluish purples. This is not what the simple direct intentionalist would say about color sensation. But there is no other way to plausibly account for the intuitive and commonsense Aristotelian resistance to the once new and shocking proposals of Galileo and his cronies. And

---

[38] Hardin (1988: 59–112); Maund (1995); Siewert (1998: 245–7).
[39] But Hill (1991: 159–85) argues that these cases cannot be assimilated.

there is no other way to plausibly account for the real semantics of many ordinary and commonsense thoughts.

The widespread resistance among contemporary philosophers, even simple direct intentionalists, to this natural and hoary view is, I believe, rooted in the worry that it implies that ordinary experience and the ordinary thoughts rooted in that experience are false at least in certain respects.

There are various ways to respond to this worry. My own response, which at a certain level of abstraction I share with simple direct intentionalists, who characteristically deploy it somewhere if not in the case of color, is this: If experience is false in some respects, it need not be false in all respects.[40] Any plausible account of sensory content must admit that there are artifacts of our experience, features of that experience that are non-veridical even if apparently representational. Push your eyes together and you will see double, but there aren't in fact two of everything you see. I just apply the admission that there are such possibilities in a more straightforward and general way, which I think is hence a more antecedently plausible way, than simple direct intentionalists, who, because of the direction of explanation they favor, have a harder time accommodating widespread artifacts of experience.

But another way to respond to the worry in question, which even simple direct intentionalists often favor in isolated cases like color, involves what seem to me to be alterations of the commonsense semantics of terms for experienced properties, or even of commonsense conceptions of what makes something true in general. I suggested in Chapter 4 that some superfine details of truth don't matter, so these are not proposals that I can dismiss out of hand. But there are no genuine differences from the commonsense notion of truth in the cases under discussion that are introduced by my official jargon 'match', and I claim to be using color terms like the common man.

The most traditional way to introduce alterations is to claim that colors of specific sorts are the standard causes of the normal human experiences of such colors. We have already seen why this involves some modification of the commonsense meaning of color terms. Otherwise Galileo and his cronies would not have put their discoveries about color perception in such a radical way, and claimed there were no colors. Aristotelians would not

---

[40] But see Mendola (1997: Part Three).

have been so resistant. Perhaps you think there was a shift in the meaning of color terms between Aristotle and the present. But then my students wouldn't be so surprised when I tell them about the differences between the objective bases of reddish purples and bluish purples. This modification also posits contents that are much too complicated and sophisticated to plausibly appear within our ordinary sensory experience.

So perhaps Brian Loar's alteration is preferable. He distinguishes between the introspectible internal intentionality of experience and its merely referential features.[41] And perhaps the first captures commonsense colors while the second respects the scientific facts. Loar says that

> I can imagine what it is like to be an isolated brain that is a physical duplicate of my own brain. What I imagine includes not just that brain's nonintentional phenomenal states, its flutters and pains, but also states and events that correspond to my own *outward-directed* thoughts and perceptions. I imagine my isolated twin's states and events as subjectively representing things *in the same manner as* those thoughts and perceptions of mine.... [T]he internal intentionality of perceptions and thoughts consists in their apparent *directedness*, in their *purporting subjectively to refer* in various complex ways.[42]

If we are permitted in Loar's case of the isolated brain to include what intervenes between our brain and skin's end, I agree that there is something like this internal intentionality in our experience. But I disagree with Loar's contention that external conditions predominate in assigning to internal intentional features of our experience particular references and truth-conditions,[43] so that his envatted twin can successfully refer to radically different things than he can, through the mediation of perceptions sharing internal intentionality with his own. Loar isn't simply considering perceptions whose content is something traditionally indirect, like 'the cause of a sensation of X type'. He rather thinks that the sensed properties are themselves given to us via internal intentionality. But he thinks that 'none of the twin brain's concepts pick out physical-objecthood or spatial properties'.[44] He presumes it to be an open question whether his twin's apparently 'spatial concepts refer to some non-standard properties and relations—e.g. properties of the visual system itself—or fail of reference entirely'.[45] But I claim that the body in the vat can only match real spatial

---

[41] Loar (2003). [42] Loar (2003: 230–1). [43] Loar (2003: 231).
[44] Loar (2003: 250). [45] Ibid.

relations through the mediation of his phenomenal spatial concepts, and that there are limits to the kinds of spatial relations that can cause various features of his spatial experience if that experience is to be veridical. If the body in a vat shares qualitative experience with Loar while Loar experiences a green tea cup or a purple igloo, but the body's experience is caused in as radically different a way as the experience of someone deceived by Descartes' evil genius, then the body's beliefs are largely false, no matter how systematic the pattern of correlations between the actual causes of the features of its experience and those features. Loar seems to be talking about the same qualia as I am, but to be motivated to a different view of their semantic significance by theoretical and case-based arguments for externalism that we have already discarded. And even if his subtle and quite unintuitive distinction between internal intentionality and reference might protect some positive value for commonsense views of color even in light of scientific developments, it is not the value that common sense presumes. His model cannot plausibly explain the disputes between Galileo and his opponents, which involved reference and truth.

One relatively moderate revisionary proposal is David Chalmers'. He suggests that even if an Aristotelian world is a kind of primary truth-condition for a color experience, it need not be the only admissible truth-condition.[46] Color claims can be true even if it is not an Aristotelian world, though in some sense an Aristotelian world is the best and central case for color claims. But this proposal is explicitly motivated by an attempt to retain truth for commonsense claims in the face of what would otherwise be contrary evidence. And that is not adequate motivation, because science has in fact shown us that our sensory experience is misleading about the world in certain ways about which common sense is affronted. Consider once more the apparent similarity of bluish purples and reddish purples. Consider the structure of unique hues. These are non-veridical artifacts of our experience, but they don't seem that way to common sense. What's more, if we are generally prepared to reinterpret commonsense claims so that they come out true in the face of otherwise contrary evidence, then we will end up insisting that God exists and that people are immortal simply because most people think so. And maybe the world once was flat.

---

[46] Chalmers (2006). This is a variant of the earlier and more ordinary proposal in Chalmers (2004b) that colors are the standard causes of certain color experiences.

Of course, many simple direct intentionalists join me in general opposition to Loar's and Chalmers' ingenious proposals, and also to traditional indirect causal stories about the semantics of terms for at least many experienced properties, even if not in the specific case of color. They think that our experience generally gives us a more or less direct access to features of the world.[47] So the rest of this section will juxtapose MS and simple direct intentionalism in cases other than color.

Various established ways of characterizing forms of intentionalism can be used to more finely specify my view. Block introduced a distinction that Byrne calls a difference between intermodal and intramodal intentionalists.[48] Only the former insist that any differences between the phenomenal content of experiences in different sense modalities are differences in representational content. Byrne also distinguishes between restricted and unrestricted intentionalists, where the first deny and the second assert that intentionalism 'applies to bodily sensations like headaches, itches, pinpricks, and orgasms'.[49] Like Byrne, I am an intermodal unrestricted intentionalist.

This company has a possible cost for me. Some of the standard objections to familiar forms of simple direct intentionalism, and especially to intermodal unrestricted intentionalism, are also objections to my view. But in fact MS can evade these objections more naturally than simple direct intentionalism.

It may seem that some obviously subjective features of our experience, for instance the painfulness of pain, are not at all analogous to allegedly representational properties of visual experience. I treat physical pains and pleasures at considerable length in *Goodness and Justice*, in a way friendly to qualia empiricism, and I also discuss there the troubling case of the itch.[50] But the short version is that pains and pleasures involve the presence in experience of a certain kind of apparent spatially-localized badness and goodness, throbbing right there in your arm or lips. Unlike orthodox simple direct intentionalists, I don't think that the content of pain is bodily damage per se, and this makes my view less subject to objection on grounds that many pains don't represent such damage. But the spatiality of physical pains and pleasures does plausibly underwrite their possession of representational content.

---

[47] Defense of intentionalism includes Tye (2000); Byrne (2001).
[48] Block (1996); Byrne (2001: 205).   [49] Byrne (2001: 205).
[50] Mendola (2006a: 139–83).

Christopher Peacocke has developed a number of more obviously world-directed cases that seem to spell trouble for intentionalism generally. Perhaps his most revealing case is this: 'Suppose you are standing on a road which stretches from you in a straight line to the horizon. There are two trees at the roadside, one a hundred yards from you, the other two hundred. Your experience represents these objects as being of the same physical height and other dimensions; that is, taking your experience at face value you would judge that the trees are roughly the same physical size.'[51] But there is surely something different in your experience of the two trees. This suggests to Peacocke that there is a kind of non-representational content in which your experience of the two trees differs.

Like simple direct intentionalists, I claim to the contrary that your experience of the two trees differs in a kind of representational content. But the exact nature of the difference on my view is much simpler, and I claim for that reason preferable, to standard proposals. MS can admit the existence of widespread non-veridical artifacts in our experience. But simple direct intentionalists must stretch and strain to treat cases so that they involve as few non-veridical artifacts as possible, because of the direction of explanation that they pursue. It leads them to make implausibly complex claims about the nature of some raw sensory contents.

Christopher Hill suggests this:

It is possible to say that Peacocke's two trees look to be the same size and also that the first tree looks larger than the second. These statements are compatible because 'looks' involves a different adverbial modifier in the first statement than it does in the second. When we say that the two trees look to be the same size, we mean that they look the way trees that are the same size look when they are seen from different distances. And when we say that the first tree looks larger than the second, we mean that the first tree looks roughly the way that a tree that is larger than the second tree would look if it were the same distance from the observer of the second tree. It is clear that there is no incompatibility here.[52]

Michael Tye makes a second suggestion and reports a third:

[T]he experience represents the nearer tree as having a facing surface that differs in its view-point relative size from the facing surface of the further tree, even though it also represents two trees as having the same viewpoint-independent size. The

[51] Peacocke (1983: 12).   [52] Hill (1991: 199).

nearer tree (or its facing surface) is represented as being *larger from here*, while also being represented as the same objective size as the further tree.... Frank Jackson has suggested... [that t]he two trees look the same objective size, but the nearer tree looks nearer.[53]

But I hold that in the most primitive sense of phenomenal visual size, relevant to the raw content of visual experience in this case, the second tree looks smaller, period. It seems progressively smaller in that sense as you back away. It is just that we are so accustomed to this particular artifact of our visual (but not tactile) experience, that our judgments correct almost automatically for this fact. Indeed, if we were holding on to an object as it recedes, the overall content of our complete sensory experience might overrule the raw visual component.

We have complex spatial-visual capacities to which we will return in Section 7.6, which make the tendencies underlying this correction in judgments central in a very basic way to our capacity for many common thoughts. As Peacocke says, we would *judge* that the trees are of the same height. But that is not, as he also says, a matter of taking our experience at face value, but rather of being quite used to the way in which we should not take our visual experience at face value. While there aren't the sophisticated complexities in raw visual experience that Hill, Tye, and Jackson propose, which seem motivated by a desire to preserve the veridicality of visual experience, still much of what they say about how the trees look does plausibly capture how we immediately judge or are disposed to judge objective sizes on the basis of our visual experience of the trees.[54]

Despite what I've said about the trees, I do not deny that there is some depth present in our visual experience. Consider another of Peacocke's cases, 'an example in which a wire framework in the shape of a cube is viewed with one eye and is seen first with one of its faces in front, the face parallel to this face being seen as behind it, and is then suddenly seen, without any change in the cube or alteration of its position, with that former face now behind the other.'[55] I think that this aspect switch involves a difference in the qualitative and hence representational content of visual

---

[53] Tye (2000: 78–9).
[54] My criticism of course presumes that by 'experience' is meant the content of sensation.
[55] Peacocke (1983: 16).

experience, though it is clearly causally responsive to our judgments. There is a qualitative similarity between our experience before and after the switch, but not an identity.[56] To put it colorfully, visual sense data bulge in a limited way. And if they bulge in the wrong way because of a mistaken judgment, that can generate another sort of non-veridical artifact in our experience.

Another of Peacocke's cases is this: 'When you see a two-dimensional array of elements as grouped in columns rather than rows, your experience has the... content that certain elements that are in fact vertically arranged are collinear. But there need not be any difference in [representational content] between the case in which the array is seen as grouped in columns and that in which it is seen as grouped in rows.'[57] But I claim that there is a difference in the qualitative and hence representational content of experience in these cases, somewhat analogous to the difference that occurs when something becomes the center of one's visual attention. But this also involves a difference in visual experience that we learn quickly to disregard as a mere artifact, since we know there is no ghostly difference in the array of objects when it shifts in our experience from one grouping to the other.

Simple direct intentionalism does not factor, and that is one advantage it shares with MS. But simple direct intentionalism cannot admit such a straightforward treatment of cases like these, because it is not hospitable to widespread non-veridical artifacts of experience. That is one relative advantage of MS.

7.5

The internally determinate qualia deployed by MS are potentially shared by veridical perceptions, hallucinations, and sensory illusions. They can match or fail to match features of the world.

There are mind-based externalist theories that we have yet to consider, which are in various ways less reductive than both MS and the mind-based externalist theories that we have discussed. And they also constitute objections to this simple intentionalism of MS.

---

[56] I also favor this analysis of Siewert's case of experience of a trompe l'oeil painting before and after discovery that it is an illusion. See Siewert (1998: 230–1).

[57] Peacocke (1992: 79).

First, some claim that knowledge is a more basic mental state than belief or experience, that for instance mere belief is a kind of failed knowledge, so that the very existence of belief perhaps requires the existence of knowledge.[58] Since knowledge requires truth, and truth often involves external conditions, knowledge is frequently a mental state for which no internalist account is plausible. And so this may be grounds for externalism. Perhaps even experience aims at knowledge in some way that requires externalism. Perhaps sensory content is richly and crucially teleological in this way, contrary to MS.

One proponent of the conception that knowledge is basic is Gilbert Harman. He says this: 'The most primitive psychological notions are not belief and desire but rather knowledge and successful intentional action. Belief and intention are generalizations of knowledge and success that allow for mistake and failure. We conceive a creature as believing things by conceiving it as at least potentially knowing things, and similarly for intention.'[59]

But this is not an adequate theoretical basis for externalism, because these claims are consistent with internalism. Internalists need not deny that creatures potentially or even actually know things. And even if we are able to conceive of a creature as believing something only by our being able to conceive of it as potentially or even actually knowing that, still that doesn't imply that conceiving of the creature as believing something requires that it or anyone actually knows that. People believe things that are false, and which hence no one knows. And if Harman is only claiming that someone could only believe something if they knew something else, still even internalists need not deny that belief requires knowledge of internal states. What's more, the notion of Euclidean flat space is a more primitive notion than the notion of the curved space of General Relativity, which is indeed plausibly rooted in a generalization of that more primitive notion, but that doesn't imply there is any Euclidean flat space. A desire for immortality aims at immortality, and the notion of a desire for immortality is conceptually dependent on the notion of immortality. And yet it is certainly consistent to believe that there are such desires and no immortality.

Nevertheless, perhaps there are legitimate theoretical grounds for externalism in the arguments that support this position. Harman's own arguments

---

[58] For a survey, see Gibbons (2006b).   [59] Harman (1999: 226).

are versions of arguments we have already considered and dismissed,[60] but other proponents of the claim that knowledge is basic have other arguments.

Timothy Williamson argues that if knowledge is unanalyzable in terms of necessary and sufficient conditions including belief, it will be possible to provide a case in which knowledge is causally and hence explanatorily inequivalent to belief plus other non-knowledge conditions, for instance truth and justification.[61] Hence there are probably actions under certain characterizations that only knowledge, if it is unanalyzable, will explain. But we should not be surprised, especially in light of the standard externalist response to the Argument from Explanation to which we will return in the next chapter, that by broadening or narrowing an *explanans* we will broaden or narrow its potential *explananda*. So this is insufficient grounds for externalism.[62]

Still, John Gibbons presses the point.[63] Perhaps the proper explanations of *all* intentional actions (rather than of intentions or attempts) characteristically involve not just beliefs and desires, but knowledge.

You might intend to run over your uncle, and this may lead you to back your car out of your driveway to drive to his house. But if, unknown to you, your uncle is napping behind the wheels of your car, you will run him over; but you will not, in this case, run him over on purpose. Your intention to A is causally related to your A-ing, but not in the right way, so you do not intentionally A.... You correctly believe that backing out of your driveway will lead to running over your uncle. Given your plan, the belief, we may say, is justified. But the belief does not constitute knowledge. If it is just an accident that your belief is true, and if you act on the belief, then it will just be an accident that your attempts are successful, if they are successful at all. To get intentional action, your means-ends beliefs must constitute knowledge.[64]

But note that it is uncontroversial that the truth of means-ends beliefs is often a necessary part of the full explanation of an intentional action rooted in those beliefs, and that truth is characteristically external. You wouldn't have intentionally gotten back to the barn if your beliefs about a passable route had been mistaken. And these uncontroversial facts are not enough to show that internalism is false. Ditto for Gibbon's story.

---

[60] Harman (1999: 226). [61] Williamson (2000).
[62] For difficulties with Williamson's treatment of experience, see Mendola (2007).
[63] Gibbons (2001b; 2006b). [64] Gibbons (2006b: 90).

The recently popular claim that knowledge is more basic than belief does not really imply that externalism is true, let alone that MS is false, nor is it supported by arguments that show that. Indeed, the claim that belief or sensation aims at knowledge in particular is in tension with the even more popular claim that we can know things merely by hearing them from others, since we prefer to consult real experts who haven't merely heard things. And our worries about details of truth from Part I suggest that knowledge, which implies truth, sometimes involves dark details that are not and should not be of any psychological significance. So let's turn to other mind-based externalisms.

There is a classical argument that entwines considerations of sensation and cognition in a way that may support externalism. In some of its developments, it also suggests a different account of the content of experience than MS. This is the 'Refutation of Idealism' that Kant added to the second edition of *The Critique of Pure Reason*.[65] The refutation is addressed to the skeptic of Descartes' First Meditation. There Descartes considers the possibility that all his sensory experience is mere illusion, like a dream or the hallucination of a madman, while yet he can certainly know himself to exist as a thinking thing. And the refutation aims to 'prove the existence of objects in space outside' on at least roughly the basis of such a Cartesian consciousness of one's own existence.[66] This suggests externalism, even about experience.

Unfortunately, this argument is an even deeper exegetical tangle than the Private Language Argument. Kant himself was sufficiently dissatisfied by his presentation of the refutation to amend it by a long note to the preface of the second edition.[67] And even so, he continued to work on the argument after the second edition appeared.[68] It is clear that any reconstruction of the refutation is by necessity highly interpretative. But however the exegetical details turn out, Kant's argument should be read so that its conclusion is consistent with his very characteristic transcendental idealism about space and time, about persisting objects outside in space. It seems that, according to Kant, experience can meet conditions sufficient for self-consciousness and such that it is as of persisting objects in space, even if there aren't in fact any real objects out there with that nature. What

---

[65] Kant (1998: 326–9: B274–B279). [66] Kant (1998: 327: B275).
[67] Kant (1998: 116–22: Bxxix–Bxli). [68] Kant (1998: 72).

is out there according to Kant, the thing in itself, is neither spatial nor temporal. And this suggests that Kant's refutation does not really support externalism of the sort with which we are concerned. Perhaps there must be *some* noumenal world out there if Kant is right, and just conceivably that is a conclusion of the refutation, but if that commitment is all that is required to be an externalist, then externalism is trivially true, and trivial. Of course, the refutation is aimed at the First Meditation. And a reading like this may suggest that Kant's argument cannot connect with Descartes. But perhaps we are supposed to see by the refutation that the skeptical meditator is attempting to entertain a situation (that during ordinary experience—experience meeting all ordinary tests of coherence, regularity, and stability—he is yet a dreamer or a madman) that he cannot coherently believe, since he also must take himself to be aware of objects in space, whether or not there really are any.

This quick way with Kant's argument is obviously not the last word on the subject. We will return to work stemming from the refutation in Section 7.6, where it will help elaborate the proper response to the final mind-based theory that we need to consider.

That is the disjunctive theory of perception or experience, originally developed by Hinton and Snowdon.[69] It holds that the contents of veridical experiences are object-dependent, in the sense that they involve the very objects perceived. But it also holds that perceptual illusions and hallucinations are not object-dependent. There is no single mental state with a single content that can be present in hallucinations and veridical experiences, contrary to MS. Hence the disjunction. And externalism is required by this treatment of veridical experience.

Some disjunctivists, for instance Putnam, deny that hallucinations and perceptual illusions can be phenomenally indistinguishable from veridical perceptions.[70] But this is implausible, since then we could introspect that the similarity of reddish purples and bluish purples is merely apparent. Then we could introspect our color blindness. Most disjunctivists more plausibly maintain that in such cases there are two very distinct sorts of mental states which are yet phenomenally indistinguishable. For instance, M. G. F. Martin has developed the claim that there are hallucinations

[69] Hinton (1973); Snowdon (1980–1, 1990, 1992).   [70] Putnam (1999).

and illusions that are indiscriminable from veridical experiences, but have different contents.[71] And even the contents of two veridical perceptual states directed at distinct but completely indistinguishable objects would differ according to most disjunctivists.

I, to the contrary, hold that perceptual illusions and hallucinations can share one sort of basic semantic content with veridical experiences, a kind of putative object-directedness, and that veridical experiences of indistinguishable objects can share the same such content. I think that phenomenal indiscriminability, perhaps specifically Martin's 'indiscriminability through reflection', is good test for sameness of sensory content. Something like this has also been suggested by Martin Davies.[72]

Disjunctivists have proposed a variety of arguments for their alternative. Some are distant from our concerns. Bill Brewer suggests that veridical perceptual beliefs provide epistemic reasons that phenomenally indistinguishable perceptual illusions do not.[73] This is not obvious to me,[74] but in any case in the next part I grant that there may be epistemically relevant differences that are not a matter of a difference in mental states, that you can have different evidence if you simply have something else in your pocket. But all this seems irrelevant to internalism in philosophy of mind.

Still, one cluster of arguments for disjunctivism is central to our topic. One foundational text is John McDowell's claim that without object-dependent contents 'there is a serious question about how it can be that experience, conceived from its own point of view, is not blank or blind, but purports to be revelatory of the world we live in'.[75] He also says that otherwise it is all darkness in the interior.[76]

McDowell's primary physicalist target is the internalist component of views that factor content into internally determinate conceptual or functional roles on the one hand, and, on the other, genuinely representational contents delivered by externalist mechanisms that we have already dismissed.[77] But my proposal has a very different form, with qualia rather than darkness inside. What's more, since the force of McDowell's charge resides in metaphors, the same metaphors that are often used to express the nature of zombies, it is more a challenge than an argument.

[71] Martin (2004: 74–81).   [72] Davies (1991).   [73] Brewer (1999: 232).
[74] But see Sturgeon (2000: ch. 1).   [75] McDowell (1998: 243).
[76] McDowell (1998: 250).   [77] Like McGinn (1982).

But the challenge has been developed into arguments by William Child and John Campbell.[78] Child worries that views like MS treat 'experiences as states of a type whose intrinsic mental features are world-independent;...mak[ing]...no reference to anything external to the subject. But if that is what experience is like...how can it so much as put us in position to think about [an objective world beyond experience]?'[79] But, I reply, there are two senses of world-independence in question. My view is that experience is as of a world of external objects, but isn't constituted by those external objects. And it is the first sort of object-involvement that is semantically crucial, not the second sort on which Child fastens.

Still, perhaps the question is how this is possible. Campbell says this: 'Experience of objects has to explain how it is that we can have the conception of objects as mind-independent.... On [views like MS], all that experience of the object provides...is a conscious image of the object. The existence of the conscious image is in principle independent of the existence of the external object. The existence of the image, though, is dependent on the existence of the subject who has the conscious image. So if your conception of the object was provided by your experience of the object, you would presumably end by concluding that the object could not have existed had you not existed, and that the object exists only when you are perceiving it. We cannot extract the conception of a mind-independent world from a mind-dependent image.'[80] But I reply that the content of the experience is what is semantically relevant, not the state that has the content, and that according to MS it is not a part of the content of a sensory state that it is mind-dependent. Campbell admits this possibility, but further complains that for sensory content to be intentional in this way requires the assimilation of sensation to thought. But I do not mean 'intentional' in this restrictive way. I think that sensation has content that is object-directed without sensation being thought.

Yet, despite my quibbles about the details of these arguments, the guts of the puzzle may seem untouched. How can the qualia delivered by MS be about the world? Consider a case. I claim that the content of a visual experience can present a kind of spatial pattern of colored

---

[78] Child (1994: 140–77); Campbell (2002a) and (2002b: 114–31).
[79] Child (1994: 146–7). [80] Campbell (2002a: 135).

shapes. And I claim that such a pattern might match the world or not. Campbell complains of Locke's analogous invocation of resemblance that '[t]his desperate manoeuvre has no hope of success, and Berkeley's stricture, that there can be no intrinsic resemblance between an idea and a physical property, seems perfectly reasonable'.[81]

But there is no obvious reason to think that the content of an experience and a thing in the world cannot both involve the same properties. Aristotle certainly thought that color just as we experience it is out in the world, and even an adverbial account of the realization of our color experience is consistent with Aristotelian color being out there. Some might worry that the world is not at all how we experience it to be. But that is not a happy position for disjunctivists, who think that veridical perception is open to the world.

So what is the worry? Perhaps that the spatial array of colors present in visual experience according to MS will not focus specifically on any particular pattern of things out in the world. If experience has the kind of content I have suggested, then it may not seem that it can reach out to particular objects in the world, and it may even seem that sensory images could as well be mere daydreams as immediate perceptions directed on the immediate environment. This worry requires more mechanism of qualia empiricism.

7.6

Sensations are not the only mental states that are not mediated by language. And thoughts without language can answer the worry of the disjunctivists, partly through resources explored by the Strawsonian tradition of Kant interpretation.

It is useful to distinguish several layers of such thoughts.

First is a kind of proto-judgment closely tied to immediate experience and action, which embeds visual experience in a certain way. But begin with visual experience itself.

The shapes and colors present in the contents of immediate visual sensation themselves have spatial and temporal relations. The temporal

---

[81] Campbell (2002a: 129).

relations present in that experience over time plausibly correspond to temporal relations of the physical states that realize the experience. Perhaps also some features of the spatial relations present in that experience are dependent on spatial relations in realizing structures. But a more important point for current purposes is that the raw sensory content of visual experience has a kind of generality; it is plausibly shared by the experience of physical duplicates. And it is also important that, as we saw in our discussion of Peacocke, the rudimentary spatiality of visual sensation involves a kind of deformation of any spatial structure plausibly found in the world itself. These facts invite our disjunctivist worry. Such content is not obviously focused on a particular region of the world, and it misrepresents the space of the world.

Still, there are other senses, and also motor capacities. Tactile experience has a more obviously three-dimensional spatial structure, focused on objects that are available to the internalist. And we can also move our bodies and limbs in ways that constitute a crucial internalist resource. These capacities are entwined with our visual experience in the kind of proto-judgment that was already suggested by our discussion of Peacocke. As I reach out to catch a red frisbee or a wafting green umbrella, there is no real mystery about what positions in the world I take the experienced colors to occupy. My limbs are an internalist resource, and occupy positions in the world that I can even sense from the inside.

There is a type of generality possessed by even the contents of the thoughts these capacities allow us. If you were moved about in the world or rotated while preserving your internal physical states, your thoughts would retain the spatial contents in question. Such contents have a kind of egocentric spatial structure, which moves with you. Catching two indistinguishable frisbees would involve no differences in content of this sort. And hallucinations or perceptual illusions of frisbees could also share the relevant content. On the other hand, your physical twin, made of different particles, might be said to share such content with you, but also to differ in another sort of internally determinate content because of those internal differences. That last point will be relevant later.

In proto-judgment, the colors you experience are projected to particular locations in the world relative to the orientation and location of your body, and so the content of the proto-judgment matches the world or fails to match. And this is sufficient to answer the worry of the disjunctivists. Even if the umbrella and frisbee are yet out of reach, you can be prepared to catch them in a certain way or to run and get them by certain movements of your limbs, which allows some extension of the relevant projections even out beyond immediate action, and out beyond the moment.

It is controversial to claim that there can be full-blown thought without language. But even such a fervid fan of linguistic mediation as Michael Dummett has recognized this first layer of proto-judgments, and noted some relevant details: 'The sublinguistic level of proto-thought is essentially spatial... [b]ut it is also essentially dynamic.... For this reason... we observe objects as differentiated according to the general type of material of which they consist: whether they are rigid or flexible, elastic, brittle or plastic, cohesive like a lump of sugar or a heap of grains like caster sugar,... and so forth. The reason that we use visual cues to project these properties, even though unaided vision does not disclose them, is precisely that they bear on the dynamic possibilities.'[82]

While it is not needed to answer the main disjunctivist worry, there is also a second layer of relevant, word-free thoughts. If, like most but not all humans, you have visual imagery as well as motor imagery, you can practice a catch in imagination before you make it. You can imagine acting in certain ways given certain visual experiences. Call your ability to do this 'the primary imagination'.

The disjunctivist M. G. F. Martin thinks that the existence of such a faculty is grounds for a new objection to intentionalism.[83] He plausibly claims that we imagine things from a point of view, say with something to the left and something else to the right. But he further claims that this implies that visual imagination is an imagination of someone's experiencing something. Because there is a difference between experiencing something and its being there, he then concludes that the intentionalist, unlike the disjunctivist, cannot properly explain how such a visual imagination is taken to be of what is seen in imagination. Why is this? Because, he also plausibly assumes, the intentionalist must explain the apparent presence in actual sensory experience of the world itself as due not to the presence of an actual object but rather to a certain way of taking that experience, as genuine experience of a world rather than mere imagination. And in the case of visual imagination we cannot take an experience as genuine veridical

---

[82] Dummett (1993a: 124). See also Dummett (1993b: 148–9).   [83] Martin (2002).

experience in that way. But yet we do take the imagined experience to be veridical within the imagined realm, so to speak. It is that last point which the intentionalist allegedly cannot explain.

But, I reply, this just points to some details of the proper intentionalism. First, visual imagination may involve a point of view, but it doesn't present something as involving experience per se. Second, the taking of such an exercise in imagery as the imagination of *experience* of the thing experienced is the dependent mode, which requires an explicit response to the imagery in question, say a proto-judgment. Visual sensation and hence visual imagery has the content as of the object perceived, albeit implicitly from a point of view because of the spatial artifacts present in visual experience relative to its projection in proto-judgment.

The primary imagination provides you with the capacity for thoughts with contents like the proto-judgments of the first layer, but which you do not take to be true. However, it also helps provide resources for a capacity for thoughts you take to be true in a different way, thoughts which hence match other bits of the world or other times than those you currently occupy. This involves a complex third layer of thoughts unmediated by words.

Even without the mediation of language, we seem capable of thoughts of relatively complex concrete worlds or scenarios with three spatial dimensions as well as a temporal dimension and with various properties in various locations, which outrun anything that would fit within the experience of a moment. We also seem so capable of the conception of various paths through such a world, various persisting concrete objects which take various paths, various ways things would seem if we moved around in certain ways or the objects moved around in certain ways. We can even so conceive the dark side of a moon that seems from here green-tinged 'like a drifting dolphin's eye seen through a lapping wave'.[84] Though this is somewhat more doubtful, it would appear that we are even so capable of explicitly conceiving ourselves and our fellows in the guise of things that move through the world and have various experiences of it.

Thought that is not mediated by words can yet have a kind of fact-like complexity. It is not primarily the kind of discursive complexity found in

[84] Hardy (1998).

a linguistic proposition, though something like that may become involved when we think of persisting concrete objects with changing properties. It is primarily a kind of spatio-temporal complexity. And partly through that complexity it can match or fail to match the world.

Even in the third layer, the most obvious sorts of thoughts involve egocentric spatio-temporal structures with the same sort of generality as the first layer of proto-judgments. We are also somehow capable of conceiving concrete situations that we ourselves do not occupy, more objective conceptions of a world we do occupy, and a kind of individuality that is introduced into our thought by our differences from physical twins and 'dthat'. But for the moment we can leave unresolved whether these sorts of contents are available without the mediation of language. Perhaps even our conception of ourselves and our fellows involves word-mediation. But I doubt it.

I will develop some details of my crude sketch of the third layer in the next part. But some of its more controversial elements can also be fleshed out by reference to the Strawsonian tradition of Kant interpretation, and its treatment of the Refutation of Idealism. Kant was not an externalist and did not maintain that thought required the mediation of language. But while many in the Strawsonian tradition do not agree, this element of their views is not what is crucial.

Strawson himself reads the refutation as suggesting that a certain sort of self-consciousness requires experience of continuing objects distinct from the self.[85] This seems plausible, as long as we maintain with Kant that it is awareness *as of* relatively permanent distinct objects and a continuing self, rather than awareness of *actual* relatively permanent distinct objects and a continuing self, that is crucial. To be aware of oneself as having certain experiences may require being aware that sometimes one's experience is of objects that yet may also exist unexperienced, or at least exist in a form that is different than experience suggests. At some moments, one's experience and the object coincide, and at some moments, they do not. And the notions of both an object that is independent of one's experience and of one's experience as a psychological state of oneself plausibly are correlative notions, which depend on one another, as suggested by that second sort of moment.

[85] Strawson (1966: 125–32).

A second relevant reading of the refutation is due to Jonathan Bennett. It does not focus, like Strawson's, on the need for a difference between one's own sensation of an object and the object itself, but rather on the need for a difference between one's memories and facts about one's past experience.[86] This reconstruction also seems to me to capture a plausible mechanism that is Kantian in spirit. And by its focus on the past it better captures that particular element of Kant's obscure formulations.

Strawson's reading stresses the kind of objectivity that involves a possible difference between one's own experience and the object of one's experience. Other people are not involved. One concern of the next part, Wittgenstein's Private Language Argument, in some interpretations stresses the kind of objectivity that involves a possible difference between one's own experience and that of other people. Bennett's reconstruction involves a kind of intersubjectivity within the subject, across time, which puts it midway between Strawson's reconstruction of Kant (which involves no intersubjectivity) and Wittgenstein's argument (which involves multiple subjects who are different people).

John Campbell develops an interrelation between certain aspects of the two forms of objectivity introduced by Strawson and Bennett and another form involving the conception of the self from the outside, rather than from the inside as in Bennett.[87] Campbell says of the first two forms that there 'is a kind of objectivity possible in spatial thinking that has to do with the possibility of assigning causal significance to spatial properties and relations at a reflective level removed from the immediate practical demands of interaction with one's surroundings. This kind of reflective or objective spatial thinking turns out to be demanded by thought about the past, about the history of oneself and one's surroundings.'[88] But he further claims that the capacity to understand the first person as an objective entity in the physical world is intertwined with this framework, and involves 'grasp of the two dimensions of one's causal structure [as an entity with a history which affects its present and which has effects on other things] and also its connection with self-knowledge and ordinary social interaction'.[89]

As I said, my belief is that the third layer of thoughts unmediated by words sometimes includes such advanced sorts of objectivity. And one

---

[86] Bennett (1966: 202–18). [87] Campbell (1999).
[88] Campbell (1999: 2). [89] Ibid.

way to develop such a conception would be by juxtaposition with José Luis Bermúdez' work, in which the Strawsonian tradition intersects with empirical psychology, and in which Strawsonian mechanisms are freed of any reliance on linguistic mediation.[90] But because of our special interests, I will focus for now on another possibly worrisome point about these otherwise attractive resources.

Kant was a transcendental idealist, and hence not an externalist. But, as I've said, the Strawsonian tradition often has externalist trappings, and so my invocation of this literature may seem to suggest new mind-based grounds for externalism. All of the Strawsonian mechanisms that we have considered are in fact capable of internalist variants that involve the mere awareness as of objects. But there are contrary arguments.

Gareth Evans' *The Varieties of Reference* develops Strawson's understanding of Kant in such a way that our thought of objects is supposed to crucially require a capacity for a kind of fundamental identification of persisting objects in a space in which we are also located.[91] And that is supposed to involve real persisting objects in real space. And Evans provides some arguments for this externalist conception.

Kant would have claimed that one can have a demonstrative thought as of a specific material object with certain experienced properties even in the absence out in the noumenal world of such a distinct object, and that in general the identity of thoughts is independent of the identity of objects out in that real world. But Evans claimed that, in the absence of a real object out in the world, a putative demonstrative thought could at most, like a similar hallucination, involve merely a failed demonstrative thought, no real thought at all. And he made similar points about the identity of thoughts. Consider a case involving a persisting place:

A person might lie in bed in hospital thinking repeatedly 'how hot it was here yesterday'—supposing himself to be stationary in the dark. But his bed might be very well oiled, and be pulled by strings, so that every time he has what he takes to be the same thought, he is in fact thinking of a different place, and having a different thought. It is ... essential, for us to have the ability to think of places in the demonstrative way that we do, that in fact we do not usually get moved about in this way very often.[92]

---

[90] Bermúdez (1998, 2003).   [91] Evans (1982: 89–301).
[92] Evans (1982: 201–2).

But we should oppose the dark doctrine of failed thoughts. You and I can share experience of even a particular green fir tree projected as a hologram, indeed even though it isn't a representation of a real tree, indeed even though nothing in the world is green, indeed even though nothing in the world is a tree. Of course, it may be that demonstrative thought of a particular green fir tree distinct from all other qualitatively indistinguishable trees requires linguistic mediation. And perhaps to share a reference in the case of the hologram requires a shared source, which is external, or at least causal interaction. But that does not imply the existence of an objective *referent* of the experience. There is perhaps no particular green fir tree out there in the world. On such a non-referential basis, we can even share a demonstrative thought that *that* tree is green. So we have more than merely Evans' failed thoughts in such a case. What's more, if Kant's conception of transcendental idealism were true, our shared demonstrative thoughts would generally be just like that. And indeed even weaker conditions would suffice for more than mere failed thoughts. Even causally unconnected hallucinations of the same sort of tree can share one sort of intuitive general content. And an individual hallucination without an external source can even have one kind of internally determinate demonstrative content, so that now—or even later today if we allow consideration of your individual history—you can refer to a specific one of the two pine trees that you hallucinate at this moment.

Each day as the earth spins, revolves around the sun, and speeds around the center of our galaxy which is itself rapidly moving in space, we are all quite like the man on Evans' slippery bed. Or at least our flat-earther ancestors were. No matter how comforting it would be for philosophers, who in our specialized world sometimes lack an adequate understanding of physics, we cannot develop transcendental arguments that limit the ability of the physical sciences to tell us shocking things about the nature of the world we inhabit. If General Relativity and Quantum Mechanics tell us that there are no spatial or temporal relations of the commonsense sort that Evans' theory of reference requires, but there remains the experience of such relations that we know we have, then that mere experience will have to suffice to help constitute our relevant thoughts. If someday physics tells us that Kant was right to think, though for the wrong reasons, that there are no temporal and spatial relations of the sort that he denied of things in themselves,[93] then still there surely is our experience as of persisting objects in space.

Externalism may be rooted in the constitution of one's thoughts by external objects generally, or by other people in particular. In this part, we have been considering mind-based externalisms, which naturally focus most on the former possibility. To consider theoretical arguments for social externalism, and to properly understand the bearing of intersubjectivity among different people on thought and externalism, it is natural to turn now to the public medium of language, and to language-based externalisms. This will also involve a natural shift in our vantage point, from one person on the inside looking out at the world as in the Refutation of Idealism, to people on the outside looking in at another person as in radical interpretation. But it will also involve looking at oneself.

---

[93] Mendola (1997: Part Three) argues that these are not idle possibilities.

PART III

Language-Based Externalism and Thought Content

8

Private Language and Privileged Access

The positive role of this part is to sketch qualia empiricism's third component: Non-Epistemic Internalism or NEI. NEI is an internalist account of our capacities for thoughts beyond experience that can bridge qualia and rigidified description clusters. But this part also has negative roles. It will critically survey language-based externalism and its theoretical motivations, and also examine the standard objection to an important semantic role for qualia: Wittgenstein's Private Language Argument. These roles are linked. The Private Language Argument is an important theoretical rationale for language-based externalism. And theoretical mechanisms developed by language-based externalists have internalist echoes in NEI.

8.1

The word-free thoughts of Section 7.6 are key elements of NEI. But we need a better sense of them. In particular, we need to see how capacities for such thoughts aid RDC, and help constitute word-mediated thoughts to which RDC does not apply. Chapter 10 gathers together these and other features of NEI, developed dialectically throughout this part.

NEI is a double modulation of familiar externalist proposals. First, standard accounts of thought beyond experience crucially deploy epistemic notions. They focus on knowledge, justified belief, or good evidence. But I will urge a withdrawal from this 'epistemicism'. A shift of focus to mere belief or even idle imagining is required. Perhaps belief requires evidence, but certainly not good evidence. And in any case our most central focus is the conditions required for thought contents, not specific kinds of thoughts, not even mere beliefs.

Second, there are various externalist resources on the outside of the convoluted surface of an individual, but they frequently have internalist echoes inside, and externalist resources in the past often have internalist echoes in the present. Outside there are colored objects with spatial and temporal complexity, but inside there are color qualia and Strawsonian mechanisms. By exploiting symmetries like these, I will hijack the detailed theoretical imagination of externalists for my internalist ends. My positive sketch of NEI will involve mechanisms adopted with variation—often inversion—from externalists.

This positive goal explains my general negative strategy towards externalist motivations in this part: co-option. Our topic is vast, but it helps that we won't be trying to build some new city, even out of old boards and bricks, but simply holding up a mirror to an old one. I will accept the core motivations for various externalist mechanisms, but divert them towards support of internalist analogs.

It is natural to believe that at least many of our thoughts are mediated by the words in which we formulate such thoughts, by which I mean that our outer or inner speech is part of what constitutes such thoughts. But words have meanings in public languages, with many speakers. They reflect and refract many different perspectives of many different people. Because natural languages are in various ways outside the speaker, their importance to thought suggests grounds for externalism. And this vague worry can be made precise in various ways that constitute theoretical objections to internalism.

Some of Part I's externalist cases suggest that when individual speakers misunderstand or incompletely understand the public meanings of words in natural languages, they yet retain capacity for thought mediated by those words that reflects their public meanings. But of course incomplete understanding or misunderstanding also suggest individual differences in thought. And RDC can deal with those cases.

RDC also suggests an immediate generalization. While it is characteristic of language-based externalism to hold that *all* mental states inherit their content from the meaning of public languages, even an honest internalist should grant that *some* of our thoughts are plausibly mediated by words that we say to ourselves or out loud. But while our complex social environment is causally responsible for our individual capacities for meaningful speech, and while some aspects of language meaning are public phenomena, it is not obvious that any facts that *constitute* my individual speech as *relevantly* meaningful are outside my skin. Perhaps rather our individual and internally determinate speech dispositions—our dispositions to say thus and so under various actual and hypothetical conditions, perhaps even to say thus and so in our mind's ear and throat in the presence of various actual and hypothetical qualitative experiences—are sufficient to constitute our individual speech as at least meaningful enough to mediate our thought. Or perhaps they are sufficient when augmented with other internal resources.

Still, to many externalists this moderate conception will seem wrongheaded, and for reasons worth considering. The first two chapters of this part will critically examine these theoretical motivations for language-based externalism, along with prominent theories with which they are entwined. There are three parallel ways in which my negative discussion of language-based externalist theories is organized.

The first reflects disputes about the nature of linguistic meaning, and hence the contents that word-mediation contributes to thought. The two dominant views of linguistic meaning focus on truth-conditions of sentences and on their conditions of proper use.

There is variation within the truth-condition tradition. Russell, and Wittgenstein in the *Tractatus*, held that two true sentences are characteristically made true by distinct facts, that a true sentence says something that corresponds to a particular fact, while a false sentence does not.[1] But Frege held that all true sentences refer to a single entity: The True.[2] And Davidson was hostile to facts in a way more obviously hospitable to physicalism. Even friends of facts have disputes. Some externalists focus on the actual referents of sentence terms, while the *Tractatus* introduced a concern with conditions that *would* make a sentence true.

The match of sensory contents, proto-judgments, and Strawsonian spatial thoughts to the world involves a correspondence analogous to that suggested by the *Tractatus*, though involving spatial rather than discursive complexity. And RDC extends this model to thoughts mediated by terms that purport to refer, by developing resources first suggested by Wittgenstein's *Investigations*. But the *Investigations*, and Wittgenstein's preliminary studies in *The Blue*

[1] Russell (1956). [2] Frege (1960).

and Brown Books,[3] also founded a second semantic tradition, focused on use rather than truth-conditions, that I will also exploit.

The use tradition too spans variation. Some think there is no proper general semantic theory, just the detailed use of each sentence. But some propose general semantic theories deploying other central notions than truth, for instance the conventional consequences of utterances or their conditions of epistemically justified assertion.[4] For terms that do not purport to refer, NEI makes use of a relatively general notion of proper use, though not a specifically epistemic one.

In Chapter 9, I will develop NEI's ecumenical semantic conception by contrast to well-developed externalist accounts. And I will adopt non-epistemic, internalist variants of two very contrasting externalist alternatives: Davidson's fact-less externalist truth-conditional account, and Brandom's externalist inference-based theory.

These two theories are also a natural foil along a second axis of our concern. The best-developed language-based externalisms, including Brandom's and Davidson's, are versions of interpretationism, the view that the contents of someone's thoughts or the meanings of their sentences are constituted by proper radical interpretation or translation of that person. So Chapter 9 will also focus on interpretation, especially by others. Self-interpretation will be our concern later in this chapter, partly through consideration of Wright's development of Wittgenstein's view of self-avowals.

A focus on interpretation will allow us to develop elements of NEI involved in our capacity to conceive the mental states of ourselves and others. Interpretation seems crucial to many because it is our epistemic access to thoughts, and so interpretationism is frequently a form of epistemicism, and not just externalism. But we will see that the dominant interpretationisms can be modulated into better forms that are neither epistemicist nor externalist, and can be incorporated into NEI.

Interpretation is also related to our final axis of negative concern: the Private Language Argument. The dominant language-based externalist theories rest heavily on a pair of roughly Wittgensteinian observations, that only public languages are possible, and that this constrains the nature of our thoughts. But there are various ways to interpret these observations. While

---

[3] Wittgenstein (1969).   [4] Dummett (1981: 359–63).

the Private Language Argument in the *Investigations* is thought by many to be the major theoretical buttress of language-based externalisms, and a central objection to any internalism deploying qualia, different theorists interpret this textually obscure argument in very different ways.

There is even disagreement about the conclusion of the argument. One traditional understanding is that it is that there are no private experiences—such as the qualia of MS may seem to be—because such things could not be talked about.[5]

But qualitative experience in my sense is constituted by relevantly public physical states, characteristically has general and shareable content, and at most involves only the individuality of constituting physical states. It isn't very private. And we should accept no transcendental deduction of the impossibility of the color blind. And it is not good evidence that something does not exist that it has features that make it impossible to talk about.

So for our purposes another traditional understanding of the conclusion of the Private Language Argument is more relevant, which in any case is a lemma in arguments leading to the first traditional conclusion. This is that qualia can play no semantic role, that for instance they cannot be talked about. And that may seem a central objection to qualia empiricism.

But there remains disagreement about the nature of the argument that leads to this conclusion. We will survey nine possible interpretations. Seven are embedded in our discussion of externalist language-based theories in Chapter 9. But two important, interrelated interpretations are discussed in this chapter and Chapter 10. Various reconstructions elaborate various hints present in Wittgenstein's complex text. What I will call Private Language Argument 1, and discuss in this chapter, is an argument that qualia are semantically irrelevant because they could vary among the behaviorally identical. This is a way of arguing that certain internal and 'private' differences that must be crucial to thought according to certain forms of internalism, including qualia empiricism, are not in fact significant. In Chapter 10, we will consider another version of the Private Language Argument, PLA9, which is generalization of PLA1. It demands from the internalist an account of how individuals who apparently share only reference and have detailed internal psychological differences yet share thoughts. PLA3 and 4, and Davidson's PLA2, are based on another general

[5] Robinson (1994: 91–118).

idea. They claim that the kind of correctness required of language capable of truth and falsity must be rooted in social correctness. But they differ in certain details. Chapter 9 not only discusses these arguments, but also considers versions of the Private Language Argument rooted in two other general ideas. PLA5 suggests that there are no facts about types of linguistic phenomena except through social determination. PLA6 and 7 develop in different ways Kripke's understanding of Wittgenstein's argument. They allege that internal dispositions of the sort I will deploy in NEI cannot deliver the infinity and normativity of thought. Brandom's PLA8 sums together in a novel way various elements deployed in the other reconstructions.

My general strategy of response to these Private Language Arguments, as to the other theoretical considerations apparently supporting language-based externalism, will be to accept the guts of the concrete considerations adduced as relevant to linguistic meaning and thought content by various language-based externalists, but only when those considerations are modulated into an appropriately internalist and non-epistemic form.

8.2

This chapter considers the simple private language argument PLA1. This argument bears an interesting relation to the Arguments from Introspection and from Explanation that are often deployed against externalism. We will see that this argument against internalism fails because those familiar arguments against externalism fail. In other words, this chapter considers three general arguments that may seem to quickly resolve the issue between internalism and externalism without recourse to my more complicated indirect procedure in this book. And it shows that such arguments fail, and for the same reason. That's the interesting part.

This discussion will involve a part of the positive story that NEI will tell about self-awareness, or rather about one's beliefs or even idle imaginings regarding one's own mental states. And our discussion will also yield an important positive clue to the general nature of NEI. But though our discussion will reveal various symmetries between externalism and internalism that I will eventually exploit in a positive way, my primary focus will be negative.

My strategy against PLA1 will be this: I will begin by discussing the two familiar general arguments against externalism. We will see in Sections 8.3 through 8.5 that these arguments fail, but only if externalists respond in a certain way. And then, as we will see in Sections 8.6 and 8.7, externalists must lose one familiar general theoretical argument for externalism and against internalism, which is PLA1. That's the central symmetry between externalism and internalism that this chapter aims to reveal.

The two familiar general arguments against *externalism* that are our first concern are the Argument from Introspection and the Argument from Explanation. The first supposes that a person has introspective and hence 'privileged' access to the contents of their thoughts, but not to the conditions that externalists hold necessary to the constitution of those thoughts. The second presumes that thoughts explain behaviors, and argues that what's merely contemporaneous and internal explains behaviors.

These arguments are not decisive, because externalists have developed a variety of responses that leave these claims in doubt. For instance, Davidson and Burge have suggested that external conditions fix not only the contents of introspected thoughts but also the contents of introspecting thoughts, so that externalism is consistent with introspective access to contents.[6] Dretske, Millikan, and Stalnaker have developed conceptions of psychological explanation that are friendly to externalism.[7]

But variants of the Argument from Introspection and the Argument from Explanation *can* show that introspective access and proper explanation of certain *specific* kinds are inconsistent with externalism. Indeed, we might link these two variants in a single argument, which goes like this:

Differences in the contents of two thoughts must be introspectible in a way that can make a difference to *narrow* behavior, to behavior at skin's end. If someone thinks y rather than z, then there must be circumstances in which they would hence move in a different way. Since you and your Twin Earth double would never move differently, you hence do not think differently.

Since I will rely on this argument for organizational purposes, it is worth considering natural resistance. It might seem that being introspectible has little or nothing to do with making a difference to behavior. Not everything that makes a difference to our behavior need be introspectible, of course,

---

[6] Davidson (1984a, 1987); Burge (1988). [7] Dretske (1988); Stalnaker (1989); Millikan (1993c).

since there might be deeply unconscious beliefs and desires. But that is not required by the argument. A more pressing objection is that there are possible forms of introspection that would be causally inert in this particular way. If there are differences in qualia that make no difference at skin's end, or distinct references that make no difference there, still there are conceptions of introspection according to which such qualia or references can be introspected. Indeed, those conceptions include those often favored by friends of qualia, and the externalist proposals of Davidson and Burge.

Nevertheless, the argument that I have given is deployed against externalists. Indeed, it is hard to see what other sorts of understandings of introspection and explanation than those it incorporates could be deployed against externalists. And the close parallel between qualia and external reference is a part of what I want to stress. While such specific conceptions of introspection and explanation as this argument deploys involve deniable subtleties, the key point is that this very argument can also be deployed against reasonably plausible forms of *internalism*.

Presume for instance that experience of qualia is not physically reducible, and has no causal effects on the physical world, so that epiphenomenal dualism about qualia is true. Then consider the differences in qualitative experience involved in a red-green qualia inversion between physical twins. One twin is normal, and like the rest of us. The other sees as red what we see as green, and sees as green what we see as red. A color wheel that the second experiences is flipped around on its blue-yellow axis. Those differences cannot be revealed in behavioral differences, we can presume. An internalism that holds that nevertheless such differences are relevant to believing something is green or is red does not meet the conditions that our combined form of the Arguments from Introspection and Explanation demands. Such differences are intuitively introspectible in one sense, but not in a way that affects narrow behavior.

Dualism is false, I presume, even epiphenomenal dualism about qualia. But note that the same sort of argument can be deployed against internalist forms of physicalism that can yield differences in qualia that are not revealed in behavior, say if qualia inversion depends on neurological details that are characteristically irrelevant to behavior, which is more or less what I believe.

Considered at a certain level of abstraction, this is perhaps the central theoretical objection to internalism. Here is the complaint put abstractly: Internalists must claim that there are differences in content when those differences are not relevant to the explanation of behavior and hence not relevant to commonsense belief-desire psychology; internalism cannot properly explain the evident and intuitive psychological similarities of those who are internally quite different. We will return to this abstract form of the objection in Chapter 10. But a more specific form of this objection is one simple and reasonably persuasive reading of Wittgenstein's Private Language Argument, which is indeed plausibly present in the text of the *Philosophical Investigations*. That is PLA1.

Wittgenstein seems to argue, among other things, that differences in qualia between behavioral duplicates are not semantically relevant. He also seems to argue for related limitations on the introspection or memory of qualia, in particular that introspective errors about one's past qualitative experience would be unknowable.

Parallels between PLA1 and the familiar general arguments against externalism will be my eventual point. The Arguments from Explanation and Introspection are indecisive against externalism, I think. But the best externalist replies to those arguments make claims and invoke resources that are closely analogous to internalist resources and claims against PLA1. Because the Arguments from Explanation and Introspection are indecisive against externalism, so too PLA1 is indecisive against internalism.

The next three sections will focus, for economy's sake, primarily on the Argument from Introspection against externalism. Section 8.6 will turn to PLA1 and internalism.

8.3

The Argument from Introspection, generally characterized, is that externalism is inconsistent with our introspective access to our thoughts. But we need to consider this argument more closely.

The first complicating fact is that there are a variety of things that introspective access might be. 1) Truth is a necessary condition of knowledge, and so pretty clearly we can't introspect whether our beliefs about the external world are knowledge. But our central concern here is not access to whether we know things, but rather access to the *content* of thoughts that may be ill-founded beliefs, or even idle imaginings, as well as access to the *content* of perceptions, veridical or otherwise. 2) And introspective access need not be infallible or immediate access to the contents of all our beliefs. Consider unconscious or Freudian repressed beliefs, past beliefs, or non-occurrent beliefs. 3) Nor is it obvious that we have introspective access to all features of the contents of even our conscious, occurrent, and present beliefs and conscious perceptions. Does the content of my particular perceptual experience of a particular building involve an odd or even number of bricks? Are two experienced color-patches of *exactly* the same shade? Perhaps we only have introspective access to central features of the contents of certain sorts of beliefs and perceptions. 4) And there are a variety of things that introspective access might be, even once we figure out what its relevant objects are. For instance, as a foe of epistemicism, I think that we should not start out presuming that our introspective access characteristically yields knowledge or even justified belief about our own mental states. And yet I think that self-understanding, if I can call it that, is still revealing.

It would seem that a suitably robust and intuitive introspective access would be assured if the following two rough conditions obtained:

First, we can immediately report the contents of our current sensations in at least general detail. Note that it is only given certain deniable internalist theories that this phenomenology would literally involve a looking inwards. But it is an intuitive part of introspection. This ability seems also to encompass the contents of proto-judgments, the primary imagination, and to a degree our complex, Strawsonian spatial thoughts.

Second, we can sit in an armchair and introspect to at least a large degree the contents of those of our beliefs that are expressed in characteristic declarative sentences that we assert out loud or to ourselves. We can tell by some appeal to the mind's eye and ear what we say or would say about various possible circumstances that might arise. We can to some degree access our speech dispositions.

There are details that matter: Can we sit in our armchairs and conceive all the relevant possible situations that might arise? In one sense yes; we are capable of conceiving each relevant situation. In one sense no; unprompted, many of us would never have thought of the Twin Earth scenario or the arthritis case, despite the fact that we were in the first sense capable of thinking of them.

Are we infallible in our armchairs about what we would in fact say about a given situation? Are our armchair claims about our thoughts epistemically indefeasible? No, though it does seem that in fact we do have pretty good accuracy, and our claims have some epistemic weight. I'm not sure if it is enough weight to make such claims generally epistemically justified.

I believe that there is roughly the sort of introspective access that I have just described. It fits quite well with qualia empiricism. In this chapter, I will hereafter call it 'a priori knowledge', to maintain suitable contact with the dominant vocabulary of the relevant literatures, even though there are problems with this terminology. I don't know whether these armchair claims characteristically constitute knowledge, and frankly I don't care. And introspective access of this sort seems to involve perception and memory, which are not intuitively a priori. Still, these terminological details won't matter for our present purposes. So I will retain the customary nomenclature.

There are at least apparent reasons to worry that even such a limited and qualified introspective access is inconsistent with externalism. But before we consider those apparent reasons, there is also a second complicating fact about the Argument from Introspection we must briefly note. There are at least two sorts of Arguments from Introspection. What I will call 'general' and 'particular' Arguments from Introspection differ in the abstraction of the externalist considerations they deploy.

8.4

Perhaps the canonical statement of a general Argument from Introspection is due to Michael McKinsey:[8]

(1) Oscar knows a priori that he has a thought with a certain content.
(2) According to the externalist, a necessary condition of Oscar having that thought is some external condition E.
(3) If E is necessary for having that thought, then that is knowable a priori.

Hence

(4) According to the externalist, Oscar can know E a priori.
(5) But Oscar cannot know E a priori.[9]

[8] McKinsey (1991). [9] This argument is suggested by McKinsey (1991: 16).

There are a number of possible externalist replies to this general argument. One might claim that Oscar can know E a priori in the relevant sense.[10] But that is unintuitive. One might deny that a priori warrants can be transmitted in the way the argument requires.[11] But such transmission seems intuitively appropriate at least in the argument in question, especially given its focus on the claim that Oscar *can* know E a priori and not that he *does* know E a priori. I will focus rather on three other possible replies that seem more plausible.

One might deny that Oscar knows a priori that he has a thought with the particular content in question, deny that he has introspective access to that fact. But it is important to see that there are a variety of ways to do this. A straight-up Ryle-style denial of introspective access may be intuitively implausible, but there are subtler strategies. We have already noticed that it seems implausible to claim that we have introspective and infallible access to all features of the contents of our beliefs or perceptions. Remember the many bricks of the building and the two color-patches. An externalist might similarly deny that some features of a content, in particular those that are externally fixed, are introspectively accessible, while yet not denying the existence of much introspective access to other features. While some have thought that just the ability to say and then repeat the words that express a belief constitutes sufficient access to its content, there is a more intuitive and less deflationary externalist possibility. Presume for the moment Burge's extension of Putnam's Twin Earth case. Perhaps introspective access to one's thought that water is wet requires more robust capacities than just the ability to resay the words, more than just the ability to follow utterances of 'water is wet' with utterances of 'I think that water is wet'. But perhaps introspective access requires less robust capacities than some internalists presume. Perhaps it isn't necessary to know by introspection of one's water thoughts that one is thinking that H-O-H as opposed to XYZ is wet, even if the difference between XYZ and H-O-H is relevant to whether one is in fact thinking that *water* is wet.[12] Perhaps the difference between thoughts about water and thoughts about Putnam's twin water needn't be introspectible, though the difference between thoughts about water and thoughts about ash cans must be.

---

[10] Sawyer (1998). Perhaps this claim could be vindicated by the Splitting the Difference strategy discussed below, in a form that relies on irrelevant alternatives.
[11] Davies (1998); C. Wright (2000).   [12] Burge (1988); Falvey and Owens (1994).

I will call this first strategy of response, which delivers a roughly intuitive introspective access consistent with externalism, 'Splitting the Difference'. We will return to it repeatedly. I think that it would be sufficient to defend externalism.

There is a second strategy of response that is at least potentially distinct. But in fact its cogency depends on Splitting the Difference, so in its best forms it isn't really distinct. This is to claim that one can have suitably a priori access to the fact that one is thinking of water, even as opposed say to thinking of XYZ, although one can't introspect that difference, when the possibility that the locally watery stuff is XYZ is not an epistemically relevant alternative.[13] It is thought by many that the fact that one might conceivably be in a Cartesian demon scenario or mad or dreaming does not suffice to deliver an epistemically relevant set of alternatives in many ordinary situations, that the fact that ordinary evidence is insufficient to rule out these scenarios is not sufficient to show that we ordinarily lack perceptual knowledge. Perhaps when such wild scenarios are introduced into discussion, they become relevant scenarios, but not under ordinary circumstances. Likewise, although the fact that ordinary introspectively available evidence—say that available to the chemically ignorant in 1600—is insufficient to rule out the possibility that XYZ is the locally watery stuff, perhaps that is not sufficient to show that the chemically ignorant in 1600 lacked introspective knowledge that they were thinking of water, even if water is of necessity H-O-H.

I think that this strategy, which I'll call 'Irrelevant Alternatives', is a second plausible strategy of response for externalists, especially those enamored of epistemicism, but only if a further condition is met. Even the chemically ignorant in 1600 must have been capable of telling with something approximating certainty that they weren't thinking about entities with the general perceptible features of ash cans when they thought 'water is wet'.[14] They needed firmer a priori or armchair or introspective access to *those* features of the content of their thought, which could not be disrupted by the introduction of wild scenarios analogous to those involving XYZ, or at the very least could not be as easily disrupted. If we take this firmer sort of introspective access to be what is meant by 'a priori access', this

---

[13] Burge (1988); Warfield (1992, 1997); Falvey and Owens (1994); Sawyer (1999).
[14] Sawyer (1999) grants this proviso.

means that the cogency of Irrelevant Alternatives presumes Splitting the Difference. But in any case they are very similar responses.[15]

There is a third and apparently distinct possible reply, or cluster of replies, to McKinsey's argument. That is to deny premises (2) or (3). Perhaps the externalist truths are contingent. And even if they are necessary, perhaps they are necessities that are only knowable a posteriori.[16] Call this pair of strategies 'A Posteriori Externalism'.

Chapter 1 admits that the issue between internalism and externalism is contingent and a posteriori. In Aristotle's world, externalism would be true. But one possible difficulty for A Posteriori Externalism is that the important case-based arguments for externalism certainly look like armchair arguments. Still, perhaps we bring to our armchairs certain relevant empirical presumptions. So my point about this cluster of replies is something else: There is a surprising link, indeed a pair of links, between the best forms of even this strategy and Splitting the Difference. And so Splitting the Difference is a crucial strategy for the externalist. It is the core of all three viable externalist replies to the Argument from Introspection.

To uncover the interaction of A Posteriori Externalism and Splitting the Difference, it will be useful to turn from a discussion of McKinsey's general argument to the first of two particular Arguments from Introspection due to Paul Boghossian.[17] Our discussion will reveal the entwining of the two responses that I have promised.[18]

8.5

Boghossian's first argument focuses on the concept of water as understood by the paradigmatic externalist. Its focus on a particular externalist model of a particular concept is why it counts as a *particular* Argument from Introspection. And these particularities help reveal the entwining we seek.

---

[15] Brown (2004: 136–55) argues that while Irrelevant Alternatives is generally a plausible strategy, it is not a plausible response in a few cases. The strategy is alleged to fail in cases where we have perceptual demonstrative thoughts, say that a particular apple that we see is red when there are yet many other apples around from which we could not discriminate that particular apple if the apples were rearranged. But it is surely relevant that we do in fact discriminate that apple from the others in the actual perceptual situation in question. So the qualification seems not sufficiently well motivated.
[16] Brueckner (1992).   [17] Boghossian (1998).
[18] McKinsey (2002: 112) stresses differences between his argument and Boghossian's. But they do not affect the particular link I allege between Splitting the Difference and A Posteriori Externalism.

Boghossian presumes that Twin Earth intuitions drive externalism. And he presumes that concepts are individuated finely, so that water and H-O-H are not the same concept even if all water is H-O-H. Given that background, here is his argument:

Compatibilists hold that introspective access is compatible with externalism. Assume that Oscar is a pre-chemical compatibilist. Boghossian claims this:

Oscar is in a position to argue, purely a priori, as follows:

(1) If I have the concept water, then water exists.
(2) I have the concept water.

Therefore,

(3) Water exists.

Since the conclusion is clearly not knowable a priori, one of the premises in Oscar's evidently valid reasoning had better be either false or not knowable a priori.... [But] Oscar... *qua* compatibilist... is committed to both premises (1) and (2) and to their being knowable a priori.[19]

There are a variety of possible responses to this argument. Burge suggests that the pre-chemical might have the concept of water in two ways, either by residing on a planet wet with water with which they perceptually interact, or by deference to experts who have the appropriate chemical conception of H-O-H even on a completely dry earth.[20] But Boghossian's plausible response to this reply is just to generalize his argument to cover the relevant disjunction.[21]

Let me focus, rather, on the interaction of Splitting the Difference and A Posteriori Externalism as possible replies. Boghossian very quickly dismisses the possibility that Oscar doesn't have a priori knowledge that he has the concept water, on the grounds that this simply denies introspective access.[22] But since this possibility can be understood to encompass some forms of Splitting the Difference, we know this to be too quick. I think that this provides a reasonable externalist reply in this context. Perhaps Oscar has a priori knowledge that his concept water isn't the concept of an ashcan, but not that his concept water is distinct from closer competitors. And perhaps

---

[19] Boghossian (1998: 275).   [20] Burge (1982: 116).   [21] Boghossian (1998: 276).
[22] Boghossian (1998: 275).

that is grounds to deny that he has a priori knowledge that he has the concept of water in particular.

This will sound familiar. Still, Boghossian's discussion does reveal how Splitting the Difference is entwined with forms of A Posteriori Externalism, to which he pays greater explicit attention.

Boghossian considers the possibility that though the Twin Earth argument is apparently a priori, still perhaps there are conditions that are only knowable a posteriori—which I will call 'a posteriori conditions'—on a term being Twin Earth-eligible, that is to say properly governed by Twin Earth intuitions. The details of his discussion of this form of A Posteriori Externalism matter to us.

He not implausibly claims that some of the conditions required for a term to be Twin Earth-eligible are a priori accessible: '[I]t has to be a word that expresses an atomic concept. It also has to aim to name a natural kind. Furthermore, the user of the word must be indifferent about the essence of the kind that his word aims to name; he must be chemically indifferent.'[23] At least in a different Burge-style social determination case, we might raise worries about the introspective or a priori accessibility of the first two conditions that Boghossian cites, and I will return to this point in a minute. But we have already seen, in Part I as modulated by Section 8.3, that there is a plausible set of analogous conditions that are relevantly accessible from armchairs.

For now the key point is that it may be that Twin Earth-eligibility requires that a word actually name a natural kind. That is apparently only knowable a posteriori.

Boghossian replies that we can run a Twin Earth case on an *empty* natural kind term, by considering a hypothetical situation in which it names a particular kind.[24] But he admits that this merely points us towards other apparently a posteriori conditions on Twin Earth-eligibility.

[If] we can run Twin Earth experiments even on terms that fail to refer, then how do we know a priori that water is required for 'water' to express water? We can't infer that claim merely from the fact that 'water' is Twin Earth-eligible.... [W]e know that only by virtue of our knowledge that 'water' does name a natural kind.... And that, of course, is something that we could only have come to know empirically.[25]

---

[23] Boghossian (1998: 278). [24] Ibid. [25] Boghossian (1998: 279).

So far we have come to this apparent fact: Whether empty kind terms are Twin Earth-eligible or not, there plausibly seem to be presumptions about a posteriori conditions carried into our armchairs in Twin Earth arguments.

But Boghossian does not agree. His further negative discussion of the possibility that while empty kind terms are Twin Earth-eligible, still there are relevant a posteriori conditions for that, helps reveals the particular link we seek between A Posteriori Externalism and Splitting the Difference.

Boghossian begins with Dry Earth—'a planet just like ours on which, although it very much seems to its inhabitants that there is a clear, tasteless, colourless liquid flowing in their rivers and taps and to which they confidently take themselves to be applying the word "water", these appearances are systematically false, and constitute a sort of collective mirage.'[26] He then constructs a dilemma. On the one hand, an externalist might say that under dry conditions there is no determinate concept associated with the term 'water'. But that is in real conflict with our introspective access to whether or not our terms express determinate concepts. On the other hand, an externalist might say that there is a compound concept associated with the term 'water' on Dry Earth but not on Earth, a concept approximately like that of the clear, tasteless, colorless liquid that flows in taps and rivers around here. But that conflicts with our introspective access to whether or not our terms express compound concepts or rather atomic concepts.

But there is an externalist answer to this dilemma. Externalism can Split the Difference between the introspectible features of the contents of these thoughts, which are shared between Earth and Dry Earth, and non-introspectible features that are not. In fact, they can do so in two different ways, which correspond to both horns of Boghossian's dilemma. We have already seen that this is consistent with adequate introspective access. Externalists can claim that the non-introspectible differences between the concepts are due to the a posteriori conditions presumed by their externalism. If Boghossian is right about key details, this will require either that we split the difference regarding the determinacy of a concept, or that we split the difference regarding its atomicity. But there is no obvious reason why externalists cannot do either. We have many concepts that are not obviously determinate, and it may be that

[26] Ibid.

the semantic value of a concept shifts in a crucial way when it is not empty.

What seems the best A Posteriori Externalist response to Boghossian's first type of Argument from Introspection is linked in this way to the Splitting the Difference response. The relevant conditions that are only knowable a posteriori constitute only differences in content that are not introspectible.

Boghossian also deploys a second type of particular Argument from Introspection: 'traveling case' or 'switching' arguments.[27] They take a variety of specific forms, but if we focus on the most telling response to the most telling forms, we can discern other roles for Splitting the Difference.

Imagine that you live in pre-chemical times, pre-1750. Imagine that while sleeping you are secretly transported to Twin Earth. Most externalists agree that if you were to remain there long enough, you would develop a concept of twin water, of XYZ. But it also seems plausible that you would retain your concept of water, at least if you are never told of the switch. Here is John Gibbons making that case: 'Suppose I say "I remember the first time I went swimming in the ocean as a child. The water was really salty." It seems fairly clear to me that if I went swimming in water as a child, I am now thinking about water, even if I have been switched.'[28] On this conception, after the switch you can introspect properly the contents of your various first-order thoughts about water or twin water, and yet have no idea that there is a difference in content between them. That is one kind of Splitting the Difference.

But Boghossian argues that, in such a switching case, externalism would implausibly imply that you cannot know your past, pre-switch thoughts.[29] And the necessary externalist reply to his argument reveals another detail that is of use to us. Boghossian claims that there is this inability to know because after you acquire the concept of twin water, you might be told about the switch, but not when it happened. If asked whether last year you were thinking about water or twin water, you clearly wouldn't know. But then it seems you never knew.

Gibbons plausibly suggests instead that before being told about the switch you knew, and you lost the capacity for this knowledge upon being

---

[27] Boghossian (1989, 1994).   [28] Gibbons (1996: 295).
[29] Boghossian (1989: 22–3). Boghossian makes other arguments. For criticism see Gibbons (1996).

told about the switch. This seems to rest on the mechanism of Irrelevant Alternatives. And consider the details of his reply: Your concepts of water and twin water have both changed, because you 'do not take [your] beliefs about water as evidence for and against [your] beliefs about twin-water'.[30] 'These two concepts may be more functionally similar than two different individuals' concepts of water are. But one difference outweighs all of the similarities.... [You] believe that the kinds picked out by the concepts are distinct.... Thoughts involving one concept do not count as evidence for and against thoughts involving the other without the mediation of other thoughts.'[31]

It seems to me that internalists should admit that we do not know that Gibbons is wrong in this reply to Boghossian. But we should also note this response to Boghossian incorporates Gibbons' treatment of the case in which you are not told about the switch, and we have already seen that this turns crucially on a version of Splitting the Difference. It also seems to depend on a version of Irrelevant Alternatives, but we earlier saw that viable forms of this response depend for their plausibility on Splitting the Difference.

Where are we? It seems plausible that some differences in content are not introspectible in a firm and straightforward way, while others are. Splitting the Difference is a crucial element of the defense of externalism against various Arguments from Introspection. It is presumed by all viable externalist responses. And remember the connection of that cluster of arguments with one key form of the Argument from Explanation, which I noted in Section 8.2. Such non-introspectible differences in content cannot be revealed in different narrow behaviors. That's okay too, it seems.

8.6

But such replies have a cost, which the externalist must pay. To see this, we need to turn now to a standard objection to *internalism*. A central theoretical objection to internalism is that people can intuitively share thoughts even when their conceptions of things are very different. To focus on the complex ideology inside our heads, as internalists plausibly

[30] Gibbons (1996: 306).   [31] Gibbons (1996: 307).

must, may seem inappropriate, because it surely differs when our intuitive beliefs do not. We can both believe that water is wet and yet have radically different understandings in our heads of what it is to be water and to be wet. Put in such a general way, this is PLA9.

This objection to internalism is sometimes associated with the roughly Fregean conception that a name will share not only a reference but a sense for different speakers of a language, even if there are differences in the speakers' ideas of the thing named, so that 'Hesperus' has the sense 'the evening star' for all speakers. But in fact Frege says that actual proper names in actual natural languages plausibly involve variations in sense across individuals,[32] and that ideas differ from one person to another not necessarily in content but by definition.[33] Perhaps a more plausible original source is Locke, who may also have been the first to propose the more specific version of this argument that we will soon trace.[34]

But, whoever first formulated the objection, it is at least in a general way pressing and intuitive. It surely has at least this much legitimate force: To be plausible, internalism must provide a positive account of how contents are shared despite ideological differences. The answer I prefer will come in Chapter 10.

For now, my focus will be on a more specific version of this general argument. This is PLA1, and it is arguably present in the text of the *Philosophical Investigations*, in the pages spanning remarks 239 to 317. It is a reasonable objection to a certain kind of internalism, indeed to my kind of internalism.

First, let me note three elements of necessary background. There is some obvious historical context for the argument. Aristotle thought that color just as we experience it is on the objects we see. Galileo changed our minds about that. Still, conservative philosophers came to think that objective color was on the objects even though color just as we experience it—phenomenal color that is such that reddish purple and bluish purple are very similar despite the fact that they correspond to very different surface properties of objects and very different sorts of visible light—was merely in the mind's eye, was merely on the qualia under our hats. And these qualia came, in the guise of sense data, to seem semantically quite important. So internal qualia came to seem a natural resource for a certain sort of

---

[32] Frege (1960: 58 n.).   [33] Frege (1956).   [34] Locke (1975: Bk. II, chap. XXXII, sec. 15).

internalism, which holds that our beliefs that things are green are closely dependent in content on our experience of green. I am urging a return to something like this now unpopular conception.

We can construe Wittgenstein as arguing that such qualia are not semantically important. But note a second element of background for his argument: Wittgenstein considers two cases that are superficially quite different: pain qualia and color qualia. But in remark 312 he explicitly suggests that these differences are merely contingent and in that way superficial. If the surfaces of things had patches that reliably produced pain in all of us, then we would speak of pain patches on those things. And we should also remember Berkeley's argument that the qualia associated with extreme heat and with certain pains are the same. So it will be appropriate if I treat pain qualia and color qualia symmetrically in my reconstruction of Wittgenstein's argument.

One last piece of background: Remark 272 introduces the possibility that people may vary in the qualia associated with their sensation of red, even when they exhibit no behavioral differences. Call such people 'qualia variants'. And remark 293 even introduces the possibility of zombies, who lack qualia. I believe that these remarks are meant to introduce into Wittgenstein's argument the fairly wild possibility, which also plays a role in contemporary arguments for dualism about qualia, that there are qualia variants or even perhaps zombies among us, who yet behave in all the ways proper for speakers of English who share common beliefs.

Now on to the reconstruction: In remark 243, Wittgenstein introduces the topic of a private language, which only one person can understand, and in which private sensations and hence qualia play a crucial semantic role. Presume for the moment that he is discussing someone with variant qualia. Then he has two arguments that such a private language, understood only by the variant because only the variant has the necessary qualia, wouldn't be possible. I am calling the conjunction of these two arguments PLA1.

One runs roughly from remarks 271 to 279, and surfaces again at 293 and 294. It is an argument that qualia variants, as well as zombies, would share a language and relevant thoughts with all the rest of us. This seems to me reasonably intuitive. They talk and walk like the rest of us, and it isn't silly to think that is all that is required to share English.

Another argument involves the sensation language or 'S language', in which the qualia variant attempts to name his or her qualia. It runs from about remark 258 to remark 271. The suggestion seems to be that there can be no difference between correct and incorrect use of such a language, and hence that there can be no such language. If we grant Wittgenstein's questionable premise that language must always be capable of incorrect use, still one might object that the speaker's use might become incorrect over time, that it might deviate from its original use. It might become attached to different qualia. I believe that remark 271 introduces a possible reply to this objection, that such a speaker might then have the relevantly same sort of relationship to a past self that we have to a presumed zombie or qualia variant among us, and hence that the alleged difference in use is really semantically irrelevant because of the first argument I noted.

The first argument in my reconstruction, on which the second in some sense depends, presumes hypothetically that there are in fact qualia variants or even zombies. What if, much more plausibly, there aren't? There are color blind people, but they are behaviorally detectable. If qualia in fact are shared at least by all the behaviorally normal, might qualia be semantically relevant? They wouldn't be private then in the full sense. If qualia are semantically relevant to a language but all behaviorally normal people share the qualia, then at least behaviorally normal people could all understand the language in question.

As far as I can see, Wittgenstein gives no plausible direct reasons to think that shared qualia could not be semantically relevant. But perhaps his point is that we cannot exclude the epistemic or perhaps the real possibility of behaviorally-normal variants or even zombies, and that that is enough to show qualia always semantically irrelevant, even while we presume there are some. Even the physicalism of MS involves merely a posteriori and fallible constitution claims, and of course merely neurophysiological differences may not be behaviorally detectable. And perhaps Wittgenstein's further point is that the possibility of variants or zombies is a key premise in many arguments for qualia.

To summarize, Private Language Argument 1 is that since qualia are subject to possible variations that yet leave behaviors stable and appropriate, such qualia are hence semantically irrelevant even if they exist. They introduce possible differences in thought content or the understanding of language that are yet not manifestable in behavior. So such differences are not genuine semantic differences, genuine differences in thought or speech.

There are traditional ways to buttress this argument that are quite suspect. If Wittgenstein thinks that the S language cannot be deployed in the same way over time unless it can be *known* to be so applied, that seems rooted in unfounded verificationism.[35] And it also seems that while we might not know with certainty that we are using our private terms over time in the same way, memory provides pretty good evidence about that.[36] And it finally seems that memory is our crucial evidence for claims about the past or even about some present objects.[37] But I think that when unaccompanied by suspect epistemicism, PLA1 has some force.

8.7

Internalisms of a certain kind, in which qualia play a crucial role, including qualia empiricism, face PLA1. How can they respond? Our previous discussion of plausible externalist replies to the Argument from Introspection shows the way, along with our earlier discussion of the identity of certain forms of the Argument from Introspection and the Argument from Explanation.

The externalist, we have seen, must Split the Difference. Some differences between contents are introspectible in a way that can make a difference to narrow behavior, and some are not. But the internalist who thinks that behaviorally undetectable qualia play a semantic role can Split the Difference also. Qualia inversions or other analogous variations introduce differences in content that are not introspectible in the particular way that can make a difference to narrow behaviors. But that doesn't matter.

A pair of qualia variants who are physical twins behave in that sense in the same way, and even neurophysiological differences between qualia variants may be behaviorally undetectable. But Putnam's twins also in that sense behave in the same way. We can describe the behaviors of Putnam's twins differently, as pursuing H-O-H or XYZ. But likewise our pair of qualia variants can be described as fleeing pain or variant pain.

Of course, there are some differences in the cases. My claim that the qualia in question cannot be introspected may sound absurd. But the qualia

---

[35] Fodor (1975: 70).   [36] Robinson (1994: 99–101).
[37] Strawson (1954); Soames (2003: 74).

deployed by the internalist are only introspectible in a different sense than that which is most immediately relevant. They are not revealed in behavior at skin's end. And in Section 8.2, we noted a close parallel between the kinds of introspection that make no difference to narrow behavior and are favored by fans of qualia, and those favored by externalists who adopt the Davidson-Burge conception of introspection.

Still, there are some differences. The qualia are, the internalist thinks, inside, and they make a difference to our experience. Our qualia are accessible to us in our armchairs in something like the sense that I sketched in Section 8.3. But, even if externalists do not deploy the Davidson-Burge conception, they can point out that XYZ and H-O-H are outside, and generally accessible to public scrutiny.

To each their own favored position, I say, outside looking in or inside looking out. But in light of my standing complaint about epistemicism, let me put it this way: There are two *semantic* standpoints that are at least potentially relevant to the contents of thoughts about thoughts, from the outside looking in at another's thoughts, and from the inside looking in (or out) at one's own. Both perspectives seem fallible, though the details will depend on whether we end up externalists or internalists. Perhaps neither standpoint allows us to have epistemically adequate justification for our thoughts about thoughts, nor such knowledge. But that doesn't matter to a foe of epistemicism like me. Such a conception allows that we have the kinds of access to thoughts, from the inside and the outside, that we plausibly have, whether or not it is epistemically justified knowledge.

There are disanalogies between internalism and externalism that may be revealed by situations somewhat different from those that PLA1 deploys. If half of someone's current qualia were inverted, it may plausibly seem that would cause a difference in their narrow behavior, while if half of their references were switched in the manner of Twin Earth, that would not. But that case makes assumptions about causal mechanisms of introspection, involving causally discriminable differences between the two types of experience, that are in tension with PLA1. One way to see this is to note that quick oscillations of qualia over time would be unknown according to PLA1, and that that plausibly requires that such differences in the moment would be likewise. As Howard Robinson notes, 'there is no clear distinction between present recognition and memory: If I judge that two simultaneous sensations remain the same for two seconds, is that a memory judgment or a direct one?'[38] And even if you cannot believe that differences in the moment could be unknown, still there is a symmetry here. Partial switch of external referents is accessible from the outside, and can from the outside cause a difference in narrow behavior, though evidently via different special mechanisms than a partial switch of qualia might.

In any case, I don't endorse PLA1. I just claim that it reveals one key symmetry between externalism and internalism. And there are other detailed parallels in PLA1-type cases. 1) Gibbons suggests that the recognition that one has been switched to Twin Earth may cause one to lose knowledge. Likewise, the recognition that someone's qualia may have been switched may cause one to lose knowledge of the contents of their mind. 2) Boghossian considers difficulties introduced by externalism for knowledge of one's past thoughts. But Wittgenstein considers difficulties introduced by an internalism rooted in qualia for knowledge of one's past experiences. 3) And on both sides the differences that must be split reflect natural empirical presumptions of cases that support the view hence defended. Qualia inverts are pretty implausible, but so too are Putnam's twins. Scenarios of absent or differing qualia are no more compelling than scenarios that involve Dry Earth, or quasi-water that differs in chemical composition rapidly over time while its superficial properties remain the same.

Internalists who deploy qualia and externalists are in the same abstract boat, and should paddle together against the behaviorist. The issue between externalists and such internalists must be resolved somewhere else. If the Argument from Introspection and the Argument from Explanation fail against externalism,[39] and I believe that they do, then so too does PLA1 fail against internalism. It is appropriate to split all the differences in question.

8.8

Section 8.3 suggested that our introspective access is such that we can immediately report the contents of our current sensations, proto-judgments,

---

[38] Robinson (1994: 117).

[39] There may be forms of the Argument from Explanation that still seem to have some purchase. And we discussed some in the last chapter that even some externalists favor. But all these arguments involve reasonably deniable claims about the proper *explananda* of psychological explanations, and so are indecisive.

primary imaginations, and to some degree our complex spatial thoughts. We can also introspect to at least a large degree the contents of those of our beliefs that are expressed in sentences that we assert out loud or to ourselves, including those governed by RDC. We can tell by some appeal to the mind's eye and ear, and with some degree of success, what we say or would say about various possible scenarios that might arise.

But let me say a little more about our access to our word-mediated thoughts according to NEI. Both speech in the mind's ear and content present to the mind's eye at least often involve inner images that are at least analogous to sensory qualia, respectively presenting concrete auditory tokens of words and possible concrete conditions under which we would say various words. This involves the primary imagination. You can in some sense 'quasi-experience' some things that you merely imagine saying, that you are merely disposed to say, and actual inner speech also involves quasi-experience or images of actions in the mind's throat.

But our access to our word-mediated thoughts also involves our Strawsonian capacity, unmediated by words, for thoughts with more complex spatio-temporal structures, and even perhaps forms of intersubjectivity, that cannot be present in our sensory experience in any immediate way. It is quite plausible that such complex thoughts can include those of many of the semantically crucial scenarios under which we would say various things. Such complex thoughts apparently entwine sensory experiences and quasi-experienced inner images in complicated ways, for instance when we imagine how the world would look from elsewhere, or at another time, or to another person.

This suggests the very general outlines of a qualia-rooted conception of many of our thoughts. It is the skeleton of NEI. We will steal refining mechanisms from externalists in the next chapter. But there are various interactions among word-mediated and concrete spatial thoughts that complicate even our own access to our thoughts, and are immediately evident.

First, it is clear that some of the hypothetical scenarios under which we would say various things are not concrete in the manner of the contents of sensation or spatial thoughts, but rather are themselves word-mediated. Various complex interactions between words are possible, but it would seem that in the basic case the scenarios can be presented in vocabulary whose content does not rest on the words uttered in response to the scenarios.

A second evident complication is that while it is likely that the basic phenomenon in question involves assertion of *statements* in response to scenarios, we can also consider scenarios as candidate extensions of *terms*, as for instance in the Twin Earth case.

Third, as Dummett has insisted, the use of a statement involves not merely the conditions under which one would assert the statement, but also 'what constitutes acceptance of it, i.e. the consequences of accepting it. Here "consequences" must be taken to include both the inferential powers of the statement and anything that counts as acting on the truth of the statement.'[40] These features of the use of statements seem available to us in something like the same manner as their conditions of assertion.

Fourth, there are recognitional capacities that are not word-mediated, for instance as we recognize some contemplated concrete scenario as home.

Fifth, there are various relatively subtle ways in which current thoughts or sensations that are not word-mediated may constrain the contents of word-mediated thoughts, and in ways we can access from the inside. John Campbell has plausibly proposed that the reference of one's terms is sometimes constrained by the current focus of one's perceptual experience.[41] And mechanisms of that general type can provide NEI with an inverted analog of Paul Grice's mechanism for segregating features of word use that are not relevant to core meaning from those that are, but focused on psychologically-relevant content rather than meaning.[42] Grice appeals to complex conversational contexts and to psychologically-implausible intentions and inferences to fix differences between what is said and what is merely implicated—either conventionally or non-conventionally—by one's utterances. In particular, a key subclass of non-conventional implications is supposed to be due to general principles that govern conversations, for instance that one should make conversational contributions that are as informative as required for the current purposes of an exchange, but not more informative than is required.[43] But for us a focus not on conversation with others but on thinking through words that one speaks to oneself is more revealing, and suggests different mechanisms for dividing core content from peripheral implications. One's concrete take on one's situation may be quite relevant to the proper interpretation of the *content* of one's words

---

[40] Dummett (1981: 453).   [41] Campbell (2002b).   [42] Grice (1989).
[43] Grice (1989: 26).

in a situation in which that content is closely related to things one doesn't very literally say. To mention one currently popular case, this may help explain why some waiter who says 'The ham sandwich needs some coffee' may be referring to a customer, and can know that.[44]

But a sixth form of interplay is most relevant to our current focus on self-understanding. Wittgenstein suggests a certain conception of self-knowledge that has been developed by Crispin Wright, indeed as an attack on such a conception of word-mediated thought—as involving dispositions to respond—as NEI incorporates:

The dispositionalist account... misrepresents the intuitive epistemology of self-ascriptions of understanding.[45]

Self-ascriptions of a specific mode of understanding of some expression, like self-ascriptions of a large class of beliefs, intentions, and sensations, are a kind of *avowal*.... [S]ubjects are credited with special authority for their avowals.... [W]e think of the knowledge which they thereby express as groundless and immediate. It is hard to see what justification there could be for this practice if what one ascribed, in self-ascribing a particular understanding of some expression, was a *disposition*.[46]

This basic conception is developed in Wright's later work on self-knowledge. The central claim noted is qualified in necessary ways, and a certain explanation (or intentional non-explanation) for it is broached:

[I]t is just primitively constitutive of the acceptability of psychological claims that, save in cases whose justification would involve active self-interpretation [such as Freudian analysis might occasion], a subject's opinions about herself are default-authoritative and default-limitative; unless you can show how to make better sense of her by overriding or going beyond it, her active self-conception, as manifest in what she is willing to avow, must be deferred to.[47]

The first qualification is hence that there are conditions under which the default authority of these avowals may be overridden. But there is also a second:

[T]he success of a language game which worked this way would depend on certain deep contingencies. It would depend, for instance, on the contingency that taking the apparent self-conception of others seriously, in the sense involved

---

[44] Stanley (2005).   [45] C. Wright (2002b: 123). See also C. Wright (2002a).
[46] C. Wright (2002b: 122–3).   [47] C. Wright (2002d: 368–9). See also C. Wright (2002c, 2002e).

in crediting their apparent beliefs about their intentional states, as expressed in avowals, with authority, almost always tends to result in an overall picture of their psychology which is more illuminating...than anything which might be gleaned by respecting all the data *except* the subject's self-testimony. And that in turn rests on the contingency that we are each of us, ceaselessly but—on the proposed conception—subcognitively moved to opinions concerning our own intensional states which will indeed give good service to others in their attempt to understand us.[48]

To understand this suggestion of Wright's, it is crucial to understand what conditions are those that might defeat presumptive self-avowals. I propose the following internalist account: Conditions that might defeat presumptive self-avowals include suitably dissonant dispositions of the sort NEI deploys. It is also crucial to understand what deep contingencies allow these avowals to provide good service to others. I propose that the relevant deep contingencies are that one's avowals are generally linked to one's own internal dispositions in at least roughly informative ways. So I have interpreted Wright's claims in a plausible internalist and indeed dispositionalist way, and still, it seems, preserved the particular epistemic privilege on which Wright insists. It hence appears that Wright's attack on dispositionalism generally, including my internalist variant, is not successful, even though there is little doubt that my internalist interpretation of his claims is not what he intends.

I think that something like this development of Wright's proposal is plausible. As might be expected, I favor a non-epistemic construal, whereby this mechanism concerns an important semantic standpoint on oneself and not self-*knowledge* per se. As I have developed Wright's proposal and the more traditional conception of introspective access suggested in Section 8.3, there isn't enormous difference between them. Still, there is some, and an internalist and non-epistemic variant of Wright's suggestion seems a plausible constraint on the nature of our thought. Self-avowals take up some slack left by other internally determinate facts about one's own states, so that a kind of self-avowal is partly constitutive of some thoughts, I think.

This mechanism can play several useful roles for NEI. One important application is to provide a kind of default authority to one's own sense that

[48] C. Wright (2002e: 313).

one's quasi-experience counts as an imagination, a memory, a conception of how the world looks from elsewhere, or of how it looks to someone else.

Despite these various complications, my proposal here is more conservative than some proposals that tempt internalists. Siewert, Tienson, Horgan, and Pitt have sketched quite robust phenomenologically-based conceptions of thought.[49] Tienson, Horgan, and Pitt suggest that there is something distinctive that it is like to believe any particular propositional content, and indeed to have any particular attitude towards that content. Siewert proposes that sensory content itself is much more robust than the crude sensory content I propose. But qualia empiricism, like traditional empiricism, makes do with differences in more primitive sensory experiences and quasi-experiences and their relations, and differences in dispositions for those things, and differences in various ways of responding to and hence taking such things. That is for the simple reason that those are the only things that I can introspect.

[49] Siewert (1998); Horgan and Tienson (2002); Pitt (2004).

9

Language, Truth, and Inference

Introspective access is a standpoint friendly to internalism. But an interpersonal standpoint is also revelatory, and friendlier for externalists.

Psychological and semantic idioms are important tools whereby we deal with one another, so it is not unreasonable to believe that the facts of meaning and psychology are constituted in the eye of the suitably sensitive beholder deploying those idioms. Much of what we do with that vocabulary is attempt to understand one another, so we can get on better in the world. And that is not entirely unlike what we do when we try to interpret or translate a foreign speaker or a book. So to consider acts of interpretation or translation the key to mental phenomena is not unmotivated.

In any case, the highly-developed language-based externalisms that will be our principal focus here—those of Davidson and Brandom—are forms of 'interpretationism'. That is the view that the contents of someone's thoughts or the meanings of their sentences are constituted by proper radical interpretation or translation.

9.1

Forms of interpretationism differ along several axes.

First of all, interpretationism can focus on thoughts or on language. We aren't *directly* interested in language, just mental states. But since some thoughts are mediated by meaningful speech, even interpretationism about language is relevant to our concerns. There are also possible interpretationisms that focus solely and directly on thought, and hence might provide a route to externalism that isn't strictly language-based. But it is quite natural to use speech as a clue to the interpretation of thoughts, and since some thought is mediated by speech, that seems inevitable anyway. So our focus will be forms of interpretationism that focus on thoughts but are yet recognizably language-based.

There is relevant variety even among these dominant forms. For one thing, they may suggest with Brandom and Sellars that the content of thoughts is inherited from the meaning of public languages, or more ecumenically with Davidson that the content of someone's thoughts and the meaning of their sentences are fixed all at once by their proper interpretation. But other differences will play a greater role in our discussion.

One crucial variety of forms spans externalism and internalism. Since interpreters are, in the obvious cases, other people than the interpreted, interpretationism may seem to suggest theoretical grounds for externalism. And interpretationism is also paradigmatically externalist in other ways. For instance, it may maintain that the contents of beliefs be fixed by a principle of charity that requires that beliefs be largely true. Dennett claims that 'normally, more often than not, if x believes p, then p is true'.[1] Since most beliefs are about conditions in the world external to the skin, these forms of interpretationism are externalist.

But I will argue that the proper development of interpretationism in fact supports internalism. Interpretationism and its reasonable motivations do not properly motivate externalism, and, if rightly understood, these considerations give us some insight into the correct form of internalism. And while the most familiar forms of internalist interpretationism have epistemicist elements, we will see how to avoid them.

Another crucial axis of differences will provide the principal structure for our discussion. There are forms of interpretationism that allow abstraction from the individual peculiarities of interpreters, so that proper interpretations or translations are not substantially interpreter-relative. And there are substantially interpreter-relative forms. Davidson's and Brandom's accounts span this range, and also constitute well-developed truth-conditional and use-based semantical theories. A focus on these theories will also provide the opportunity to consider several forms of

[1] Dennett (1978: 18).

the Private Language Argument, and other language-enmeshed theoretical motivations for externalism.

9.2

The division between non-relative and relative forms suggests a dilemma for interpretationism: The characteristic difficulty of forms that are not interpreter-relative is that it is hard to see how a focus on the act of interpretation or translation is in that case much beyond dispensable and potentially misleading window-dressing. The differences among translators or interpreters don't really matter. But the characteristic difficulty of interpreter-relative forms is an obvious threat of circularity, impredicativity, or incoherence, for instance if specific thoughts exist merely relative to interpretations and yet interpretations themselves involve particular thoughts.

One way to try to avoid this dilemma is to be a skeptic about thoughts independent of interpretation, but less skeptical about some linguistic medium of interpretation that allegedly presumes no thought. Some hold that proper translations must be relativized to particular translation manuals, and that the translation manuals must deploy otherwise uninterpreted syntax. But such skepticisms are more a radical rejection of our issue between internalism and externalism than views about it.

Another and more certain way to avoid the dilemma is to be modest about what interpretation delivers. Indeed, a modest interpretationism is one element of NEI.

I think that we are to attribute to Karl or Friedrich *some* beliefs and desires, call them 'core thoughts', on the basis of hard constraints suggested by the other elements of qualia empiricism. Such attributions are required of any full and proper interpretation. But given the fixed basis of those core thoughts, a range of different detailed psychological stories about Karl or Friedrich can properly be told by different interpreters, in light of the interpreters' differing interests or psychological vocabularies. And these differing interests and psychological vocabularies can themselves be underwritten by core thoughts of the interpreters, so that there is no danger of circularity or impredicativity.

One account of this general sort is due to Adam Morton. He suggests that there are different 'styles' of psychological explanation, which highlight different features of someone. Here are two of Morton's evocative alternative characterizations of Aida's final act:

2. Calculating. Aida realized that if she did nothing she would live, in captivity, and Radames would die. She found this no better than not living at all, because she would be subject to the will of her enemies and separated from her lover. There was an alternative, to be with her lover and spite her enemies, which she found preferable, since it gave her autonomy and closeness to Radames. She therefore took it.

3. Social. Aida's jealousy of Amneris made the prospect of life as a prisoner of Amneris's father intolerable, and her frustrated love for Radames made her willing to do anything to join him. When the opportunity arose, then, to defy the Egyptians and join her lover, it suited both her jealousy and her love.[2]

It seems to me different explanations like these might be equally true, and on internalist grounds. A plausibly moderate internalist relativism maintains that there are some thoughts that are fixed by the non-relative internal facts, but that different sorts of descriptions and elaborations of those basic psychological states might be appropriate within different styles of description. That can include merely hypothetical styles, so it is no grounds for an externalism involving actual interpreters. It is implausible to think of the fixed internal thoughts as *evidence* for any given interpretation, since an actual interpreter may be more familiar with someone's behavior than with the internal facts that constitute that person's core thoughts, and that is why I will call such internal facts 'proper grounds' for interpretation instead.

Further, we would beg no questions against externalism, or the existence of unconscious thoughts, if we presumed that at least minimal grounds for proper interpretation of someone include whatever internal conditions constitute the psychological materials sketched in the preceding chapter: sensory experiences, proto-judgments, the primary imagination, Strawsonian spatial thoughts, word-mediated thoughts with introspectible contents, and complicating phenomena like self-avowals. We will work in this chapter towards an understanding of how something like those resources

[2] Morton (1980: 46–8).

can root the interpretation of other sorts of thoughts, and in the next chapter we will see in particular how interpretation on such grounds can deliver the rigidified clusters of RDC. So in fact NEI also incorporates a modest non-relative interpretationism, whose modesty involves the use of proper grounds that constitute thoughts that we have already discussed to fix other core thoughts.

So there are two routes around our dilemma, and I will take the second: modesty. I think that there are, because of the dilemma, genuine problems of coherence for interpretationisms that are neither modest nor skeptical. But because the dominant forms seem to oscillate in and out skepticism in a way that is not illuminating for us, because I intend to borrow some of their mechanisms, and for purposes of discussion, I will waive these difficulties hereafter.

We have discovered a modest relativist interpretationism, and also a modest non-relativist form, that can help flesh out NEI. But our principal concern will be with less modest forms, which can tell us more about the semantic structure of word-mediated thoughts. We will begin, in Sections 9.3 through 9.6, with a key non-relativist account.

9.3

There are semantic views, including that of the late Wittgenstein, according to which it is impossible to construct any systematic theory of meaning, because there is just the complicated use of individual words and sentences, and nothing very general to say about it. If that were true, then the apparatus for word-mediated thought sketched in the last chapter would be adequate, though unilluminating. But I will presume that there is a central semantic notion that underwrites the core content contributed to thought by terms and sentences, and that other elements of the use of sentences, for instance the force of commands in Frege's sense, are somehow rooted in that core. Still, there is a diversity of views about the core.

Truth is the central externalist element of Davidson's prominent non-relativist interpretationism. It is a very natural resource for language-based externalism, since truth involves the world.

But there is a textual complication. Early Davidson stressed merely the importance of truth in the opinion of the interpreter,[3] which suggests interpreter-relativity. Only the possibility of omniscient interpreters was supposed to generate a link with truth itself.[4] But in Davidson's later work, the link to truth became more direct, and interpreter-relativity largely fell away. He said that in 'sharing a language, in whatever sense this is required for communication, we share a picture of the world that must, in its large features, be true'.[5] He thought that we should interpret Karl and Jenny so that their perceptual judgments, especially, are largely true. And the truth of their perceptual judgments involves the state of their environment.

We need to consider the advantages of this non-relative externalist conception versus those of internalist alternatives. We don't have far to look to find one alternative. Quine's discussion of radical translation, itself a skeptical development of proposals by Carnap, is the immediate root of Davidson's view.[6] Quine's dominant concern was linguistic meaning and not thought content, but the issues are closely linked.[7] And Quine's interpretationism was internalist. The basic semantic resources Quine deploys are the 'stimulus meanings' of sentences that report immediate observations. *Word and Object* says that stimulus meanings involve not rabbits out in the world but rather sensory irritations, activities in the sensory organs at skin's end: 'It is important to think of what prompts... assent... as stimulations and not rabbits. Stimulations can remain the same though the rabbit be supplanted by a counterfeit. Conversely, stimulation can vary... because of variations in angle, lighting, and color contrast, though the rabbit remain the same.... A visual stimulation is perhaps best identified... with the pattern of chromatic irradiation of the eye.'[8]

There are problems with this. First, Quine suggests that the meaning or meaning-analog of a sentence reporting a perceptual observation is the stimulation of sense organs and not some environmental fact. And that is highly unintuitive. If I see an earth mover and say so, my belief and sentence are not intuitively about the patterns of chromatic irradiation of my eye. Second, because facts about linguistic meaning are supposed to be facts about translatability, and proper translations must preserve stimulus

---

[3] Davidson (1984b). [4] Davidson (1984d). [5] Davidson (1984c: 199).
[6] Quine (1960: 26–79). Quine attributes the principle of charity to N. L. Wilson (1959). But Davidson denied that his view was based on Quine's.
[7] On Quine see Mendola (1997: 202–8). [8] Quine (1960: 31).

meanings, this view implies that no translation is possible of, and hence no meaningful language is possible for, someone different enough from a translator in sensory capacities.

Quine's later work addressed these worries. 'My observation sentences are and were about the distal external world.... My concern with the proximal was epistemological rather than semantical.... The explanation of... harmony at the proximal pole... is an intersubjective harmony of our subjective standards of perceptual similarity of neural intakes.'[9] But at least the second worry persists. The color blind do not enjoy such an intersubjective harmony with the normal. And if there is no intersubjective harmony at the proximal pole, it is certainly not obvious how Quine can deliver shared distal reference and avoid the first worry.

It is not surprising that Quine initially deployed a radically revisionary basic semantic conception, since his account was quite skeptical. He thought that whatever facts there are about meaning are captured by proper translations, but also that there is an indeterminacy of propriety among intuitively quite distinct translations of someone, corresponding to intuitively different 'translation manuals'.

But there is a relevant subtlety. If, like Quine, we stress the indeterminacy between the propriety of different translations, this is a kind of skeptical internalism. However, since interpretation manuals are outside the interpreted, if we stress the relativization of proper translation to an arbitrarily-adopted translation manual, the same facts suggest a certain kind of externalism. Still, in any case, interpreter-relativity of that sort will be our concern later on.

Quine seemed to take his late shift towards 'the distal external world' from Davidson. As Davidson said, 'the notion of stimulus meaning plays no role in my method, but its place is taken by reference to the objective features of the world that alter in conjunction with changes in attitude towards the truth of sentences'.[10] Hence Davidson's externalism in its paradigmatic form.

We are enquiring after proper grounds for that externalism. And we have isolated a reasonable initial motivation. Quine's focus on sensory irritations does not deliver intuitive contents for perceptual beliefs, and Davidson's externalist account is better motivated in that respect.

---

[9] Quine (1999: 74–5). See also Quine (1995: 20–1).   [10] Davidson (1984b: 136).

But there is another obvious internalist alternative, developed by another intellectual descendent of Quine, and it is not skeptical. David Lewis' account also developed over time. In its first period, best represented by the paper 'Radical Interpretation', it is probably not internalist.[11] Still, it will aid exposition to begin with that paper.

Lewis took radical interpretation to go like this: We the interpreters are given complete knowledge of Karl's physical state. There are a number of constraints on radical interpretation set by our commonsense theory of persons, which tell us how 'beliefs and desires and meanings are normally related to one another, to behavioral output, and to sensory input'.[12] These implicitly define our concepts of belief, desire, and meaning.[13] In particular, two important constraints are the Principle of Charity and the Rationalization Principle. The Principle of Charity mandates that Karl 'should be represented as believing what he ought to believe, and desiring what he ought to desire... making allowances for the likelihood that Karl's circumstances—his life history of evidence and training... —may have led him understandably into error.'[14] The Rationalization Principle requires that Karl 'should be represented as a rational agent; the beliefs and desires ascribed to him... should... provide good reasons for his behavior.'[15]

There is an immediate moral. Davidson deploys principles of charity and rationality that rest on truth. But Lewis' view indicates that such principles can rest not on truth, but on evidence. As long as evidence meets internalist strictures, internalists can deploy such principles. Perhaps sensory irritations are viable in this role, but, after the last part, we might as well use qualia.

There are two externalist elements in the first period version of Lewis' view. First, there is some role for truth by the interpreter's lights as a baseline for proper attribution, against which deviations are sanctioned by Karl's different history of education. This will involve external facts, or at least the external interpreter's view of those facts. Second, Karl's *history* is crucial even to those proper deviations.

But these externalist elements are later abandoned. The paradigmatic statement of Lewis' late view is 'Reduction of Mind'.[16] By then we are

---

[11] Lewis (1982).   [12] Lewis (1982: 111).   [13] Lewis (1982: 112).
[14] Ibid.   [15] Lewis (1982: 113).   [16] Lewis (1994).

supposed to share thoughts not only with our Twin Earth twins, but also with Davidson's Swampman, and even with brains in bottles who share our internal states.[17] Some externalist elements remain in the penumbra of Lewis' late view.[18] First, the laws of nature are supposed to have a regularist basis and yet to be relevant to proper interpretation. Second, Lewis' analysis of mad pain suggests that it matters whether or not you are a typical member of your kind.[19] But these relatively idiosyncratic commitments of Lewis as a systematic philosopher do not occlude his basically internalist interpretationism.

Davidson has characteristic and I think reasonable complaints against the semantic centrality of evidence. If someone claims that evidence rather than truth is primary in the theory of meaning or content, say in the manner of verificationists who explicate the meaning of a claim in terms of characteristic evidence for that claim, Davidson complains that they misrepresent or misunderstand the central semantic notion.[20] As a foe of epistemicism, I agree. But Lewis deployed evidence in a different way, to help constitute conditions of realization for beliefs that have full-blown truth-conditions. Still, perhaps Davidson had an argument that tells against even such a position, at least when it is allied with the kind of sensory contents that MS delivers.[21] It may lead to epistemic skepticism, and Davidson held that to be a reason to think it false. Put that way, I don't think that is much of an argument. It isn't enough reason to believe a philosophical position that if it were true it would imply the truth of something else that we want to be true but lack sufficient reason otherwise to believe. It isn't adequate evidence for the view that being human constitutes happiness that it would be nice if we were all happy. But there is a better way to put Davidson's point. While controversial, it is not unreasonable to worry that our internally determinate sensory evidence, our qualia, are insufficient to warrant our beliefs about the external world. But surely even the Cartesian skeptic should grant that we have such beliefs. And so perhaps an evidential role for internally determinate sensory experience cannot deliver through a Lewis-style architecture the facts of perceptual belief. This seems to be a reasonable motivation for externalism, and it is related to a second and

---

[17] Lewis (1994: 423–5).　[18] Lewis (1994: 425).　[19] Lewis (1980).
[20] Davidson (2005b: 58).　[21] Davidson (2005b: 56–7).

more certain problem with a Lewis-style account, at least when such an account is allied with an internalist account of sensory contents as qualia. To claim that our perceptual beliefs about the external world are rooted in inference on the basis of our qualia is psychologically unrealistic. Nor are qualia the sole or most intuitive sort of evidence. We certainly don't *think* our evidence is internally determinate.[22] We intuitively think that there are differences in the evidence we possess due merely to external differences, say in the notes in our pockets.[23]

So Davidson's externalist proposal does at least on the surface seem preferable to both Quine's initial proposal and to Lewis' somewhat epistemicist internalism, at least when Lewis' conception is allied with what we have seen to be the correct conception of sensory contents. But perhaps there is another internalist architecture that is preferable to Davidson's.

Another famous internalist interpretationism is Daniel Dennett's, despite its focus on truth.[24] Dennett, another intellectual descendant of Quine, favors a kind of modalized ET. Your internal state fixes its own ideal possible evolutionary history, which in turn fixes the content of your mental states in the manner suggested by ET. But we are done with ET. So let me float another sort of account, which shares a certain abstract form with Dennett's proposal.

It deploys an internalist conception of sensory experience as qualia, but in a different way than a Lewis-style account. It deploys qualia not as evidence, but rather to fix a kind of ideal truth, or, to be precise, to fix a kind of putative match. In light of Davidson's concerns, internalists about qualitative experience should hold that a principle of charity to qualia governs proper belief attribution, but not in a way that invokes qualia merely as characteristic evidence for perceptual beliefs. If you have qualitative experience as of a green square, then you must be ascribed the corresponding perceptual belief, at least if you can be coherently ascribed it given all the other constraints that govern proper belief ascription. Such an attribution has a kind of default propriety. What once were held to be epistemically basic beliefs in fact are rather attributionally basic.[25] The standard for proper charity in interpretation is fixed not by the evidence available to the interpreted as in Lewis, nor by the truths of the world

---

[22] Gibbons (2006a).   [23] Clark and Chalmers (1998).
[24] Dennett (1969, 1982, 1989, 1991).
[25] Mendola (1997: 279–95) develops both externalist and internalist versions of this.

as in Davidson, but rather by the apparent truth to the interpreted of the contents of their own perceptual experience. Externalists like Davidson sometimes stress that things in the world are not mere evidence for beliefs but rather partly constitutive of those beliefs, and internalists should deploy this Davidsonian suggestion with an internalist twist. Not the surface spectral red on a perceived wheelbarrow but the phenomenal red in my experience of the wheelbarrow helps to constitute my perceptual belief that it is red.

NEI can incorporate this suggestion. To a certain degree, it already has. One detailed difficulty for this model involves the kinds of spatial corrections in perceptual judgments that we make quite automatically, introduced in Chapter 7. But in the next section we consider resources that will help with this complication.

The general architecture that I am proposing is a form of internalist interpretationism that slides in between familiar externalist and internalist forms. Like familiar internalist forms, it deploys qualitative experience. But like familiar externalist forms, it focuses on something at least analogous to truth, not on evidence. In this way, it can evade the characteristic problems of both familiar forms. The characteristic problem of familiar internalist forms is their invocation of implausible forms of epistemicism. But Davidson's advantages over Lewis are not advantages over my non-epistemic proposal, which deploys the internally determinate contents of sensory states to help constitute the conditions required for allied perceptual beliefs to match the world. One characteristic problem of familiar externalist forms is that, given the physical facts, it is hard to see how they can deliver our perceptual beliefs involving color, which for instance underlie the general normal human belief that bluish purples and reddish purples are very similar. Generally shared perceptual errors are not a natural fit with these forms of externalism. Another related problem is that such views have no obvious means to deliver the differences in spontaneous perceptual beliefs of the normal and the color blind. But Lewis' advantages over Davidson in these respects are not advantages over my proposal.

Davidson's account is the paradigm non-relative externalist interpretationism. But so far we have found fewer grounds for its externalism than may be apparent, since a new internalist alternative has its advantages without its disadvantages. This element of NEI evades the dilemma for interpretationism with which we began only because the role of the interpreter can fall out as irrelevant. But that is probably inevitable for any non-relative interpretationism.

9.4

There are other beliefs than perceptual beliefs. And Davidson's account of these may involve more adequate motivation for his externalism.

To hold a sentence true closely reflects belief. Radical interpretation of Karl at t was supposed by Davidson to yield for each sentence S held true by Karl at t a Tarskian truth-sentence 'S is true iff p', where S is a sentence in the object language and p in the language of the interpreting theory. The basic evidence for proper interpretation according to Davidson is what sentences Karl holds true under what circumstances and at what times. We are to interpret him so that he is right, at least as far as we can tell, as much as possible.

For the case of perceptual beliefs, we have developed an internalist alternative, and seen that it is preferable. But there are other cases, and other relevant details of Davidson's account. According to Davidson, in proper interpretation we do this:

First we look for the best way to fit our logic, to the extent required to get a theory satisfying [Tarski's] Convention T, on to the new language; this may mean reading the logical structure of first-order quantification theory (plus identity) into the language, not taking the logical constants one by one, but treating this much of logic as a grid to be fitted on to the language in one fell swoop. The evidence here is of classes of sentences always held true or always held false by almost everyone all of the time (potential logical truths) and patterns of inference. The first step identifies predicates, singular terms, quantifiers, connectives, and identity; in theory, it settles questions of logical form. The second step concentrates on sentences with indexicals; those sentences sometimes held true and sometimes false according to discoverable changes in the world. This step in conjunction with the first limits the possibilities for interpreting individual predicates. The last step deals with the remaining sentences, those on which there is not uniform agreement, or whose held truth value does not depend systematically on changes in the environment.[26]

[26] Davidson (1984b: 136).

While this is reminiscent of Quine's procedure in *Word and Object*, there are several differences. Davidson does suggest that we focus, unlike Quine, on some differences and similarities between individuals, and that is an element of externalism. But in later writings he backed away from a focus on the interpretation of public language, towards the radical interpretation of individual idiolects,[27] so that cannot be the proper Davidsonian route to externalism. Davidson specifically noted these differences with Quine:

> [T]he semantic constraint in my method forces quantificational structure on the language to be interpreted, which probably does not leave room for indeterminacy of logical form; the notion of stimulus meaning plays no role in my method, but its place is taken by reference to the objective features of the world which alter in conjunction with changes in attitude towards the truth of sentences; the principle of charity, which Quine emphasizes only in connection with the identification of the (pure) sentential connectives, I apply across the board.[28]

In addition to the characteristically Davidsonian preference for objective features of the world over stimulus meanings or sensory contents, which we have already discussed, the use 'across the board' of a charity principle formulated in terms of truth implies externalism. And charity applied across the board, even to beliefs far removed from perception, seems like a plausible alternative to Lewis' and Quine's focus on the evidential relations of non-perceptual beliefs to perceptual beliefs. It is characteristic of at least one side of Davidson to claim that a focus on evidential relations involves an inappropriately epistemic conception of what constitutes the truth-conditions of non-perceptual beliefs. And as a foe of epistemicism, I am sympathetic.

But there is a complication. Davidson does not stably endorse a difference with Lewis and Quine on this point. For instance, he says that while we are to interpret in such a way as to minimize disagreements that lead to a failure of understanding,

> [s]ome disagreements are more destructive of understanding than others, and a sophisticated theory must naturally take this into account. Disagreement about theoretical matters may (in some cases) be more tolerable than disagreement about what is more evident; disagreement about how things look or appear is less tolerable than disagreement about how they are; disagreement about the truth

---

[27] Davidson (2005a, 2005d).   [28] Davidson (1984b: 136 n. 16).

of attributions of certain attitudes to a speaker by that same speaker may not be tolerable at all, or barely. It is impossible to simplify the considerations that are relevant, for everything we know or believe about the way evidence supports belief can be put to work in deciding where the theory can best allow error, and what errors are least destructive of understanding. The methodology of interpretation is, in this respect, nothing but epistemology seen in the mirror of meaning.[29]

Lewisian internalist interpretation, focused on evidential relations rather than truth, also deploys epistemology seen in the mirror of meaning. Besides such quotes, another factor that supports this second reading of Davidson is that the texts in which his view most clearly evolves away from a focus on charity in light of the interpreter's beliefs to charity in light of truth—texts we will discuss in the next two sections—involve perceptual judgments only. That is relevant because beliefs farther removed from perception are more likely to be where individual differences between the interpreter and interpreted are to be expected and properly accepted, especially if such beliefs aren't constrained by truth. And so a focus on evidential relations rather than interpreter-relativity seems more plausible for these cases. There is also a third current in Davidson that underwrites this picture. Some key texts[30] indicate that interpreters should take account of explicable errors and the relative likelihood of various mistakes, which seems to reflect evidential considerations.

I think that the best way to interpret Davidson overall, in light of these various sorts of passages, is as proposing a complex amalgam of two oversimplified initial models, one that deploys evidential relations exclusively to constitute the contents of non-perceptual beliefs, and one that deploys charity rooted in the world exclusively. The truth of the world is supposed to be one constraint, and epistemology seen in the mirror of meaning is supposed to be another, which also provides for explicable mistakes. And both constraints are supposed to work together to fix the proper interpretation of non-perceptual beliefs.

This may seem to provide motivation for externalism. But these features of Davidson's proposal can be co-opted by NEI.

Internalists characteristically focus on evidence. And even with my resistance to epistemicism, I think that inferential relations between the

---

[29] Davidson (1984d: 169).
[30] Davidson (1984b: 136–7). This element of Davidson is systematized by Henderson (1999).

sentences to which one assents are sometimes partly constitutive of what one thinks through uttering such sentences. For instance, I think that proofs are partly constitutive of the meaning of some mathematical sentences and the content of thoughts mediated by such sentences. In our dispositions to variously assent to verbally characterized scenarios, NEI already has one mechanism that can underwrite these facts.

But the rub is this: I claim that content-characterizing inferences are sometimes epistemically inappropriate, and hence that the epistemic status of a characteristic inference is irrelevant. For example, consider some of the inferences quite characteristic of superstitious beliefs in our mundane world. I think that Aquinas' Five Ways are pretty bad arguments. But I also think that they are forms of inference that are quite characteristic of a certain sort of religious belief. I have no idea whether there are even hypothetical and humanly comprehensible conditions that could constitute good evidence for such a belief. And the Strawsonian mechanisms are unlikely to deliver a concrete conception of God. But I have no doubt there are such beliefs. You may prefer other examples. But my general point is that claims are made for which even the most characteristic evidence is awful. The linguistic division of labor is not the only cognitive phenomenon with a dark side.

The second element of our Davidsonian amalgam is a role for the world itself in fixing judgments other than immediate perceptual judgments. And an internalist variant of this element can help with the necessary complications involving perceptual distortions left hanging in the last section, and also in other ways. NEI deploys a particular internalist echo of the world: complex thoughts of the concrete spatio-temporal way the world is, of the sort suggested by our earlier discussions. We each have a concrete conception of the way the world is that is not mediated by words.[31] Though it is enormously incomplete, and also inconsistent in various ways, still we each have a rough conception of how things look and feel and sound from various places and times, times and places that are related in various ways and by various paths, say to where we are now. Some evidence for this is that we have the internally determinate capacity to draw appropriate rough sketches of how things are and how they look elsewhere, and to move in ways that would be appropriate to other times and places. We are also able to conceive other concrete ways that the world might have been.

[31] Normal humans are in question.

Consider your take on concrete reality. Such a concrete scenario will match or not match the world itself in various ways. But whether it matches the world or not, it constrains by a kind of charity across the board what you believe by your asserted sentences. And your word-free concrete conception of the world provides some constraints on the proper interpretation of even your perceptual beliefs, which helps the qualia-based mechanism of the last section answer worries about the obvious spatial distortions in visual experience. And what you would believe via sentences you would be disposed to assert of a given hypothetical concrete scenario is constrained by charity on the basis of that scenario.

My central point about this second bit of quasi-Davidsonian mechanism is that externalism does not own a concern with truth across the board, or analogous things like match, though sometimes Davidson wrote as if it does. And so there are fewer grounds here for Davidson's externalism than may meet the eye.

What's more, there are grounds to prefer my internalist variant. Error, Davidson said, is what gives belief its point, but error must be quite limited:

> The reason for this is that a belief is identified by its location in a pattern of belief; it is that pattern that determines the subject matter of the belief, what the belief is about.... False beliefs tend to undermine the identification of the subject matter.... To take an example, how clear are we that the ancients—some ancients—believed that the earth was flat? *This* earth? Well, this earth of ours is part of a solar system, a system partly identified by the fact that it is a gaggle of large, cool, solid bodies circling around a very large, hot star. If someone believes *none* of this about the earth, is it certain that it is the earth that he is thinking about? An answer is not called for.[32]

But the externalism of this conception is in one way merely skin deep, and in another way quite implausible. We should all share with most externalists the intuition that the ancients believed false things about the Earth. It is that intuition which stands behind some of the most forceful of the famous externalist cases. Perhaps radical Kuhnians think the ancients shared no world with us, and perhaps those who favor paradigm case arguments think the ancients' belief that the Earth is flat was true even in our shared world. But most of us think otherwise. Davidson's account requires a shared world, and the translatability of the ancients, and no

---

[32] Davidson (1984d: 168).

massive error. Perhaps he thought 'an answer is not called for' because of massive indeterminacy, which is a skeptical element of his view that I am mostly suppressing, but which isn't relevant in a context in which we are trying to develop a positive account of thought content. Perhaps he thought an answer not called for because the positive answer his externalist view suggests is the very unintuitive suggestion of the paradigm case argument. Or perhaps he thought no answer was called for because his view suggests that the ancients couldn't believe that an actually round earth was flat. But in any case, Davidson's view does not accommodate the plausible and indeed characteristically externalist intuition that we and the ancients share reference to a planet, and that they were massively wrong about it.

NEI can better accommodate this plausible intuition. The gross difference between the ancients and moderns about the shape of the Earth is clearly reflected in the concrete scenarios, unmediated by words, that we accept and they accepted. They took themselves to stand on something with a different shape.

We should conclude, I claim, that Davidson was right to focus on truth rather than primarily on evidence. But he was somewhat wrong in his externalist way of doing so.

One might object to NEI, even though it is centered on truth or match. As external interpreters of someone, we only have epistemic access to their sensory experience by observing their evident behavior in their external environment. We can't interpret them on the basis of their qualia or other internal and hence observationally inaccessible states. But the explicitly epistemic focus of this complaint undercuts its relevance to our issue. We are pursuing an understanding of what in fact constitutes mental states. Epistemic concerns, which are admittedly very naturally invoked by interpretationism, only suggest externalism about *the facts* of mental content if we presume a very controversial and tendentious form of verificationism, which almost no one now accepts, which no one has strong reason to accept, and which would not be at all characteristically Davidsonian.

9.5

There are other aspects of Davidson that may suggest grounds for externalism. Radical interpretation as so far characterized focuses dominantly on the semantics of belief and the way in which belief is responsive to the world. But belief also figures in the explanation of action, and Davidson wrote not merely *Inquiries into Truth and Interpretation* but also *Essays on Actions and Events*.[33] Indeed, in its full and canonical formulations his account of interpretation is a unified theory of the interpretation of belief, preference, and meaning.[34]

The basic data for interpretation in that full account are the varying circumstances that lead the interpreted to prefer that one rather than another sentence be true.

Jeffrey's version of decision theory, applied to sentences, tells us that a rational agent cannot prefer [the truth of] both a sentence and its negation to [the truth of] a tautology, nor a tautology to both a sentence and its negation. This fact makes it possible for an interpreter to identify, with no knowledge of the meaning of the agent's sentences, all of the pure sentential connectives, such as negation, conjunction, and the biconditional. This minimal knowledge suffices to determine the subjective probabilities of all of the agent's sentences—how likely the agent thinks those sentences are to be true—and then, in turn, to fix the relative values of the truth of those sentences (from the agent's point of view, of course). The subjective probabilities can then be used to interpret the sentences. For what Quine calls observation sentences, the changes in probabilities provide the obvious clues to first order interpretation when geared to events and objects easily perceived simultaneously by interpreter and the person being interpreted. Conditional probabilities and entailments between sentences, by registering what the speaker takes to be evidence for his beliefs, provides the interpreter with what is needed to interpret more theoretical terms and sentences.[35]

This conception involves less concern with charity across the board and more concern with evidential relations than the alternative Davidsonian proposal that we discussed in the last section, and it is interesting that this seems characteristic of his more decision-theoretic formulations.[36] But focus on another point.

According to Davidson, it is crucial for interpretation that there be a match between preferences that are verbally expressed and non-verbal actions. That may suggest some new grounds for externalism, since non-verbal action may not only affect but crucially involve the external world.

[33] Davidson (1980).
[34] Davidson (1990, 1999b, 1999c, 2004a, 2005e: 7–75). See also Hopkins (1999).
[35] Davidson (2004b: 127).   [36] For a late example, see Davidson (2005e: 49–75).

But since action may also be complete at or within skin's end, that depends on the nature of the non-verbal actions in question.

Davidson gave this example: 'A drill master who says, "Left, right, left, right" makes clear to someone who does not understand these abbreviated sentential utterances which one he prefers to have made true from moment to moment. (Someone who does not think imperatives have truth-values will have no difficulty figuring out what the drill master wants made true.) Commands, demands, and requests are among the most pressing uses of language we are apt, as children and aliens, to be exposed to.'[37] But notice that the drill master's preferences can be revealed by his own marching, no further out than skin's end, and that his dissatisfaction with a soldier's contrary performance is also likely to be quite evident there. Marching takes some time to accomplish, but dispositions to march further may be present even in a moment. Of course, this is just one example. Still, it is Davidson's example.

NEI will incorporate a version of this mechanism. Causal notions are traditionally difficult for empiricists. But there are classical empiricist conceptions of causal notions, rooted either in expected regularities like Hume's or in individual action like Berkeley's. And NEI incorporates an internalist physicalist conception of our thought about causes that shares an abstract structure with Berkeley's idealist view,[38] as well as with Davidson's focus on action.

We have some thoughts only because we have sensory experience, and the characteristic phenomenal content of perceptual belief is paradigmatically incoming. But we also have causal thoughts because we do things, and so causal content is paradigmatically outgoing. What we do we most immediately do by moving our muscles inside our skins, and we can be disposed to a temporal trajectory of such motion even before we perform it. Your causal thought about the force of an oncoming wind or a blast wave is displayed at least in part in your motor preparations for meeting their force, regardless of what in fact is outside you. Individual actions complete at skin's end, and preparations for such action are a useful resource for the internalist physicalist, as you trace a square with your finger, grab a frisbee, or press hard into the blowing rain.

---

[37] Davidson (1999b: 331).
[38] Mendola (1997: 143–65) further develops this conception.

There is also another sort of parallel between the phenomenal and the causal. Just as there are mere phenomenal images or quasi-experiences, so too, I think, there are mere motor images or quasi-intentions, for instance when you rehearse in imagination what you would physically do in a certain circumstance that isn't in fact present.

These basic causal resources enrich our capacity for concrete thought unmediated by words. In fact, it seems crucial that the complex spatial scenarios that we have the capacity to conceive in a way unmediated by words involve a conception of how things would look if we *moved* in various ways. These resources also seem to help constitute the introspectible facts about what we would say under various hypothetical scenarios, and what we do say in the mind's throat.

9.6

Davidson was an externalist, but so far the roots of his externalism seem shallow. Are there other grounds for externalism in Davidson?

In 'Three Varieties of Knowledge',[39] Davidson split the Principle of Charity into a Principle of Coherence and a Principle of Correspondence, which holds that a speaker's beliefs are about those conditions that regularly cause them. While at first we hear merely that the 'Principle of Correspondence prompts the interpreter to take the speaker to be responding to the same features of the world that he (the interpreter) would be responding to under similar circumstances',[40] we are eventually more specifically informed that 'the stimuli that cause our most basic verbal responses also determine what those verbal responses mean, and the content of the beliefs that accompany them',[41] where stimuli are 'events and objects in the environment'.[42] And in 'Could There Be a Science of Rationality?', Davidson says that 'the truth conditions of my sentence "The moon is gibbous", or of my belief that the moon is gibbous, depend in part on the causal history of my relations to the moon. But it could happen that two people were in relevantly similar physical states (defined just in terms of what is inside their skin), and yet one could be speaking or thinking of our moon, and the other not.'[43]

[39] Davidson (2001c). [40] Davidson (2001c: 211). [41] Davidson (2001c: 213).
[42] Davidson (2001c: 212). [43] Davidson (2004b: 121).

We have already discussed Davidson's eventual preference for a focus on the true state of objective stimuli, but this mechanism is somewhat richer. Only the narrow-minded will be disconcerted to see the primary partisan of interpretation morphing into a causal-informational theorist before our eyes. Only the carping will mind if external stimulus events are suspiciously like facts, while Davidson denies that there are facts. But it is reasonable to remember that we discussed all adequately developed externalist causal-informational accounts in Part II, and saw that they are false.

Still, perhaps Davidson can be taken as proposing a new conception of proper causes. Much of his late work developed the notion of triangulation, which seems to support forms of externalism, and also to play a crucial role in fixing content.[44] Perhaps it is Davidson's account of proper causes.

What is triangulation, and what is it supposed to accomplish? It comes in levels. Consider a human child—capable of robust interaction with adult interpreters—looking at ambient furniture. We begin with first-level triangulation, involving

> three similarity patterns[: t]he child finds tables similar; we find tables similar; and we find the child's responses in the presence of the tables similar.... The relevant stimuli are the objects or events we naturally find similar (tables) which are correlated with the responses of the child we find similar. It is a form of triangulation; one line goes from the child in the direction of the table, one line goes from us in the direction of the table, and the third line goes between us and the child. Where the lines from child to table and us to table converge, 'the' stimulus is located.[45]

So far this suggests merely an interpreter-relativity of stimulus, which removes indeterminacy in one sense, but is indeterminacy in another. But there are more complicated conditions that are, according to Davidson, required for thought. What I will call Level 2 triangulation requires that the interpreted also perform interpretation on the interpreter. Level 3 requires in addition that the two 'interact' in a way 'available' to the interacting creatures.[46] And Level 4 triangulation requires that this interaction be by communication.[47] Each must speak to and be understood by the other, though given the possibility of radical interpretation, they needn't speak the same language.

---

[44] Davidson (2001a, 2001b, 2001c).   [45] Davidson (2001b: 119).
[46] Davidson (2001b: 120).   [47] Davidson (2001b: 121).

These extra levels of triangulation remove certain sorts of relativity and indeterminacy, it would seem. That was one of Davidson's reasons for thinking triangulation is important, and perhaps this suggests a new account of proper causes. And note that the non-relative stimulus determinacy delivered by Level 4 triangulation involves both the world and another cognizer. Those are external conditions, so we have two new possible roots for externalism in Davidson.

There is indeed another possible root for externalism that involves triangulation. Davidson suggested that the proper general understanding of Wittgenstein's Private Language Argument is this: It must be possible to make a distinction between thinking that one means something and actually meaning it, and this requires that in general one judge and mean as others in one's community do.[48] Error must be possible, and error is social deviance, so there can be no private language or thought. This general understanding is shared with other reconstructions we will consider, but Davidson's own version, PLA2, takes a specific and suitably Davidsonian form, which reflects an argument for the necessity of language to thought first broached in 'Thought and Talk'.[49]

The argument goes roughly like this: There is no belief without the conception of belief, because belief requires an understanding of the possibility of mistake. And we have the idea of belief only from its role in the interpretation of language, so someone must be in a speech community to have the concept of belief.

This argument was eventually developed by Davidson through the concept of triangulation. We then heard that belief requires the concept of belief because belief requires the possibility of surprise, and this in turn requires the concept of belief.[50] And we also heard that the concept of belief requires language, because the capability for linguistic communication is sufficient for the possession of concept via the upper levels of triangulation required for thought, and there is no other plausible sufficient condition.[51]

So triangulation suggests various grounds for externalism. But there are various difficulties with these routes.

PLA2 is too hasty. Shock, say the shock of pigeons or squirrels, seems capable of constituting surprise, and yet doesn't require possession of the

---

[48] Davidson (2001b: 117).   [49] Davidson (1984d: 170).
[50] Davidson (2001a: 103–4).   [51] Davidson (2001a: 105).

concept of belief. And while Davidson repeatedly says that belief requires the concept of belief and that possible error requires the conception of error, so that there can be no creatures who lack semantic self-consciousness but who have beliefs, that claim is not well motivated. There is no obvious reason why there might not be those who are capable of error but incapable of recognizing that possibility.

But from our perspective the key point is something else. Certainly there are alternative conceptions of error possible, in which a belief lacks a kind of fit with the world that isn't somehow rooted in social deviance. Consider Lewisian brains in bottles, most of whose beliefs are false. Indeed if, as Lewis suggests, brains in bottles can have the same thoughts in some intuitive sense that we do, then neither the world nor other people are necessary to thought, nor even to thought rooted in interpretation, whatever Davidson says about triangulation. I don't know about brains in bottles. That's too internalist even for me. But NEI incorporates internal capacities that deliver thoughts of complex concrete scenarios, which can match or not match the world in various ways. And that involves no social deviance. Even sensory content itself provides a capacity for incorrectness.

But let me be more positive about this aspect of Davidson's view. Triangulation as developed by Davidson involves intersubjectivity in ways that have important internalist analogs, which will eventually help us answer PLA9. I doubt that these internalist analogs characteristically involve language, so I will suppress that Davidsonian detail.

Triangulation is supposed to involve external conditions in two ways. Focus first on the apparent role of the world. And imagine that all people share a hallucination, enforced by a Cartesian demon. To help preserve reference across the individuals, we can presume that there is some causal interaction among the deluded mediated by the deceiver, acting a bit like Berkeley's god. Such individuals might perform something a lot like mutual interpretation involving even something quite like Level 4 triangulation, without the world itself playing any genuine role in the practice. The shared illusion of a world will do.[52]

While Wittgenstein made some think that idiosyncratic sensory states should be semantically irrelevant, it might be that only the contents of

[52] Stroud (1999) makes this point, but suggests on page 160 that the 'question of whether our beliefs are all or for the most part true cannot consistently be asked with the possibility of reaching a negative answer'. See also Davidson (1999a).

sensory states are shared, while worldly referents vary wildly or are absent. Then the worldly referents would be irrelevant, and on what seems even better grounds. While such a scenario may seem highly unlikely, still it is revealing. And of course the zombies and qualia inverts of Wittgenstein's worries are pretty unlikely too.

Of course, Davidson may not have granted that such a scenario is a coherent possibility. But other interpretationists, including Lewis, do not agree. Davidson does have one argument apparently focused against this possibility, the notorious omniscient interpreter argument. An omniscient interpreter must charitably interpret creatures by his or her own lights, and truth by his or her own lights is truth. But of course a truly omniscient interpreter would know the contents of any internally determinate sensory experiences deployed by internalist interpretationists, who favor other sorts of charity principles.[53]

So much for the world. Triangulation requires not the sharing of a world but rather of a conception or experience of the world. Now consider the alleged role of the interpreter in triangulation.

There is a puzzle about the robust role for interpreters that triangulation suggests, which reflects our opening dilemma for robust forms of interpretationism. If the condition of the interpreter plays an important role, then there is interpreter-relativity of a stronger sort than is customarily associated with Davidson. And if the point of Davidson's extra levels of triangulation is rather to remove robust interpreter-relativity or corresponding indeterminacy, then we should be able to ignore the presence of an external interpreter. Each individual's own state, and hence arguably internal state, will rather fix a sufficiently restricted range of merely possible interpreters for that individual, and of proper interpretations of that individual. The role of the interpreter is hence merely hypothetical, and so no real grounds for externalism. This returns to one horn of our opening dilemma for interpretationism. Non-relative forms of interpretationism seem not to essentially involve interpretation at all.

Still, I think that the social aspects of triangulation do suggest an internalist echo that is crucial in the constitution of our capacities for certain sorts of thoughts. We do seem capable of considering how things look to one

---

[53] For a late presentation of the argument and something like this objection see Davidson (2005c: 43–4).

another, and that is entwined with our conception of a world that we share in something like the way Davidson suggests.

Let me give one example that is quite obviously purged of tendentious externalist baggage. In a dream of some New Jerusalem, I might have an understanding of how things are in the world of the dream and of what others in the dream are dreamed by me to see, and by a kind of internal echo of externalist triangulation. We will develop a somewhat better conception of this capacity during our discussion of Brandom, and it is also related to Bennett's version of the Refutation of Idealism.

Triangulation provides no proper root for externalism in Davidson, unless perhaps it rests on robust interpreter-relativity. Indeed, it suggests yet another resource for NEI.

Davidson was an externalist. But our exploration of his paradigmatic and well-developed non-relativist externalist interpretationism, which is also one of the best-developed truth-conditional externalisms, has discovered no legitimate motivations for externalism, and many helpful resources for NEI.

9.7

Robustly interpreter-relative interpretation naturally assures externalism. That is because, except in the case of self-interpretation discussed in the last chapter, interpreters are outside the interpreted, and because a robust, immodest role for interpreters implies that there are no internally determinate core thoughts.

The best-developed robustly interpreter-relative externalism is Robert Brandom's view, which is also a usually well-developed externalist account of linguistic meaning as proper use. But in contemporary discussions there are four other sorts of apparently robust relative non-skeptical externalist interpretationisms that focus on interpretation by others. They relativize respectively to best current theories, to best theories of the society of the translator, to local situations and concerns, and in a different way than Brandom to the individual cognitive configuration of the interpreter. Before we turn to Brandom's account in Sections 9.8 through 9.13, we will give brief consideration to these four forms.

The first involves an unusual reading of the Twin Earth case. Perhaps not truths about natural kinds, but rather our best contemporary theories about natural kinds, determine the extensions and references of our ancestors' words. Gary Ebbs suggests something like this, though with a skeptical spin that probably makes it non-robust.[54] Still, a robust version is possible. Since best theories may change with time, a theory of this sort would support over time the proper ascription of different extensions to a single term of a single ancestor uttered in a single moment.

The second sort of relativism is a variant of the first. Perhaps the relativity of meaning isn't due to the different relationships of different successors to a given set of ancestors within a community over time, but rather due to the different relationships of different translating communities to a given translated language. Mark Lance and John Hawthorne have proposed that there are sentences that different translators in different communities that have different theoretical commitments might appropriately translate so that they come out false in one translation and true in the other.[55]

Charles Travis suggests a third form of apparently robust relativity.[56] He defends a unified conception whereby the propriety of belief ascriptions, their proper interchangeability, and also the existence and identity of thoughts, are 'occasion sensitive', which means that these things are all relativized to occasions. Indeed, he believes that the meanings of all sentences and their synonymy[57] are also occasion sensitive in this way. Declarative sentences say how things are from among alternatives, but the range of alternatives is itself occasion sensitive.[58]

Sometimes, he suggests, being blue and being painted blue count as different alternatives, say when we are worrying about Darwin's appearance and whether he is choking.[59] Sometimes they count as the same alternative, as when we are choosing a car or contemplating a new building. Sometimes being blue ink is a matter of how ink looks in the tube, and sometimes of how it will look on the page.[60] So there are different possible understandings of the claim 'this is blue', and indeed of the thought that

---

[54] Ebbs (1997: 179–222).
[55] Lance and O'Leary-Hawthorne (1997: 44–54). But note the qualifications regarding dual translation on 81–2, and the exchange between Byrne (2002) and Lance and O'Leary-Hawthorne (2002).
[56] Travis (2000).
[57] Travis doesn't call the relation of interchangeability of sentences 'synonymy', but for no cited reason.
[58] What then is shared and stable? Merely the words.
[59] Travis (2000: 72).   [60] Travis (2000: 126).

this is blue. Sometimes thinking that this is blue and thinking that this is painted blue count as the same thought, and sometimes as different thoughts.[61]

Some of the occasions to which thoughts are relative, for instance the cases I've already given, are contexts that don't seem to imply any interesting interpreter-relativity. The interpreted person is merely as a matter of non-relative fact in one sort of relevant context or another. If the contexts in question are external, that would be grounds for a novel form of externalism, but not one that is firmly supported by Travis' cases, since there are plentiful internal echoes of these contexts. Consider the internal psychological differences between worrying about someone choking and buying a car.

But occasions in general, according to Travis, involve 'such things as the point, or purpose, in identifying relevant ways for things to be, the functions which talking of the ways to be identified would serve, our reasons for speaking of the world as being one way or the other'.[62] And at least sometimes this is supposed to involve robust interpreter-relativity. Here is his case: Unbeknownst to Pia, Max is in fact Moriarty. She would flee Moriarty under that name. But she welcomes the news that Max is coming to the party. In these conditions, there are obvious reasons for many ascribers to distinguish two thoughts that Pia might have, that Max is coming to the party and that Moriarty is coming. But consider this:

> Two of Moriarty's henchmen, Alf and Rod, have followed with interest his clever and successful deception of Pia—pretending that he is named Max, that he is a lawyer, and so on. They know that if she thinks *he* is coming to the party, she will be all aflutter. Alf asks, 'Does she know that Moriarty is coming?' Rod answers 'Yes.' In the circumstances, Rod counts as having stated truth. If he does, there then counts as just one thing there is to know, or to think, which is one thing Pia does know or think.[63]

I think that these three relativist proposals are interesting. And they suggest the relevance of future external conditions, which I promised to consider in this part. But the cases provided are insufficient to motivate externalism

---

[61] Travis (2000: 129–44). And a certain attitude towards a content may be thinking it on some understandings and not on others. See 149–50.
[62] Travis (2000: 89).   [63] Travis (2000: 188).

rooted in robust interpreter-relativity.[64] They rather suggest that there was something psychological and fairly robust about our ancestors and about Pia that is preserved among the various alternative interpretations occasioned by various new theories, or various translator communities, or various purposes of various interpreters. They rather suggest that there are stable psychological states that don't turn on what interpreters in the future will do, which will not change (while yet sitting in the past) with the succession of various future interpreters deploying different theories or having different purposes.

Internalists need merely split the difference in these cases, at least when considering core thoughts.[65] They should focus on contents that abstract away from details that would be fixed by various possible future histories, and hence by pressures of the sort that Travis, Hawthorne, Lance, and Ebbs invoke. And so these cases support something more analogous than it may initially appear to modest interpretationisms like Morton's. To the degree that the future-oriented relativisms are well motivated, they aren't plausibly robust.

There is a fourth form of relativism. 'Projectors'[66] claim that proper attributions of content are made by an interpreter via the method of considering the attitudes that the interpreter would have under the circumstances of the interpreted. They suggest that an interpreter work outward from the self, rather than inward from the world. Perhaps this allows a robust role for the idiosyncrasies of interpreters. Two views that at least on the surface seem to be of this sort are found in early Grandy and early Stich.[67]

Grandy's and Stich's views were expressed in a relativist way, as indeed were Quine's and even Lewis' views on occasion. But that seems like an unimportant feature of all of these proposals. Grandy seems to have been dominantly concerned to modify an emphasis on Principles of Charity in an already relativized sense, principles that require that we aim to maximize agreement between ourselves and the interpreted, in the direction of Principles of Humanity, which require that we aim to maximize the similarity of the imputed pattern of relations among beliefs, desires, and the world to our own.[68] This would help us to take proper account of

---

[64] Ebbs, Lance, and Hawthorne appeal to arguments that share a form with PLA5b, 6, and 8. But we will see that this is insufficient motivation for externalism.
[65] Splitting the Difference when capitalized is a view about privileged access. [66] Levin (1988).
[67] Grandy (1973); Stich (1980, 1981, 1982, 1983, 1984, 1985). [68] Grandy (1973: 443).

idiosyncrasies in the evidential situations and histories of training of others when ascribing beliefs. While both Principles of Charity and Principles of Humanity as so characterized are relativized to the ascriber, still Lewis' account, which in its final form is not relativized to ascribers, shows that concerns with the rationality of responses to evidence and training needn't take such a form. Indeed, if I know myself to be seriously and unusually irrational in some relevant way, it would seem that I shouldn't focus on similarity to myself in making ascriptions. So it seems that the main thrust of Grandy's position was neither deeply externalist nor relativist, and is preserved in Lewis' non-relative and more or less internalist account.

Stich's account grew out of the observation that issues about proper interpretation reflect issues about content similarity and not just identity. He emphasized similarity to the thoughts of the ascriber, which introduces an element of relativization that he also emphasized. But as in the case of Grandy, this seems accidental to his central observation. That is that content similarity can matter as well as content identity. That might be true even if such similarity isn't a matter of relative similarity to the interpreter, and possible idiosyncrasies of the interpreter would again suggest that it isn't centrally so. Stich also and plausibly emphasized that the interpreted cannot reasonably be held to very strict canons of rationality. But of course the possibility of irrationality in interpreters is reason to think that the proper degree of rationality in the interpreted shouldn't be determined by the standing psychological idiosyncrasies of interpreters.

The relativism of these classic views seems an artifact of their surface expression. We need to look elsewhere for genuinely robust interpreter-relativity.

9.8

Brandom's account will require considerable exposition.[69] It involves a fifth sort of robustly relative externalist interpretationism, but it will take a while to properly understand this, and also certain elements of Brandom's proposal that I will hijack for NEI.

[69] Brandom (1994, 2000).

Brandom's proposal has four broad features that we will consider in a general way in this and the following four sections, before discussing three crucial details in Section 9.13.

First, Brandom's account is in the tradition that focuses on proper use rather than truth. And Brandom's account is in particular an inferentially-based account. Rather than starting with the notions of reference or truth and working towards the notion of a good inference, Brandom starts with good inference and works towards reference and truth. And, indeed, Brandom suggests a particular form of inferentially-based account:

> The kind of inference whose correctnesses determine the conceptual contents of its premises and its conclusions may be called, following Sellars, *material* inferences. As examples, consider the inference from 'Pittsburgh is to the west of Princeton' to 'Princeton is to the east of Pittsburgh'.... It is the contents of the concepts *west* and *east* that make [that] a good inference.... Endorsing [this inference] is part of grasping those concepts.[70]

Two other broad features of Brandom's account are also inherited from Sellars.[71] The second feature is that it is firmly language-based. The content of *all* thoughts is supposed to be inherited from the meaning of public language. The third feature is that the account is normative in a sense that is supposed to resist naturalistic reduction. But the fourth broad feature of Brandom's account is not Sellarsian. Brandom's account, in a way we will eventually trace, is robustly interpreter-relative.

Consider the inferentialism of Brandom's account, its first broad feature. I think that, with appropriate modification, internalists should embrace it, though in a secondary role. Even Davidson does not eschew some role for inference. And while I claim that some of the inferences constitutive of some linguistically-mediated thoughts are not epistemically good ones, modification of that detail would not compromise the basic structure of Brandom's inferentialism.

NEI involves a variant of Davidson's focus on truth as semantically basic, and that may seem in direct conflict with Brandom's alternative focus on inference as basic. But if there is a central set of linguistic terms

---

[70] Brandom (2000: 52).   [71] Sellars (1997).

and sentences for which truth is the basic semantic notion, that does not imply that all terms and sentences are like that. The claim that correctness in mathematics consists of provability of some kind is consistent with anything we adopted from Davidson. Statements about proofs themselves might have content of a simple match-based sort, but statements about mathematical entities might have related inferentially-rooted content. This would imply that mathematical statements are associated with grounds for assertion even if they are not intuitively about those grounds, and hence that they can be delivered by our previous simple Chapter 8 mechanism for fixing the meaning of assertions. When presented with a proof as a relevant scenario, we may be inclined to utterance of the mathematical claim hence proven.

But there are other kinds of even assertive claims that seem to require a different treatment. The content of claims like $2 + 2 = 4$ seems to be rooted in things we do in a different way than we have yet considered, and NEI must incorporate yet more resources to account for thought mediated by such language, as we will shortly see. RDC only provides an account of the contribution to thought of terms that purport to refer, and there are many other sorts of terms that require another sort of account. Some such terms are characteristically parts of sentences that themselves have match- or at least inference-based correctness conditions. But not all are.

On a suitably inclusive understanding, inferentialism provides crucial resources to help augment the simple Davidsonian core we have already incorporated into NEI so that it can address some of these cases. And our discussion will involve consideration of resources that will help with others. In other words, we will gather various hints about how all this works from Brandom.

My ecumenical proposal is probably in conflict with more radical elements of Brandom's inferentialism. I think he would deny what seems to me the plausible claim that the very coherence of inferentialism requires that it be possible to make claims that have a basic kind of truth or match about the presence of inferences. But we will slowly return to this controversial aspect of Brandom's view. It is related to its other broad features, especially to its interpreter-relativity.

9.9

The next two broad features of Brandom's account are that it is firmly language-based, and also normative in a sense that is supposed to resist naturalistic reduction.

Sellars' simpler and more straightforward conception shares these general features. He famously held that the content of all thought is derived from the meaning of language. To think that sensory experience that is not mediated by language can constitute content for even some thoughts is to fall prey to the Myth of the Given, he claimed. And he was also skeptical of naturalist reductions of content or meaning. He said that 'the idea that epistemic facts [like sensing a particular fact] can be analyzed without remainder—even "in principle"—into non-epistemic facts, whether phenomenal or behavioral, public or private, with no matter how lavish a sprinkling of subjunctives and hypotheticals is, I believe, a radical mistake—a mistake of a piece with the so-called "naturalistic fallacy" in ethics.'[72] Epistemic facts, including facts of cognition and even of sensation in the full sense, are in the 'space of reasons', and this allegedly forbids a naturalistic reduction or analysis. Of course, constitution may occur when there is no reduction or analysis, but that was not Sellars' point.

Brandom thinks that these two general claims are linked, but in a subtle way. We will begin with Brandom's claim, adopted from Sellars, that there is very firm dependency of thought content on language meaning. It will take us a while to work back towards its connection, according to Brandom, with the denial of naturalism.

Qualia empiricism implies that our experience has one kind of fact-like structure, which makes it in one way thought-like. We experience things being certain ways unmediated by language. And we also have capacities for complex concrete spatio-temporal thoughts that are unmediated by words. Sellars' contrary claims that all thought capacities require the possession of language are not supported by any argument that I can reconstruct in a suitably sympathetic way, and are at best too idiosyncratic to detain us here.[73] But the mediation of thought by language is in any case generally consistent with internalism.

---

[72] Sellars (1997: 19).   [73] Sellars (1997: 68–79).

Speech occurs at or within skin's end, and we can even hear it through the eustachian tube. And if that doesn't seem internalist enough, presume that we sometimes speak in the mind's ear and throat, to ourselves, with appropriate sound images and tactile images engaged by motor dispositions that also sometimes result in the appropriate movements in our throats and tongues. Presume that such inner speech constitutes thoughts.[74] Further, presume that the content of such thought is whatever meaning that inner speech possesses by virtue of the internally determinate states of the speaker, including their dispositions to speak in various ways in various hypothetical circumstances, according to the general model incorporated into NEI.

Why isn't that current internal stuff, the current internal basis of our competence in languages, enough to constitute our thoughts in these cases, even if the contents of such thoughts is dependent on the meaning of language in a fairly radical way?

There are a variety of possible externalist answers to my internalist question. We've already dealt with some, but consideration of others will eventually bring us back around to the particular denial of reductivist naturalism—what I will call the 'non-reductivism'—of Brandom's account. We will only get there in stages, because Brandom's proposal is a complex specific form of externalism that we must understand by contrast with simpler forms, and because we must first understand a variety of alternative motivations for denying that the natural or physical can constitute the meaningful.

One popular externalist route from the mediation of thought by language to non-reductivism involves normativity, as Sellars' invocation of the naturalistic fallacy suggests. There is a connection that is sometimes alleged between the publicity and hence externality of language on one hand and the normativity of thought on the other, for instance by some variants of the Private Language Argument. And there are also connections alleged between that cluster of issues and irreducibility by the natural. I will start out by probing just the connection between publicity and normativity. It is the first stage of our journey back to Brandom.

---

[74] Sellars thought that not all our thought was inner speech. And he wasn't entirely sympathetic to the claim that inner speech was thought, though his objection seems merely that inner hearing of inner speech would not be thought, not that inner action in the mind's throat that was also heard would not be thought. See Sellars (1997: 90).

We begin with what is non-controversial. Language and thought have conditions of correctness of various sorts. We can utter or think truths or falsehoods; we can infer well or badly from our premises. Language also appears to be rule-governed, so that the fixed meaning of a word depends to one degree or another on the existence of a rule for use of that word.

Such forms of correctness, such forms of normativity, suggest to some that language must be social. The kind of correctness in question seems to them essentially social correctness. And if thought inherits such normativity from language, or perhaps gets it directly in some other analogous socially-based way, then it too may require the existence of the social phenomena in question. Some allege that there could not be thought with content without such social phenomena, because thoughts are normative and normativity is social. These are possible grounds for externalism.

We have already considered one form of the Private Language Argument, Davidson's PLA2, that rests on this general idea. But there are other ways to deploy the same considerations that are free of some of the problematic idiosyncrasies of Davidson's argument.

Consider the fairly straightforward PLA3: Crispin Wright once suggested that individuals can violate a standard of normative correctness for language only by being out of accord with community standards, while for 'the community itself there is no authority, no standard to meet'.[75] And perhaps the possibility of the violation of such standards is essential to meaningful speech.

John Haugeland suggested instead, in a way that would generate PLA4, that it isn't just the actual practice of a community but what is sanctioned by the community which constitutes correctness.[76] His conception allows for the possibility that a community as a whole goes astray in its practice, if not in its sanctioning activity. Of course, we might similarly think that practices of sanctioning might go astray. So perhaps externalists should invoke community practices of sanctioning sanctions, and develop another related form of private language argument. And so on until plausibility runs out.

Such claims can be deployed in support of reductionist externalist accounts of any alleged normativity of linguistic meaning inherited by thought content. They seem a natural source of social externalism.

[75] C. Wright (1980: 220).   [76] Haugeland (1982).

NEI can appeal to match as a basic source of correctness that isn't social. But some of the forms of correctness in question in these forms of the Private Language Argument may seem not to be of that sort. And so my internalist response to these arguments will be instead a kind of co-option:

Notice that we can embed such social phenomena in the skin of a single person in much the way that we earlier embedded speech. Consider Wright's proposal. And consider a natural question about Wright's proposal: What precisely is it that a community can do than an individual cannot?[77] At a particular time a single individual can be out of accord with his or her usual practice, in much the same manner that an individual can be out of accord with a community practice. And even in a moment a person can act out of accord with an (in some ways) dominant disposition. Or consider Haugeland's account. Wittgenstein can punish himself at one moment for what he did at another time. And he can punish such self-punishments, and so on. And one can have conflicting dispositions of that sort all rolled up in a moment.

If social reductive accounts succeed, it is hard to see why their appropriate reflection inside an individual in a moment cannot provide an analogous internalist reduction. Such accounts simply suggest to the internalist some complications that they should adopt, after suitable internalist modulation. That is the internalist reply I favor to PLA3 and 4.

9.10

But my reply to PLA3 and 4 may seem inadequate for this reason: Perhaps social reductive accounts of the kind of normativity in question do not succeed, while public languages are yet important to normativity in some related way. Brandom thinks this. But it will take a while for us to get back to the way this objection to internalism is supposed to work according to Brandom, which will put in play the whole of his particular non-reductivism and also its fourth general feature, its interpreter-relativity. I will focus now merely on an initial and general link between normativity and non-reductivism, in other words on the second stage of our journey

[77] This question is stressed by Blackburn (1984).

back to Brandom. The third and fourth stages will be more specific ways of defending this link.

Many now accept Sellars' and Brandom's contention that the normativity of meaning and content resists physicalist or naturalist reduction or constitution, whether such reduction takes an internalist form or is a social externalism like those we just considered. Many think that to favor either sort of reductive story is to commit something like the naturalistic fallacy, which allegedly vitiates claims that moral properties are constituted by physical properties. We've long had worries about how to fit the ethical into the physical world, and to many it now seems that we should also have analogous worries about how to fit the meaningful into that world.

I believe that this worry about naturalist reductions of the normativity of content is 'a radical mistake'. Indeed, I believe that philosophy of mind and language would be better off if all talk of reasons, rationality, normativity, and correctness were temporarily banished from the discipline, at least without ugly subscripts attached. The problem is that such words are multiply ambiguous, and we all too easily slip between their senses. Important current philosophical projects are vitiated by this. Consider our discussion of the confusion of etiological propriety and semantic propriety that underlies ET. I think that the claim that the normativity of meaning resists naturalist reduction because it is a lot like ethical normativity involves a similar equivocation.

If we are going to insist on the normativity of thought and meaning, it is important to remember that, at least on the surface, the kind of rich and problematic normativity involved in the claim that one ought morally to do something has little or nothing to do with constituting the facts about what one believes or what one says. There are a number of words—'correctness', 'norm', 'reason', 'rationality', 'rule'—used both in ethics and in discussions of mind and language. But only cursory examination is required to see that very diverse uses of those words are in play.

Take one cluster of words that includes 'reason' and 'rationality'. These two words are naturally linked, in that to be rational is in some sense to be responsive to or reflective of the faculty of reason, and the faculty of reason is perhaps the cognitive faculty that responds to reasons most directly. But there are obvious distinctions among different senses of 'reason' and among different senses of 'rationality'.

There are the reasons that explain why something, any kind of thing, happens. Call those 'explanatory reasons'. Then there are the sort of proper reasons to which the faculty of reason is properly responsive when deciding how one ought morally to act or believe. Call these 'justifying reasons'. But these are different, because at least many explanatory reasons, even psychologically explanatory reasons, are not justificatory. There may well have been explanatory reasons, rooted in his psychology, explaining why Hitler did what he did, but there is nothing in that which justifies what he did. And indeed the justifying reasons of etiquette, ethics, and epistemology seem quite distinct.

Now turn to 'rational'. Perhaps there are some sorts of minimal consistency and coherence in theoretical and practical reasoning that a person must have if they are to be capable of belief and desire. Call that 'rationality as minimal coherence'. But this certainly doesn't require that someone be fully coherent, have only epistemically justified beliefs and proper desires leading to fully justified actions. Call *that* mythical state 'rationality as justification'. And of course coherence and epistemic justification and the propriety of desire all seem quite distinct components of that state.

There are degrees of rationality. And perhaps a certain sort of idealization is involved in our attribution of beliefs and desires to people, which requires that when interpreting we pretend that people are more consistent or coherent or justified than in fact they are. But the fact of idealization requires a less than ideal reality that is more or less badly captured by the idealization, so that rationality as minimal coherence and rationality as justification are still distinct. Perhaps a person with a certain degree of self-consciousness and conscientiousness is unlikely to maintain a belief that they feel is unjustified or false, but of course we can have what are in fact false and unjustified beliefs and yet not be wildly irrational.

Take another cluster of words, which includes 'norm', 'normative', and 'correct'. What is correct in some sense may be what is in accord with norms of some sort, and norms seem to be in some sense normative phenomena, so there are natural links among these words. But again we need to be wary of obvious distinctions. The truth of a belief or a claim is a kind of correctness. So too is its justification. And we may speak of the grammatical correctness of an utterance, or the semantically correct use of a word. But the truth of an utterance, its epistemic justification, its grammaticality, and its conformity to standard usage are not the same thing. People may ungrammatically and with neologism or peculiar usage express the truth, and with grammatical and proper usage utter the false. Nor, of course, are any of these sorts of correctness the same as the kind of normative correctness of behavior that ethicists study. And, of course, the ethical norms of a social group may not track the normative truth. One can recognize the existence of social norms that one does not endorse in any way whatsoever, and should not.

There are these surface differences. Any view that denies the existence of these surface differences is false. But perhaps the surface differences are misleading and the existence of single words with such different senses is profound. Still, there is also another reason to be wary of the trendy claim that meaning is normative in a robust sense at least analogous to the ethical, so that it might reasonably seem incapable of constitution by the physical.

This reason has two branches, which are answers to different sorts of detailed resistance to naturalist reduction. I will begin with the first branch, which tells against a simpler form of non-reductivism with which Brandom's general form must be contrasted. Consideration of this simpler form will be the third stage of our journey back to Brandom.

9.11

Assume that someone has proposed a particular account of how robustly non-natural normative facts are a necessary part of what constitutes facts about minds or meanings. And assume that these involve robustly spooky properties analogous to Moorean non-natural ethical properties, which are not constituted by the physical. That is a form of what I have been calling non-reductivism, but not Brandom's form.

Such a proposal is subject to the following objection. Consider a concrete duplicate of the kind of world such a non-naturalist proposes, which has all the same concrete characteristics but lacks that extra irreducible normative something, that spooky Moorean bit. What is a concrete duplicate? Well, we presume physicalism throughout, so without begging relevant questions we might require it to be a physical duplicate. Remember that we have already seen that this will deliver qualitative experience. But you can also throw in phenomenal properties on objects if you wish—Aristotelian green right there on somebody's megaphone—or irreducible experiences of qualia.[78]

So consider a physical or otherwise concrete duplicate of our world. There is a society, in fact a series of societies, in such a concrete world, or if you insist a series of society*s, in which there are creatures just like all of us in all concrete respects, who have various concrete dispositions to speak under various conditions and to correct utterances of various sorts and who have sensory experiences such as we do. Perhaps you have a rich view of what experience requires, and think it is in the space of reasons. Still, if so, you will also no doubt grant that non-human animals have something analogous. Call it 'sentience'. So take out the experience and put in the relevant sentience. That's enough for my purposes.

If there is to be any role for irreducible normative facts in constituting the facts about meaning and mind, then that concrete duplicate of our world must lack the rich linguistic phenomena and mental lives found in our own. If you can believe that, then ask further whether we have any good reason to believe that those extra special fancy facts obtain in our world. Even if the people, or people*, in such a world lack psychologies and meanings because of some very strange peculiarities of our words 'psychology' and 'meaning', they still have something that is for all practical and philosophically-respectable purposes the same, and that is at least enough for my purposes here. People*s on another planet who were our concrete twins but lacked that extra fancy something would not be properly treated as plants, nor even as non-human animals with mere sentience. We could talk to them, and discuss their quasi-psychological states as we discuss the corresponding proper psychological states of one another here on Earth.

We have no reason to believe that the spooky non-natural properties in question are had by our minds or words. And even if they are, they don't matter very much.

This argument is an analog of our earlier argument forcing a reflection of the conditions required by an externalist language-based account of content into an individual, and we can indeed produce an internalist variant of this argument, by putting the two forms of argument together. Take someone

---

[78] Mendola (2006a) argues that some phenomenal experiences involve normative facts. But they are a relevantly special case.

just as you concretely are at this moment, with for instance your qualia and concrete physical dispositions to speak and correct speech, but presume that such a creature lacks any social environment or linguistic past in fact, or any spooky non-natural properties. Your twin, who would be systematically deceived about its social world and history, would yet possess at least some close analog of beliefs and meanings, certainly close enough for all important purposes, even if in fact there are spooky non-natural components of ordinary meaning that partly depend on external natural conditions. Maybe I am splitting a difference here, maybe I am insisting that we ignore some details of thought contents, but not big ones.

It may be objected that my internalist and naturalist twinning cases are impossible because, though there is no constitution of the normative by the concrete, yet in all possible cases the normative must of necessity supervene on its concrete basis, and yet retain its distinct existence. In other words, it may be objected that there are no possible worlds with a concrete basis such as our world exhibits and yet lacking the supervening but distinct and irreducible normative properties that help constitute meaning and content. Indeed, those who believe in the non-natural usually claim that it supervenes on the natural.

But, I reply, the non-natural is not constituted by the natural, as for instance water is constituted by H-O-H. And in our physical world there are no causal laws that link the microphysical to the irreducibly normative. Non-naturalists sometimes propose *sui generis* synthetic a priori and necessary connections, but no one else believes this at all plausible. So even if non-natural properties were consistent with the physicalism that we assume here, which I doubt, the supervenience of the non-natural on the natural could not be plausibly explained. The truly characteristic form of non-naturalism denies supervenience. The lack of supervenience is what we should expect if non-natural properties did exist. The fact that non-naturalists characteristically insist on supervenience is indeed one reason to be suspicious of their view.[79]

Another objection to my twinning arguments is most important in our current argumentative context. It may seem that all of that stuff in the concrete duplicates—the individual internalist duplicates and even the concrete social externalist duplicates—doesn't constitute meaningful

---

[79] Mendola (2006a: 144–5) further develops this argument.

speech and contentful thought, but not because that requires any special irreducible non-natural phenomena. This objection lies behind the second general form of non-reductivism we need to consider, which rests not on non-naturalism but on various kinds of interpreter-relativity.

Brandom's view is in this class, but I will consider two other venerable instances of this strategy, for purposes of illustration and contrast and so that we can survey other Private Language Arguments, before we turn explicitly to Brandom's particular strategy, which also involves interpreter-relativity of a sort. So this is the fourth stage of our journey back to Brandom.

9.12

The simplest venerable instance of this second general form of non-reductivism is present in a slight variant of an important reading of the Private Language Argument that I will call PLA5. PLA5 deploys a third sort of general consideration as the key to the Private Language Argument. It suggests that a single individual even over time cannot do what a group of distinct individuals can do, and because of a factor that I have largely suppressed in my earlier discussions. PLA5 clangs together remarks 258 and 377 from *Philosophical Investigations*:

I want to keep a diary about the recurrence of a certain sensation. To this end I associate it with the sign 'S' and write this sign in the calendar for every day on which I have the sensation.... I impress on myself the connexion between the sign and the sensation.—But 'I impress it on myself' can only mean: this process brings it about that I remember the connexion *right* in the future. But in the present case I have no criterion of correctness. One would like to say: whatever is going to seem right to me is right. And that only means that here we can't talk about 'right'.[80]

Perhaps a logician will think: The same is the same.... [But w]hat is the criterion for the sameness of the two images?—What is the criterion for the redness of an image?... For myself, when it is my image: nothing. And what goes for 'red' goes for 'same'.[81]

There is more than one way to read these remarks, and we have already considered some. But consider this reading: There is no fact of replying

---

[80] Wittgenstein (1968: I 258). [81] Wittgenstein (1968: I 377).

in the same way to the same sensation that could be constituted by a stable individual disposition that links that type of sensory experience and that particular type of mark over every day, because there is no real and objective sameness of types independent of our reactions. But somehow if the sign were socially applied, that would be different. That is PLA5.

But, on behalf of qualia empiricism, I reply that there *is* a real sameness of types in this case. Wittgenstein in fact has a red experience or not, and not because he takes it one way or the other. We do not need a social practice to provide the sort of correctness in question. Real types will do. Of course, there can be real types in the world but not available inside the skin. But Wittgenstein's case handily involves a sensory property, which might be a real internal type. And notice that even if there isn't any phenomenal purple of a certain shade within me, there might still be a natural type of experience within me, the experience of phenomenal purple of that shade, and that is all we'd really need. In fact, that seems required by the adverbialism of MS. And while one might worry that there is still a problem about real types of signs, like 'S', that doesn't seem to worry even Wittgenstein in these passages, and in fact there plausibly are internally determinate types of internal responses.

Wittgenstein could have chosen instead a case other than a sensory property, an objector may insist. But that wouldn't have helped him try to dispose of qualia as a basis of content, I reply, and qualia empiricism will of course tell a complex and dependent story about those other cases. Still, an objector may continue: Assume that there are no real types in the world. What then? But there are real types, I insist. And if there weren't, I ask, how could there be any facts about the types of moves made in a social practice?

The externalist might respond to my internalist question by iterating the proposal suggested by PLA5, and in a way that buttresses its key claims and hence provides an argument we might call PLA5b: A social practice is the same only if it is taken to be the same (according to a criterion) within the social practice in question, and that taking is the same as another only if.... And so on until plausibility or patience runs out.

I deploy real types to answer 5b, as I answered 5. But in our current context, the most important point about this externalist argument is this: It suggests that concrete duplicates of us—individual or socially embedded—do not of necessity think and talk like us, because there are no objective facts about how we think and talk. There are merely such facts from within the perspective of a certain social practice of taking things thus and so, and not across such practices. And there is such a social practice only from the perspective of a higher-order social practice in the same community. And so on. This is somewhat analogous to social relativism in ethics.

Such a view denies that the natural and physical constitute the meaningful in any straightforward non-relativist way, and so, with perhaps a little stretching, it is reasonable to call it a kind of non-reductivism. And it shares a general form with Brandom's alternative non-reductive conception. In a similar but somewhat simpler way, it links social-linguistic, non-reductivist, and interpreter-relative features.

Before we get to Brandom's version, we should consider one other contrasting form of the second general sort of non-reductivism, rooted in another kind of interpreter-relativity, which is allied to other important Private Language Arguments, and other resources useful to NEI. Begin with the skeptical argument against there being full-blown facts of meaning proposed by Kripke[82] as an interpretation of Wittgenstein's *Philosophical Investigations*. Consider a person 'K' who uses the symbol '+' as we do, and has in fact performed a number of additions in life, though never of any numbers greater than or equal to 57. It would seem that if the symbol '+' has determinate meaning for K, then it denotes the function 'plus' and not the function 'quus', where plus = $x + y$, and where quus equals $x + y$ if x is less than or equal to 57, and equals 5 otherwise. But Kripke's Wittgenstein argues that there is no fact about which of these determinate meanings '+' has for K, and that indeed there is no social fact about that either. Rather, the truth about the nature of meaning is supposed to be this: Given a background of social agreement in linguistic and mathematical practice, there are assertibility conditions for the claim that K means plus by '+', which may make that claim appropriate in one person's mouth but not another. So rather than a straightforward reduction of sameness of meaning claims, we get something more oblique, which is indeed abstractly similar to Brandom's proposal and also to the suggestions recently made in support of PLA5b. This is not so much a reply as a

[82] Kripke (1982).

response to the skeptical argument. It is a kind of social response, whose propriety would underwrite PLA6, which appends to the key presumptions of the otherwise skeptical argument the truth of that response. I myself prefer a distinct reply to the skeptical suggestions of Kripke's Wittgenstein, and in getting back to that reply, we will also come in sight of another related argument, PLA7.

To understand all this properly, we must begin with some of the details of Kripke's Wittgenstein's skeptical argument. I won't here reconstruct the whole of it, since I have done that elsewhere,[83] and much of it concerns possibilities that are irrelevant in this context. But in the course of the overall argument, Kripke's Wittgenstein considers a certain key possibility that is quite relevant to our current concerns, that K's *dispositions* to use the symbol '+' in computations determine whether K means quus or plus by '+'. While K has not in fact added out far enough to rule quus out of contention, still K has the necessary dispositions to do so, it may seem.

Dispositions might be externally constituted,[84] but we have no particular reason to think that the dispositions in question here are so constituted. Since NEI will crucially deploy internally determinate dispositions in cases like this, in accounting for the content of thought mediated by terms that do not purport to refer and even sentences that don't seem to represent concrete conditions, I should attempt to defend such a view from the onslaught of Kripke's Wittgenstein.

Dispositionalism, be it externalist or internalist, is denied by Kripke's Wittgenstein for two reasons, on the basis of two arguments. The first or 'infinity' argument goes like this: If K's dispositions to use '+' fix its meaning, then for K to mean plus by '+' is for K to be disposed, when asked for $x + y$, to give the sum of x and y as the answer, where the sum is the number yielded by the plus function, and for K to mean quus is for K to be disposed, when asked for $x + y$, to give the quum of x and y as the answer, where that is yielded by the quus function. But K's dispositions to use '+' in this way are finite, since some numbers are too large for K to add. And it follows from this that K's dispositions underdetermine whether '+' means plus or quus.

[83] Mendola (1997: 209–19) is a fuller reconstruction. [84] McKitrick (2003).

I hope it isn't churlish to point out that of course the last claim is false, at least if K is a real person. Any ordinary person has dispositions that carry him or her at least as far as the proper addition of 58 and 58, which would rule quus out of contention. But there is also an obvious reply to my quibble: Since the dispositions of an ordinary person are finite, there is *some* number that generates an analog of quus and plus between which '+''s meaning is indeterminate for that person, a number far enough out to be beyond their dispositions to add. So even if the argument as stated would be unsound if applied to any actual K, there is a sound analog of the argument available.

This reply is problematic, but it will take a moment to see why. First, consider the second supporting argument for the claim that dispositions are insufficient. The interpretation of this 'normativity' argument is controversial, but, in light of my earlier rant about the normativity of meaning, I will adopt a sober, restrained reading. If K's dispositions to use '+' fix its meaning, then for K to mean plus by '+' is for K to be disposed, when asked for $x + y$, to give the sum of x and y as the answer, where the sum is the number yielded by the plus function, and for K to mean quus is for K to be disposed, when asked for $x + y$, to give the quum of x and y as the answer, where that is yielded by the quus function. But K will have dispositions to make mistakes when adding, for instance when rushed, or distracted, or when adding large enough numbers. And such mistakes are not constitutive of what K means by '+'. Hence K's dispositions to use '+' do not determine its meaning. We cannot add a clause excluding as irrelevant to meaning those dispositions that are a source of mistakes, because this cannot be done without an independent specification of what constitutes adding, and whether that is available for K is precisely the issue at hand.

The normativity argument, as I have construed it, claims that dispositions to use '+' may involve dispositions to make mistakes in calculations that are not constitutive of the meaning of '+'. The obvious reply is that the dispositions that should be held to fix the meaning of '+' include not merely dispositions to use it in calculations of the canonical sort, but also dispositions to correct such use, to correct such corrections, and so on. Indeed, yet other dispositions, for instance to count in certain ways, to give certain proofs, to make statements of theoretical constraints on the nature of addition, to add in other than the canonical way, and so on, seem also to help determine the meaning of '+' for K.

One person who has insisted on the significance of these 'surrounding dispositions' is Simon Blackburn.[85] But let me add a slight twist, and a slight concession to the meaning skeptic. I claim, against both the infinity and the normativity arguments, and in a manner analogous to our earlier twinning arguments, that any way in which any ordinary speaker can see that some of K's dispositions are insufficient to mean plus by '+' is a case where that ordinary speaker has some internally determinate disposition that constrains the use of '+' beyond the way it is constrained by K's dispositions. It is intuitive that we understand how additions work even out beyond cases we can actually add explicitly, at least in the canonical way favored by Kripke's Wittgenstein. But if all *our* dispositions to talk about additions and infinities and deploy '+' in additions and to correct those additions, and all the inferences we are disposed to make between arithmetical sentences and more mundane counting sentences like 'there are three apples on the table', leave the interpretation of what we mean by '+' indeterminate in some particular way, then it is not in fact determinate in that way. And if there is some vagueness in what we mean, that does not imply that we mean nothing. We can always split the difference in cases like this, in the sense that we can posit contents that are indeterminate across the range of possible fine determinacies in question. Not just the normativity argument, but the infinity argument also, are inadequate for this reason, and so the dispositionalist story about '+', and indeed the internalist version of the dispositionalist story about '+' that is now an element of NEI, are unscathed.

That is what I believe. That is what I deploy as a response to PL6. What reason does Kripke's Wittgenstein provide for thinking that this is wrong, that all of K's dispositions together, not just to add but to do all the rest a plausible K would plausibly be disposed to do, underdetermine their meaning plus by '+'? None explicitly, but perhaps his claim would be that an individual's dispositions even to correct, even to correct corrections and so on, might be in error. For instance, they might not meet our community standards for what '+' means. But if K is to mean what we as a community mean by '+' in such a case, if '+' is not for K a phrase in an idiolect

---

[85] Blackburn (1984).

that K's dispositions alone fix, then it seems likely that the dispositions not merely of K but of K's entire linguistic community should be relevant to fixing the meaning of '+'. Hence, of course, externalist determination occurs, and so this route might provide grounds for externalism. This last argument is PLA7, which is reminiscent of PLA2, 3, and 4. It has some surface plausibility. It doesn't make obvious sense to say that an entire linguistic community's dispositions to use '+' and to correct such uses could underdetermine whatever meaning it has in that community.

But I reply to PLA7 by reference to my earlier individual twinning reply to PLA3 and 4, being willing if necessary to split remaining differences. Our recent elaboration of the dispositionalist response to the infinity and normativity arguments has helped defend and elaborate my earlier response. The real types that I deployed against PLA5 and 5b also help.

Kripke's Wittgenstein's conclusion about meaning is different but analogous to that incorporated in PLA7, and hence leads to the different but analogous PLA6, since PLA6 folds conditions of general social agreement into the presumed background for meaning claims that have not truth-conditions but rather assertibility conditions, and suggests that different individuals within the community might properly assert apparently conflicting meaning claims about a given individual, as they variously project agreement or disagreement in practice with the interpreted. I have already said how I reply to PLA6.

But what if we think, as Brandom thinks, that it does make sense to say that even all the social resources deployed in PLA5, 5b, 6 and 7, plus the internal dispositions that I favor, together underdetermine whatever meaning '+' has in the community in question? Then this is yet another opportunity to link together social-linguistic externalism, non-reducibility, and robust interpreter-relativity, in an analogous but somewhat different way than both the relatively simple social relativist conception incorporated into PLA5b and the individually-varying proper assertion conditions incorporated into PLA 6. At long last, with all the necessary elements and contrasts in place, we are back to Brandom.

Consider a social group from the outside. They act and sanction acts; they have various dispositions to use words and correct uses and make mathematical calculations and correct other calculations. But presume that there are no sufficiently robust facts in the world to type their mathematical practices and thoughts and talk in any very fixed way, as involving adding rather than some suitably inaccessible alternative we might call 'schmadding', especially when we remember that their practice could conceivably have gone astray. Still, perhaps there is a sense in which their practice might be properly seen as addition from one perspective and schmadding from another.

Consider three distinct interpreters. One might interpret them as adding pretty well, another as schmadding pretty well, and another as quadding pretty badly. Perhaps the third would be too far outside the community, and for that reason would lack authority. But at least the first two might be inside the community, and from their internal and hence weighty and yet different perspectives, which help perhaps to constitute two somewhat different yet mostly overlapping communities, they each see a 'fact' about meaning that is not available from the perspective of the other interpreter. Given facts of agreement aren't crucial in this conception, unlike PLA6, or at least aren't sufficient. It isn't that the propriety of each interpreter's claim rests on projected similarity or dissimilarity between the interpreted and the interpreter. Rather, the propriety of an interpretation rests on a relatively free choice by the interpreter.

On such a conception, there is no reduction of meaning or thought to objective physical or concrete facts, and social community is crucial in more than one way, and interpreter-relativity is assured. But there are no spooky Moorean non-natural normative properties involved. And the role that the community plays in this proposal is somewhat different than its role in the other non-reductive externalisms that involve interpreter-relativity. PLA5b involves no alternative internal perspectives within the community, and PLA6 involves different sorts of variation in internal perspectives.

Brandom thinks something with this general structure, though involving a crucial detail that I will introduce only in the next section.

But, I complain, such a linkage of sociality, non-reducibility, and interpreter-relativity fails to be the correct response to the issues in play, and fails to deliver a successful PLA8. I've already said why. Partly, it is incorrect because there are real types that can play a semantic role consistent with internalism. Partly it is because there are limited but real semantic facts, constituted in part by the internal dispositions we have explored here, that ignore the differences between various plausible relativized interpretations that Brandom might suggest. While we haven't yet considered the details of Brandom's position, we have seen that externalism with the general structure he suggests is not sufficiently well motivated.

9.13

Three details of Brandom's account require our consideration. The first is that his account is expressivist in roughly the sense that non-cognitivism in ethics is expressivist. This expressivism is a particular form of the relatively abstract pattern of Brandom's interpreter-relativity discussed at the end of the last section. It is his detailed form of non-reductivism. It is related to some forms of interpreter-relativity already discussed in something like the way that non-cognitivism in ethics is related to subjective relativism.

Ascribing meaning or belief is expressing a state of mind of the interpreter, Brandom thinks, in particular a recognition of commitments made by the individual interpreted. Unlike ordinary ethical expressivists, Brandom can't deploy facts about meaningful expressive discourse to root such a structure. Expressivism about linguistic phenomena cuts back against itself. It must be expressivism all the way down.

Since ascribing meaning or belief is something that we do inside linguistic communities, according to Brandom, and the theorist looking on but ascribing meanings or beliefs is hence in some sense in the community in question, but yet there are relatively free choices for those inside the community about what meanings or beliefs to ascribe, this is a structure of interpreter-relativity such as we considered in the guise of PLA8, which delivers a kind of reasonably plausible non-reducibility entwined with social externalism. Nevertheless, we already noted problems with this general strategy as a root for externalism. And there is now another. We can ascribe beliefs to Hitler without in any normatively robust sense recognizing his commitments. Still, Brandom suggests in at least one place that the kind of recognition of commitments that he deploys is not rich in that way.[86]

Consider a second, and I think a deeper and more interesting, specific feature of Brandom's account. There is another element of normativity in the account which yet suggests nothing non-reductive, and which

[86] Brandom (2000).

interacts with its social externalism and indeed with its central feature—its inferentialism—in ways that are relevant to NEI. It also suggests other grounds for externalism.

Brandom says that '[p]ropositional contentfulness must be understood in terms of practices of giving and asking for *reasons*.... [S]uch practices must be understood as social *practices*—indeed as *linguistic* practices. The fundamental sort of move in the game of giving and asking for reasons is making a *claim*—producing a [linguistic] performance that is propositionally contentful in that it can be the offering of a reason [for a further inference in theoretical or practical reasoning], and reasons can be demanded for it.'[87] This is one reason Brandom is an externalist. Claiming is crucial and claiming is a social game.

If we don't presume too highfalutin a conception of reasons, it seems clear that humans have such capacities as Brandom suggests. And though there are clearly other plausible conceptions of what it might be to have a belief, still let me grant Brandom's claims about claims for purposes of discussion. What I suggest rather is that we perform one of our twinning procedures on this conception. Take the image of Brandom's social picture and project that into a single individual. One speaks in the mind's ear out of one's internal dispositions and makes a claim, offering a reason for a conclusion to oneself for which further reasons can be demanded.

Why doesn't that produce an adequate internalist analog of Brandom's conception? Because, he might say, one will only have made a claim if one's commitments and entitlements in making the claim are recognized by someone else. We must be scorekeepers of commitments if there are to be commitments. To 'treat a performance as an assertion is to treat it as the undertaking or acknowledging of a certain kind of commitment—what will be called a "doxastic"... commitment. To be doxastically committed is to have a certain social status.... Such statuses are creatures of the practical attitudes of the members of the linguistic community.'[88]

But, I reply, one could keep score on oneself. And indeed Brandom suggests that himself.[89] Still, Brandom might object again. Such scorekeeping involves keeping score on how those to whom speech acts are addressed *change* their commitments and entitlements. But, I reply, one could address oneself in such a way when reasoning, even all in the present.

---

[87] Brandom (1994: 141). [88] Brandom (1994: 142). [89] Ibid.

I believe that the central reason why Brandom believes that such a squashed internalist analog of his account will not work is the same reason he believes that his inferentialist conception can deliver representations. This is a third detail of his account, which like the second is interesting and relevant to NEI. The story goes like this:

> Deontic scorekeeping is ... a kind of interpreting. But it is implicit, practical interpretation, not explicit theoretical hypothesis formation [as in Davidson].... [W]e can often just understand what others are saying (without theorizing about it), but where just understanding them crucially depends on being able to substitute one expression of a remark for another.... [A] sentence in one person's mouth does not typically have the same significance as that same sentence emerging from another person's mouth.... [T]he inferential articulation of conceptual contents is such that what someone becomes committed to by uttering a certain expression can be assessed only against a background of collateral commitments available as auxiliary hypotheses that can be brought in as other premises in drawing the inference. Even where people share a language ... there will still be some disagreements, some differences in the commitments that people have undertaken. We each embody different perceptual and practical perspectives and so will never have exactly the same doxastic and practical commitments.... Even in the smooth untroubled cases of communication, if you want to understand what I say, you have to be able to associate with it a sentence that in your mouth expresses the claim that the sentence I uttered expresses in mine. For your understanding it ... involves your being able to trace out the inferences the claim is involved in, the evidential significance of what I have said, in order to know what I am committing myself to. That means knowing how it could function as evidence for you, as well as for me ...[90]

Deontic scorekeeping is essential to language meaning, and essentially involves smooth substitutions and translations across different perspectives and hence different people. Brandom gives various examples of this phenomenon, including the smooth substitution of personal pronouns and demonstratives in conversation, and being able to give *de re* specifications of the content of someone's claim.

A crucial question is whether we can provide a squashed internalist analog of this mechanism, which can be incorporated into NEI. Otherwise, there may be theoretical grounds for externalism, if social substitutions are in fact essential to meaningful language. Perhaps such a mechanism must track

---

[90] Brandom (1994: 510).

evidential significance, but remember that characteristic evidence need not be good evidence.

Fortunately, Allan Gibbard has already plausibly sketched the necessary internalist analogs: 'Perspective shifts... needn't be impersonal. Individual memory too requires some mastery of them: Early in the morning, I experience myself eating breakfast; in mid-morning I conclude from memory not "I am eating breakfast", but that I ate breakfast a while ago.'[91]

Brandom might reply that he is concerned with shifts over changes in background belief, and perhaps minor temporal shifts are not enough to provide that, no more than the changes in reasoning suggested earlier. But Gibbard has two more cases: 'A lone thinker... will need to cope with shifting perspectives if it is to engage hypotheticals: to understand, say that had one not eaten breakfast today, one would now be hungry—and so come to realize that one has eaten.'[92] Possibly Brandom's understanding of how hypotheticals work will leave that case also disanalogous, but if necessary there is a last resort for the internalist. Even if there is no real social environment, we can consider hypothetical social environments. As Gibbard suggests, we can consider the hypothetical situation of non-existent others whose auxiliary beliefs are as different as required.[93] And of course we can do that in the present.

So we can develop a proper twinning argument, and deliver a squashed internalist version of Brandom's account. And we have uncovered no reason to prefer Brandom's externalist version to this internalist analog.[94] But we have discovered new resources for NEI.

---

[91] Gibbard (1996: 704).   [92] Ibid.   [93] Gibbard (1996: 705).
[94] Dowell (2006) develops another dual of Brandom.

10

Qualia Empiricism

I think that the correct internalism is qualia empiricism. And we have seen that neither case-based nor theory-based arguments provide genuine support for externalism, with the possible exception of PLA9. Section 10.1 reviews qualia empiricism, and especially NEI. Section 10.2 responds to PLA9. Sections 10.3 and 10.4 contrast my proposal with close alternatives.

10.1

Qualia empiricism has three components.

MS maintains that sensory contents are qualia, and that qualia are constituted by internal physical states, in a necessary but a posteriori manner. These physical states of experiencing have a modal structural architecture, and intentional contents.

RDC maintains that there is a set of properties that is constituted by the internally determinate dispositions of a speaker to be positively relevant to what counts in their judgment as the referent of a given term. And there are various relative weights of those properties in determining what counts as the referent under various conditions, also determined by the internally determinate dispositions of the speaker. The relevant properties and their weights are the description cluster of the term for the speaker at the time. The content contributed by the term 'X' with a putative reference to thoughts that it mediates can be captured by 'dthat [best satisfier of the description cluster for "X"]', as long as 'dthat' is understood not to obliterate the semantic contribution of the description.

Non-Epistemic Internalism, or NEI, includes:

1) from Chapter 7, proto-judgments, the primary imagination, and a capacity for word-free but relatively complex spatial thought, perhaps enriched in various way explored in the Strawsonian tradition;
2) from Chapter 8, a general qualia-based model of word-mediated thoughts, augmented by Wrightian self-avowals, and by other forms of interplay among thoughts that are and are not mediated by words;
3) from Chapter 9,
    a) an elaboration of the general qualia-based model of Chapter 8 into an ecumenical model of the core content of word-mediated thoughts, based partly in Davidson and partly in Brandom,
    b) moderate Morton-style interpreter-relativity,
    c) an internalist version of Davidsonian triangulation,
    d) motor capacities as the root of causal thoughts,
and
    e) an internalist variant of the Brandomesque capacity to track preservation of reference over changes in point of view, and to perform other sorts of deontic scorekeeping.

This mechanism works together to provide the resources required by RDC, in a way that is not merely partially evident from our armchairs but is also the focus of relevant scientific investigation. Let me elaborate certain elements of this story in a way that will eventually bring us back to RDC.

The most basic resources of qualia empiricism are the qualia of MS, whose realization is to be understood on the basis of empirical work on color vision. But the primary imagination is an extension of that first resource. While there are some individual differences regarding whether people can imagine colors in this way, everyone is capable of some sort of quasi-experience of this general sort, if only of words heard in the mind's ear. We can tell this from our armchairs. But neurophysiological investigation of this capacity has made it reasonably clear that it involves activity in some of the same higher brain areas involved in sensory perception.[1]

Another basic resource is an inverted, outgoing analog of incoming sensory qualia, which we might call 'motor intentions'. We have motor

---

[1] Farah (1988); Kosslyn, Alpert, Thompson, Maljkovik, Weise, Chabris, Hamilton, Rauch, and Buonanno (1993); Palmer (1999: 611–13).

capacities of various sorts, capacities to move our limbs and bodies and tongues and mouths in various ways, which are constituted internally, by the muscular-skeletal structure inside our skin and the neurophysiology that controls it. And these constitute our capacities for one elementary sort of causal thought. While some elements of this resource are evident from our armchairs, there are also relevant empirical surprises.[2] For instance, while it may seem obvious that motor control is organized in outgoing hierarchies, involving motor intentions with contents at different levels of abstraction, it is surprising that very different sorts of fine muscle movements are required so that we can retain the personal characteristics of our hand-writing even when writing in very different media.[3] There is also both empirical and armchair evidence that such motor intentions are sometimes quasi-present, even when actual motor activity is not.[4] Consider activity in dreams, or when you rehearse some dance step mentally without actually undertaking it. This involves what we might call 'quasi-intentions', analogous to quasi-experiences.

Modal notions, for instance notions of causation, are difficult for empiricists. But of course not only for empiricists. And motor intentions provide NEI with an internalist physicalist analog of Berkeley's conception of the root of our causal notions. We have causal thoughts because we can do things, in particular perform certain basic actions complete at skin's end. Of course, there are other modal notions. These basic causal elements are a long way from 'dthat'. But we will come back to 'dthat'.

Qualia, motor intentions, quasi-experience, and quasi-intentions are the most basic elements deployed by qualia empiricism. But they are linked into complex thoughts through the machinations of various capacities that have not been adequately explored by traditional empiricists.

Some simple sorts of spatial and temporal structure appear within our experience. But one crucial component of NEI is our capacity for more complex spatio-temporal thought that is yet not mediated by words. This is a capacity for conceptions of at least rough three-dimensional concrete scenarios, including persisting and mind-independent objects with colors and shapes and other experienced properties, among which we can move, pan, and zoom in imagination, and of which we can imagine various

---

[2] Jeannerod (1997); Passingham (1993); Rosenbaum (1991). [3] Rosenbaum (1991: 229).
[4] Jeannerod (1997: 94–125); Rosenbaum (1991: 67–8).

experiences from various angles and points. Think now of your kitchen, and of what's in the cabinets.

This capacity involves an internally determinate linkage of experiences, quasi-experiences, motor intentions, quasi-intentions, and underlying dispositions. There are at least two sorts of organization that this capacity seems to exploit. First, we have viewer-centered abilities to understand how the whole visual scene would change if we moved about the variously-changing world in various ways, of how it would look from other places or times. Externalists and various enemies of empiricism have been unusually sensitive to this sort of organization, but NEI incorporates internalist and empiricist variants. Second, there is object-centered organization, which is relevant when we consider how a particular object looks from various sides. This element was well explored from the armchair by traditional empiricists and phenomenalists, perhaps best by H. H. Price.[5] We can adopt much of that work when it is shorn of epistemicist distortions. But the armchair is not the most important tool for studying this capacity. That it can be internally determinate should be less surprising to those who enjoy complex video games or digital illusions at the movies than it would have been to Hegel. There are relevant computational models, psychological studies, and neurophysiological work.[6]

This capacity for conceiving complex spatio-temporal contents seems to be entwined with our capacity to conceive at least some of the mental states of others, for instance their experience of the world from another point. Our capacity for intersubjective thought involves an internalist variant of Davidsonian triangulation, for instance as you conceive what someone else sees within your dream. In fact, it seems mostly an analytic convenience to distinguish the basic features of this capacity from that we previously discussed. For instance, Strawson plausibly combined one understanding of the Private Language Argument with an understanding of Kant's Refutation of Idealism, suggesting that experience as of *public* and persisting objects in space is crucial to our capacity for thought.[7]

---

[5] H. H. Price (1932: 170–321).

[6] Kosslyn (1980, 1994); Shepherd and Cooper (1982); Mel (1986); Finke (1989); Carruthers (1996); Carruthers and Boucher (1998); Hauser and Carey (1998); Ristau (1998); Palmer (1999: 143–462 and 602–10).

[7] Strawson (1959: 15–116). For relevant debates, see Carruthers and Smith (1996).

Commonsense thought concerns such things as my coffee and my orange here on the table. And that thought is supposed by qualia empiricism to be rooted in a conception of a three-dimensional world of colors and shapes and other properties that appear in sensory experience. But it may be hard to see how such a rudimentarily concrete three-dimensional scenario can deliver in particular *coffee* on a table, at least if the coffee tastes and smells flat enough. And certainly thought about my orange might be associated in my imagination with a concrete conception matched as closely by someone else's orange.

But we have various internal capacities that help introduce the specific complexities of coffee and my orange into my thought, and help to dispose of this worry. They include recognitional capacities, word-mediated responses, squashed Brandom capacities to track references over changes in point of view, and a capacity sketched in Part I to think of particular objects. Still, I should admit that the natural temptation to talk in an ordinary way about the basic three-dimensional contents that qualia empiricism crucially deploys, in a commonsense language that speaks of banquets and my orange and cups of coffee, would misrepresent my claims. A more primitive qualia-based language is really required.

It should speak, I believe, of phenomenal elements and causal elements in certain spatio-temporal arrangements, in order to capture the crucial and semantically basic contents: those of our qualitative experiences, motor intentions, quasi-experiences and quasi-intentions, and above all those of the more complex concrete scenarios, or at least the concrete bases of those complex scenarios, which will also involve the persistence of particular concrete objects over time. Such concrete basic contents provide a kind of semantic basis from which the contents of other thoughts, especially those that are linguistically mediated, can be constructed, in ways that mirror dependencies in our capacities for such thoughts of the sort I have already introduced. In *Human Thought*, I develop in considerable detail a language that attempts to capture basic contents,[8] though it must be extended to properly account for the dynamic properties Dummett notes as elements of proto-judgments, to properly allow for some of the structure of continuing objects and even persons allowed by our Strawson-style mechanisms, and probably to allow for the individuality that can accrue

---

[8] Mendola (1997: 97–165).

to our thoughts on the basis of resources like our own individuality and 'dthat'.

Another very large component of qualia empiricism is a story about linguistically mediated thoughts. First, we can say not only out loud but to ourselves, in the mind's ear and throat, various sentences that sound different in different languages. This is obvious from our armchairs, and also scientifically supported.[9] And in this part I have sketched an ecumenical story about how such words have content that is consistent with internalist and physicalist strictures. We can hold such sentences to be true and false, and be disposed to assert them or not assert them, under various concrete actual and hypothetical scenarios of the sort with which our capacity for complex spatio-temporal thought provides us. We can also so respond to word-mediated scenarios. And we can be disposed in various ways to react to sentences. We can also be disposed in various other ways to use sentences. These dispositions are regulated by dispositions to correct responses, and to correct corrections, and many other sorts of surrounding dispositions. We also have internal squashed Brandomesque capacities to keep deontic score and to understand one another across differences in theoretical and other perspectives.

It goes without saying that such a conception requires empirical elaboration. Chomsky's internalist explorations of our complex syntactic capacities might help flesh out this vague proposal, even if Chomsky is sometimes skeptical about the significance of the robustly semantic interests of philosophers.[10] And the diverse empirical disciplines that study language and its neural basis are coalescing in a way that promises to provide significant illumination of the workings of our internal capacities for meaningful speech.[11]

But perhaps the main remaining point from our perspective is how these resources work to support RDC. RDC is a semantic proposal about the content of terms that purport to refer, not a psychological mechanism. And such terms have their contents fixed by proper interpretation on the grounds discussed in the last two chapters, especially on the basis of our dispositions to assert sentences containing such terms of various hypothetical concrete and word-mediated scenarios, and also to directly name and

---

[9] Levelt (1999). [10] Chomsky (1995).
[11] Key elements are discussed in Brown and Hagoort (1999); Carruthers and Boucher (1998); Carruthers (1996); Pinker and Bloom (1992).

describe various scenarios. That there are two sorts of scenarios—concrete and word-mediated—is one reason that the clusters have the hierarchical structure we have discerned.

What of 'dthat'? The basic resources that its mastery requires are a capacity to entertain merely hypothetical scenarios—which is to entertain thoughts outside of the mode of belief—and a capacity to understand stability of reference between such scenarios, which is byproduct of our Brandom-style capacities to keep deontic score and to understand the preservation of reference over differences in background belief.

There are some elements incorporated into NEI for which there is currently little scientific sanction, though they seem to be plausible resources supported by historical evidence: for instance modest Morton-style interpreter-relativity and internalist Wrightian self-avowals. But this story is of course very incomplete. I have said nothing about conative states like desire. And while I have focused on conscious thoughts, I do not mean to imply that there are no wholly unconscious thoughts of the sort favored by cognitive science or even by Freud. I have simply told a partial internalist story, which I think is one plausible model for all we know now, about the cognitive thoughts that we most certainly have.

10.2

We still face PLA9. It may seem that it is only public references and not any narrow contents that we share when we intuitively share thoughts.

There are several components of my reply. First, the bare possibility of behavioral duplicates with different or absent qualia doesn't show that there are any. Normal humans plausibly share qualitative experience to a relatively large degree, and hence normal human qualitative experience is in fact plausibly 'private' in only a much attenuated sense. Qualitative sensory experience can play a central role in public language and shared thought, since we suitably share such experience.

There are the color blind. But we learned from Kripke, Putnam, and Burge that one can use a public language term to say and even think something whose public meaning one doesn't completely understand, and so the fact that the color blind can speak English doesn't show that the color qualia of the normal don't play a crucial semantic role in English.

It merely suggests that the meanings of the terms of the color blind are dependent on other people. This in turn may suggest that their thoughts are not internally determinate. But remember that we have an internalist strategy for dealing with analogous examples. When a color blind person, at least after recognizing their non-normality, thinks of purple through the mediation of the word 'purple', they may be thinking of dthat [property called 'purple' in my community]. Even if there are a few color inverts among us who are behavioral duplicates of normal percipients,[12] they also share such metalinguistic contents with others.

Still, we are situated in different locations and in different orientations, and hence have different experiences. And there are many ideological differences among even the normal. The possibility of shared qualia is not enough. We refer to the same things and intuitively share thoughts even when we have very different internally determinate understandings of what those things are and very different sensory experiences of them. And so there must be other components of my reply.

When we intuitively share thoughts, there are often narrow contents that we literally share, which may be somewhat abstract. And there are other sorts of crucial relations between contents that we can recognize, and that can constitute the relevant sharing of thoughts even when narrow contents are not literally shared. Let me explain both of these points.

Consider first word-mediated thoughts. RDC provides some details of the way that shared content works for key cases of that sort. Occasionally, members of language communities share whole rigidified clusters, distinguished from other elements of their complicated individual psychologies and theories by the very words by which they are mediated. The rigidified clusters go term by term, and that blocks any general holism of thought that would plausibly prevent the sharing of narrow contents across distinct individuals who speak the same language. Of course, in the usual case, there are differences between the clusters corresponding to a single term for different speakers of a language. Still, there are often shared elements between the relevant rigidified clusters. The hierarchical structure of the clusters sometimes helps in this respect, and at the very least, there is a shared metalinguistic element. Slightly more abstract shared narrow contents can also bind speakers of different languages, as we saw in Chapter 2

---

[12] Nida-Rümelin (1996).

during our discussion of Burge. Two specific resources that we can borrow from externalists to help block a general holism of inferential roles even when terms are not shared between two speakers, and even when we are considering terms and even claims that do not purport to refer, are Fodorian asymmetric dependence of internal inferential roles—so that inferential roles less crucial to content are asymmetrically dependent on those that are—and Gibbons' direct inferential interaction, interaction without the mediation of other thoughts. In this way, two terms may share semantically dominant inferential roles even if not all inferential roles.

But the most important resource in this context is the squashed internal Brandom capacity. This gives us the ability to recognize other sorts of crucial relations between different narrow contents of thoughts that are linguistically mediated, that constitute other sorts of intuitive sharing of thoughts that do not require the literal sharing of narrow contents, sometimes not even abstract ones. We deploy this capacity all the time as we understand one another, in just the sorts of linguistically-mediated cases on which Brandom focuses. We make suitable intersubjective projections.

But there remains this worry: Aren't there shared thoughts that aren't mediated by words, even when we share nothing like identical sensory experiences?

Indeed there are, and our capacity for word-free spatial thought, perhaps augmented in the ways explored in the Strawsonian tradition, along with non-linguistic aspects of the squashed Brandom capacity, are the key to their existence. You and I can have beliefs with complex spatio-temporal contents that match the same objects in the world, say the same orange tree. Sometimes narrow contents of such thoughts are literally shared. But other kinds of cases are more prevalent. Since there are many orange trees in the world that look much the same, and our thoughts aren't *enormously* complex, it is important that the spatio-temporal contents in question often have a kind of indexical element. Yours is centered on you and mine on me, and that tree behind you may be in fact also the tree in front of me. Such contents overlap in the external world; they match the same object. But part of our capacity for intersubjective understanding is our ability to make projections and identifications between one person's view of the world and another, even in the absence of a genuine referent. We also have a similar ability to understand projections and make identifications across our experience of the world from one point or time to another, and even across hypothetical possibilities. No words need be involved. This non-linguistic Brandomesque capacity gives us the ability to understand that we share thoughts that are not mediated by language even when our narrow contents are not literally shared.

These are internalist capacities. We can have a sense of shared reference by the use of our squashed Brandom capacities even if in fact the world is a shared hallucination, though unless the hallucinations of different people are causally linked or rooted in a common cause, we only do this successfully by accident. Indeed, even if only one person exists, their individual deployment of these capacities allows what would hence be illusory social understanding of illusory others.

10.3

My solipsistic proposal has contemporary company, though I think that company suffers a little from epistemicism.

David Chalmers has developed his version of two-dimensionalism in one related way. He suggests that certain beliefs crucially involve phenomenal experiences, and that these beliefs have an important general cognitive role.[13] He has developed an allied conception of narrow content,[14] juxtaposed with Frege's notion of sense,[15] and sketched a general semantic framework in which to embed it.[16]

There are a number of differences between Chalmers' proposal and my own. First, Chalmers is concerned only to articulate contents that are something like Carnapian intensions, functions from something like possible worlds to something like extensions, while my rigidified description clusters are more like traditional descriptions. And this implies a second difference. While we both allow that there may be variability between different individuals in the content expressed by a given word, I think that some elements of the narrow content of a thought that matches the world may yet be false.

But two other differences are more important from our current perspective, though they are complicated by the presence of a related similarity.

---

[13] Chalmers (2003). [14] Chalmers (2002b). [15] Chalmers (2002c).
[16] Chalmers and Jackson (2001); Chalmers (2002a, 2004a).

The two important differences are two ways in which Chalmers deploys the epistemic notion of a prioricity, while I deploy a semantic notion that is closely analogous to analyticity. This is a kind of generalization of the notion of the semantic a priori applied earlier to rigidified description clusters. But these important differences are embedded in a significant structural similarity. According to Chalmers, there is a space of scenarios, crucially involving various configurations of basic physical and phenomenal facts, that plays a kind of foundational semantic role. Thoughts not explicitly about such basic physical and phenomenal facts, say your belief that there is water in your glass, are yet 'verified' or 'falsified' by such basic scenarios. Likewise, in my conception, there is a semantically basic set of contents, and the contents of all our thoughts are rooted in, are dependent on, this basic set of contents. However, Chalmers provides an epistemic characterization of both crucial elements in this semantic architecture, of both the basic scenarios and the form of dependence of other contents on basic scenarios. But I think that neither should be epistemically characterized. Those are the two important differences that I mean.

Two-dimensionalism is a space of semantic views that hold that there are two semantic values for terms, characteristically expressed in terms of possible worlds. We have already discussed Frank Jackson's version of robust two-dimensionalism. But if we broaden our focus to include less robust forms, I can express my important differences and similarity with Chalmers in this way: In the typography of Gendler and Hawthorne, I favor a *semantic* two-dimensionalism, or something closely analogous, while Chalmers favors an *epistemic* two-dimensionalism.[17]

Kripke taught us to distinguish genuine metaphysical possibilities from mere epistemic possibilities. He convinced us that it is metaphysically necessary that water is H-O-H and that Hesperus is Phosphorus, even though for someone who is suitably ignorant, it is epistemically possible, possible for all they know, that water isn't H-O-H and that Hesperus isn't Phosphorus. And Chalmers' semantic conception is rooted in epistemic as opposed to metaphysical possibilities. According to Chalmers, a scenario corresponds to a maximally specific way that the world might be for all that can be known a priori.[18] And a scenario verifies a statement when it

---

[17] Gendler and Hawthorne (2002).
[18] Chalmers (2004a: 176–7). I am suppressing complications about centering.

can be ruled out a priori that the scenario is actual but the statement is not true.[19]

But the basic contents I propose are generated in the way I sketched earlier, by the nature of our internally determinate capacities and the interdependencies among them. I don't think that epistemology has much to tell us about the nature of basic contents. Instead, the basic contents correspond to maximally specific ways that the world can be thought by us to be, which span a range fixed by our internally determinate psychological capacities. And I think that there are more or less analytic relations of dependence between certain contents and others, which can in principle be assessed a priori or at least from armchairs, but only when conditions are right. Epistemic status is not what is central. The basic contents are at the bottom of chains of dependency of a specifically semantic sort, and these dependencies are constituted by allied dependencies in our internal capacities for such thoughts.

One example involves the hierarchical structure of RDC's clusters. The capacity for thought mediated by a particular word that purports to refer, for a particular speaker at a particular time, depends upon capacities for conceiving at least some of the properties in the relevant cluster, and its match is likewise dependent. Another example is that we would not be able to conceive relatively abstract things, for instance monetary inflation, if we were not capable of thought of things that would properly count as their relatively concrete realization in the world.

There is much work to be done in properly developing and assessing both epistemic and semantic two-dimensionalisms. But there are various *prima facie* reasons to prefer a non-epistemic conception of basic contents and also of the relations among contents.

First, the nature and existence of a priori knowledge are quite controversial, and so too is what is a priori knowable. The fate of Chalmers' proposal depends on the resolution of these controversies. But regardless of the fate and complexities of a priori knowledge, there are the sorts of basic contents that my account delivers on the basis of our internal capacities and their relations. Second, the content of a thought seems to be a prior fact that helps determine whether it can be a priori knowledge. For instance, it is not an accident that analytic truths are perhaps the best case for a

[19] Chalmers (2004a: 182).

priori knowledge. This suggests that the a priori is not what is basic. Third, something is presumably a priori knowable in the relevant sense only if it is true. And the truth of even a priori claims can involve the external world in a way that is irrelevant to thought content. Remember the dark details of the social determination of truth and reference, details that internalism properly ignores. Fourth, there are some thoughts, for instance, the thought that there are thoughts, that are knowable a priori in standard senses—that can be known independent of experience or at least independent of any experience beyond that required to possess the concepts in question—but yet that are not true in all basic semantic possibilities. Fifth, according to standard understandings, the a priori justification of some thoughts, and also defeating conditions that prevent such justified true beliefs from being knowledge, may involve external conditions in a way that is irrelevant to the content of the thoughts. Perhaps the mathematicians in the next building have recently undercut my apparently a priori knowledge of some mathematical truth by conceiving a ground-breaking set of apparent counterexamples that is now receiving much public discussion, but that I have not considered.

Chalmers has a reply available to my fourth and fifth complaints. His own conception of what is a priori knowable is probably sufficiently unusual to evade these particular worries. For instance, he seems to think that claims about the internal nature of bat experience, claims that humans could not even form the concepts to understand, are yet a priori knowable in a way relevant to the semantics of human thought, perhaps because bat-like creatures could know them a priori. And he discusses cases analogous to my thought-that-there-are-thoughts case and, despite the fact that such a treatment seems to be in tension with his general characterizations of a priori knowability, regiments them out of consideration.[20] But such replies have a cost. The unusual nature of Chalmers' conception of a priori knowability provides other grounds for hesitation about his proposal, which are indeed the sixth *prima facie* reason to prefer my alternative.

For instance, Chalmers must deploy enormous idealizations to deliver semantic relations of dependence by capacities for epistemic a priori inference, when no real human can in fact make the inferences in question.[21] If some abstruse mathematical claim is provable in some way that no human

---

[20] Chalmers (2002a: 168) and (2004a: 208–9). [21] Chalmers (2002a: 147–9).

could ever survey and understand, yet it counts as relevantly knowable a priori for Chalmers. If no finite human could ever come even to believe that there is a dependency between one particular quite complex content of their thought and another quite complex content of their thought, yet that dependency is knowable a priori in the relevant sense.

But I think that facts of content dependency are constituted by the cognizer's actual internal states, capacities, and dispositions, or there are no such facts of semantic dependency in their case.[22] Consider our discussion of arithmetical sentences and Kripke's version of Wittgenstein in Chapter 9. If all of one's internal states, capacities, and dispositions, say to utter mathematical sentences and to use them in proofs of one sort or another, do not determine that one's thought has one content that might potentially be distinguished from another in such a case, then one's thought is indeterminate in that way. What an infinite superbeing would be able to infer is not relevant to the content of our finite thought. And, on the other hand, the actual complex interdependencies of our internal capacities for thought may give the contents of our thoughts a kind of actual complexity of semantic dependency that we could not reflexively understand or formulate, and hence that we could never know a priori or even believe without enormous idealization of our nature.

There is another important class of differences that I have with Chalmers, which is also complicated by the presence of a related similarity. Perhaps the most immediately important of these differences is this: Chalmers holds that dualism about qualia obtains because the truth of physicalism doesn't a priori entail the existence of qualia.[23] But I think that the constitution of qualia by the physical involves a posteriori necessities, despite the lack of such an entailment. So my account of narrow content does not aim always to deliver the facts of constitution in an a priori manner. I think that cannot always be done. But, on the other hand, I also think that Chalmers is right about some other significant examples of constitution.

Consider four different sorts of cases. I think that there is a coherent and consistent content in which Hesperus is not Phosphorus, if we mean by that a situation in which the *narrow* content of my ignorant thought that

---

[22] Mendola (1997) allows recombinatorial idealization in the configuration of the full range of basic semantic contents, rooted in realistic dispositions to activities that are potentially infinitely iterated. That realistic rooting is a relevant difference.

[23] Chalmers (1996).

'Hesperus is not Phosphorus' is true, a thought that we might conceivably capture by the narrow content expressed by 'dthat [heavenly body called "Hesperus"] is not identical to dthat [heavenly body called "Phosphorus"]'. And there are basic semantic contents whose truth would suffice more or less analytically for the truth of that narrow content. But Hesperus is in fact Phosphorus. So if we presume the standard view that all identities of this sort are in fact necessary, then there is no metaphysical or real possibility corresponding to this semantic possibility. The actual referents of two components of the narrow content of my thought rule out the real or metaphysical possibility of that thought. A crucial component of the most intuitive candidate for a worldly truth-maker for that thought in our world, Venus not being itself, is trivially incoherent. This set of claims is closely analogous to Chalmers' treatment of this case.

But I do think that thoughts characteristically have at least two sorts of content, both a narrow content and also a wide content that can incorporate their actual worldly truth-maker, or rather, I should perhaps officially say, their actual worldly match-maker. And to understand clearly some of the complications that this introduces, consider the thought that 'dthat [heavenly body called "Hesperus"] *is* identical to dthat [heavenly body called "Phosphorus"]'. That involves a contingent narrow content for whose truth the truth of a range of basic semantic contents would suffice. And in fact it is true. It has an intuitive worldly truth-maker that includes the necessary and trivial fact of Venus being itself, but also the metalinguistic features in question, which are not obliterated by dthat. The wide content of this thought is contingent too, because it includes not just Venus being itself but also those contingent metalinguistic features. The conjunction of a necessary truth and most contingent truths is a contingent truth. And so I think that no single proposition in this case is both necessary and knowable only a posteriori. I agree with robust two-dimensionalists, such as Frank Jackson, about that. And while such a claim is suggested by some features of Chalmers' early discussions in *The Conscious Mind*, he has subsequently distanced himself from it.

I also think that there is a narrow content, a semantic possibility, corresponding to zombies, who are physically just like us but lack qualitative experience. But, unlike Chalmers, I think that there is no metaphysical possibility corresponding to that thought. And yet I think there is an asymmetry between this case and the case of Hesperus and Phosphorus.

We can entertain a narrow content in which 'dthat [heavenly body called "Hesperus"] is identical to dthat [heavenly body called "Phosphorus"]'. And we can entertain a basic semantic content that would suffice for the truth of that. But there is no basic semantic possibility generated by my proposal in which our physical states are sufficient to assure the existence of our qualitative experience, despite the fact that what is actual must be metaphysically possible, despite the fact that our physical states do constitute our qualitative experience, and despite the fact that I believe that. My belief in these relations of constitution has content, and indeed true content, if I can put it that way, but it must be delivered by my semantic proposal in an unusual orthogonal way. There are no semantically basic contents that assure that this constitution occurs. That is why we can never fully understand the constitution of our experience by our neurophysiology, as I do think we can fully understand how H-O-H constitutes water. So in this case there is a real metaphysical possibility, indeed a fact, in some sense without a corresponding semantic possibility, that is without a basic semantic possibility that would assure it. Chalmers agrees that there is an asymmetry between the case of Hesperus and Phosphorus and the case of qualia,[24] but we disagree considerably about its nature.

On the other hand, I agree with Chalmers that there is no basic narrow content, no basic semantic possibility, in which, holding microphysical laws fixed, being H-O-H isn't sufficient to assure being suitably water-like, isn't sufficient to assure being wet and runny and clear and water-like enough to count as the referent of 'water' if only you are in enough of the streams and lakes around here. And I agree with him that this guarantees that there is no corresponding metaphysical possibility either. If we can see by armchair reasoning that being H-O-H would be semantically sufficient for water-likeness, then it would be sufficient in fact. What's more, I agree with Chalmers that if we see that being H-O-H would not be sufficient in a similar way for fire-likeness, then it cannot be sufficient in fact. There are content dependencies here that are analogous to analytic relations, and that can be assessed more or less a priori, at least in principle and with enough idealization of finite human capacities.

What's the difference between this case and the case of qualia? It is partly that the qualia case either involves a constitution relation between distinct

---

[24] Chalmers (2004a).

sorts of elements (phenomenal and physical-causal) present in semantically basic narrow contents, or alternatively an orthogonal linkage not between elements of basic contents but between one sort of element and the *experience* of another sort, between physical-causal properties and the experience of phenomenal properties. Either somehow physical surface properties must constitute phenomenal colors, but in a way we cannot fully understand in the manner of ordinary cases of constitution, or, more plausibly, internal physical properties of someone must constitute the experience of mere phenomenal colors in a way we cannot fully understand. And the fire and water cases are not like that. The notions of fire and water and H-O-H are all of the same causal-physical sort, and so their relations of constitution and possible constitution are a normal sort of case. But the constitution of qualia by the physical is not a normal case.

Like Kripke and Chalmers, I differ from contemporary orthodoxy because I believe there is an asymmetry here. But I have a different understanding of the difference than Chalmers. And I think that Kripke got his cases backwards.

But let me stress again my principal agreement with Chalmers in this area. One of the most controversial features of Chalmers' account has been the way in which his scenarios are supposed to entail a priori other contents. According to Chalmers, it is supposed to be a priori true that H-O-H is suitably water-like, so that it can count as water if only it is actually in all the lakes and falls from the air, and also a priori true that XYZ would be suitably water-like too. As I just said, I believe, aside from our differences about qualia, that Chalmers gets this point more or less right. I also think, as Chalmers thinks, that many relations of possible constitution can be assessed a priori, or in our armchairs, at least in principle and if we idealize away from the finitude of real humans.

So objections to this feature of Chalmers' account—which was earlier suggested with qualifications involving a posteriori necessities such as I favor by Terry Horgan[25]—are sometimes also objections to my view. Still, the fact that I favor an analog of semantic two-dimensionalism is an advantage in this context, since that helps me answer the most important of these objections.

[25] Horgan (1984).

The deepest source of resistance to this so-called cosmic hermeneutics, which has been articulated by, among others, Ned Block, Robert Stalnaker, Alex Byrne, and James Pryor, is the thought that there can be no factoring of world and narrow content whereby narrow content delivers the necessary sorts of dependencies in an a priori fashion.[26]

The charge can be detailed in various distinct ways. Block and Stalnaker claim that '[i]t is a part of the semantics of natural kind terms that they are natural kind terms, but it may also be part of the semantics of these terms that this is a defeasible condition. What is not plausibly a part of the semantics, something we all know in virtue of knowing the language alone, is what to say in all the myriad cases in which the defeasible condition is defeated. In these cases, what we say will no doubt be dictated by principles of "simplicity", conservativeness, etc.'[27] And Block and Stalnaker suggest that while armchair reflection may suffice to determine how we would respond to various hypothetical microreductive scenarios, which would deliver my sort of semantic a prioricity, still 'our reasoning about the proper epistemic response in various counterfactual situations is informed not only by our concepts, but by implicit and explicit theories and general methodological principles that we have absorbed',[28] by general empirical background knowledge.

I agree. And indeed I think that some of the things we would say if confronted with these situations are not even as epistemically rational as Block and Stalnaker seem prepared to grant. Some depend on what we saw in Chapter 4 to be the irrational or arbitrary influence of historical accidents and social quirks that undercut the significance of the details of reference and truth that result. I think that Block and Stalnaker are too easy on Chalmers, given his stress on knowledge and rational inference, at this point.

But epistemicism is a mistake, and the correct form of two-dimensionalism is semantic rather than epistemic. Whether our dispositions to say things are a matter of epistemic rationality or irrational quirks, the crucial relations between contents in question are semantic and not epistemic, and are constituted by our internally determinate psychological capacities and their relations of dependency. Perhaps sometimes we can make a priori or

---

[26] Byrne (1999); Block and Stalnaker (1999); Yablo (2000); Byrne and Pryor (2006).
[27] Block and Stalnaker (1999).   [28] Block and Stalnaker (1999: 43).

at least armchair judgments that track these relations, but that epistemic fact does not constitute the semantic relations in question.

Block and Stalnaker complain that some of our armchair judgments in these cases aren't something that all we speakers know. And so it is also relevant to point out that on my account there may be differences in the kinds of semantically relevant relations that different speakers will be disposed to recognize among thoughts mediated by shared words, which reflect genuine differences in the detailed semantics of the speakers' thoughts. What is a priori in the semantic sense built on these dependencies can differ from one person to another. And since the semantic a priori merely delivers weighted elements of a cluster for terms that purport to refer, some things that are semantically a priori can even turn out false and unsuited to our world in a way that the speaker will come to recognize. So what is a priori in my sense need not be something that 'we all know by virtue of knowing the language alone', as Block and Stalnaker suggest.

Chalmers also maintains that there is variation in what is a priori between those who know the language. But it is harder for him, with his focus on a priori knowledge, to evade one aspect of Block and Stalnaker's complaint, isolated in Byrne and Pryor's worry that Chalmers' proposal is subject to one of Kripke's famous objections to description theories of reference, that there may be error in the descriptions that seem to introduce a difference in cognitive role for co-referring terms.[29] What is a priori may perhaps differ from one individual to another, as Chalmers claims. But knowledge is true, and it is harder to say that truth will differ in the same way from one individual to another. But the clusters of RDC can incorporate error.

If a sentence is analytic, then that is because of the meaning it has, and that depends on the nature of what provides meaning to sentences. When a thought content dependency is like an analytic relation, then that is because of the contents involved and the nature of what provides thoughts with such contents. We must work up from a theory of what might be called the realization of thoughts, of what constitutes creatures to have them, to an account of content dependencies, dependencies of the sort that for instance assure that H-O-H would be suitably water-like. This may in turn support some a priori or at least armchair inferences. But because of relatively subtle differences among the contents of the thoughts of different

[29] Byrne and Pryor (2006).

individuals mediated by the same words, the relevant armchair inferences of different people may conflict, and they may be mistaken. And in any case, the epistemology of these dependencies is not their basic and defining element. It is secondary. A generalization of semantic aprioricity is more fundamental than epistemic aprioricity in this context.

10.4

Steve Yablo has developed, though not exactly endorsed, an account of conceptual necessities analogous to analyticities that is even closer to my proposal than Chalmers' is.[30] Before noting a contrast, let me take the opportunity to reinforce my arguments against Chalmers' more deeply epistemological alternative, by appeal to Yablo's plausible claim that there are cases of something like analyticities involved in constitution relations that yet do not allow for a priori knowledge. These involve paradigm instances of what he calls response-enabled concepts.

Cassinis are a class of figures, defined by a specific equation, which look oval. And our concept of an oval is supposed to be an example of a response-enabled concept.

A thing... is oval if it is of a shape that would strike *me* [and other actual normal humans] as egg-shaped were I (with my sensibilities undisturbed) given a chance to look at it.... Could things have turned out so that cassinis were not oval? If ovality... is purely a function of shape, then the answer is no. 'Cassinis are oval' is... conceptually necessary. But... it is very far from a priori that cassinis are oval. To determine whether they are oval, you have to cast your eyes over (some of) them, and see how they look to you. There is no other way to do it. 'Cassinis are oval' is an analytic (conceptually necessary) truth that we are in no position to know a priori.[31]

I'm not confident that I know how to distribute the notion of the epistemic a priori in cases like these. Chalmers says that a priori knowability is knowability independent of experience, and these cases certainly seem to involve experience in a crucial way. Only experience will tell you whether cassinis are ovals. But Chalmers has replied to Yablo that it is knowable

---

[30] Yablo (2002).   [31] Yablo (2002: 467–9). I have suppressed paragraph breaks.

a priori that eliciting an ovality response in a certain sort of epistemically possible world would be sufficient to constitute something's being an oval in that world.[32] Perhaps even those who are incapable of the experience in question can know this a priori. On the other hand, he hasn't replied that cassinis are ovals in all epistemically possible worlds, that it is epistemically necessary that cassinis are ovals. He hasn't replied that it can in fact be known by anyone a priori, or known by any idealization of any of us a priori, that cassinis are in fact ovals.

Perhaps in such cases the familiar notion of the epistemic a priori is pulled in two. Still, such cases are not a problem for an internalist like me, who deploys a semantic conception of the relevant content dependencies. Dispositions to such responses are internally determinate, and perhaps to a limited degree even assessable in armchairs. In all semantic possibilities, cassinis are ovals, because of content dependencies analogous to analyticities. But these cases do suggest that we cannot assess these dependencies in some of the ways characteristic of the epistemic a priori. I think that's a bigger problem for Chalmers than he thinks it is. But it's certainly okay by me.

Despite stealing his case, I think that even Yablo is a bit too epistemically oriented. The fact that cassinis are ovals is a conceptual truth. It is constituted as true for someone who has the concepts in question by their internally determinate conceptual capacities, including their recognitional capacities, and so is closely analogous to an analytic truth. So far, I agree with Yablo. But he generalizes from the case of ovality in a certain way. He seems to think that other concepts that have a similar epistemology of application have a similar semantic nature. And this seems to me to be a mistake.

While Yablo never claims (or denies) that the constitution of qualia by the physical is analytic, he applies the response-enabled model of a concept, based on ovality, to the case of pain qualia. And the two concepts do arguably involve a similar epistemology of application, in that the best way to know if something is pain is to experience it. Still, I think that the dependencies among our conceptual capacities make the constitution of the feeling of pain by the physical a very different sort of case than the case of oval cassinis, and certainly no analyticity. And many share with me Chalmers' plausible feeling that the pain case isn't much at all like a conceptual necessity. I think it is a mistake, a mistake revealed by the nature

[32] Chalmers (2002a: 191).

of our thought contents and the psychological capacities that root them, to group concepts on the basis of their epistemology of application. Even that degree of epistemicism is too much for me. But such an epistemological grouping is suggested by Yablo's terminology, and by his uniform treatment of what seem quite different cases.

Yablo also suggests a similar treatment of theoretical predicates. Consider the issue of what sorts of microphysical configurations could count as energy.

The extension of 'energy'... is a function of what the correct scientific theory is. To find that theory, one must appeal at some point to considerations of naturalness, simplicity, nonarbitrariness, and the like—in a word, to considerations of *reasonableness*.... [But r]easonableness is... response-enabled [like ovality]. You can't hand responsibility over to 'rules of reasonableness'.... You have to let yourself be led to some extent by your gut.[33]

This treatment also rests heavily on epistemic similarity to the case of ovality. But I have been arguing for a different treatment. In cases like this one, the facts of what can constitute what are conceptual truths. But they are not conceptual truths that rest on an epistemic notion like reasonableness. They are fixed by semantic dependencies of contents that reflect dependencies of capacities for such thoughts. They are so fixed even if the epistemology of application of the concept of energy, at least to strange cases, normally involves your gut. It is not the epistemology of that concept that matters semantically, at least according to my gut.

10.5

Neo-empiricists should cast out the spirit of epistemicism, along with externalism and the ghost in the machine. If you are interested in mental content, don't worry about what knowledge or justified belief requires. Don't even worry about evidence. Consider rather what is required merely to believe something, or even just to think it.

Qualia empiricism is a form of empiricism, in the tradition of Hobbes, Locke, Berkeley, Hume, Mill, and Russell. But there are many grounds for claims to that name, and I do not invoke all of them.

---

[33] Yablo (2002: 478).

As is suggested by its dalliance with verificationism, traditional empiricism developed an account of the epistemic justification of thoughts. But I make no claims about justification. I do not endorse some sort of epistemic empiricism. While I claim that the contents of our thoughts rest crucially on the qualitative contents of our experiences, I do not believe that my qualia are my sole or ordinary evidence. And I am not what is sometimes called an extreme epistemic empiricist, as opposed to a rationalist. I think that there is a good deal of armchair knowledge that is more or less analytic, and which, ovality aside, it is not unreasonable to consider a paradigm of a priori knowledge.

Empiricism is also associated with claims about the causal genesis of our concepts, about their history.[34] Some think that all thoughts are rooted in experience in a way that implies that there are no innate concepts, or at least no innate concepts beyond those that are required by that experience itself. But I make no claims about the causal genesis of our concepts. As an internalist, I think that an intemperate focus on causal sources and history is a Hegelian nightmare of the nineteenth century from which we should finally awake.

Rather, I think that we should focus on possibility or necessity in two different ways. We should focus on the nature of our capacities or potentials for thoughts. And we should focus on necessary connections between such capacities. It is not that a capacity for thought logically implies a capacity for sensation, at least for all I know. Perhaps it is not even necessary that where there is thought there is sensation. But the capacity for thoughts with the particular contents that our thoughts have necessarily requires, I think, the capacity for sensory contents such as we have. Our peculiar human experience is in that sense a necessary root of our all too human thought.

[34] Prinz (2002).

Bibliography

Ackerman, Diana/Felicia (1979a), 'Proper Names, Essences and Intuitive Beliefs', *Theory and Decision* 11, 5–26.

——(1979b), 'Proper Names, Propositional Attitudes and Non-descriptive Connotations', *Philosophical Studies* 35, 55–69.

——(1980), 'Natural Kinds, Concepts, and Propositional Attitudes', *Midwest Studies in Philosophy* 5, 469–85.

——(1985), 'Plantinga's Theory of Proper Names', in J. Tomberlin and P. van Inwagen (eds.), *Alvin Plantinga* (Dordrecht: Reidel), 187–98.

——(1989), 'Content, Character, and Nondescriptive Meaning', in J. Almog, J. Perry, and H. Wettstein (eds.), *Themes from Kaplan* (New York: Oxford University Press), 5–21.

Adams, Fred, and Kenneth Aizawa (1994), 'Fodorian Semantics', in Stephen P. Stich and Ted A. Warfield (eds.), *Mental Representation* (Cambridge, Mass.: Blackwell), 223–42.

Agar, Nicholas (1993), 'What Do Frogs Really Believe?', *Australasian Journal of Philosophy* 71, 1–12.

Allen, Colin, Marc Bekoff, and George Lauder (eds.) (1998), *Nature's Purposes* (Cambridge, Mass.: MIT Press).

Almog, Joseph (1991), 'The Subject-Predicate Class I', *Nous* 25, 591–619.

Alpern, M., K. Kitahara, and D. H. Krantz (1997), 'Perception of Colour in Unilateral Tritanopia', in Byrne and Hilbert (1997: ii. 231–48).

Ayers, Michael (1991), *Locke, Epistemology and Ontology*, vol. ii (London: Routledge).

Bach, Kent (1981), 'What's In a Name', *Australasian Journal of Philosophy* 59, 371–86.

——(2002), 'Giorgone Was So-Called Because of His Name', *Philosophical Perspectives* 16, 73–103.

Bennett, Jonathan (1966), *Kant's Analytic* (Cambridge: Cambridge University Press).

Bermúdez, José Luis (1998), *The Paradox of Self-Consciousness* (Cambridge, Mass.: MIT Press).

——(2003), *Thinking without Words* (New York: Oxford University Press).

Berry, A. J. (1954), *From Classical to Modern Chemistry* (Cambridge: Cambridge University Press).

Bertoldi, F., W. Altenhoff, A. Weiss, K. M. Menten, and C. Thum (2006), 'The Trans-Neptunian Object UB313 is Larger than Pluto', *Nature* 439, 563–4.

Bigelow, John, and Robert Pargetter (1987), 'Functions', *Journal of Philosophy* 84, 181–96.

Blackburn, Simon (1984), 'The Individual Strikes Back', *Synthese* 58, 281–301.

Block, Ned (1996), 'Mental Paint and Mental Latex', *Philosophical Issues* 7, 19–49.

Block, Ned, and Robert Stalnaker (1999), 'Conceptual Analysis, Dualism, and the Explanatory Gap', *Philosophical Review* 108, 1–46.

Boghossian, Paul (1989), 'Content and Self-Knowledge', *Philosophical Topics* 17, 5–26.

—— (1994), 'The Transparency of Mental Content', *Philosophical Perspectives* 8, 33–50.

—— (1998), 'What the Externalist Can Know A Priori', in Crispin Wright, Barry C. Smith, and Cynthia MacDonald (eds.), *Knowing our Own Minds* (Oxford: Clarendon Press), 271–84.

Bourse, Christopher (1976), 'Wright on Functions', *Philosophical Review* 85, 70–86.

—— (1977), 'Health as a Theoretical Concept', *Philosophy of Science* 44, 542–73.

Braddon-Mitchell, David (2003), 'Qualia and Analytical Conditionals', *Journal of Philosophy* 100, 111–35.

Braddon-Mitchell, David, and Frank Jackson (2007), *The Philosophy of Mind and Cognition*, 2nd edn. (Cambridge: Blackwell).

Brandom, Robert (1994), *Making It Explicit* (Cambridge, Mass.: Harvard University Press).

—— (2000), *Articulating Reasons* (Cambridge, Mass.: Harvard University Press).

Braun, David (1993), 'Empty Names', *Nous* 27, 449–69.

Brewer, Bill (1999), *Perception and Reason* (Oxford: Clarendon Press).

Broackes, Justin (1997), 'The Autonomy of Color', in Byrne and Hilbert (1997: i. 191–225).

Brown, Colin, and Peter Hagoort (eds.) (1999), *The Neurocognition of Language* (New York: Oxford University Press).

Brown, Jessica (2000), 'Against Temporal Externalism', *Analysis* 60, 178–88.

—— (2004), *Anti-Individualism and Knowledge* (Cambridge, Mass.: MIT Press).

Brueckner, Anthony (1992), 'What an Anti-Individualist Knows A Priori', *Analysis* 52, 111–18.

Burge, Tyler (1979), 'Individualism and the Mental', *Midwest Studies in Philosophy* 4, 73–122.

—— (1982), 'Other Bodies', in A. Woodfield (ed.), *Thought and Object* (Oxford: Clarendon Press), 97–120.

—— (1986a), 'Individualism and Psychology', *Philosophical Review* 95, 3–45.

———— (1986b), 'Intellectual Norms and Foundations of Mind', *Journal of Philosophy* 83, 697–720.
———— (1988), 'Individualism and Self-Knowledge', *Journal of Philosophy* 85, 649–63.
———— (2007), *Foundations of Mind* (Oxford: Clarendon Press).
Byrne, Alex (1999), 'Cosmic Hermeneutics', *Philosophical Perspectives* 13, 347–83.
———— (2001), 'Intentionalism Defended', *Philosophical Review* 110, 199–240.
———— (2002), 'Semantic Values?', *Philosophy and Phenomenological Research* 65, 201–7.
Byrne, Alex, and David R. Hilbert (eds.) (1997), *Readings on Color*, vols. i and ii (Cambridge, Mass.: MIT Press).
Byrne, Alex, and James Pryor (2006), 'Bad Intensions', in M. García-Carpintero and J. Maciá, *The Two-Dimensional Framework: Foundations and Applications* (Oxford: Oxford University Press), 38–54.
Campbell, John (1987–8), 'Is Sense Transparent?', *Proceedings of the Aristotelian Society* 88, 273–92.
———— (1999), *Past, Space, and Self* (Cambridge, Mass.: MIT Press).
———— (2002a), 'Berkeley's Puzzle', in T. Gendler and J. Hawthorne (eds.), *Conceivability and Possibility* (Oxford: Clarendon Press), 127–43.
———— (2002b), *Reference and Consciousness* (Oxford: Clarendon Press).
Carruthers, Peter (1996), *Language, Thought, and Consciousness* (Cambridge: Cambridge University Press).
Carruthers, Peter, and Peter K. Smith (eds.) (1996), *Theories of Theories of Mind* (Cambridge: Cambridge University Press).
Carruthers, Peter, and Jill Boucher (eds.) (1998), *Language and Thought* (Cambridge: Cambridge University Press).
Casullo, Albert (1987), 'A Defense of Sense-Data', *Philosophy and Phenomenological Research* 48, 45–61.
———— (2003), *A Priori Justification* (New York: Oxford University Press).
Chalmers, David (1996), *The Conscious Mind* (New York: Oxford University Press).
———— (2002a), 'Does Conceivability Entail Possibility?', in T. Gendler and J. Hawthorne (eds.), *Conceivability and Possibility* (Oxford: Clarendon Press), 145–200.
———— (2002b), 'The Components of Content', in David Chalmers (ed.), *Philosophy of Mind* (New York: Oxford University Press), 608–33.
———— (2002c), 'On Sense and Intention', *Philosophical Perspectives* 16, 135–82.
———— (2003), 'The Content and Epistemology of Phenomenal Belief', in Q. Smith and A. Jokic (eds.), *Consciousness: New Philosophical Perspectives* (Oxford: Clarendon Press), 220–72.
———— (2004a), 'Epistemic Two-Dimensional Semantics', *Philosophical Studies* 18, 153–226.

Chalmers, David (2004b), 'The Representational Character of Experience', in B. Leiter (ed.), *The Future for Philosophy* (New York: Oxford University Press), 153–81.

—— (2006), 'Perception and the Fall from Eden', in Tamar Szabo Gendler and John Hawthorne (eds.), *Perceptual Experience* (Oxford: Clarendon Press), 49–125.

Chalmers, David, and Frank Jackson (2001), 'Conceptual Analysis and Reductive Explanation', *Philosophical Review* 110, 315–61.

Child, William (1994), *Causality, Interpretation, and the Mind* (Oxford: Clarendon Press).

Chisholm, Roderick (1957) *Perceiving* (Ithaca, NY: Cornell University Press).

Chomsky, Noam (1995), 'Language and Nature', *Mind* 104, 1–61.

Church, Alonzo (1950), 'On Carnap's Analysis of Statements of Assertion and Belief', *Analysis* 10, 97–9.

Clark, Andy, and David Chalmers (1998), 'The Extended Mind', *Analysis* 58, 10–23.

Clark, Austen (1993), *Sensory Qualities* (Oxford: Clarendon Press).

—— (2000), *A Theory of Sentience* (New York: Oxford University Press).

Conant, James Bryant (ed.) (1966), *The Overthrow of the Phlogiston Theory* (Cambridge, Mass.: Harvard University Press).

Crimmins, Mark (1992), *Talk about Beliefs* (Cambridge, Mass.: MIT Press).

Cummins, Denise Dellarosa, and Colin Allen (eds.) (1998), *The Evolution of Mind* (New York: Oxford University Press).

Cummins, Robert (1975), 'Functional Analysis', *Journal of Philosophy* 72, 741–65.

—— (1989), *Meaning and Mental Representation* (Cambridge, Mass.: MIT Press).

Dalton, John (1964), *A New System of Chemical Philosophy* (New York: Philosophical Library).

Davidson, Donald (1980), *Essays on Actions & Events* (Oxford: Clarendon Press).

—— (1984a), 'First Person Authority', *Dialectica* 38, 101–11.

—— (1984b), 'Radical Interpretation', in *Inquiries into Truth and Interpretation* (Oxford: Clarendon Press), 125–39.

—— (1984c), 'The Method of Truth in Metaphysics', in *Inquiries into Truth and Interpretation* (Oxford: Clarendon Press), 199–214.

—— (1984d), 'Thought and Talk', in *Inquiries into Truth and Interpretation* (Oxford: Clarendon Press), 155–70.

—— (1987), 'On Knowing One's Own Mind', *Proceedings and Addresses of the American Philosophical Association* 60, 441–58.

—— (1990), 'The Structure and Content of Truth', *Journal of Philosophy* 87, 279–328.

—— (1999a), 'Reply to Barry Stroud', in Lewis Edwin Hahn (ed.), *The Philosophy of Donald Davidson* (Peru, Ill.: Open Court), 162–5.

—— (1999b), 'Reply to Deborah Soles', in Lewis Edwin Hahn (ed.), *The Philosophy of Donald Davidson* (Peru, Ill.: Open Court), 330–2.

—— (1999c), 'Reply to Jim Hopkins', in Lewis Edwin Hahn (ed.), *The Philosophy of Donald Davidson* (Peru, Ill.: Open Court), 286–7.

—— (2001a), 'Rational Animals', in *Subjective, Intersubjective, Objective* (Oxford: Clarendon Press), 95–105.

—— (2001b), 'The Second Person', in *Subjective, Intersubjective, Objective* (Oxford: Clarendon Press), 107–21.

—— (2001c), 'Three Varieties of Knowledge', in *Subjective, Intersubjective, Objective* (Oxford: Clarendon Press), 205–20.

—— (2004a), 'A Unified Theory of Thought, Meaning, and Action', in *Problems of Rationality* (Oxford: Clarendon Press), 151–66.

—— (2004b), 'Could There Be a Science of Rationality?', in *Problems of Rationality* (Oxford: Clarendon Press), 117–34.

—— (2005a), 'A Nice Derangement of Epitaphs', in *Truth, Language, and History* (Oxford: Clarendon Press), 89–107.

—— (2005b), 'Meaning, Truth, and Evidence', in *Truth, Language, and History* (Oxford: Clarendon Press), 47–62.

—— (2005c), 'Method and Metaphysics', in *Truth, Language, and History* (Oxford: Clarendon Press), 39–45.

—— (2005d), 'The Social Aspect of Language', in *Truth, Language, and History* (Oxford: Clarendon Press), 109–25.

—— (2005e), *Truth and Predication* (Cambridge, Mass.: Harvard University Press).

Davies, Martin (1991), 'Individualism and Perceptual Content', *Mind* 100, 461–84.

—— (1998), 'Externalism, Architecturalism, and Epistemic Warrant', in Crispin Wright, Barry C. Smith, and Cynthia MacDonald (eds.), *Knowing our Own Minds* (Oxford: Clarendon Press), 325–61.

Dennett, Daniel C. (1969), *Content & Consciousness* (London: Routledge).

—— (1978), 'Intentional Systems', in *Brainstorms* (Montgomery, Vt.: Bradford Books), 3–22.

—— (1982), 'Beyond Belief', in A. Woodfield (ed.), *Thought and Object* (Oxford: Clarendon Press), 1–95.

—— (1989), 'Reflections: About Aboutness', in *The Intentional Stance* (Cambridge, Mass.: MIT Press), 203–11.

—— (1991), *Explaining Consciousness* (Boston: Little, Brown).

Donnellan, Keith (1974), 'Speaking of Nothing', *Philosophical Review* 83, 3–31.

Dowell, J. L. (2006), 'Making It Totally Explicit', *Philosophical Papers* 35, 137–70.

Dretske, Fred (1986), 'Misrepresentation', in Radu Bogdan (ed.), *Belief* (Oxford: Clarendon Press), 17–36.

Dretske, Fred (1988) *Explaining Behavior* (Cambridge, Mass.: MIT Press).
―― (1995), *Naturalizing the Mind* (Cambridge, Mass.: MIT Press).
―― (2000), *Perception, Knowledge, and Belief: Selected Essays* (Cambridge: Cambridge University Press).
Ducasse, C. J. (1942), 'Moore's Refutation of Idealism', in P. Schilpp (ed.), *The Philosophy of G. E. Moore* (Chicago: Northwestern University Press), 223–51.
Dummett, Michael (1981), *Frege: Philosophy of Language*, 2nd edn. (Cambridge, Mass.: Harvard University Press).
―― (1993a), *The Origins of Analytical Philosophy* (London: Duckworth).
―― (1993b), *The Seas of Language* (Oxford: Clarendon Press).
Ebbs, Gary (1997), *Rule-Following and Realism* (Cambridge, Mass.: Harvard University Press).
―― (2000), 'The Very Idea of Sameness of Extension Across Time', *American Philosophical Quarterly* 37, 245–68.
Egan, Frances (1991), 'Must Psychology Be Individualistic?', *Philosophical Review* 100, 179–203.
―― (1992), 'Individualism, Computation, and Perceptual Content', *Mind* 101, 443–59.
Ehrlich, E., S. B. Flexner, G. Carruth, and J. M. Hawkins (1980), *Oxford American Dictionary* (Oxford: Oxford University Press).
Enç, Berent (1982), 'Intentional States of Mechanical Devices', *Mind* 91, 161–82.
Ereshefsky, Marc (2001), *The Poverty of the Linnaean Hierarchy* (Cambridge: Cambridge University Press).
Evans, Gareth (1982), *The Varieties of Reference* (Oxford: Clarendon Press).
―― (1985a), 'The Causal Theory of Names', in *Collected Papers* (Oxford: Clarendon Press), 1–24.
―― (1985b), 'Understanding Demonstratives', in *Collected Papers* (Oxford: Clarendon Press), 291–321.
Falvey, Kevin, and Joseph Owens (1994), 'Externalism, Self-Knowledge, and Skepticism', *Philosophical Review* 103, 107–37.
Farah, M. J. (1988), 'Is visual imagery really visual?', *Psychological Review* 95, 307–17.
Finke, R. (1989), *Principles of Mental Imagery* (Cambridge, Mass.: MIT Press).
Fisher, Justin C. (2007), 'Why Nothing Mental is Just in the Head', *Nous* 41, 318–54.
Fodor, Jerry (1975), *The Language of Thought* (Cambridge, Mass.: Harvard University Press).
―― (1980), 'Methodological Solipsism Considered as a Research Strategy in Cognitive Science', *Behavioral and Brain Sciences* 3, 63–109.

—— (1984), 'Semantics, Wisconsin Style', *Synthese* 59, 1–20.

—— (1987), *Psychosemantics* (Cambridge, Mass.: MIT Press).

—— (1990a), 'A Theory of Content I: The Problem', in *A Theory of Content and Other Essays* (Cambridge, Mass.: MIT Press), 51–87.

—— (1990b), 'A Theory of Content II: The Theory', in *A Theory of Content and Other Essays* (Cambridge, Mass.: MIT Press), 89–136.

—— (1991a), 'A Modal Argument for Narrow Content', *Journal of Philosophy* 88, 5–26.

—— (1991b), 'Replies', in B. Loewer and G. Rey (eds.), *Meaning in Mind: Fodor and his Critics* (Oxford: Blackwell), 255–319.

—— (1994), *The Elm and the Expert* (Cambridge, Mass.: MIT Press).

—— (1998), *Concepts* (Oxford: Clarendon Press).

—— (2000), *The Mind Doesn't Work That Way* (Cambridge, Mass.: MIT Press).

Frege, Gottlob (1956), 'The Thought: A Logical Inquiry', trans. A. M. and Marcelle Quinton, *Mind* 65, 289–311.

—— (1960), 'On Sense and Reference', in Max Black and P. T. Geach, *Translations from the Philosophical Writings of Gottlob Frege*, 2nd edn. (Oxford: Basil Blackwell), 56–78.

Galileo (1957), 'Excerpts from The Assayer', in S. Drake (ed.), *Discoveries and Opinions of Galileo* (Garden City, NY: Doubleday).

Gazzaniga, Michael, Richard Ivry, and George Mangun (2002), *Cognitive Neuroscience*, 2nd edn. (New York: Norton).

Gendler, T., and J. Hawthorne (2002), 'Introduction', *Conceivability and Possibility* (Oxford: Clarendon Press), 1–70.

Gibbard, Allan (1996), 'Thoughts, Norms, and Discursive Practice: Commentary on Robert Brandom, *Making It Explicit*', *Philosophy and Phenomenological Research* 56, 699–717.

Gibbons, John (1996), 'Externalism and Knowledge of Content', *Philosophical Review* 105, 287–310.

—— (2001a), 'Externalism and Knowledge of the Attitudes', *Philosophical Quarterly* 51, 13–28.

—— (2001b), 'Knowledge in Action', *Philosophy and Phenomenological Research* 62, 579–600.

—— (2005), 'Qualia: They're Not What They Seem', *Philosophical Studies* 126, 397–428.

—— (2006a), 'Access Externalism', *Mind* 115, 19–39.

—— (2006b), 'Knowledge, The Priority of', *Encyclopedia of Philosophy*, vol. v, 2nd edn. (Detroit: Macmillan Reference), 86–90.

Godfrey-Smith, Peter (1991), 'Signal, Decision, Action', *Journal of Philosophy* 88, 709–22.

Godfrey-Smith, Peter (1993), 'Function: Consensus Without Unity', *Pacific Philosophical Quarterly* 74, 196–208.

—— (1994), 'A Modern History Theory of Functions', *Nous* 28, 344–62.

Gordon, James, and Israel Abramov (2001), 'Color Vision', in E. Bruce Goldstein (ed.), *Blackwell Handbook of Perception* (Oxford: Blackwell), 92–127.

Grandy, Richard (1973), 'Reference, Meaning and Belief', *Journal of Philosophy* 70, 439–52.

Grice, Paul (1989), *Studies in the Way of Words* (Cambridge, Mass.: Harvard University Press).

Guerlac, Henry (1975), *Antoine-Laurent Lavoisier* (New York: Scribners).

Hansford, S. Howard (1968), *Chinese Carved Jades* (Greenwich, Conn.: New York Graphic Society).

Hardin, C. L. (1988), *Color for Philosophers* (Indianapolis: Hackett Publishing Company).

—— (1997), 'Reinverting the Spectrum', in Byrne and Hilbert (1997: i. 289–301).

Hardy, Thomas (1998), 'The Pedigree', in *Selected Poems*, ed. Robert Mezey (London: Penguin), 117–18.

Harman, Gilbert (1973), *Thought* (Princeton: Princeton University Press).

—— (1999), '(Nonsolipsistic) Conceptual Role Semantics', in *Reasoning, Meaning, and Mind* (Oxford: Clarendon Press), 206–31.

Harrison, Bernard (1973), *Form and Content* (Oxford: Blackwell).

—— (1986), 'Identity, Predication and Color', *American Philosophical Quarterly* 23, 105–14.

Haugeland, John (1982), 'Heidegger on Being a Person', *Nous* 16, 15–26.

Hauser, Marc, and Susan Carey (1998), 'Building a Cognitive Creature from a Set of Primitives', in Cummins and Allen (1998: 51–106).

Hawthorne, John (2002), 'Advice for Physicalists', *Philosophical Studies* 108, 17–52.

Henderson, David K. (1999), *Interpretation and Explanation in the Human Sciences* (Albany, NY: SUNY Press).

Hill, Christopher S. (1991), *Sensations* (Cambridge: Cambridge University Press).

Hinton, J. (1973), *Experiences* (Oxford: Clarendon Press).

Hopkins, Jim (1999), 'Wittgenstein, Davidson, and Radical Interpretation', in Lewis Edwin Hahn (ed.), *The Philosophy of Donald Davidson* (Peru, Ill.: Open Court), 255–85.

Horgan, Terence (1984), 'Supervenience and Cosmic Hermeneutics', *Southern Journal of Philosophy Supplement* 22, 19–38.

Horgan, Terence, and John Tienson (2002), 'The Intentionality of Phenomenology and the Phenomenology of Intentionality', in David Chalmers (ed.), *Philosophy of Mind* (New York: Oxford University Press), 520–33.

Howard, Ian P. (1982), *Human Visual Orientation* (New York: John Wiley & Sons).

Hsia, Yun, and C. H. Graham (1997), 'Color Blindness', in Byrne and Hilbert (1997: ii. 201–29).

Hull, David L., and Michael Ruse (eds.) (1998), *The Philosophy of Biology* (Oxford: Oxford University Press, 1998).

Jackman, Henry (1999), 'We Live Forwards but Understand Backwards: Linguistic Practices and Future Behavior', *Pacific Philosophical Quarterly* 80, 157–77.

—— (2005), 'Temporal Externalism, Deference, and Our Ordinary Linguistic Practice', *Pacific Philosophical Quarterly* 86, 368–80.

Jackson, Frank (1975), 'On the Adverbial Analysis of Visual Experience', *Metaphilosophy* 6, 127–35.

—— (1977), *Perception* (Cambridge: Cambridge University Press).

—— (1994), 'Armchair Metaphysics', in Michaelis Michael and John O'Leary-Hawthorne (eds.), *Philosophy in Mind* (Dordrecht: Kluwer), 23–42.

—— (1998), *From Metaphysics to Ethics* (Oxford: Clarendon Press).

Jacob, Pierre (1997), *What Minds Can Do* (Cambridge: Cambridge University Press).

Jeannerod, M. (1997), *The Cognitive Neuroscience of Action* (Cambridge, Mass.: Blackwell Science).

Jeshion, Robin (2000), 'Ways of Taking a Meter', *Philosophical Studies* 99, 297–318.

Kaiser, P. K., and R. M. Boynton (1996), *Human Color Vision* (Washington: Optical Society of America).

Kant, Immanuel (1998), *Critique of Pure Reason*, trans. Paul Guyer and Allen Wood (Cambridge: Cambridge University Press).

Kaplan, David (1978), 'Dthat', in P. Cole (ed.), *Syntax and Semantics 9: Pragmatics* (New York: Academic Press), 221–43.

—— (1989*a*), 'Afterthoughts', in J. Almog, J. Perry, and H. Wettstein (eds.), *Themes from Kaplan* (New York: Oxford University Press), 565–654.

—— (1989*b*), 'Demonstratives', in J. Almog, J. Perry, and H. Wettstein (eds.), *Themes from Kaplan* (New York: Oxford University Press), 481–563.

Katz, Jerrold (1994), 'Names Without Bearers', *Philosophical Review* 103, 1–39.

Kim, Jaegwon (1993), *Supervenience and Mind* (Cambridge: Cambridge University Press).

—— (1998), *Mind in a Physical World* (Cambridge, Mass.: MIT Press).

—— (2005), *Physicalism, or Something Near Enough* (Princeton: Princeton University Press).

Kitcher, Philip (1978), 'Theories, Theorists and Theoretical Change', *Philosophical Review* 87, 519–47.

—— (1993*a*), 'Function and Design', *Midwest Studies in Philosophy* 18, 379–97.

Kitcher, Philip (1993b), *The Advancement of Science* (New York: Oxford University Press).

Kneale, William (1962), 'Modality, De Dicto and De Re', in E. Nagel, P. Suppes, and A. Tarski (eds.), *Logic, Methodology and the Philosophy of Science* (Palo Alto, Calif.: Stanford University Press), 622–33.

Kosslyn, S. M. (1980), *Image and Mind* (Cambridge, Mass.: Harvard University Press).

—— (1994), *Image and Brain* (Cambridge, Mass.: MIT Press).

Kossyln, S. M., N. M. Alpert, W. L. Thompson, V. Maljkovik, S. B. Weise, C. F. Chabris, S. E. Hamilton, S. L. Rauch, and F. S. Buonanno (1993), 'Visual Mental Imagery Activates Topographically Organized Visual Cortex: PET Investigations', *Journal of Cognitive Neuroscience* 5, 263–87.

Kripke, Saul A. (1979), 'A Puzzle about Belief', in A. Margalit (ed.), *Meaning and Use* (Dordrecht: Reidel), 239–83.

—— (1980), *Naming and Necessity* (Cambridge, Mass.: Harvard University Press).

—— (1982), *Wittgenstein on Rules and Private Language* (Cambridge, Mass.: Harvard University Press).

Kroon, Frederick W. (1987), 'Causal Descriptivism', *Australasian Journal of Philosophy* 65, 1–17.

Lance, Mark Norris, and John O'Leary-Hawthorne (1997), *The Grammar of Meaning* (Cambridge: Cambridge University Press).

—— (2002), 'Reply to Byrne', *Philosophy and Phenomenological Research* 65, 215–17.

LaPorte, Joe (1996), 'Chemical Kind Reference and the Discovery of Essence', *Nous* 30, 112–32.

Levelt, Willem J. M. (1999), 'Producing Spoken Language: A Blue Print of the Speaker', in C. M. Brown and P. Hagoort, *The Neurocognition of Language* (New York: Oxford University Press), 12–114.

Levin, Janet (1988), 'Must Reasons be Rational?', *Philosophy of Science* 55, 199–217.

Levine, Joseph (1983), 'Materialism and Qualia: The Explanatory Gap', *Pacific Philosophical Quarterly* 64, 354–61.

—— (1998), 'Conceivability and the Metaphysics of Mind', *Nous* 32, 449–80.

—— (2001), *Purple Haze* (New York: Oxford University Press).

Lewis, David (1980), 'Mad Pain and Martian Pain', in Ned Block (ed.), *Readings in Philosophy of Psychology*, vol. i (Cambridge, Mass.: Harvard University Press), 216–22.

—— (1981), 'What Puzzling Pierre Does Not Believe', *Australasian Journal of Philosophy* 59, 282–9.

—— (1982), 'Radical Interpretation', in *Philosophical Papers*, vol. i (New York: Oxford University Press), 108–21.

―― (1984), 'Putnam's Paradox', *Australasian Journal of Philosophy* 62, 221–36.
―― (1994) 'Lewis, David: Reduction of Mind', in Samuel Guttenplan (ed.), *A Companion to the Philosophy of Mind* (Oxford: Blackwell), 412–31.
―― (1999), 'Naming the Colours', in *Papers in Metaphysics and Epistemology* (Cambridge: Cambridge University Press), 332–58.
Lloyd, Dan (1989), *Simple Minds* (Cambridge, Mass.: MIT Press).
Loar, Brian (1976), 'The Semantics of Singular Terms', *Philosophical Studies* 30, 353–77.
―― (1988), 'Social and Psychological Content', in R. Grimm and D. Merrill (eds.), *Contents of Thought* (Tucson: Arizona University Press), 99–110.
―― (1996), 'Phenomenal States', in N. Block, O. Flanagan, and G. Guzeldere (eds.), *The Nature of Consciousness* (Cambridge, Mass.: MIT Press), 597–616.
―― (2003), 'Phenomenal Intentionality as the Basis of Mental Content', in M. Hahn and B. Ramberg (eds.), *Reflections and Replies* (Cambridge, Mass.: MIT Press), 229–57.
Locke, John (1975), *An Essay Concerning Human Understanding*, 4th edn. (Oxford: Oxford University Press).
Lockwood, Michael (1971), 'Identity and Reference', in M. K. Munitz (ed.), *Identity and Individuation* (New York: NYU Press), 199–211.
Lycan, William (1996), *Consciousness and Experience* (Cambridge, Mass.: MIT Press).
McDowell, John (1977), 'On the Sense and Reference of a Proper Name', *Mind* 86, 159–85.
―― (1998), 'Singular Thought and the Extent of Inner Space', in *Meaning, Knowledge, and Reality* (Cambridge, Mass.: Harvard University Press), 228–59.
McGinn, Colin (1977), 'Charity, Interpretation, and Belief', *Journal of Philosophy* 74, 521–35.
―― (1982), 'The Structure of Content', in A. Woodfield (ed.), *Thought and Object* (Oxford: Clarendon Press), 207–58.
―― (1989), *Mental Content* (Oxford: Blackwell).
McIlwain, James T. (1996), *An Introduction to the Biology of Vision* (Cambridge: Cambridge University Press).
McKinsey, Michael (1978), 'Names and Intentionality', *Philosophical Review* 87, 171–200.
―― (1991), 'Anti-Individualism and Privileged Access', *Analysis* 51, 9–16.
―― (2002), 'On Knowing Our Own Minds', *Philosophical Quarterly* 52, 107–16.
McKitrick, Jennifer (2003), 'A Case for Extrinsic Dispositions', *Australasian Journal of Philosophy* 81, 155–74.
Machery, Eduoard, Ron Mallon, Shaun Nichols, and Stephen P. Stich (2004), 'Semantics, Cross-Cultural Style', *Cognition* 92, B1–B12.

Martin, M. G. F. (2002), 'The Transparency of Experience', *Mind and Language* 17, 376–425.
—— (2004), 'The Limits of Self-Awareness', *Philosophical Studies* 120, 37–89.
Mates, Benson (1950), 'Synonymity', *University of California Publications in Philosophy* 25, 201–26.
Matthen, Mohen (1988), 'Biological Functions and Perceptual Content', *Journal of Philosophy* 85, 5–27.
—— (1997), 'Teleology and the Product Analogy', *Australasian Journal of Philosophy* 75, 21–37.
Maund, Barry (1995), *Colours: Their Nature and Representation* (New York: Cambridge University Press).
Mel, Bartlett W. (1986), 'A Connectionist Learning Model for 3-Dimensional Mental Rotation, Zoom, and Pan', *Proceedings of the Eighth Annual Conference of the Cognitive Science Society* (Hillsdale, NJ: Lawrence Erlbaum Associates), 562–71.
Mellor, D. H. (1977), 'Natural Kinds', *British Journal for the Philosophy of Science* 28, 299–312.
Mendola, Joseph (1997), *Human Thought* (Dordrecht: Kluwer).
—— (2003), 'A Dilemma for Asymmetric Dependence', *Nous* 37, 232–57.
—— (2006a), *Goodness and Justice* (Cambridge: Cambridge University Press).
—— (2006b), 'Papineau on Etiological Teleosemantics for Beliefs', *Ratio* 19, 305–20.
—— (2007), 'Knowledge and Evidence', *Journal of Philosophy* 104, 157–60.
Mervis, C. B. (1987), 'Child-Basic Object Categories and Early Lexical Development', in U. Neisser (ed.), *Concepts and Conceptual Development* (Cambridge: Cambridge University Press).
Millikan, Ruth Garrett (1984), *Language, Thought and Other Biological Categories* (Cambridge, Mass.: MIT Press).
—— (1991a), 'Perceptual Content and Fregean Myth', *Mind* 100, 439–59.
—— (1991b), 'Speaking Up For Darwin', in B. Loewer and G. Rey (eds.), *Meaning in Mind: Fodor and his Critics* (Oxford: Blackwell), 151–64.
—— (1993a), 'Knowing What I'm Thinking Of', *Proceedings of the Aristotelian Society*, suppl. vol. 67, 91–108.
—— (1993b), Part Two of 'On Mentalese Orthography', in Bo Dahlbom (ed.), *Dennett and his Critics* (Oxford: Blackwell), 108–23.
—— (1993c), *White Queen Psychology and Other Essays for Alice* (Cambridge, Mass.: MIT Press).
—— (1997), 'Images of Identity: In Search of Modes of Presentation', *Mind* 106, 499–519.

—— (1998), 'A Common Structure for Concepts of Individuals, Stuffs, and Real Kinds: More Mama, More Milk, and More Mouse' with peer commentary and replies, *Behavioral and Brain Sciences* 21, 55–100.
—— (2000), *On Clear and Confused Ideas* (Cambridge: Cambridge University Press).
—— (2004), *Varieties of Meaning* (Cambridge, Mass.: MIT Press).
—— (2005), *Language: A Biological Model* (New York: Oxford University Press).
Morton, Adam (1980), *Frames of Mind* (Oxford: Clarendon Press).
Nagel, Thomas (1974), 'What is it Like to be a Bat?', *Philosophical Review* 83, 435–50.
Nathans, Jeremy (1997), 'The Genes for Color Vision', in Byrne and Hilbert (1997: ii. 249–58).
Neander, Karen (1991a), 'Functions as Selected Effects: The Conceptual Analyst's Defense', *Philosophy of Science* 58, 168–84.
—— (1991b), 'The Teleological Notion of "Function"', *Australasian Journal of Philosophy* 69, 454–68.
—— (1995), 'Misrepresenting & Malfunctioning', *Philosophical Studies* 79, 109–41.
—— (1996), 'Dretske's Innate Modesty', *Australasian Journal of Philosophy* 74, 258–74.
Nida-Rümelin, Martine (1996), 'Pseudonormal Vision: An Actual Case of Qualia Inversion?', *Philosophical Studies* 82, 145–57.
Palmer, Stephen E. (1999), *Vision Science: Photons to Phenomenology* (Cambridge, Mass.: MIT Press).
Papineau, David (1984), 'Representation and Explanation', *Philosophy of Science* 51, 550–72.
—— (1987), *Reality and Representation* (Oxford: Blackwell).
—— (1993), *Philosophical Naturalism* (Oxford: Blackwell).
Passingham, R. (1993), *The Frontal Lobes and Voluntary Action* (New York: Oxford University Press).
Peacocke, Christopher (1983), *Sense and Content* (Oxford: Clarendon Press).
—— (1992), *A Study of Concepts* (Cambridge, Mass.: MIT Press).
Perlman, Mark (2002), 'Pagan Teleology', in Andre Ariew, Robert Cummins, and Mark Perlman (eds.), *Functions: New Essays in the Philosophy of Psychology and Biology* (New York: Oxford University Press), 263–90.
Perry, John (2001), *Reference and Reflexivity* (Stanford, Calif.: CSLI Publications).
Perry, John, and Mark Crimmins (1993), 'The Prince and the Phone Booth', in John Perry, *The Problem of the Essential Indexical* (New York: Oxford University Press), 249–78.
Pietroski, Paul M. (1992), 'Intentionality and Teleological Error', *Pacific Philosophical Quarterly* 73, 267–82.

Pinker, Steven, and Paul Bloom (1992), 'Natural Language and Natural Selection', in Jerome H. Barkow, Leda Cosmides, and John Tooley (eds.), *The Adapted Mind* (New York: Oxford University Press).

Pitt, David (2004), 'The Phenomenology of Cognition, or, What Is It Like to Think That P?', *Philosophy and Phenomenological Research* 69, 1–36.

Plantinga, Alvin (1974), *The Nature of Necessity* (Oxford: Clarendon Press).

—— (1978), 'The Boethian Compromise', *American Philosophical Quarterly* 15, 129–38.

Poirier, Jean-Pierre (1993), *Lavoisier* (Philadelphia: University of Pennsylvania Press).

Pokorny, Joel, Vivianne Smith, Guy Verriest, and A. J. L. G. Pinckers (eds.) (1979), *Congenital and Acquired Color Vision Defects* (New York: Grune & Stratton).

Preston, Beth (1998), 'Why is a Wing Like a Spoon? A Pluralist Theory of Function', *Journal of Philosophy* 95, 215–54.

Price, Carolyn (1998), 'Determinate Functions', *Nous* 32, 54–75.

Price, H. H. (1932), *Perception* (London: Methuen).

Prinz, Jesse J. (2002), *Furnishing the Mind* (Cambridge, Mass.: MIT Press).

Putnam, Hilary (1975), 'The Meaning of "Meaning"', in *Philosophical Papers*, vol. ii (Cambridge: Cambridge University Press), 215–71.

—— (1988), *Representation and Reality* (Cambridge, Mass.: MIT Press).

—— (1995), 'Introduction', in A. Pessin and S. Goldberg (eds.), *The Twin Earth Chronicles* (Armonk, NY: M. E. Sharpe), pp. xv–xxii.

—— (1999), *The Threefold Cord* (New York: Columbia University Press).

Quine, W. V. O. (1960), *Word and Object* (Cambridge, Mass.: MIT Press).

—— (1995), *From Stimulus to Science* (Cambridge, Mass.: Harvard University Press).

—— (1999), 'Where Do We Disagree?', in Lewis Edwin Hahn (ed.), *The Philosophy of Donald Davidson* (Peru, Ill.: Open Court), 73–79.

Reichenbach, Hans (1947), *Elements of Symbolic Logic* (New York: The Free Press).

Richard, Mark (1990), *Propositional Attitudes* (Cambridge: Cambridge University Press).

Ristau, Carolyn A. (1998), 'Cognitive Ethology', in Cummins and Allen (1998: 127–61).

Rizzo, Matthew, Vivianne Smith, Joel Pokorny, and Antonio R. Damasio (1997), 'Color Perception Profiles in Central Achromatopsia', in Byrne and Hilbert (1997: ii. 277–90).

Robinson, Howard (1994), *Perception* (London: Routledge).

Rosenbaum, D. A. (1991), *Human Motor Control* (San Diego: Academic Press).

Rosenthal, David (2005), 'Two Concepts of Consciousness', in *Consciousness and Mind* (Oxford: Clarendon Press), 21–44.

Rupert, Robert D. (1999), 'Mental Representations and Millikan's Theory of Intentional Content: Does Biology Chase Causality?', *Southern Journal of Philosophy* 37, 129–32.

Russell, Bertrand (1911), 'Knowledge by Acquaintance and Knowledge by Description', *Proceedings of the Aristotelian Society* 11, 108–28.

—— (1919), *An Introduction to Mathematical Philosophy* (London: George Allen & Unwin).

—— (1956), 'The Philosophy of Logical Atomism', in Robert C. Marsh (ed.), *Logic and Knowledge* (London: Macmillan), 175–281.

Salmon, Nathan (1986), *Frege's Puzzle* (Cambridge, Mass.: MIT Press).

—— (1987), 'Existence', *Philosophical Perspectives* 1, 49–108.

—— (1989), 'Illogical Belief', *Philosophical Perspectives* 3, 243–85.

—— (1998), 'Nonexistence', *Nous* 32, 277–319.

—— (2003), 'Naming, Necessity, and Beyond', *Mind* 112, 475–92.

Sawyer, Sarah (1998), 'Privileged Access to the World', *Australasian Journal of Philosophy* 76, 523–33.

—— (1999), 'An Externalist Account of Introspective Knowledge', *Pacific Philosophical Quarterly* 80, 358–78.

Schiffer, Stephen (1978), 'The Basis of Reference', *Erkenntnis* 13, 171–206.

Schwarz, Stephen (1978), 'Putnam on Artifacts', *Philosophical Review* 87, 566–74.

Seager, William (1997), 'Critical Notice of *Naturalizing the Mind*', *Canadian Journal of Philosophy* 27, 83–109.

Searle, John (1958), 'Proper Names', *Mind* 67, 166–73.

—— (1983), *Intentionality* (Cambridge: Cambridge University Press).

Segal, Gabriel (1989), 'On Seeing What is Not There', *Philosophical Review* 98, 189–214.

—— (1991), 'Defence of a Reasonable Individualism', *Mind* 100, 485–93.

—— (2000), *A Slim Book about Narrow Content* (Cambridge, Mass.: MIT Press).

Sellars, Wilfrid (1997), *Empiricism and the Philosophy of Mind* (Cambridge, Mass.: Harvard University Press).

Shepherd, R. N., and L.A. Cooper (1982), *Mental Images and their Transformations* (Cambridge, Mass.: MIT Press).

Siewert, Charles P. (1998), *The Significance of Consciousness* (Princeton: Princeton University Press).

Snowdon, P. F. (1980–1), 'Perception, Vision, and Causation', *Proceedings of the Aristotelian Society* 81, 175–92.

—— (1990), 'The Objects of Perceptual Experience', *Proceedings of the Aristotelian Society*, suppl. vol. 64, 121–50.

—— (1992), 'How to Interpret "Direct Perception"', in Tim Crane (ed.), *The Contents of Experience* (Cambridge: Cambridge University Press), 48–78.

Soames, Scott (2002), *Beyond Rigidity* (New York: Oxford University Press).
―― (2003), *Philosophical Analysis in the Twentieth Century*, vol. ii (Princeton: Princeton University Press).
―― (2005), *Reference and Description* (Princeton: Princeton University Press).
Stalnaker, Robert (1984), *Inquiry* (Cambridge, Mass.: MIT Press).
―― (1989), 'On What's in the Head', *Philosophical Perspectives* 3, 287–316.
Stampe, Dennis W. (1977), 'Towards a Causal Theory of Linguistic Representation', *Midwest Studies in Philosophy* 2, 42–63.
Stanley, Jason (2005), 'Semantics in Context', in Gerhard Preyer and Georg Peter (eds.), *Contextualism in Philosophy* (New York: Oxford University Press), 221–54.
Sterelny, Kim (1983), 'Natural-Kind Terms', *Pacific Philosophical Quarterly* 64, 110–25.
―― (1990), *The Representational Theory of the Mind* (Oxford: Blackwell).
Stich, Stephen (1980) 'Headaches', *Philosophical Books* 21, 65–76.
―― (1981), 'Dennett on Intentional Systems', *Philosophical Topics* 12, 38–63.
―― (1982), 'On the Ascription of Content', in A. Woodfield (ed.), *Thought and Content* (Oxford: Clarendon Press), 153–206.
―― (1983), *The Case Against Belief* (Cambridge, Mass.: MIT Press).
―― (1984), 'Relativism, Rationality, and the Limits of Intentional Description', *Pacific Philosophical Quarterly* 65, 211–35.
―― (1985), 'Could Man Be an Irrational Animal?', in H. Kornblith (ed.), *Naturalizing Epistemology* (Cambridge, Mass.: MIT Press), 249–67.
―― (1990), *The Fragmentation of Reason* (Cambridge, Mass.: MIT Press).
Strawson, P. F. (1954), 'Review of *Philosophical Investigations*', *Mind* 63, 70–99.
―― (1959), *Individuals* (London: Methuen).
―― (1966), *The Bounds of Sense* (London: Methuen).
―― (1974), *Subject and Predicate in Logic and Grammar* (London: Methuen).
Stroud, Barry (1999), 'Radical Interpretation and Philosophical Skepticism', in Lewis Edwin Hahn (ed.), *The Philosophy of Donald Davidson* (Peru, Ill.: Open Court), 139–61.
Sturgeon, Scott (2000), *Matters of Mind: Consciousness, Reason, and Nature* (London: Routledge).
Sullivan, Sonja R. (1993), 'From Natural Function to Indeterminate Function', *Philosophical Studies* 69, 129–37.
Thau, Michael (2002), *Consciousness and Cognition* (New York: Oxford University Press).
Travis, Charles (2000), *Unshadowed Thought* (Cambridge, Mass.: Harvard University Press).

Trout, J. D. (2001), 'Metaphysics, Method, and the Mouth: Philosophical Lessons of Speech Perception', *Philosophical Psychology* 14, 261–91.
Tye, Michael (1984), 'The Adverbial Approach to Visual Experience', *Philosophical Review* 93, 195–225.
—— (1995), *Ten Problems of Consciousness* (Cambridge, Mass.: MIT Press).
—— (2000), *Consciousness, Color, and Content* (Cambridge, Mass.: MIT Press).
van Inwagen, Peter (1977), 'Creatures of Fiction', *American Philosophical Quarterly* 14, 299–308.
—— (1983), 'Fiction and Metaphysics', *Philosophy and Literature* 7, 67–77.
Walsh, D. M. (2002), 'Brentano's Chestnuts', in Andre Ariew, Robert Cummins, and Mark Perlman (eds.), *Functions: New Essays in the Philosophy of Psychology and Biology* (New York: Oxford University Press), 314–37.
Walters, S. M. (1961), 'The Shaping of Angiosperm Taxonomy', *New Phytologist* 60, 74–84.
Warfield, Ted (1992), 'Privileged Self-Knowledge and Externalism are Compatible', *Analysis* 52, 232–7.
—— (1997), 'Externalism, Privileged Self-Knowledge, and the Irrelevance of Slow Switching', *Analysis* 57, 282–4.
Wiggins, David (1976), 'Frege's Problem of the Morning Star and the Evening Star', in M. Schirn (ed.), *Studies on Frege*, ii. *Logic and Philosophy of Language* (Stuttgart-Bad Canstatt: Frommann-Holzboog).
Williamson, Timothy (2000), *Knowledge and its Limits* (Oxford: Oxford University Press).
Wilson, Mark (1982), 'Property Meets Predicate', *Philosophical Review* 91, 549–89.
Wilson, N. L. (1959), 'Substances Without Substrata', *Review of Metaphysics* 12, 521–39.
Wilson, Robert A. (1995), *Cartesian Psychology and Physical Minds* (Cambridge: Cambridge University Press).
—— (2004), *Boundaries of the Mind* (Cambridge: Cambridge University Press).
Winston, Judith E. (1998), *Describing Species* (New York: Columbia University Press).
Wittgenstein, Ludwig (1961), *Tractatus Logico-Philosophicus*, trans. D. F. Pears and B. F. McGuinness (London: Routledge & Kegan Paul).
—— (1968), *Philosophical Investigations*, 3rd edn., trans. G. E. M. Anscombe (New York: Macmillan).
—— (1969), *The Blue and Brown Books*, 2nd edn. (Malden, Mass.: Blackwell).
Wright, Crispin (1980), *Wittgenstein and the Foundations of Mathematics* (Cambridge, Mass.: Harvard University Press).
—— (2000), 'Cogency and Question-Begging: Some Reflections on McKinsey's Paradox, and Putnam's Proof', *Philosophical Topics* 10, 140–63.

Wright, Crispin (2002a), 'Kripke's Account of the Argument Against Private Language', in *Rails to Infinity* (Cambridge, Mass.: Harvard University Press), 91–115.

—— (2002b), 'On Making Up One's Own Mind', in *Rails to Infinity* (Cambridge, Mass.: Harvard University Press), 116–42.

—— (2002c), 'The Problem of Self-Knowledge (I)', in *Rails to Infinity* (Cambridge, Mass.: Harvard University Press), 319–44.

—— (2002d), 'The Problem of Self-Knowledge (II)', in *Rails to Infinity* (Cambridge, Mass.: Harvard University Press), 345–73.

—— (2002e), 'Wittgenstein's Later Philosophy of Mind', in *Rails to Infinity* (Cambridge, Mass.: Harvard University Press), 291–318.

Wright, Larry (1973), 'Functions', *Philosophical Review* 82, 139–68.

Yablo, Stephen (2000), 'Textbook Kripkeanism & The Open Structure of Concepts', *Pacific Philosophical Quarterly* 81, 98–122.

—— (2002), 'Coulda, Woulda, Shoulda', in T. Gendler and J. Hawthorne (eds.), *Conceivability and Possibility* (Oxford: Clarendon Press), 441–92.

Yoshioka, T., B. M. Dow, and R. G. Vautin (1996), 'Neural Mechanisms of Color Categorization in Areas V1, V2, and V4 of Macaque Monkey Cortex', *Behavioral Brain Research* 76, 51–70.

Index

Ackerman, F. 36, 37 n. 42, 51–2
Adams, F. 146 n. 9
adverbial theory of perception 195–6, 294
Agar, N. 112
Aizawa, K. 146 n. 9
Almog, J. 68
analytical functionalism 187–8, *see also* functionalism
a posteriori 189–92
A Posteriori Externalism 236–40
a priori 38–9, 51–2, 179–81, 233, 316–18
Argument from Explanation 9, 19, 229–31, 245, 247
Argument from Introspection 9, 19, 228–52
Argument from Science 9, 19
Aristotle 3, 5 n., 9, 16, 107, 175, 197–200, 211, 236, 242, *see also* Modal Aristotle case
Arthritis-Tharthritis case 12, 28–30, 46–7
artifacts of experience 198, 202–4
asymmetric dependence (AD) 16–17, 143–68, 195, 313
Ayers, M. 91 n. 21

Bach, K. 36
bat experience 179–80, 187–8, 193
belief-ascription objection 47–8, 55–76
Bennett, J. 216, 277
Berkeley, G. 211, 271, 307, 326
Bermúdez, J. L. 217
Bigelow, J. 110 n. 8
Blackburn, S. 287 n., 298
Block, N. 36, 201, 322
Boghossian, P. 236–41, 247
Bourse, C. 110 n. 8, 115 n. 22
Braddon-Mitchell, D. 187 n.
Brandom, R. 19, 226, 228, 254, 277, 281–304, 310, 313
Braun, D. 70–1
Brewer, B. 209
Broackes, J. 106 n. 2
Brown, J. 90 n. 19, 236 n. 15
Brueckner, A. 236 n. 16

Burge, T. 10 n. 8, 12, 23–4, 25 n. 6, 27, 28–30, 46–50, 82, 84, 86 n., 94, 158, 229, 230, 234, 235 n. 13, 246
Byrne, A. 105 n., 201, 322

Campbell, J. 61, 210–11, 216, 249
Carnap, R. 314
Carruthers, P. 308 n. 6
Casullo, A. 39, 181, 196 n. 37
causal descriptivism 34
causal-informational accounts 15, 103–172, 174, 176, 273
Chalmers, D. 6 n., 40, 179 n., 189 n. 20, 200–1, 262 n. 23, 314–25
Child, W. 210
Chisholm, R. 11, 195
Chomsky, N. 78, 310
Church, A. 47
Clark, Andy 262 n. 23
Clark, Austen 188, 190 n. 24, 192–4
color 3–4, 6, 174, 175, 185, 197–201, 242–5, 263, *see also* color blindness
color blindness 18, 105–7, 109, 122–3, 127, 165–6, 178, 192, 263, 311–12
color inversions 179, 188–91, 230, 243
constitution 179–80, 184, 187, 189–90, 192, 292, 319–321
contingent a priori 38–9, 40, 180–1, 184, 185, 186
Crimmins, M. 60–1
Cummins, R. 110, 146 n. 9

Davidson, D. 19, 225, 226, 227, 229, 230, 246, 254, 257–77
Davies, M. 10 n. 8, 209, 234 n. 11
deep deferentiality objection 53–4, 77, 83–8
Dennett, D. 78, 254, 262
description clusters 13, 31–2, 40, *see also* Rigidified Description Clusters
direct accounts of sensory content 173–4
simple direct accounts 174–77, 196, 201–4
disjunctivism 208–11, 213–214

INDEX

dispositionalism 225, 250–2, 295–9
division of linguistic labor 27–8, 83–94
Donnellan, K. 67–8
Dowell, J. 304 n. 94
Dretske, F. 16, 108, 110–11, 118–24, 131, 133, 140–2, 229
dualism 5–6, 154, 167–8, 179–80, 230, 243, 318, *see also* physicalism
Ducasse, C. J. 195
Dummett, M. 213, 226 n. 4, 249

Ebbs, G. 90 n. 19, 278, 280
Egan, F. 10 n. 8
Elm-Beech case 27–8, 45, 164
empiricism 7, 326–7, *see also* qualia empiricism
empty names 66–75
Enç, B. 108
epistemicism 7–8, 19–20, 223–4, 232–3, 251, 261–2, 322, 326–7
Ereshefsky, M. 90 n. 20
etiological teleosemantics (ET) 16, 103–30, 133–142
Evans, G. 55, 61, 69–70, 217–19
externalism 1
  case-based 11–14, 23–99
  commonsense 2–4
  language-based 14, 18–20, 223–304
  mind-based 14–18, 103–72, 204–11, 217–19
  science-based 10–11

factoring of sensory experience 175–6, 178, 196
Falvey, K. 234 n. 12, 235 n. 13
Feynman-Gell-Mann case 12, 30, 32–5
Fisher, J. 9 n.
Fodor, J. 16, 111, 133, 143–68, 245 n. 35, 313
Frege, G. 51, 55–66, 225, 242, *see also* Hesperus-Phosphorus case
functionalism 156–9, 195, *see also* analytical functionalism

Galileo 4, 197–8, 242
Gendler, T. 315
Gibbard, A. 304
Gibbons, J. 83 n. 14, 120 n. 29, 206, 240–1, 247, 262 n. 22, 313

Gödel-Schmidt case 12, 30, 32–5
Godfrey-Smith, P. 123 n.
Grandy, R. 280–1
Grice, P. 63 n. 20, 249

Hardin, C. L. 17, 105 n., 173, 188–92, 193, 194, 197 n. 38
Harman, G. 169, 171 n. 43, 205–6
Harrison, B. 188–9
Haugeland, J. 286
Hawthorne, J. 90 n. 19, 187 n., 278, 280, 315
Henderson, D. 266 n. 30
Hesperus-Phosphorus case 51–2, 55–66, 180–1, 242, 318–19
higher-order representational accounts 174–6, 188
  higher-order experience accounts 174
  higher-order thought accounts 174
Hilbert, D. 105 n.
Hill, C. 197 n. 39, 202–3
Hinton, J. 17 n. 19, 208
Hobbes, T. 326
Hopkins, J. 270 n. 34
Horgan, T. 252, 321
Hume, D. 271, 326

inferentialism 282, *see also* use semantics
intentionalism 196–204, 213–14
internalism 1, *see also* qualia empiricism
  explanation-based 9, 19, 229–31
  introspection-based 9, 19, 228–52
  science-based 9–10
interpretationism 19, 226, 253–304
  moderate 255–7
  non-relative 254, 255–7, 257–77
  relative 254, 255–7, 277–304
  skeptical 255, 278
introspective access 231–3, 247–52, *see also* Argument from Introspection
inverted qualia, *see* color inversions
Irrelevant Alternatives 235–6

Jackman, H. 90 n. 19
Jackson, F. 34 n. 28, 36, 182, 187 n., 196 n. 36, 203, 314 n. 16
Jacob, P. 108 n. 7
Jeffrey, R. 270
Jeshion, R. 181 n. 9

INDEX

Kant, I. 17, 207–8, 215–19, 277, 308
Kaplan, D. 37–8, 71
Katz, J. 35–6, 69 n. 31
Kim, J. 5 n.
Kitcher, P. 92 n. 28, 123 n.
Kneale, W. 32 n. 23
know-how accounts 176–7, 188
knowledge as basic 205–7
Kripke, S. 11–12, 23, 30–9, 55–9, 69–70, 72, 80–1, 84, 94, 154, 180–7, 228, 295–9, 315, 321
Kroon, F. 34 n. 26

Lance, M. 90 n. 19, 278, 280
language 14–15, 31, 43–4, 223–327
LaPorte, J. 91–2
Levin, J. 280 n. 66
Levine, J. 184 n. 13, 190 n. 22, 195 n. 34
Lewis, D. 34 n. 26, 78, 171, 260–2, 265–6, 275–6
Lloyd, D. 143 n. 2
Loar, B. 36, 78, 82, 184 n. 13, 199–200
Locke, J. 211, 242, 326
Lockwood, M. 61
Lycan, W. 174

McDowell, J. 61, 209–10
McGinn, C. 25 n. 6, 108, 112, 209 n. 77
McKinsey, M. 40, 233–6
McKitrick, J. 296 n. 84
Machery, E. 12 n. 15
Mallon, R. 12 n. 15
Martin, M. G. F. 208–9, 213–14
match 79, 94, 96, 197–8, 204, 211–13, 225
Mates, B. 58
Matthen, M. 108 n. 7, 129–30
Maund, B. 197 n. 38
Mellor, D. 27 n. 10
metalinguistic internalism 13, 31–9, 41, 43–4, 47–50
Mill, J. S. 326
Millikan, R. G. 16, 61, 108, 110, 112, 113–14, 116–17, 133–6, 143 n. 1, 229
Modal Aristotle case 30–1, 35–9
modal structure architecture 188, 194

Modal Structuralism (MS) 17–18, 173–219, 305
Moore, G. E. 11, 51, 290
Morton, A. 256
multiple-contents objection 46, 55–76

Nagel, T. 193
narrow content 31, 45–6, 52, 77–80, 94
Neander, K. 108, 110, 112, 114, 116, 117, 141 n.
necessary a posteriori 173, 179–92, 318–21
  full-blown 183–4
Nichols, S. 12 n. 15
Nida-Rümelin, M. 312 n.
nomic relations 144–9, 158–60, 167–8
Non-Epistemic Internalism (NEI) 19–20, 223–327
non-reductivism 284–304

objective content of experience, *see* representational content of experience
optimality account 169–71
Owens, J. 234 n. 12, 235 n. 13

Papineau, D. 108, 133, 136–40
Pargetter, R. 110 n. 8
Peacocke, C. 202–4, 212
Perlman, M. 108 n. 7
Perry, J. 60–1, 68, 82–3
physicalism 5–6, 160, 167–8, 179–80, 183–4, 186–8, 230, *see also* dualism
Pietroski, P. 142 n.
Pitt, D. 252
Plantinga, A. 36
Price, C. 112
Price, H. H. 308
primary imagination 213–4, 248, 306
Prinz, J. 131–2, 327
Private Language Argument 7, 18–19, 207, 223, 226–8, 228–52, 274–6, 286–7, 293–301, 308, 311–14
proper cause 16, 103–172, 273
proto-judgment 211–13, 247, 306
Pryor, J. 322
Putnam, H. 12, 23, 25–8, 40–6, 81, 84, 94, 97, 131, 163, 181, 208, 234, 245, *see also* Twin Earth case

qualia 5–8, 17–18, 173–219, 230, 242–7, 260, 262–3, 320–1, *see also* color inversions
qualia empiricism 5–8, 95, 173–219, 231–3, 247–52, 255–7, 262–3, 266–9, 271–2, 275–7, 282–5, 287, 294, 296–8, 302–4, 305–27, *see also* Non-Epistemic Internalism, Rigidified Description Clusters
qualitative content of experience 175–6
quasi-experience 248
Quine, W. V. O. 258–9, 260, 262, 265, 270

reference 24–31, 77–99
Refutation of Idealism 17, 207–8, 215–19, 277, 308
Reichenbach, H. 37
representational content of experience 175–6
representationalism, *see* intentionalism
Richard, M. 59–60
rigidification 13, 31, 36–8, 52–3, 182, 184, 185
Rigidified Description Clusters (RDC) 13, 31–2, 40–2, 95, 98–9, 223–5, 283, 310–13, *see also* rigidification
Robinson, H. 227 n., 245 n. 36, 246–7
Rosenthal, D. 174
Rupert, R. 134 n. 46
Russell, B. 32 n. 23, 55, 66–75, 185 n. 16, 225, 326

Salmon, N. 62–6, 69 n. 31, 71–5
Sawyer, S. 234 n. 10, 235
Schiffer, S. 44 n. 57
Schwarz, S. 27 n. 10
Seager, W. 120 n. 30
Searle, J. 36 n. 37, 40, 44
Segal, G. 10 n. 8, 25 n. 7, 28 n. 15, 48–9, 53, 82, 91–2
Sellars, W. 282, 284–5, 288
semantic a priori 42–3, 46, 184, 323–4
sensory content 5–7, 15–18, 44, 103–30, 173–219
Siewert, C. 197 n. 38, 204 n. 56, 252
Snowdon, P. F. 208
Soames, S. 34, 52–3, 64–6, 71 n. 40, 181 n. 8, 245 n. 37

splitting the difference 235, 236, 239–41, 245, 280, 292, 298
Stalnaker, R. 36, 169, 229, 322
Stampe, D. 108, 169
Stanley, J. 250 n. 44
Sterelny, K. 27 n. 10, 112
Stich, S. 12 n. 15, 78, 280–1
Strawson, P. F. 61, 211–19, 245 n. 37, 308, 313–14
Strawsonian spatial thoughts 211–19, 248, 307–10, 313–14
Stroud, B. 275 n.
Sturgeon, S. 209 n. 74
subjective content of experience, *see* qualitative content of experience
subject-matter objection 49, 55–76
Sullivan, S. 141 n.
syntax of mental representations 144, 148, 150–60

Tarski, A. 264
Thau, M. 64 n.
Tienson, J. 252
Travis, C. 278–80
triangulation 273–7, 308
Trout, J. D. 10 n. 8
truth, *see* reference
truth-condition semantics 225–6, 257–77
Twin Earth case 12, 25–7, 40–4, 131, 141–2, 149, 163–4, 234–5, 237–41, 245, 247, 277–8
two-dimensionalism 182–4, 187, 314–321
  robust 182–4, 187
Tye, M. 169–70, 196 n. 37, 201 n. 47, 202–3

use semantics 225–6, 281–304

van Inwagen, P. 74

Walsh, D. 108 n. 7
Walters, S. 91
Warfield, T. 235 n. 13
Wiggins, D. 61
Williamson, T. 17 n. 18, 206
Wilson, M. 90

Wilson, R. 10 n. 8
Winston, J. 90
Wittgenstein, L. 7, 11, 18–19, 40, 154, 223, 226–8, 257, 275–6, 308, *see also* Private Language Argument
Wright, C. 226, 234 n. 11, 250–1, 286

Wright, L. 108, 110, 114–15

Yablo, S. 322 n. 26, 324–6

zombies 179, 243–4, 319–20